Body Studies

In recent years, body studies has expanded rapidly, becoming an increasingly popular field of study within anthropology, sociology, and cultural studies. This groundbreaking textbook takes the topics and theories from these disciplines, and combines them into one single, easily accessible text for students.

Body Studies is a comprehensive textbook on the social and cultural uses and meanings of the body, for use in undergraduate college courses. Its clear, accessible chapters explore, among other things:

- the measurement and classification of the human body
- illness and healing
- the racialized body
- the gendered body
- cultural perceptions of beauty
- new bodily technologies.

This book investigates how power plays an important role in the uses, views, and shapes of the body – as well as how the body is invested with meaning. *Body Studies* provides a wealth of pedagogic features for ease of teaching and learning: ethnographic case studies, boxes covering contemporary controversies, news stories, and legislative issues, as well as chapter summaries, further reading recommendations, and key terms. This book will appeal to students and teachers of sociology, anthropology, cultural studies, women's studies, gender studies, and ethnic studies.

Margo DeMello is a Lecturer in the Department of Communications, Humanities, and Social Sciences at Central New Mexico Community College. Her books include *Bodies of Inscription: A Cultural History of the Modern Tattoo Community*, *Encyclopedia of Body Adornment*, *Feet and Footwear*, and *Faces Around the World*.

Body Studies

An introduction

Margo DeMello

Routledge
Taylor & Francis Group

LONDON AND NEW YORK

306.4
DEM

First published 2014
by Routledge
2 Park Square, Milton Park, Abingdon, Oxon OX14 4RN

and by Routledge
711 Third Avenue, New York, NY 10017

Routledge is an imprint of the Taylor & Francis Group, an informa business

British Library Cataloguing in Publication Data
A catalogue record for this book is available from the British Library

Library of Congress Cataloging in Publication Data
DeMello, Margo.
   Body studies: an introduction/Margo DeMello. – First Edition.
   pages cm
   Includes bibliographical references and index.
   1. Human body.   I. Title.
   HM636.D46 2013
   306.4 – dc23
   2013015937

ISBN: 978-0-415-69929-7 (hbk)
ISBN: 978-0-415-69930-3 (pbk)
ISBN: 978-0-203-51960-8 (ebk)

Typeset in ScalaSans and Frutiger
by Florence Production Ltd, Stoodleigh, Devon, UK

MIX
Paper from
responsible sources
FSC   FSC® C013056
www.fsc.org

Printed and bound in Great Britain by
TJ International Ltd, Padstow, Cornwall

Contents

Figures

Preface

For many Western women (and quite a few men), Barbie played a major role in our childhoods. More than a billion dolls have been sold in the five decades Barbie was first launched in 1959, playing a major part in the socialization of millions of girls and boys, teaching them about relationships, shopping, and clothes, and, according to many critics, giving them a distorted body image as well.

Barbie's impossible body measurements – if she were a real woman, she would be 5'10" tall and weigh 110 pounds, her measurements would be 35–20–33, and her shoe size would be a size 3 (Urla and Swedlund 1995) – combined with her heterosexual and Caucasian identity, give girls (and boys) a very narrow view of what it is to be female. For many girls who can't relate to, or come close to achieving, Barbie's brand of femininity, the result is disappointment and sometimes body hatred.

In recent years, Mattell has attempted to create new Barbies with a more realistic appearance, like 2009's So In Style Black Barbie (who had a more curvy physique, fuller facial features, varying skin tones, and, in some models, curly hair). While S.I.S. Black Barbie was a hit with many African American consumers, who were pleased to finally find a doll to whom they could relate, the new doll still generated criticism; in particular, the hair-styling kit that one could purchase to straighten Barbie's kinky hair was seen as yet another condemnation of black women's natural hair.

Why does a $19.95 doll matter in terms of how we see ourselves? Barbie is seen as so critical in terms of a child's self-image and self-esteem that in late 2011 an Internet movement developed to encourage Mattell to create a bald Barbie, to help kids with cancer to feel better about themselves.

And for that matter, why do we spend so much time thinking about, and sometimes obsessing about, how we look? Perhaps as many as five million

Americans have body dysmorphic disorder, a psychological disorder in which an individual is perpetually unhappy with his or her own body, and often sees their body in a way that is totally disconnected from reality. The high rates of BDD may be linked to the increasing practice by advertisers to Photoshop models' bodies, making them seem unnaturally perfect. It may also result in growing rates of cosmetic surgery among those who can afford it, in which people change the appearance of their bodies or faces to match these unnatural and often unreachable expectations.

Courses on the study of the body are proliferating at college campuses around the world; if you're reading this book, chances are that you're taking one of these classes! Disciplines which attempt to shed light on the complexities of the human experience, such as anthropology, sociology, and cultural studies, have been interested in the subject for years.

Body Studies: An Introduction deals with the issue of bodies – thin bodies, fat bodies, sick bodies, gendered bodies, racialized bodies, sexualized bodies, globalized bodies, and healthy bodies; even living and dead bodies. It addresses how we, as individuals and as societies, deal with, represent, and understand bodies. This book covers the so-called "natural" body, the social and cultural construction of the body, bodies in historical contexts, and various metaphors of the body. It provides college students with a comprehensive and accessible resource which can be used in anthropology, sociology and cultural studies courses. It looks at the body from a historical and cross-cultural perspective, and considers the social and cultural markings on the body, and how ideas about the body have changed over time.

I want to thank Gerhard Boomgarden from Routledge, who greenlighted this book, and saw that the market needed a textbook in body studies. Emily Briggs, also of Routledge, provided assistance and support throughout the project.

I am grateful to the following colleagues and friends for providing photographs or other materials that I've included in this book. Thanks to Ian Elwood, Jeff Hayes, Lisa Brown, Teja Brooks Prebac, David Brooks, Larkin Cypher, Alex Boojor, Tamir Bar Yehuda, Nick Sanchez, Tom Young, Damien Velasquez, Bill Velasquez, Robin Montgomery, Bob Mitchell, Randy Huff, Janet Kazimir, Emily Fitzgerald, Laurence Nixon, Mary Johnson, Leigh Johnson, Samina Faheem, and Mercy for Animals for generously contributing in this way. Thanks as well to Jennifer Cray, Kit Jagoda, and Judith Pierce for connecting me with folks who provided photos. I am also grateful to the following public agencies: the Department of Defense, the Library of Congress, the National Library of Medicine, the United States Air Force, the California Department of Corrections and Rehabilitation, and the National Archives and Records Administration; many of the images in this book came from the public archives maintained by those organizations.

Finally, I am personally grateful for the support, love, and encouragement of my parents, Robin Montgomery and Bill DeMello, who have always encouraged my efforts, and from my husband, Tom Young, who puts up with my elevating levels of craziness as my deadlines approach, and for the friendship of Laura Allen, who helped with a last-minute edit just prior to the deadline.

PART I

Understanding the Body from a Social and Cultural Perspective

chapter 1

Introduction

Theorizing the body

One of the most successful horror movies of the 1950s, the era when horror movies really came into their own in the United States, was *Invasion of the Body Snatchers*. This 1956 film explores a world in which aliens from outer space invade earth by replacing human beings with new bodies that look just like them, but that are devoid of real human emotion. It's typically interpreted today as a Cold War allegory on either the threat of McCarthyism in the United States, or the dangers posed by the loss of individuality in the Soviet Union. Twenty years later, another horror film, *The Stepford Wives*, took the idea of body replacement one step further. Stepford, an "idyllic" suburban community in Connecticut, only appears to be perfect; it turns out that the husbands in the town have been killing their wives and replacing them with robots who look exactly like them, but are perfectly submissive, and thus (from the perspective of the men) are perfect wives. This film was made during the rise of **feminism** in the United States, and is clearly a statement about male fear during the era of women's liberation. Over the decades, a number of other films have also featured humans being taken over or assimilated by other life forms. In all of these cases, the films focus squarely on the body.

In fact, just a cursory look at the history of horror films shows that a remarkable number of them are indeed focused on the body – bodies that are not what they seem (*The Thing*), bodies that grow or shrink thanks to exposure to toxins (*Attack of the 50 Foot Woman*), bodies which transform into animals (*An American Werewolf in London*) or monsters (*Species*), bodies which have aliens (*Alien*) or demons (*Rosemary's Baby*) growing inside of them, and bodies which feed on the living (*The Night of the Living*

FIGURE 1.1 Sci-Fi Revoltech 001 Alien. Photo Courtesy of Toru Watanabe, via Wikimedia Commons: http://www.flickr.com/photos/torugatoru/4974295014/in/photostream.

Dead). Even films where the villain is a "normal" serial killer, and that feature no true monsters, focus on the body. From the slasher film of the 1970s to the torture porn of the 2000s, much of the pleasure and terror in these films comes from watching bodies get literally torn apart. In the 1980s, a new genre of horror film emerged called "**body horror**" which focuses on the destruction, decay, and mutations of the human body. *Re-Animator*, *The Fly*, *Body Melt*, *Videodrome*, *Splice*, *It's Alive*, *Altered States*, *Teeth*, and *Leviathan* are just a few examples of films where the body literally *is* the monster.

But why the body? In these films, bodies are torn apart, transformed, decayed, and turned inside out. It shouldn't surprise us that the largest audience for horror films has, since the 1950s, been teenagers, who are dealing with, and anxious about, their own physical and sexual trans-formations. But many adults, too, enjoy horror films because they are the most visceral movies of all, and make us feel in ways that other films don't: we tense up, we sweat, we squint, we turn away, and we jump while watching them. The experience of watching horror films, then, is **embodied**, just as the body is central to those same films. As anthropologist John Burton

a social and cultural perspective

writes, "our bodies are the perpetual medium of all that transpires in our existence, from birth until death" (2001: 3). This is the case with horror films, and it's also the case with the rest of society.

An introduction to body studies

What is the body, really? It seems like such an obvious question, and yet the answer is much more complicated than what you may think. Sure, it is a collection of cells, combined into organs, which themselves operate in systems (like the cardiovascular system, nervous system, or reproductive system) which ultimately make up the whole of the body. In humans, that body typically takes on a form with two arms, two legs, a torso, and a head.

But is that all there is when we talk about bodies? And can we really speak of bodies without also speaking of society and culture? In other words, is there such a thing as a universal, decontextualized body? A *tabula rasa*, simply awaiting inscription by culture?

The answer is no. Bodies are shaped in myriad ways by culture, by society, and by the experiences that are shared within a social and cultural context. In addition, bodies are shaped by history, and as such, they are always changing, as are our ideas about them. Bodies are contingent: molded by factors outside of the body, and then internalized into the physical being itself. This is what we call a social constructionist approach to the body. **Constructionism**, which is the perspective used in this textbook, suggests that beauty, weight, sexuality, or race do not simply result from the collection of genes one inherited from one's parents. Instead, these bodily features only take on the meaning that they have – That woman is beautiful! That man is fat! – in the context of history, society, and culture. Yes, a person may have a certain set of facial features, or weigh a certain number of pounds or kilograms. But how we think about those facial features or those pounds – are they attractive or unattractive? – comes from the time and place in which we live.

In addition, these meanings occur within a set of culturally constructed power relations that suggest that, for example, women must be attractive in order to be valuable. But this process does not just happen after we "enter" culture. Instead, it happens immediately; we are born in a particular skin, with a particular type of hair, with a particular set of eyes, a nose, and a mouth. How those features will be interpreted will then be shaped by culture, but the features themselves will already be present.

One of the reasons why this theoretical approach is often difficult for students to understand is that, since phenomena like beauty or obesity or race are expressed in the body, it seems like they must be natural. In fact, what occurs is that once something comes to take on cultural meaning, it becomes **naturalized**: we think that things are the way that they are because

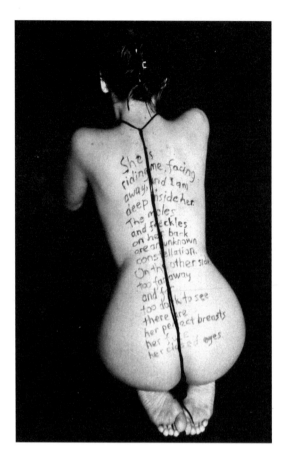

FIGURE 1.2 "Threads." Bodies can be used to represent a great many things. Photo courtesy of David Brooks.

they have always been that way, and that they are, therefore, natural. We don't realize that these meanings have been created, and that they can change, and that there's nothing natural at all about the popular belief in many Western cultures, for example, that straight hair is more attractive than curly or kinky hair. Even something that seems to be so rooted in the body as disability is partially socially constructed. There are people who have no arms, for example, and must use their feet to cook, to dress themselves, or to drive a car. That is a biological reality. But how we conceive of those people – as abnormal, or even freakish – comes from culture. There's nothing *inherently* abnormal in those people's reality.

Race is another good example. Every ten years since 1790, the United States has asked its citizens to fill out a census, which is used for redistricting, for social policy decisions and to meet a variety of legislative requirements. On every census that has so far been used, there have never been two censuses that have used the same racial categories; instead, each

a social and cultural perspective

census uses a separate set of terms (like Quadroon, Mulatto, Chinese, Mexican, or Hindu), demonstrating how arbitrary those terms really are. In Chapter 6, we will further explore the notion that race is a social construction.

This differs from what might be called an essentialist view of the body. **Essentialism** means that bodies are defined largely or entirely by their biological makeup – bones, muscles, hormones, and the like – and that much of human behavior can also be reduced to many of those biological functions. In fact, social scientists call this **reductionism**: the idea that complex human behaviors can be reduced to something as simple as, for example, hormones.

Sure, the hormone testosterone is responsible for, among other things, driving sexual behavior in both men and women, and men have more testosterone in their bodies than women. But does that alone account for the fact that men are, in many cultures, encouraged to be sexually aggressive while women are encouraged to be sexually passive, and that rape is one of the most common crimes committed against women in a variety of cultures around the world? Social scientists would argue that it is reductionist to reduce the sexually aggressive behaviors of many men to testosterone and to ignore the role that socialization, mass media, and the glorification of violence and sexual violence plays in these behaviors.

This book, using a constructionist perspective, will help you to decon-struct many of the bodily categories that seem so normal to you. We will cover the mundane – health and illness – to the frightening – torture and death – all with the aim of allowing you to understand how bodies are shaped by culture and society, and how categories like sexuality or race are constructed in relation to other categories and within systems of power. How do, for example, social institutions like politics, law, health care, and mass media shape both our perceptions of our bodies, but also how much access we have to health care, nutritious food, or safe working conditions? And what does it mean that some people, by virtue of their gender, race, class, or nationality, get greater access to those things, while other people have less access?

According to theorist Michel Thevóz, "there is no body but the painted body" (1984: 7) because the body must always be stamped with the mark of culture and society; without marking, the body cannot move within the channels of social exchange. Of course we paint the body quite literally with body paint, tattooing, makeup, and jewelry. But human bodies are never "blank" or unmarked, even when not explicitly marked through adornment or modification. Bodies can be fat or thin, dark or light, male or female, young or old, sick or healthy. In these ways, too, social position and culture is marked onto even naked bodies, in every society.

In addition, as technology changes, bodies change as well. From cosmetic surgery to organ transplantation to alternative reproductive technologies to the various practices and procedures considered within the term cyber, the body is being shaped by technology in a variety of ways today. Bodies are also changing thanks to changing perceptions, fuelled by mass media, of beauty, thinness, and muscularity, with new illnesses, practices, and obsessions emerging.

Interesting issues: born this way blog

Among those who study sexual orientation, there's no real consensus on how sexual orientation develops or is produced. It appears to have no relationship to parenting, since gay and lesbians are almost entirely raised by heterosexual parents, and gay and lesbian parents, for the most part, raise heterosexual children. And while the studies that seek to find evidence of a "gay gene" or some indication that hormones or brain structure "cause" homosexuality are thus far inconclusive, at least in some cultures, there appears to be anecdotal evidence to show that sexual orientation develops very early in life and is not a "choice." (In Chapter 8, however, we will discuss the ways that culture plays a role in how sexuality is expressed.) In 2011, DJ Paul V started a blog called "Born This Way" featuring photos sent in by gay men and lesbians of themselves as children. Many of the photos, accompanied by stories, show little boys in feminine poses and little girls with butch traits. All of the entries include statements indicating that the submitter knew that they were "different" from a very young age; whether or not they knew they were gay, they simply knew that they were not like the other kids. Paul's stated goal in the blog is to both show that being gay is not a choice, and also to create a space where gays and lesbians can feel safe about sharing their stories and where they can feel pride about themselves. He writes, "if my blog helps stop even just ONE LGBTQ person from taking their own life, or feeling bad or ashamed or unloved, then I feel I've achieved my goal." One of the criticisms of the blog is that it conflates sexual orientation with gender non-conformity; in other words, the men and women who send in their photos suggest that it's the way in which they dress or behave which challenge the norms of their gender which "prove" that they were gay. Homosexuality and gender non-conformity, however, do not always go hand-in-hand, and many transgendered people, in fact, emphasize that gender identity can be ambiguous and fluid rather than fixed and unchanging.

Embodiment

As noted in the introduction, this text will take the position that the body is, to a major extent, socially constructed. That does not mean that bodies are not biological organisms, which are subject to natural laws. It simply means that we cannot understand the biological organism without first understanding the social, cultural, and historical context in which it exists.

a social and cultural perspective

Biologist Anne Fausto-Sterling, for example, tells us that even our biological components – bone, blood, organs – are shaped by a complex relationship between biology and the physical and social environment in which we live. Our health and our behavior are shaped by both biology and history (2005). She also points out that biologists, too, the very people whose scientific analysis of the body many of the postmodern theorists now critique, are themselves socially constructed beings (as are we all), with their own biases and agendas. Science, too, is at least partially socially constructed.

This is a relatively recent theoretical development, however. For most of the history of philosophy, the body has been relatively untouched by such thinking. Instead, it is has always been seen as a biological object, and, typically, has been set aside from the mind or soul, which has generally been seen as a separate entity, subject to different laws. This was known as **mind/body dualism**, and was the typical way in which the body has been seen: as the physical being that is separate from, and inferior to, the mind. Furthermore, women have long been associated more with the body than have men, who have, historically, been seen as the more rational beings, i.e. men are more closely aligned with the mind, while women are more aligned with the body. Thanks to feminist theorizing which emerged in the 1970s, that view has been successfully challenged, but until recently the body itself was only understood within the realm of biological inquiry.

How we live in our bodies and how we experience the world through our bodies is a subject explored in the philosophical and psychological fields of inquiry known as **phenomenology**. Philosopher Maurice Merleau-Ponty, in a groundbreaking essay (1962), analysed the body in the context of the lived experience of everyday life. We do not just *have* bodies; we *are* bodies. Disability, for example, is not an external attack on the body but is experienced subjectively and is reflected in our identity. In a series of essays written by political scientist Iris Marion Young, for example, she writes of how gender plays a major role in these kinds of lived experiences. In "Throwing Like a Girl" (1977) she references studies which suggest that not only do boys and girls throw differently, but that girls and women rarely try hard when engaging in sports or other physical activities. This may be because women are expected to be objects to be looked at, rather than subjects who engage in activities. In other words, it's not because women are weaker than men that women cannot achieve, and often do not even try to achieve, some of the same things as men. It is because of the gendered norms associated with femininity – norms into which we have been socialized. It is also worth pointing out that throwing, whether one is a man or a woman, is a learned behavior, a fact which is nicely documented in a video produced by Argentinean videographer Juan Etchegaray in a short video titled simply "Men Throwing Rocks with the Other Hand" (http://vimeo.com/34678147, accessed March 31, 2013). In the video, men are filmed throwing rocks with their non-dominant hand and they do so badly, demonstrating that throwing is a skill that comes with practice – practice that not that many women engage in.

Another example of how norms of masculinity and femininity shape not just behavior, but public perceptions, has to do with Olympic weightlifter Holley Mangold. Mangold, whose 346 pounds helped her to become a world class weightlifter, experienced a huge amount of public criticism during the summer of 2012 when she performed in the Olympic Games. Commentators publicly criticized her appearance, and questioned whether she could weigh that much and still be an athlete. Mangold responded, "I'm not saying everyone is an athlete but I am saying that an athlete can come in any size." Certainly her achievements proved that point, but many people, focusing on her body size, remained unconvinced, believing that only thin people can be athletic.

Today, understanding embodiment is a task explored by sociologists, anthropologists, cultural studies scholars, and scholars interested in sex, gender, sexuality, health and illness, disability and race. In all of these cases, scholars are challenging biological reductionism – the idea that our feelings and behaviors can be reduced to our biological components – and are promoting instead an approach that takes into account our physical beings *and* how they have been shaped by culture, history, and society.

Interesting issues: apotemnophilia

Apotemnophilia is a psychological disorder in which a person has an over-whelming desire to remove a healthy limb; in some cases, it's considered to be a sexual fetish, while for many it has nothing to do with sex. Many people who have this condition experience a strong drive, which often begins in childhood, to have an arm or leg removed, and know exactly which limb must be removed in order to achieve satisfaction, and to feel normal and whole. Of men and women with this condition, a few convince a doctor to amputate their limbs, but most doctors will not knowingly remove a healthy limb, although there are a handful of underground doctors who will perform these surgeries. Many apotemnophiliacs, however, either intentionally damage their limbs enough so that they will have to be surgically removed because the limbs are damaged beyond repair. A great many remove their own limbs themselves, usually a small appendage like a finger or toe, and some convince sympathetic friends to do it for them. Sometimes they travel to other countries, where costs are less prohibitive and where doctors are bound by fewer laws, to have their limbs removed. In 1998, a New York man died of gangrene after having his leg amputated by an underground doctor in Mexico. Others don't have their limbs removed at all; they remain what the community calls "wannabes." "Wannabes" will often

a social and cultural perspective

pretend as if their limb is removed, for instance by wearing a sling or taping up a limb, either in private or in public. "Pretenders" are those who do not wish to remove a limb themselves yet pretend that they are disabled, either by hiding a limb or by using a wheelchair, brace, or crutches, in order to get attention or some other psychological satisfaction. Finally, amputee fetishists are known as devotees, and are sexually attracted to people with amputated limbs. The website Ampulove is a place for amputees, wannabees, and devotees to share stories, photos, and experiences. For people with apotemnophilia, they resist the notion that it is a disorder at all. Instead, like people who feel that having their nose reduced or their breasts enlarged, or, in the case of transsexuals, having their sex changed, will make their external selves more consistent with how they feel inside, those with apotemnophilia feel that without the limb removal, they will not be able to achieve their authentic self. This issue, which seems so odd to most people, is really just an example of many of the issues in this book. What is a normal body? How do we define what is normal, and who gets to make that decision? And what part does medical practice play in the normalization of bodies and the nature of identity?

Inscribing the social order

As we have noted, one of the major theoretical understandings of the body has to do with the idea that the body is marked by culture and society. Anthropologist Terence Turner coined the term "social skin" to refer to the ways in which social categories become inscribed onto the physical body. Through the social skin, the body becomes the symbolic stage on which the dramas of society are enacted (1980: 112).

Anthropologist Mary Douglas (1966, 1973) was perhaps the first anthropologist to centralize the cultural analysis of the body in her work and thus her influence on contemporary studies of the body is significant. Focusing primarily on traditional societies, Douglas was concerned with the universal human anxiety about disorder, and wrote that such societies respond to disorder through the classification of things both natural and social. Through the creation of categories (such as pure and impure), and their accompanying rules, people are able to contain disorder and restore order to society. For Douglas, the body is the most natural symbol for and medium of classification, and thus rules associated with controlling the body and its processes emerge as a powerful means of social control. The body, then, acts as a model for the social body such that threats to the limits of the physical body are also threats to the social body, and must be rigidly controlled. Systems of symbols, she writes, are based on bodily processes, but get their meaning from social experience. She assumes a strict homology in that people who have created a highly structured universe would also invest great meaning and find structure in the body's posture. In such societies, bodily control would be necessary because every twitch would be loaded with meaning. Further, she finds that societies with strict social limits would regard boundaries with extreme caution, and this, of course, includes bodily boundaries, inside and outside, what comes out of the body (blood, semen, etc.). There is an ongoing exchange of meanings between the two kinds of bodily experience – physical and social – so that each reinforces the other.

In sociology, a great deal of work on how the body operates as a symbol and focus of control has been done as well. Sociologist Norbert Elias says that during what he calls "the civilizing process" (1978), from the fourteenth to the seventeenth centuries, Europeans began to internalize many of the external forms of social control; instead shame and embarrassment took their place, controlling their behaviors from within. For instance, Europeans began to internalize the idea of table manners, so that no one needed to tell them that they needed to eat with a fork, or blow their nose with a handkerchief. Another sociologist, Erving Goffman (1959), developed a theory called **dramaturgical theory**, which suggests that we are all actors on a stage, at all times, and much of what we do is engage in **impression management**, during which we must monitor and adjust our own behavior in accordance with how we want others to perceive us. Goffman also noted that the body is a "sign vehicle" through which we communicate information about ourselves to others.

Three sociologists whose work has informed a great deal of work on the body in recent years are Bryan S. Turner, John O'Neill, and Mike Featherstone. Turner in particular has blended together the work of many classic sociological theorists such as Durkheim, Weber, Parsons, Elias, and Goffman, with the poststructural theorists like Foucault (discussed below), along with Nietzsche, Marx, and feminist theorists, to create a unified sociological theory of the body which focuses on society's need for the body to produce, reproduce, and consume. For O'Neill, there are five bodies of which we must concern ourselves – the global body, the social body, the body politic, the consumer body, and the medical body – because of the ways in which those bodies are shaped by the major social institutions of society. Featherstone, too, draws on a Marxist critique of consumer culture and positions the body within a post-industrial world in which bodies, and the maintenance of those bodies, serve as a new vehicle for the expansion of consumer culture and capitalism, and focuses in particular on body modification in his critiques.

Philosopher Michel Foucault (1979, 1980a, 1980b) was also concerned with the physical body and the ways in which it is regulated. The body is not just a text to be read but a medium for social control. But for Foucault, modern Western bodies are not subject to the same kinds of social control that Douglas describes in tribal societies. Instead they are disciplined through various controlling mechanisms located throughout the social body, such as medicine, psychiatry, education, law, or social policy, which we can then call the **body politic**. In his essay "Body/Power" (1980a), Foucault notes that, starting in the nineteenth century, the social body needed more protection, and this occurs through segregating the sick, the mentally ill, and criminals into various new institutions erected for those purposes. According to Foucault, the physical body also demanded surveillance; through these new institutions, unruly bodies would be watched, disciplined, and ultimately turned into docile bodies. But power is not just wielded by such institutions – rather, for Foucault, it is a part of all social relations. Furthermore, the body is not simply the target of power; it is the source of power as well, because as Foucault demonstrated, with the multitude of regulatory agencies available throughout society, bodies begin to discipline themselves and each other.

One of Foucault's major contributions to the field was with regard to sexuality. According to Foucault, sexuality is historically and socially constructed within relations of power. For Foucault, there is no such thing as inherent or essential sexuality. Humans created discourses about sex, and those discourses then shape our understanding of sex. He also showed how the Victorian era, although it seems like it was about the repression of sex, instead was about an explosion of interest in, and discourses about, sex. In fact, that was when we saw the rise of a variety of fetishes like foot fetishes, as well as an explosion of interest in pornography. He also pointed out that control over the body, and particularly over sexuality, can be dangerous, because it also engenders an intensification of desire. He says that the revolt of the sexual body is the reverse effect of this power play and the response on the side of power has been to economically exploit eroticization so that the body is no longer controlled by repression, but by stimulation. Foucault's work has since been considerably expanded and complicated by the work of a great many theorists, including, most notably, feminist and queer theorists.

Foucault's contribution to an understanding of the body in culture has been tremendous, as can be seen by much of the recent scholarship on the body (Polhemus 1978; Turner 1984; Armstrong 1985; O'Neill 1985; Berger 1987; Featherstone et al. 1991). Other writers (Grosz 1990; Mascia-Lees and Sharpe 1992), again following Foucault, demonstrate that the body is a canvas on which patterns of significance are inscribed and counter-inscribed. Mascia-Lees and Sharpe, for example, literalize this notion in their discussion of how the tattoo is a visceral example of how culture writes on the body. For them, the body serves also as allegory for culture because of its factualness: it is borrowed to lend an aura of realness to cultural constraints when there is a crisis in society.Anthropologists Nancy Scheper-Hughes and Margaret Lock, in their essay "The Mindful Body" (1987), bring together many of the pieces we have so far discussed. They propose three types of bodies: the lived-in individual body, the social and representational body, and the controlled and disciplined body politic.

Another stream of research on the body in culture has focused on the class(ed) body. The most important thinker here is certainly Pierre Bourdieu, and in particular his book *Distinction: A Social Critique of the Judgement of Taste* (1984). Bourdieu uses a concept called "**habitus**," developed by sociologist Marcel Mauss, which refers to the ways in which the lifestyle, values, and tastes of a social group are acquired through experience and reflected in the form and habits of the body. Mauss wrote, "the body is man's first and most natural instrument" (1979: 104). Bourdieu also gives us the notions of **cultural capital**, the experiences, knowledge, skills, and even ways of speaking that a person has developed which may be differentially valued by the culture around them, and **physical capital**, one's skin color, body shape, beauty, or grace, all of which, again, will be differentially valued by the society in general.

Medical anthropologists Philippe Bourgois and Jeff Schonberg borrowed from Mauss and Bourdieu's concept of habitus, but used it in a slightly different way. They used what they call "ethnic habitus" to explore the behaviors of homeless heroin injectors in San Francisco (2007). They found that white and black addicts had different ways of dealing with one of the problems of chronic heroin users – the difficulty of finding veins which could still be used for injecting. For white users, they turned to intramuscular or subcutaneous injections when usable veins could no longer be found, while black users spent more time and effort locating a good vein; it was worth the time and effort for the black users because the experience of injecting into the vein was more satisfying than injecting intramuscularly. These different bodily techniques result in different outcomes, and result from different values and beliefs.

Another theorist who uses the concept of habitus is sociologist Loic Wacquant, who wrote about African-American amateur boxers in Chicago. What Wacquant calls the "pugilistic habitus" refers to "a virtual punching machine, but an intelligent and creative machine capable of self-regulation while innovating within a fixed and relatively restricted panoply of moves as an instantaneous function of the actions of the opponent" (Wacquant 2004: 95). Wacquant himself, through the course of his fieldwork, acquires such a habitus and even fought in a Chicago Golden Gloves tournament.

Beyond the contributions of Bourdieu, Russian philosopher Mikhail Bakhtin's work (1984) has also informed the work of a number of contemporary studies which deal with the difference between lower-class and upper-class bodies (Stallybrass and White 1986; Fiske 1989; Kipnis 1992). Bakhtin wrote his doctoral dissertation about the French Renaissance

FIGURE 1.3 Dressing a mannequin. Photo courtesy of Tom Young.

writer François Rabelais and his work *Gargantua and Pantagruel,* focusing on the institution of carnival and the grotesque realism in Rabelais' work. What made this work so important for body studies theorists is how Bakhtin described the use of the body, and in particular his focus on the grotesque body. According to Bakhtin's reading of Rabelais, the grotesque body is the open, protruding, extended, secreting body, which is opposed to the classical body, which is static, closed, and sleek. The grotesque body gives birth, grows fat, grows old, and dies. It is this body which is associated with the lower and working classes, while the upper classes embrace a body which does not change, which remains young and beautiful and without flaws.

Theorizing the female body

Many recent studies on the body have taken as their target the gendered body (Russo 1985; Martin 1987; Gallop 1988; Jaggar and Bordo 1989; Bordo 1990; Butler 1990; Mascia-Lees and Sharpe 1992). These studies take on

introduction: theorizing the body   15

topics such as the role that fashion plays in the construction of the female body (Silverman 1986; Wilson 1987; Gaines 1990), how women's experience of their bodies is shaped in part by being subjects of the "**male gaze**" (Mulvey 1975), or how women's bodies are constituted through the discourses of science (Martin 1987; Jaggar and Bordo 1989; Bordo 1990). In general, these studies look at both how women shape and control their own bodies (or discipline them, using Foucault's language) in order to meet mandated social norms, but also how, in some cases, they derive pleasure from that disciplining and policing. In addition, for scholars like Judith Butler, these practices not only reinforce gendered norms, but actually *create* them.

For example, Emily Martin, in her work on medical constructions of the female body (1987), looks at how social control over the body has moved from the legal realm of corporal punishment, as per Foucault, to the medical realm of science. She argues that women's bodies are now not only fragmented into parts through sexualization but also through medical practices.

Jane Gaines, in her work on fashion (1990), suggests that women are often defined completely by their clothing – a woman is what she wears. This comes in part from the fact that women must, in Gaines' words, "carry the mirror's eye within the mind" (1990: 4) because they know they are always on display, both from their own experiences of being constantly watched, but also from looking at images of other women in the media. Fashion is paradoxical because while women dress and make themselves up, dress and makeup can also be seen as a sign of the enslavement of women. In any case, fashion both shapes the undressed body, and in turn, the body gives existence to the dress, "for it is impossible to conceive of a dress without a body" (ibid.). Entwistle and Wilson, paraphrasing Kaja Silverman (1986) wrote "clothing makes the body culturally visible" (2001: 82).

On the other hand, nudity may be just as important in some traditional cultures as clothing is in ours. For example, the Nuba, a pastoral tribal group in the Sudan in Africa, wear elaborate body painting as a sign of their social and cultural accomplishments. Nuba men, then, must be naked in order to display their masculinity, strength, and virility. For the Nuba, only the old or the sick wear clothing (Faris 1972).

Feminist critic Susan Bordo points out that because women must spend so much time managing their bodies in order to achieve an artificial feminine ideal, they are diverted from other, more important, concerns, resulting in "bodies whose forces and energies are habituated to external regulation, subjection, transformation, 'improvement'" (1993: 166). A woman's daily activities are focused around diet, fashion, makeup, and other forms of self-improvement, and yet, in reality, it results in a feeling of defeat as a woman

a social and cultural perspective

never really can be good enough. It also results in a female body which is docile and easy to control. For Bordo, as for other feminist scholars, the body is a continuous and important site of struggle; through the body women can resist gender domination.

Feminists have, it can be argued, played the largest role in redefining body studies in recent years. It makes sense that this has been a focus of feminist scholars because of the ways that women have been, historically and in the present, largely defined by their bodies. Whether we look to a time when women were encouraged to forgo higher education, because the female brain would pull valuable resources from the uterus and thus render them unable to bear children, or whether we look at how modern women's accomplishments are still often seen as secondary to their physical appearance, it makes sense that feminist scholars would want to resist and challenge any sort of biological determinism. In fact, virtually every policy debate over women in the Western world today still centers at least in some way on women's bodies, and, in particular, on their reproductive ability. Should women have access to birth control or abortion? Should women be able to serve in the military, and should they be allowed to fight alongside men? Can a woman serve as the President of the United States, especially if she's a mother/is menstruating/is menopausal?

Feminist scholars today do not deny the importance of the body in terms of shaping the experiences of women, however. They recognize that the same capabilities that once restricted (and continue to do so in much of the world) women – their capacity to menstruate, get pregnant, give birth, and breast feed – also result in very different lived experiences for men and women. Whether it's because women must constantly monitor their appearance and behaviors in order to please men, under whose gaze they continuously operate, or whether it's because they must take into account the ways in which their reproductive abilities influence the activities that they engage in, women are always aware of their bodies in ways that men are not.

For example, feminist philosopher Judith Butler (1990) points out the ways in which even the most essential aspects of the body – hormones, organs, genes – are already inserted into a discourse about those aspects, and that discourse is already shaped by pre-existing ideas about gender, sex, and power. She notes that bodily materiality is constructed through what she calls a "gendered matrix" where the woman is more grounded in nature and materiality while the man is not. Matter itself, the body itself, is already shaped by gender, and can never really be seen objectively. In other words, there is no biological reality that is separate from social meanings.

Other feminist theorists take the perspective that women's bodies are not problematic, but that those same characteristics that are used to not just define but oppress women – their reproductive abilities – should instead be seen as a source of strength and power and pride. This perspective, shared by scholars like Adrienne Rich and Audre Lord, suggests that women are more "naturally" nurturing and has been embraced by eco-feminists, peace activists, and others. However, these perspectives can be seen as just as reductionist as those which suggest that women cannot achieve certain things because of their bodies. Luce Irigaray is another theorist who focuses on the difference between male and female bodies. She proposes that the differences between those bodies may be linked to differences in thought patterns between men and women. Theories like this are known as "**sexual difference theories**" because they suggest that female embodiment and male embodiment are qualitatively different experiences, with very different results which must be attended to, rather than denied. One of the focuses here is, again, to call attention to the fact that historically, male bodies, and male experiences, have been seen as the norm, a practice which must be overcome.

Counter-inscription

Both Mary Douglas and Michel Foucault also realized that the body can also be a site of resistance, or counter-inscription, as people can, and do, mark their own bodies in ways that threaten the existing social order, and this becomes an important focus in much of today's scholarship on the body.

For example, many of the Cultural Studies scholars of the 1970s and 1980s looked at subcultures like punks and mods and argued that clothes, hair, and makeup could be used as a form of resistance to social oppression; what Dick Hebdige called "ornamentation as social offense."

In these approaches, practices like anorexia, obesity, or corseting are examples of practices which can be seen as self-destructive, yet can also be read as statements of refusal to conform to bodily norms. Other recent works emphasize the ongoing struggle for control over the female body, as women challenge, through their bodies, dominant notions of beauty, femininity, or respectability. For example, Mary Russo (1985) focuses on female bodies that challenge conventional notions of beauty and propriety; bodies which through self-marking, are seen as "subversive" or "out of bounds." Russo borrows the concept of the grotesque body from Bakhtin, but with respect to women. She talks about how women sometimes make spectacles of themselves, and how making a spectacle of oneself is a uniquely female danger. Whereas men can expose themselves, it tends to be a deliberate act. For women, it is inadvertent, and involves a loss of boundaries (fat thighs, visible bra strap, loud voice, heavy makeup). Russo points out that women, because they are already marginalized, are already associated with danger (which explains why their bodily fluids are so polluting);

thus women's bodies are already transgressive. In my own work on tattooed women (1985), I use this same argument to suggest that heavily tattooed women do the same thing: by borrowing the tattoo from men, and using it to turn their bodies into a masculine, and quite offensive, sign, they are challenging the dominant notion of femininity to which all women are expected to conform.

In fact, a great many of the bodies that this text deals with can be considered subversive or deviant. Whether female, fat, criminal, non-white, disabled, old, anorexic, poor, tattooed, veiled, or pornographic – society, or certain elements in society, may find these bodies to be troublesome, and thus subject to extra levels of social control. At the same time, some of these same bodies may then respond by fighting back with a variety of forms of corporeal challenge: new uses of the body which challenge the control of the state, the church, the society, or the family.

But we also have to remember that a body that is subversive at one time or place was not so in another time and place. Social categories are, by definition, socially constructed, so a "pervert," for example, is just a social category that didn't exist before the nineteenth century (just like pornography didn't exist as a category before the nineteenth century). As philosopher Ian Hacking says in an essay called "Making Up People," "people spontaneously come to fit their categories" (1995: 151). As social categories are created, people begin to fit into those categories.

Foucault points out, however, that as bodies resist control, power responds with an entirely new mode of control, and the struggle continues (Foucault 1980). For example, even as inner city rappers, underclass punks, or zoot-suited Latinos use their sartorial practices to challenge middle- and upper-class norms and values, those same practices are often incorporated by the fashion industry and commodified. According to Kaja Silverman, however, just because deviant dress is often absorbed by the fashion industry, that doesn't mean that "absorption means recuperation or neutralization." Instead, she suggests that even when a subcultural practice has been commodified, it still may be a victory. She writes, "It is no small thing to effect a change in mainstream fashion" (1986: 149).

Today, the body is no longer simply thought of as a model or template for culture or social organization. Thanks to the work of feminist theorists and other postmodern theorists, as well as the on-the-ground work of punks, riot grrls, and other subversives, it is a full-blown site for cultural war. And as we'll see in the chapters to come, the way in which bodies are used, contested, and their meanings disputed, points to the ways in which bodily meanings forever continue to shift, often in interesting and uncomfortable ways.

Key terms

Body Horror

Body Politic

Constructionism

Cultural Capital

Dramaturgical Theory

Embodiment

Essentialism

Feminism

Habitus

Impression Management

Male Gaze

Mind/Body Dualism

Naturalization

Phenomenology

Physical Capital

Reductionism

Sexual Difference Theories

Further reading

Bakhtin, Mikhail. (1984). *Rabelais and His World*. Bloomington, IN: Indiana University Press.

Bordo, Susan. (1993). *Unbearable Weight: Feminism, Western Culture, and the Body*. Berkeley, CA: University of California Press.

Bourdieu, Pierre. (1984). *Distinction: a Social Critique of the Judgement of Taste*. Cambridge, MA: Harvard University Press.

Butler, Judith. (1990). *Gender Trouble: Feminism and the Subversion of Identity*. New York: Routledge.

Douglas, Mary. (1973). *Natural Symbols: Explorations in Cosmology*. New York: Vintage.

Douglas, Mary. (1966). *Purity and Danger: An Analysis of Concepts of Pollution and Taboo*. New York: Praeger.

Foucault, Michel. (1980a). *Power/Knowledge: Selected Interviews and Other Writings. 1972–77*. Brighton: Harvester.

Foucault, Michel. (1980b). *The History of Sexuality: Volume I, An Introduction*. New York: Pantheon Books.

Gaines, Jane and Herzog, Charlotte, (ed.). (1990). *Fabrications: Costume and the Female Body*. New York: Routledge.

Martin, Emily. (1987). *The Woman in The Body: A Cultural Analysis of Reproduction*. Boston, MA: Beacon Press.

Russo, Mary. (1985). *Female Grotesques: Carnival and Theory*. Milwaukee, WI: Center for Twentieth Century Studies, University of Wisconsin-Milwaukee.

Young, Iris Marion. (2005). *On Female Body Experience: "Throwing Like a Girl" and Other Essays*. New York: Oxford University Press.

PART II

The Scientific and Biomedical Body

chapter 2

Healthy and Diseased Bodies

In 2010, the United States Congress, after months of bitter debate, passed two major pieces of health care legislation, the Patient Protection and Affordable Care Act and the Health Care and Education Reconciliation Act, which together opponents call "Obamacare." These two bills were intended to make health care more affordable for Americans and to reduce the number of uninsured Americans (at about 48.6 million in 2012). The bills include provisions to expand Medicaid eligibility for the poor, subsidize insurance premiums for the middle class, provide incentives to businesses that provide employee health care benefits, mandate that Americans purchase health insurance, and prohibit insurance companies from denying coverage to those with pre-existing conditions or instituting caps on coverage. While Democrats largely supported the legislation (although many Democrats wanted universal single payer coverage instead), Republicans overwhelmingly oppose it, and want to see it repealed and replaced by market-based solutions.

The debate over health care, and whether health care should be a right of all citizens (as it is in most Western nations) or a privilege for those who can afford it, continues to rage in the United States. Fueling the debate are issues like abortion and birth control – should these be part of a woman's health care, covered by her public or private insurance? And what, in general, should be defined as health care?

These discussions cannot really be considered without first defining health and illness. When we talk about health and illness, most of us tend to think in terms of biology, science, or medicine. Health and illness seem like objective conditions; either one is healthy or one is not. However, both health and illness are at least in part socially constructed. Both conditions depend in large part on how a given society, at a given time, defines what it is to be healthy. Furthermore, what is healthy for one person may be an indication of illness for another.

The social construction of health and illness

From a biological or medical perspective, illness is the condition of poor physical, emotional, or mental health. But in order for a condition to be perceived as an illness, it must be defined that way first by one's culture. The kind and incidence of diseases vary among societies, and cultures interpret and treat illness differently. What one culture sees as an illness – for instance, talking to God, which in the West is a sign of mental illness – another culture may interpret as a religious calling.

In the United States, in recent years we have seen a number of new illnesses emerge, such as pre-menstrual syndrome, post-traumatic stress disorder, postpartum depression, restless leg syndrome, attention deficit disorder, obsessive compulsive disorder, and social anxiety disorder. While many of these are clearly recognized as serious medical conditions today, the fact that they have emerged in recent years (sometimes through the pharmaceutical company that created the drug which treats them) is an indication that many illnesses are, at least in part, socially constructed. For instance, homosexuality was once considered to be a mental disorder but was declassified as such by the American Psychiatric Association in 1973.

Another way that illness is culturally constructed is that we see that the spread of, treatment of, and prevention of illness is often constrained by cultural values, cultural practices, and the social and economic position of the patient. In Japan, because of the concept of *gotai*, which is the ideal of maintaining bodily integrity, people not only do not get their ears pierced, they very rarely undergo voluntary surgery, and they don't tend to donate their organs after death. Japan also has an illness known as *kikomori*. Translated as "school refusal syndrome," this condition primarily affects young men who stop going to school and begin withdrawing socially, ultimately locking themselves in their homes for months. While it may sound like agoraphobia, and has been compared to conditions like autism, researchers feel that it is linked to social conditions found exclusively in Japan such as the intense pressure on Japanese men to succeed and the financial support provided by middle-class Japanese parents for their children.

In the United States, on the other hand, agoraphobia is largely a woman's disease, and tends to emerge historically at times when women are subject to extremely tight levels of social control, as in the late nineteenth century, or in the 1950s. Feminist scholar Susan Bordo (1989) sees both agoraphobia and anorexia as female responses to the enforcement of domesticity and dependence as the female ideal.

In many cultures, sickness is a disruption not just to one's physical health, but to one's social health as well. In many cultures, the sick occupy what is called the **sick role**; they must spend their time making sure that they do not make others around them uncomfortable; they must be cheery and pleasant to be around. Barbara Ehrenreich, in her writing on breast cancer, notes that breast cancer patients in particular must work hard to be cheerful and positive to those around them, and the breast cancer community, enabled as it is by corporate sponsors, plays a major role in encouraging women to stick with the positive message: "cheerfulness is more or less mandatory, dissent a kind of treason. Within this tightly knit world, attitudes are subtly adjusted, doubters gently brought back to the fold" (2007: 409).

Sickness, and the time during which one is sick, is a **liminal** space: one is neither here nor there, one's whole life is on hold. Even the hospital is set up as a marginal space, removed from outside society; the patient is stripped of all identity and status, and is forced to get well. According to cultural critic Susan Sontag (1991: 3), we all hold dual citizenship in the "kingdom of the well and the kingdom of the sick;" at some point in our lives, we must trade in our passport to the former world and begin using the passport from the latter.

For many traditional cultures, the root of disease is found in violations of order, and how through illness the social order is disturbed. Similarly, disease is a disturbance of the natural order, particularly diseases brought about by the intrusion of an alien object in the body. Many cultures also believe that the patient has brought about his own illness, and if he does not get well, it's seen as his fault. Even in our own culture, the idea that diseases have a moralistic component – especially seen in respect to HIV/AIDS – or that they are a form of God's punishment, is still with us today. (Evangelist Jerry Falwell once famously said that AIDS is "God's judgment on a society that does not live by his rules.") The corollary to that belief is the idea that those who, say, overcome cancer are somehow heroic or especially deserving of their reprieve from death.

In the United States, thanks to the power and influence of the pharmaceutical industry, we have a tendency to see most conditions and behaviors as medical problems which can be treated with drugs. **Medicalization** refers to the practice of redefining conditions as medical conditions. Once a condition has been defined as a medical (or psychiatric) condition, and once a drug has been prescribed to treat that condition, then people will tend to develop the condition, thus reinforcing and reifying the condition, leading to its spread in society. Especially today, with the ubiquity of pharmaceutical advertisements on television, on the Internet, and in magazines, as the public sees ads for restless leg syndrome drugs, the idea that restless leg syndrome is a common medical condition becomes not just more normative, but, in fact, more common among the populace. This concept helps explains the growth of certain illnesses and even epidemics in our history, such as the rise of "hysteria" among women in the nineteenth century or the current popularity of the diagnosis of attention deficit disorder today. With hysteria, by the way, Victorian middle- and upper-class women were diagnosed as moody, nervous, emotional, and frigid. It should not surprise us that the root of the word "hysteria" is the same as the root of "hysterectomy" and in fact the removal of the uterus was often the cure for the condition.

Social anxiety disorder is another good example of this process. At one time, people who were uncomfortable in groups of strangers, or speaking in public, were simply considered to be shy. Today, those behaviors are symptomatic of social anxiety disorder, a mental condition which can be treated with anti-depressants. Not surprisingly, with that diagnosis, and with the availability of drugs intended to treat this condition, more Americans have become diagnosed with social anxiety disorder, leading to drugs like Celexa skyrocketing in popularity.

One result of medicalization is the over-prescription of medication, and the increasing practice of people diagnosing their own illnesses on the internet and shopping for the "appropriate" medications. Another way of looking at it could be that some of the symptoms that are interpreted medically – stress and anxiety are now signs of psychiatric condition – could instead by interpreted socially. In other words, what if we saw the rising number of anxiety disorders as indicative of a social system that produces too much stress? In contemporary Western society, we work more hours than ever before, we take work home, answering work emails at all hours of the day and night, and multi-task at a level that our parents would have found incredible. Is it any wonder we are under so much stress? By medicating those symptoms, rather than dealing with them on a societal level, the underlying problems are not solved; they are simply covered up.

Interesting issues: schizophrenia in Ireland

In 1977, medical anthropologist Nancy Scheper-Hughes wrote a book called Saints, Scholars and Schizophrenics: Mental Illness in Rural Ireland that looked at some of the cultural causes of mental illness. She outlined many of the cultural conditions within this isolated, rural community – the emigration of the young, the breakdown in the extended family structure, the lack of intimacy between men and women – as well as the global changes that made small family farms

the scientific and biomedical body

like those found in that community economically unproductive. The confluence of these factors, according to Scheper-Hughes, as well as the socialization process which coerced and shamed last-born males, was partly responsible for the high rates of depression, suicide, and schizophrenia, especially among bachelor farmers who were alone responsible for inheriting the family farm and caring for their elderly parents. At the time, schizophrenia was thought to be primarily an internal psychological disorder, so Scheper-Hughes' analysis, which placed it in the context of the social, cultural and economic surroundings, was groundbreaking. Even though the book was written in the 1970s, the issues it covers are still relevant today as we grapple with how much culture plays a role in physical and psychological illnesses.

Culturally specific illnesses and conditions

Ethno-etiologies refer to cross-cultural variations in causal explanations for illnesses. Every culture has their own ethno-etiology to explain their own culture's illnesses. Some cultures have what is called a **naturalistic disease theory** to explain illness; naturalistic disease theories see illness as caused by an impersonal, external force such as bacteria or viruses, and also see the body and the mind as separate entities. This is the approach found in Western **biomedicine**, and in this approach, only the body is treated, in isolation from the mind, the environment, or one's social relationships. Professionally trained physicians treat patients within this system, using the standardized body (typically the middle-class, male body) as the norm, focusing primarily on symptoms and using a combination of drugs and surgery. In this approach, the body is typically seen as a machine, and the doctor a mechanic who fixes the machine.

In other cultures, other theories of illness tend to be prominent. For example, many cultures have what are called **personalistic disease theories** which see agents like witches, ancestral spirits, or sorcerers as being the cause of illness. While these are, like bacteria, external agents, they are *personal* – a sorcerer would only cause a person's illness if he or she had something against the victim. Treatment for illness in this system would involve ascertaining who has caused the problem, and ensuring that the patient remedy the social problem which has led to the illness. Sometimes a form of counter-magic might be prescribed, and people might wear amulets or talismans to protect them from magical harm. Another example of this is the idea, found in some Asian cultures, that a child is born with a disability because of the sinful behavior of the parents. In cultures with beliefs like this, healers are not professionally trained doctors. Rather, they are religious practitioners with experience in diagnosing – generally via **divination** – and treating, illnesses of a supernatural nature.

Another disease theory found in other cultures is what is called the **emotionalistic disease theory**. In this case, a person becomes ill thanks to an emotional experience that they have had. The Latin American disease *susto* is an example of this; susto is a disease where the victim is frightened by something, causing the soul to become separated from the body, resulting in physical illness. Women and children are more likely to experience susto, which manifests itself in insomnia, anorexia, despondency, and nervousness. Susto is treated by bringing in a *curandero*, or a native healer, who asks the victim to recount the frightening experience, while he or she brushes the person with special herbs and recites prayers. Susto is an example of what we call **somatization** – whereby the body absorbs stress and manifests it through physical illness. *Nervoso* is another example of a similar condition, which means nervous, hungry, emotional, and/or weak. Anthropologist Nancy Scheper-Hughes (1993) described the prevalence of nervoso among shantytown dwellers in Brazil as a natural response to the violent, demeaning, and impoverished conditions of the people's lives. Scheper-Hughes also points out that while *hunger* is not a subject that can be openly discussed in a clearly poverty-stricken region like the shantytowns of Brazil, where food (i.e., the cure) is unavailable, nervousness is a topic for discussion. That's because medicine is now readily available, thanks to Brazil's socialized health care system. So nervoso is now interpreted as nerves rather than hunger, is treated with drugs, and the unequal and unfair social system is left intact.

Finally, **disharmony theories** are found primarily in Asia, and suggest that illness is caused by the body's natural balance being disrupted. For instance, acupuncture is an Eastern medical technique involving the insertion of needles into the body's acupuncture points. The theory behind acupuncture states that the body has an energy force running through it known as *Qi*, which includes spiritual, emotional, physical, and mental aspects. The Qi travels through the body along special pathways or meridians, and if the Qi is unbalanced or lacks strength, or its travels are disrupted, ill health can occur. By balancing and repairing the Qi, the patient can be healed.

Disability and the normative body

Disability, too, is at least partially a social construct. The whole notion of disability only makes sense within a context in which the standardized or "normal" body has already been defined. If a normal body is a body which has two fully functioning arms and legs, for example, then a body which lacks those features will be defined as disabled.

Sociologists consider disability to be a **master status**: For those who are disabled, they find that disability is not simply a physical affair, it is their condition of being in the world. People who become disabled experience an

the scientific and biomedical body

FIGURE 2.1 U.S. Marine Corps Cpl. Anthony McDaniel races around the track during practice for the 2012 Warrior Games in Colorado Springs, Colo., April 23, 2012. McDaniel suffered a bilateral leg and partial hand amputations from an improvised explosive device in Afghanistan 2010. He is competing in track and wheelchair basketball. Photo courtesy of the Department of Defense.

extreme drop in social status and self-worth; they acquire what sociologists call an "**embattled identity**," where the sense of who and what a person is is no longer dominated by past social attributes but by present physical defects. And just as the bodies of disabled people are permanently impaired, so are their social standings. That's why so many people do not look at those who are disabled; they become **socially invisible.**

Anthropologist Robert Murphy, in his 1990 book *The Body Silent*, wrote about his journey into disability after he was diagnosed with a spinal cord tumor. He writes that the disabled represent humanity reduced to its bare essentials; disability is not just a physical malady, it is a social malady. He writes about the fact that when one is healthy, one takes one's body for granted, but when one is ill, it can no longer be taken for granted, for it has become a problem. In his moving and eloquent text, Murphy notes that the body is the foundation upon which we build our sense of who and what we are, and it is the instrument through which we grapple with and create reality. The newly disabled person experiences not only an altered body, but an altered consciousness as well, resulting in a damaged self. According to this model, disabled people can be seen as subverters of an American ideal which demands movement, able bodies, and accomplishment, just as the poor are betrayers of the American dream. As disabled people depart from the

healthy and diseased bodies

ideal, they become ugly and repulsive to the able bodied. Thanks to his own disability, Murphy writes about the damage to the ego he experienced, as he felt an extreme drop in social status and self-worth, as well as changes in his relationships with his former colleagues and even his wife, who moved from his lover to his caretaker.

Many disabled people and advocates for the disabled see the real problem with disability being not the disability itself, but society's response to the disability. We could, for example, view disability as an inevitable part of one's life course: most of us, if we live long enough, will experience a loss of functioning of some, or many, parts of the body. We may lose our eyesight, or our hearing, or our ability to walk. At some point, unless we die too soon, every able-bodied person will themselves be disabled. That's one reason why those who are disabled are so stigmatized; because they remind us of our own vulnerability. Taking this perspective, which is known as the **social model of disability**, we might instead focus on the role that society plays in stigmatizing the disabled, or how societies could, if they chose, provide the disabled with greater access to services and resources. Clearly, the difficulty of living with a disability would be greatly lessened by living in a society which provides equal access to all, and which does not discriminate against or stigmatize non-normative bodies.

Another way of looking at disability would be to move away from the idea that bodies should all look the same and work the same way. We know that there is a wide diversity in terms of physical and mental capabilities in humans. In fact, the 2012 Paralympics, and the participation of South African athlete and double-amputee Oscar Pistorius in the 2012 Olympic Games, may have played a role in changing public opinion about disabled people. If we were to respect that diversity, then disabled people would feel both more included and would not be subject to discrimination and disadvantages.

People with disabilities are not just stigmatized because their bodies are different. Men and women with disabilities also find that their bodies challenge **normative ideals about gender**, making society even less tolerant of them. In many societies, men, for example, are expected to be strong, independent, and self-sufficient. Disabled men, however, are often seen as less-than-men because their bodies are not necessarily strong and they are not necessarily self-reliant. Women, on the other hand, are not expected to be strong and independent; in fact, dependence in women is often seen as a plus. However, women are expected to be sexually attractive, and since they are defined so intensely by their appearance, then having a body that falls short of the norms of beauty is a heavy burden for a woman to carry. Disability, then, can de-masculinize men and de-feminize women. In addition, disabled people are often infantilized – treated as children by well-meaning strangers.

"C H A N G" AND "E N G"
THE WORLD RENOWNED UNITED
S I A M E S E   T W I N S.

FIGURE 2.2 "Chang" and "Eng" the world-renowned united Siamese twins. Portrait of the twins with nine vignettes along the border depicting them in such activities as hunting, boating, plowing, and with their respective families. New York: Currier & Ives, 1860. Photo courtesy of the National Library of Medicine.

People with disabilities do not just suffer from lack of access to public services. In the past, the disabled were targeted by medical professionals and political leaders who did not want to see them as part of society. In the United States, for example, the physically and mentally disabled were subject to mandatory sterilization policies in which tens of thousands of individuals – mostly women – were sterilized from the 1900s to the 1970s, to prevent them from giving birth to disabled children; Germany and Sweden did the same thing, sterilizing hundreds of thousands of their citizens in the 1930s and 1940s. This mass sterilization project was part of a larger **eugenics** movement in which sterilization and selective breeding were encouraged to minimize "defective genes."

While mandatory sterilization is no longer legal in the United States, the prospect of giving birth to children with defects is still a major reason for

therapeutic abortions. Amniocentesis is routinely recommended to pregnant women today (especially women who get pregnant later in life), in order to detect conditions like Down's syndrome; women bearing fetuses with such conditions are then given the choice to terminate their pregnancies. These issues will be discussed more fully in Chapter 4.

There's a very real reason that for the last few hundred years, up until just a few decades ago, disabled people were one of the most popular attractions found in circus and carnival sideshows. Human freaks, because of their extreme corporeal differences, helped to define and construct "normality" for their audiences. By visibly displaying what were once called dog girls, lobster boys, human torsos, and Siamese twins, the sideshow allowed the audience to take comfort in their position as normal, and ideal, while turning the disabled bodies into spectacles. Disability is so troubling because, according to disability scholar Rosemarie Garland Thomson, "disability is the unorthodox made flesh, refusing to be normalized, neutralized, or homogenized" (1997: 24).

Freaks, monsters, and freak shows

In the West, the disabled were displayed in inns, taverns, and at local fairs throughout Medieval Europe. The first such freak to be displayed in the United States was Miss Emma Leach, a dwarf who was exhibited in Boston in 1771. In the nineteenth century came Chang and Eng, the first conjoined twins who were displayed starting in 1829. Around 1840, human oddities became joined into what is now known as the freak show, thanks especially to the work of P. T. Barnum who established the American Museum in 1842.

When being displayed in a sideshow, freaks are what the talker or manager or showman makes them. The disabled, known as born freaks, were rarely in charge of their own careers or destinies, and indeed joined circuses or carnivals typically because it was the only way they could make a living for themselves. The "exotic" presentation is one form of displaying a freak, by appealing to people's interest in the unexplainable and bizarre. For example, Tom Thumb was displayed as an 11-year-old English boy, while he was actually a 4-year-old American, and the original Wild Men of Borneo were actually mentally disabled brothers from Ohio.

Human abnormalities were explained scientifically by a number of theories, including the idea that if a pregnant woman was scared, her child may be born with an abnormality relating to what scared her. In the eighteenth century, the science of **teratology** developed, which was the scientific study of monsters. This led to a new understanding of freaks that saw them as part of God's natural order, a belief that was later discarded in favor of the missing link theory that developed after Darwinism, which saw freaks as being literal half-human, half-animal creatures, which gave rise

the scientific and biomedical body

to the freak known as the "wild man."

In the twentieth century, with the rediscovery of Mendelian genetics and the rise of modern science, born freaks began to be understood from a biological and cultural perspective and this began to adversely affect attendance at freak shows. Notions of pity, humane impulses, and the desire to lock away all undesirables led to its eventual decline. The use of the physically disabled in American freak shows finally ended in the 1960s when the American Civil Liberties Union brought public attention to the freak shows and caused their demise; many U.S. states now prohibit the exhibition of disabled people for entertainment.

In Germany, thanks to the rising eugenics movement, freak shows were restricted or banned as early as 1911, and especially after World War I when clean-cut showgirls emerged as a new form of entertainment. Some freaks fled the country, but others were most likely euthanized as part of the Nazis' program to clean up the country's hospitals from 1939 to 1941 when an estimated 70,000 physically and mentally disabled people were killed; the deaths were called *Gnadentod* or "mercy deaths."

Today, while disability has not disappeared, the disabled as performative object is not as popular as it once was. But the idea that disability is outside of the norms and bounds of society remains with us, through the idea that disabilities should be cured through surgery, making disabled people "normal." Still, the extraordinarily disabled remain objects of public fascination, as stories of conjoined twins who are separated through surgery make international news, and in 2012 TLC began airing a television show featuring Abby and Brittany Hensel, two 22-year-old conjoined twins. We also continue to stigmatize and discriminate against the disabled. **Disablism** refers to the various ways in which society is constructed to favor the able-bodied and to marginalize the disabled. Even well-meaning events such as the Paralympics set the disabled aside as outside of the accepted norms of society, even while, perhaps, contributing to society's greater acceptance of disabled men and women.

Gender, morbidity, and mortality

Health, like so many other social institutions, is gendered. How women and men get sick depends in large part on the social roles played by men and women.

Around the world, women live longer than men, because of a combination of biological and social factors. Men engage in riskier behaviors than women, leading to more deaths from homicides, car accidents, gun accidents, and the like. Men tend to have more type-A aggressive personalities, and tend to hold in their emotions, which contributes to heart disease. Men visit the doctor less often than women because of differential role expectations (women visit for children as well as themselves, and women's reproductive lives come under greater medical scrutiny than men's); in addition, seeking medical help is often seen as a sign of weakness for men. In addition, men who engage in sports have greater chance of injury. Many health practices that are bad for us, like drinking, eating junk food, or smoking are also found more commonly among men. And finally, men are less likely to seek mental or emotional health care, leading to greater risk of depression or suicide.

Poor men and men of color live shorter lives than everyone else. Working-class men work in more hazardous conditions than most women (and middle-class men), increasing their exposure to toxins and the likelihood of workplace accidents. Men of color, because they're disproportionately poor, are more likely to live and work in unhealthy conditions, to live and work in dangerous environments, to be victimized by crime, to lack health insurance, and to have an unhealthy lifestyle. (These issues will be discussed further later in this chapter.)

When Olympic cyclist Lance Armstrong was diagnosed with testicular cancer in 1996, it was a wake-up call for many men, because of the fact that many men do not attend to their health. In addition, health issues that involve the genitals are among the least discussed of all health issues, thanks to the shame associated with them. After Armstrong so publicly survived his diagnosis (going on to win yet more gold medals), many men began to see testicular cancer differently, and testicular cancer diagnosis rates began to rise. Of course the fact that he admitted to using performance-enhancing drugs in 2013 has somehow confused the issue of how much of a role those drugs played in his "heroic" victories.

While women live longer than men, paradoxically, they often are sicker than men. Again, the reasons for this tend to be both social and biological. For women, there are a number of conditions that impact women's bodies in ways that do not, or rarely, impact men's bodies, including obesity and size issues, and of course reproductive health. Women alone experience pregnancy, menstruation, menopause, and childbirth, all of which come with a number of complicating health factors. The demands of looking a certain way make women more susceptible to certain problems, such as eating disorders, issues related to cosmetic surgery, and problems related to other ways that women try to beautify themselves like high heels or corsets. In general, beauty practices aimed at women have always had health repercussions, from foot binding to skin whitening for African-American women to skin tanning for white women. These practices are both gendered and racialized and will be discussed further in Chapters 6, 7, and 10.

Poor women, like poor men, are more disadvantaged because of their living conditions, working conditions, and lack of access to health care. And since women disproportionately make up the poor in this country, they will

the scientific and biomedical body

be less likely to have health insurance, and will be less healthy overall. Women working in factories where mostly women work are often exposed to greater dangers than men, since those workplaces, like garment factories, are historically less protected than male workplaces. More women than men die and are injured in workplace homicides, because they are more often found as clerks, where they are subject to the rage of violent customers and employees, and also because they're killed or injured by their partners.

Finally, in many cultures, girls are fed less than boys, leading to chronic malnourishment for girls in developing cultures. This continues into adulthood, because in a great many societies, men eat first, and women eat their leftovers, leading girls and women overall to be less healthy. In addition, in some parts of the world, female babies have a smaller chance of survival into adulthood than male babies thanks to the almost universal preference for male babies and the practice of **female infanticide** and selective neglect. In addition, the number of girls conceived is much lower than the number of girls actually born, given selective aborting of female fetuses (known as **female feticide**) after amniocentesis in countries like India and China, and the wider practice of selecting female fetuses found around the world, including in the West.

One disease that disproportionately affects women is breast cancer. Journalist Barbara Ehrenreich has written about the commercialization of breast cancer in the United States, and the proliferation of businesses and non-profits that – while encouraging women to fight the disease – also ignore the causes of the disease (2007). She points out that what she calls the "pink-ribbon marketplace" offers thousands of pink products that infantilize women with breast cancer, and at the same time minimize or ignore one of the most likely causes of the disease: environmental carcinogens, caused by corporate pollution. Because so many companies that sell beauty products to women both sponsor breast cancer research yet also contribute to this pollution, the breast cancer industry cannot afford to focus attention on the problem. The result is that billions of dollars will continue to be spent in the United States and other Western nations to find a cure for cancers like breast cancer, while almost no money or resources are spent trying to find – and mitigate – the causes. Perhaps this is because there is no money to be made by pharmaceutical companies and hospitals in prevention. It's only the sick, after all, who generate money for the health industry.

HIV/AIDS: a bodily, social, and cultural phenomenon

Since the 1980s, HIV/AIDS has become one of the deadliest epidemics of the last few centuries. The HIV virus destroys a person's immune system, leaving the body vulnerable to a variety of opportunistic infections and cancers, which can be fatal. HIV is spread through bodily fluids like semen, blood, and vaginal secretions, and is passed through sexual contact or through the exchange of blood. It is also passed perinatally from an infected woman to her baby before or during birth, or after birth by breast feeding.

HIV is particularly dangerous because, after a brief flu shortly after infection, the virus tends to go dormant. With an incubation period lasting up to about 11 years, many people who are infected do not realize that they carry the virus, and, if they engage in unprotected sex, can transmit the virus to countless other people. Eventually, however, if untreated, the virus will deplete the immune system and the person develops the symptoms associated with full-blown AIDS.

AIDS is the sixth leading cause of death among young people in the United States, and continues to infect 50,000 people per year in the United States. Worldwide, 25 million people have died from the disease since the 1980s, and today there are approximately 34 million people living with HIV or AIDS. Almost three million new people become infected every year, and about two million people die each year from the disease.

Since the 1990s when AIDS emerged as a health threat, scientists have learned a great deal about its transmission and its symptoms, and have developed a number of medications, called **anti-retroviral drugs**, that can hold the virus in check, keeping many people from developing full-blown AIDS. However, there is no cure for AIDS, which is still a fatal condition, and as of this writing, there are no successful vaccines.

Sociologists and anthropologists have also studied AIDS – not from a medical perspective, but from a social and cultural perspective. Using this perspective, they have been able to uncover many of the social and cultural factors that help spread the disease; this information, in turn, is being used to fight it.

Sub-Saharan Africa is, today, the region of the world with the greatest number of new infections, greatest number of deaths, greatest number of people living with the disease, and perhaps most tragically, greatest number of children – over 11 million – who are orphaned thanks to AIDS. Sixty-eight percent of all people living with AIDS live in southern Africa, and 76 percent of all deaths occur there. Why would this region be associated with such high numbers?

In Africa, unlike the United States, most transmissions occur through heterosexual sex, with women being the hardest hit – they make up about 59 percent of all victims in the region. The reasons are complex, but have to do with a number of ancient and modern cultural and economic patterns in Africa. For example, **polygyny** – a marriage of one man and multiple wives – was once the most popular marital practice in Africa. Even when monogamy is practiced, men often still have multiple female sexual partners,

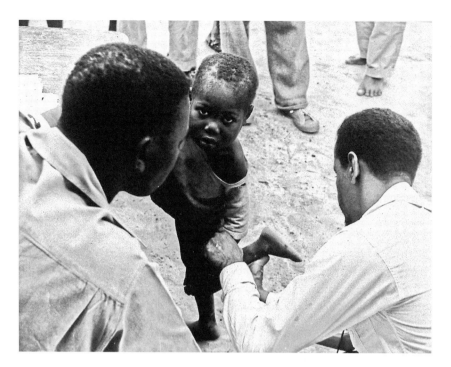

FIGURE 2.3 Two men are examining the feet of a young boy. Yaws is the disease of poverty and filth. The first victims are always the children. WHO photo by Paul Almasy, courtesy of the National Library of Medicine.

which contributes to a high rate of sexually transmitted infections. In recent years, many men have left their home villages to seek work elsewhere; because of that, many have resorted to using prostitutes for sex, which is also a major factor in the spread of the disease – first to the men who pay for sex, and next to their wives at home.

Gender plays another part in the spread of the disease in Africa. Because of a gendered power differential, men dominate women in sexual relationships, forcing women to have sex when they may not want to. In addition, many women cannot ask their partners to wear condoms, because doing so would imply that he (or she) may be unfaithful in the relationship. To make such an accusation, even implicitly, may get a woman beaten. And because so many women in Africa are dependent on men for economic support, they cannot afford to lose their partners by denying them sex. Finally, condoms, which are the primary method of AIDS prevention (other than abstinence), are impractical for women who are expected to get pregnant and provide their husbands with a child.

Sexual violence is another facet of male dominance in Southern Africa, and also plays a major role in the spread of AIDS. In particular, when children are raped, the probability of the child incurring the disease is increased. In

healthy and diseased bodies

fact, child rape is often a preferred form of sex in the region, thanks to the widespread belief that AIDS can be cured by having sex with a virgin. Other misconceptions about AIDS include the belief that AIDS is caused by witchcraft or sorcery. Misinformation like this only helps to spread the disease further.

No matter what the belief about the cause of AIDS, many Africans experience high degrees of discrimination if they are thought or known to be carrying HIV. Because of a lack of education about the causes and methods of transmission, men, women, and children with the virus are ostracized, and can be kicked out of their homes or villages. This stigma keeps many people from being tested for the disease, and allows it to spread even further.

Finally, poverty is a major factor in the spread of AIDS in Africa. When people are struggling for daily survival, their health care will not be a primary concern to them. In addition, desperate people are more likely to engage in behaviors – like selling their bodies for money – that spread the disease. And because the anti-retroviral drugs that can keep HIV from developing into AIDS are so expensive, without government intervention it would be prohibitive for the average African to be able to afford them.

Using knowledge gained from social scientists, it is clear that simply promoting abstinence or even condom use to fight AIDS is impractical in Africa. Instead, programs that focus on empowering women, fighting poverty, fighting stigma, reducing sexual violence, and providing education about AIDS have a greater chance of success.

Stigma, by the way, is not just associated with AIDS in Africa. One of the reasons why effective treatments for AIDS took so long to develop in the United States in the 1980s and 1990s was that it was largely viewed through a moral, rather than a medical, lens. Because AIDs was seen as a "gay disease" and was associated with practices – men having sex with men, unprotected sex, sex outside of marriage, and IV drug use – that many Americans frowned upon, fighting the disease was not a priority for many politicians. It was not until it became a major public health crisis, and the political landscape in the United States changed, that people began focusing less on the moral aspects of the illness and more on how to stop it. Even today, many young straight people still do not practice safe sex because they think that safe sex and AIDs-prevention messages only apply to "other people," i.e., gays or injection drug users, and many people in charge of educating our kids do not want to provide condoms or information about safe sex to them because they think it will encourage promiscuity.

In fact, whether we are discussing AIDS in Sub-Saharan Africa, the site of today's epidemic, or AIDS in the United States, where it first appeared and where, as of 2009, 1,200,000 people continue to live with the disease, social and personal practices continue to shape its transmission, and cultural values continue to play a role in its containment.

In the United States, sex workers, IV drug users, men who have sex with men, women who have unprotected sex with men, and African-Americans all remain at high risk for the disease. Poverty, unprotected sex, a lack of knowledge about the disease, multiple sex partners, a lack of testing, and inequality in sexual relationships are all factors involved in the spread of the disease in the United States.

Class matters: illness and inequality

As we have seen in our discussion of AIDS in Africa, economic factors like poverty can play a major role in shaping the health of a population. In fact, sociologists have long known about the links between illness and inequality. We call these the **social determinants of health**: those social and demographic factors like race and class that determine our health, illness, and even death.

Many cultures understand these links, seeing in their illnesses the larger structural forces that are causing them. *Sufriendo del agua*, for instance, is known as "suffering from water," and it's an illness defined and experienced by poor Mexican peasants who do not have access to clean water to cook, wash, and drink. This means that people suffer from health problems caused by a lack of access to clean water, and on top of that, they are anxious and nervous, creating yet other health problems.

On a broader level, we know that wealthy nations suffer from different illnesses than poor nations. Wealthy nations suffer from heart disease, cancer, and other diseases related to prosperity, pollution, obesity, and aging. Poor nations, on the other hand, suffer from illnesses related to poverty and poor sanitary conditions. Consequently, infectious diseases like tuberculosis, malaria, and AIDS are the leading causes of death in those countries, alongside of violence and malnutrition – both also caused or exacerbated by poverty.

Even though the United States spends more money on health care – including private insurance, out of pocket costs, and government programs like Medicaid and Medicare – than any other nation in the world, the country's life expectancy is dropping compared to other industrialized nations. This is because the poor will tend to have personal habits that are less healthy – like smoking, excessive drinking, poor nutrition, and drug use – than the middle class or the rich, and tend to live and work in less healthy, more toxic, and more dangerous, environments. Diabetes is associated in the United States, for example, with the poor quality, inexpensive diets eaten by the poor, and asthma is found most commonly in poor communities with poor air quality. Lead poisoning is found predominantly in poor communities, because of the poor housing there. Finally, the lower a person's income in the United States, the less likely they are to exercise. It should not surprise us, then, that the American south has the highest obesity rates, highest poverty rates, and highest death rates in the nation. And because they are sicker, the poor are more likely to miss more school when young and work when older, which impacts their educational and income opportunities.

Another factor is that people who work in low-income jobs tend to have very little control over their jobs, or for that matter their lives. Great Britain's influential **Whitehall Study** demonstrated that lack of control over one's life, regardless of access to health care, is associated with higher degrees of stress, which itself is correlated with higher death rates from heart attack and stroke. And in 2012, a study was published in the *Archives of Internal Medicine* which shows that those who are unemployed, even for only a short period of time, are at a higher risk of heart attack than the general population.

The poor also are less likely to have health insurance – in fact, 48 million Americans, at the time of this writing, lack health insurance – and subsequently visit the doctor less often. They do not get preventative health care, and when they do visit the doctor, they do so at free clinics or crowded emergency rooms, where they are less likely to get quality treatment. Lack of prenatal care among America's poor is associated with the high rates of infant mortality in poor communities; Memphis, Tennessee, for example has the highest rate of infant mortality in the nation. The city operates a public graveyard called "Babyland" where poor black babies are buried with taxpayer dollars, because their mothers cannot afford the cost of their burial.

Because dental care is not offered in the emergency room, the millions of uninsured Americans – and billions of others around the world – either pay for dental care themselves, or, for the poor, just do not get it. The result is that missing and rotten teeth are becoming more and more common for poor people, and bad teeth are becoming a visible mark of poverty. Unfortunately, bad teeth mean more than just a bad smile: it means less of a chance of a job where appearance is important; it means less ability to eat fruits and vegetables; and it leads to the use of alcohol or drugs to cope with the pain of toothaches.

Because health care is so expensive, medical bills are now the leading cause of bankruptcy in the United States. Yet, at the time of this writing, the U.S. Supreme Court is hearing a challenge to the Affordable Care Act, and millions of Americans oppose the idea of having any sort of government regulation of health care. The American health insurance industry is among the most profitable industries in the world, so while health care costs rise, their profits also rise. Still, Americans are devoted to the idea of private enterprise and freedom of choice – so much so that they will vote against legislation that provides them with better health care and longer lives.

In Chapter 3, we'll move into another issue that deals with health, aging, and we will see that, like health and illness, aging and youth are also socially constructed. We will also note the ways in which certain bodies – like the able bodied – are privileged, and how that impacts all of those who do not have, or no longer have, those bodies.

Interesting issues: man robs bank to get health care

In the summer of 2011, a 59-year-old unemployed truck driver named Richard James Verone walked into a North Carolina bank, handed a teller a note saying that he had a gun and was demanding $1, and sat down on a chair to await the arrival of police. He planned the robbery so that he would be arrested and sentenced to a prison term, during which he could get health care for his herniated disc, a growth on his chest, a foot injury, and arthritis. Since he was unemployed and had no health insurance, he could not afford to see a doctor, so he thought that getting care in prison was his only option. Because he only demanded $1, and did not have a gun, he was only charged with larceny, rather than robbery, so he most likely will not get the three-year sentence that he was hoping for. Instead, Verone now plans to use his upcoming trial to highlight the poor condition of the American health care system.

Key terms

Anti-retroviral drugs
Biomedicine
Disablism
Disharmony Theories
Divination
Embattled Identity
Emotionalistic Disease Theory
Ethno-Etiologies
Eugenics
Female feticide
Female Feticide
Female Infanticide
Liminality
Master Status

Medicalization
Naturalistic Disease Theory
Normative Ideals about Gender
Personalistic Disease Theory
Polygyny
Sick Role
Social Determinants of Health
Social Invisibility
Social Model of Disability
Somatization
Teratology
Therapeutic Abortions

Further reading

Bogdan, Robert. (1988). *Freak Show*. Chicago, IL: University of Chicago Press.

Ehrenreich, Barbara. (2007). "Welcome to Cancerland." In *Feminist Frontiers*, ed. Verta Taylor, Nancy Whittier, and Leila Rupp. New York: McGraw Hill, 35–7.

Fan, Hung. (2013). *AIDS: Science and Society*. Sudbury: Jones & Bartlett Learning.

Garland Thompson, Rosemary (ed.). (1996). *Freakery: Cultural Spectacles of the Extraordinary Body*. New York: New York University Press.

Murphy, Robert F. (1987/1990). *The Body Silent*. New York: Henry Holt, 1987; W.W. Norton, 1990.

Nettleton, Sarah. (2013). *The Sociology of Health and Illness*. Cambridge: Polity.

Scheper-Hughes, Nancy. (1993). *Death without Weeping: The Violence of Everyday Life in Brazil*. Berkeley, CA: University of California Press.

chapter 3

Aging Bodies

After Japan surrendered to the United States on September 2, 1945, ending World War II, hundreds of thousands of American soldiers returned to the United States to their wives and girlfriends. Thanks to the brand new **G.I. Bill,** which gave returning soldiers access to higher education and low-cost home loans (most of which were, thanks to segregationist policies, only available to whites), this triggered the largest baby boom this country had ever seen; 77.3 million children were born from 1946 until 1964. Today, the oldest of this generation are nearing retirement age, and, thanks to increases in life expectancy because of medical advances, are living longer than ever. These so-called **Baby Boomers** are impacting America's culture and economy in a variety of ways.

From an economic standpoint, this population will put a strain on the Social Security system over which politicians are already arguing. Because Social Security benefits for the currently retired are paid for by the currently employed, as the Baby Boomers continue to age, and Americans continue to have fewer children, and thus fewer future workers, there will be less money to pay for the benefits of the Boomers, as well as future generations of retired people. This is called the **old age dependency ratio** – the ratio of elderly people to working-age adults – and it is growing. At this point, the Social Security Administration expects that the Social Security Trust Fund will be depleted by 2041, while the Congressional Budget Office estimates the year to be 2052. In either case, something has to change in order for the system to remain solvent, because, according to the Economic Policy Institute, Social Security is the major source of income for 60 percent of all retired Americans. (One easy change would simply be to apply the Social Security tax to all income above $106,800, where it currently stops today; in other words, the wealthy pay Social Security taxes on only a very small

FIGURE 3.1 Damien Velasquez. Humans live longer than many species, and the advanced years show on our faces. Photo courtesy of Bill Velasquez.

percentage of their income; by having all income taxed, the fund would be increased greatly.) This aging process, by the way, is happening in nations around the world where the median age of the global population is rising, creating more health care and other social costs.

From a cultural standpoint, the aging of the Baby Boomers is fascinating to watch simply because of its invisibility. Baby Boomers, unlike every generation before them, have worked diligently to deny that they even are aging. From cosmetic surgery to youthful clothing, exercise, diet, and makeup, older Americans today are putting off aging in a way that we have never seen before. This is both a result of, and a contributor to, the **American culture of youth**.

In addition, the fear of aging, and the concerns over what many politicians are calling the Social Security crisis, puts the blame on seniors for somehow "taking" money from other "hard-working" Americans, when in reality today's seniors earned the money that went into the Social Security fund. But because our society focuses on current earners, as opposed to previous earners, and young people, as opposed to future seniors, it is difficult for us to recognize that all of us will eventually not only age, but need the funds that were set aside for that very purpose.

the scientific and biomedical body

How we age

All living creatures age, but humans are one of the longest-lived species. With the exception of some species of tortoises, fish, whales, and parrots, some of which can live over 200 years, humans live a relatively long life. What makes us especially unusual is that human females live many more years after the end of our reproductive lives, which is extremely atypical. In our case, we may stop reproducing early so that we can continue to help rear our offspring into adulthood, and then help raise our grandchildren. It may also be that for women, the post-reproductive years are the years during which we can focus on other important social and cultural activities, without the need to focus on children.

In any case, humans age, just as other animals do, and the signs of aging are found in our bodies and faces. But how we deal with the signs of aging are very different, and are culturally and historically specific. Humans are considered to be "old" at different times in different cultures. In the United States, for example, we typically mark the senior years with the age of retirement at 65. But long before that time, our bodies are aging, and much of that aging can be seen in our faces.

The signs of aging include wrinkles, sun spots, drooping eyelids, and jawlines, dry skin, and what Americans call turkey neck. Much of this is caused by the changes in skin tone and texture as skin loses collagen during aging, leading to a loss in elasticity. In addition, facial fat begins to move around, leaving hollow pockets on the face that are exacerbated by bone loss.

The signs of aging appear at different times for different ethnic groups. For instance, dark skin shows discoloration associated with aging much later than lighter skin, and wrinkles appear later in darker skinned people. In addition, when skin is exposed to a great deal of sun, the signs of aging will be more severe than when skin is sheltered from the sun during youth. The same goes for smoking: smokers' skin will age more quickly than will the skin of non-smokers.

In the United States, aging is seen by many, and especially by women, as something to be avoided. Because women in particular are valued in part by their appearance, aging is viewed very negatively for, and by, American women. For example, the older women get in the West, the less represented they are on television, in movies, and in other forms of mass media. In the United States, in 2012, 47 percent of the population is over 40, yet 71 percent of the women on television are under 30. Feminist and media scholars call this **symbolic annihilation**: the underrepresentation or elimination of a specific demographic group in the mass media, which results in a distortion of the public's understanding of that group; in this case, aging women.

The double standard of aging is not universal, however, and is found in Western cultures more than in non-Western cultures. One reason for the concern about aging in the West is that, starting in the nineteenth century, as doctors began managing illness and health, they also began managing life-cycle changes. Birth, adolescence, and aging are all managed by health care professionals now and are all increasingly medicalized. That means that if aging, or menopause in women, is now considered to be a diseased state, then the young, pre-menopausal body is the normal state, and to achieve that body (or a semblance of it), a regimen of pills and/or surgical techniques must be prescribed.

On the other hand, many cultures value aging in both men and women because age brings wisdom and thus respect and status. In Japan, for example, reverence and respect for the elderly is common, so the aging process is much less fraught with anxiety than in the United States. In fact, in most traditional agricultural societies, women and men both age naturally, applying little to no makeup and not attempting to hide their wrinkles. Aging is seen as a natural and normal process, and older people are honored for having lived so long and for the wisdom that they have obtained.

Even in the United States, standards for aging differ. In the south, for example, "well bred" southern ladies maintain a higher standard of beauty than do women in other parts of the country, and that standard is not relaxed as they age. Older ladies are expected to continue to coif and color their hair, make up their faces, and maintain other grooming and beauty standards well into old age.

The culture of youth

In the United States, and the West in general, youth is valued, treasured, and revered, and in all cultures, youth is considered to be beautiful. Many of the signs of female beauty are actually just signs of youth: large eyes, puffy red lips, pink cheeks, thick hair, and clear skin are all indicators of youth in girls. Boys have that same kind of beauty when they are young too, and both boys and girls grow out of it as they get older. But only women are expected to remain perpetually young.

Even in cultures where aging is respected, youth is also valued. That's why in many cultures girls marry very young, often between 12 and 15, when their youth and fertility is at its visible peak. In the United States, as men get older, wealthier, and more powerful, they often divorce their first, aging wife, and trade up for a newer, younger version. On average, for men who divorce and remarry, each subsequent marriage involves a younger wife. This is called **hypergamy**: the process of women trading their youth and beauty to marry older men, who in turn trade their wealth for their wives' youth and fertility. Donald Trump, Hugh Hefner, and any number of kings and princes, and other monarchs are examples of this practice. This results in a far larger dating pool for men than it does for women.

the scientific and biomedical body

In cultures in which **polygyny**, the marriage of one man to multiple wives, is practiced, the same process occurs, except without the divorce. A man marries a woman who is typically a few years younger than him. This is because she is marriageable shortly after menstruation while he must typically wait until he can put together the goods needed for a **brideprice** to pay her family. After being married to her for a few years, and amassing some property or wealth, he may marry a second wife, who will be younger than the first. Each subsequent wife will be younger than the previous wife, and the wealthier the man, the more numerous, and the younger, his wives will be.

In the United States in particular, youth is the model to which all women should aspire. It should not surprise us that many of the most famous supermodels since the 1980s were discovered and got their start when they were in their early teens. Brazilian model Adriana was discovered when she was just 13; Kate Moss and Gisele Bündchen both began modeling when they were just 14. These girls, because of their youth, had all of the signs of beauty, youth, and fertility that most cultures value, and were then at the high point of their marketability. From there, sadly, it's all downhill, as for them, as for all women, their skin loses its dewy freshness, their eyes no longer seem so large, their lips begin to lose their plumpness, and their hair starts to thin. Aging, assuming we live long enough, is the only universal to which we will all be subjected, other than death. Thankfully, we have a multibillion dollar industry devoted to making up for what nature takes away.

FIGURE 3.2 A variety of anti-aging products. Photo courtesy of the author.

In countries like the United States, there is an enormously profitable market in makeup, pharmaceuticals, and cosmetic surgery which is intended to reverse or slow down the signs of aging on the face and body. By far the most popular anti-aging products available today are cosmetics and surgical procedures. Cosmetics include anti-aging lotions, creams and oils, which are intended to rejuvenate the skin and reduce the signs of aging. Surgical procedures include facelifts, brow lifts, botulism injections, facial fat transfers, chemical face peels and laser resurfacing, cheek tightening, eyelid lifts, lip enlargement procedures, and injections of collagen or other fillers into the face to fill wrinkles or hollows. Other procedures include hormone injections and nutritional supplements. For the most part, women partake of these procedures, while men are left to age "naturally." As with makeup and other ways of hiding the aging process, cosmetic surgery procedures do not actually reverse aging nor do they contribute to longer life; they simply camouflage the external signs of aging. (It is a good thing, by the way, that the richest among us cannot just buy immortality; can you imagine what would happen if some of us lived forever? We would experience shortages of food, housing, water, and medicine, unemployment would skyrocket, and Social Security and Medicare would collapse. On the other hand, the wealthiest among us can in fact buy longer, healthier lives and the mortality disparities that we currently see will most likely increase into the future.)

Men, on the other hand, do not typically fear the signs of aging on the face; instead, they fear the loss of power and virility that often comes with aging, and which are not seen on the face. In fact, in many cultures, men gain power as they age. (We call societies where the elderly rule **gerontocracies**.) That's why erectile dysfunction (once called impotence; a term loaded with moral significance, and rarely used today) is so frightening to so many men – because it signified a loss of sexual power. And that's also why advertisements for erectile dysfunction drugs like Viagra and Cialis do not feature old men or images associated with aging. Instead, they feature virile, healthy-looking men surrounded by icons of masculinity: cars, beautiful women, athletic gear, and alcohol. Sports, in particular, are the most pervasive theme in erectile dysfunction product advertisements because they suggest fitness, health and masculinity, rather than disease, aging, or loss.

Interesting issues: the cougar

*The **cougar** is a term that just emerged in popular culture in the last few years to refer to an older woman who dates younger men. Implied in the term is not just the idea, however, that she dates or prefers younger men, but that she preys on them, like a dangerous, carnivorous cat. Actress Demi Moore, when she was married to the 15-year younger actor Ashton Kutcher, was called a cougar, and*

the scientific and biomedical body

at least two reality shows so far have featured "cougars" either competing against younger women for the romantic attentions of young men (Age of Love) or, in the case of The Cougar, 20 young men competed to win the favor of a 40-year-old cougar. There's now an online dating site called CougarLife that promotes itself as a way for young men, called "cubs," to hook up with older women. While some women embrace the concept of older women dating or hooking up with younger men as being liberatory – why not encourage the idea of older women continuing to be sexual beings? – others see the term as demeaning and point out that the practice is heavily ridiculed in popular culture, making the women look not just predatory but desperate. (Men, on the other hand, never look desperate when dating younger women.) On Age of Love, for example, a 30-year-old tennis player named Mark Philippoussis chose from a group of "kittens" in their twenties and a group of cougars in their thirties and forties. Even though Philippoussis was closer in age to the cougars, he eventually chose a kitten as the winner.

Problems facing the elderly

In the United States, while seniors do wield considerable voting and political clout, individual seniors often face huge burdens that younger people in this country do not experience. As the economy has suffered in the past few years around the world, retirement has become more difficult for many elderly people, who have lost a substantial part of their retirement savings – some even lost their homes – and some have found that they need to keep working beyond the age that they had hoped to retire. In addition, while Social Security is available to most American workers, the amount of Social Security benefits that one receives depends on one's income during one's working years, so low-income workers get lower benefits than high-income workers. For women who did not work in the workforce, but worked at home and were supported by their husband's wages, they only receive half of their husband's Social Security benefits after their deaths, so elderly women are doubly disadvantaged.

At the same time, seniors are viewed by many, especially in Western countries, to be less competent and more troublesome than younger workers (even though studies (such as James, McKechnie, and Swanberg 2008) show that this is not the case), so they are less likely to be hired than younger people. In addition, they will have more health problems than young people, and thus will cost companies and health insurance companies more money. In 2005, an internal memo was leaked from Walmart discouraging Walmart managers from hiring older workers as a way to keep health care costs down, even though Walmart only provides health insurance for less than half of its employees anyway.

FIGURE 3.3 As they get older, many seniors lose their mobility, their health worsens, and they become isolated, lonely and depressed. Having a companion animal can help them remain healthy, and keep up their spirits. Photo of Lea Johnson and Koko, courtesy of Gina Georgousis.

For those seniors who are still working, companies, which cannot by law fire older workers in the United States, can encourage them to quit by changing their shifts to less desirable time periods, demoting them, or requiring additional work from them. And we know that when workers over 55 lose their jobs, it takes them longer to find new jobs than for workers under 55. Some seniors are simply pushed into early retirement because they cannot find jobs, and if they do not have enough retirement savings built up, they may not be able to afford to retire early. It's worth pointing out that when Social Security was first instituted in 1935, the average American only lived two years after retirement. Today, we live an average of 15 years after retirement, which means those Social Security payments, and any other investments we have, have to stretch much further today.

the scientific and biomedical body

Health care is a major concern for the elderly because the elderly have, by far, a greater number of health problems than any other age group, including problems specific to the elderly like dementia. The good news is that, overall, Americans are healthier in their senior years than they used to be, leaving their sickest years to the very last years of their lives, a phenomenon called the **compression of morbidity**. But once they do get sick, that sickness is expensive. In the United States, as discussed in Chapter 2, health care is not a right but a privilege, so one's access to health care is determined by one's class, one's income, one's job, one's race, and other social factors. In addition, each year, health care gets more and more expensive and costs a greater percentage of our income as a country, as individuals, and as employers. For seniors, at least, they have access to a federal program called **Medicare** which covers much of the health care for seniors. In fact, thanks in part to Medicare, which was passed in 1965, the percentage of elderly living in poverty dropped from 33 percent in 1967 to just 11 percent in 2010, according to the Pew Research Center.

Medicare has a number of problems, however. With the aging of the Baby Boomers, the system itself will be increasingly stressed, and even today it does not cover all of seniors' health costs or prescription costs. Physicians, too, get very low reimbursement rates for seeing Medicare patients, which makes them less likely to accept them as patients. One of the reasons why costs are expensive is that thanks to the Medicare Modernization Act, passed in 2005, the federal government cannot negotiate with pharmaceutical companies for lower costs on drugs; consequently, the American government pays more to American drug companies than any other country does. (The bill was created and steered through Congress by Congressman Billy Tauzin, who immediately retired after the bill's passage and took a $2 million per year job as president of the lobbying group for the pharmaceutical industry, the Pharmaceutical Research and Manufacturers Association.) Another cost factor is the very expensive medical technology that Americans have access to.

Another problem facing the elderly in the United States is that as the elderly live longer, it is becoming less common for families to care for their aging relatives, leaving many to be institutionalized in their final years. The cost to live in nursing homes is expensive, and thus out of reach for the elderly poor, and in some nursing homes, the standard of care is questionable at best. In addition, sociologist Philip Cohen (2011) has written of **care vacuums**, by which he refers to the recent closures of large numbers of nursing homes in poor and minority communities. This makes it both harder for people of color to find nursing homes for their aging relatives, or to visit them once they're in long-term care. In addition, for many seniors, living in a nursing home is less a solution than a curse; the idea that they may just be left in an institution to die without family and friends is more frightening than death itself. For others, however, the physical care that seniors find in nursing homes, combined with the social life provided by spending time with others in their age group, can be deeply satisfying.

Age norms

Age norms are the socially constructed expectations and guidelines regarding what people in specific age groups are allowed to do. Age norms determine how we should dress, how long we should wear our hair, how sexual we should be, what kinds of entertainment we should engage in, and even whether we should dance in public. The older we get, the more limited our choices are in terms of all of these behaviors. Age norms are often based on stereotypes and misconceptions about the elderly which may not be based on reality, and which certainly may not be shared by the subjects of those expectations: the elderly themselves. In fact, for many seniors, aging often comes as a surprise. Feminist writer Simone de Beauvoir once said "Since it is the Other within us who is old, it is natural that the revelation of our age should come to us from outside – from others" (1970: 288).

We are sorted by age throughout our lives, meaning that we tend to only spend time with people of our own age group. Young people and old people rarely spend much time together so the knowledge that young people have about old people is often limited and based on stereotypes. In addition, because, in the West, people think that old people are slow, stupid, and useless (there are whole websites dedicated to how funny it is that old people fall or do things wrong; visit **http://www.oldpeoplearefunny.com/**, accessed March 31, 2013, for examples of this), they are treated that way, and, in turn, many seniors begin to see themselves that way as well. Others, on the other hand, resist being called "old" (or the many negative terms used to refer to seniors like codger, fogey, and geezer), and certainly resist being labeled as incompetent or slow, and make every effort to stay involved and active in society. **Ageism** refers to being prejudiced against, or discriminating against, older people simply because of their age.

Today, for middle- and upper-class Americans, aging is becoming a very different experience than it was just a generation ago. Age norms have been changing, and are changing rapidly. In 2012, Madonna, one of the most famous pop stars of her generation, is now 54 years old. Yet she continues to dress as she did in the 1980s, with fishnet stockings, cone bras, corsets, and thigh-high stiletto boots. Clearly, Madonna is at the forefront of pushing the boundaries of what a "middle-aged" woman is allowed to do. During a performance in 2012 in Turkey, she pulled down her bra and exposed her nipple to the largely Muslim audience, shocking many observers, but also

the scientific and biomedical body

bringing up the question: who decides what is appropriate behavior for what age? And is it ageism to suggest that just because a woman, for example, is in her 50s, she cannot wear her hair long, or should not wear a short skirt, or must not, in Madonna's case, show off her breast during a performance? Even for those seniors who are not wearing mini-skirts or going to punk shows, many are still living lives that seniors just a couple of generations ago would never have dreamed of.

Interesting issues: Helen Mirren's bikini

In 2008, British actress Helen Mirren was photographed on vacation in Italy. What made this particular paparazzi photograph so notable was that Mirren, who was 62 at the time, was photographed in a bright red bikini, and looked, according to all accounts, terrific. The photo received wide coverage in the press and there was a great deal of discussion about whether it was "okay" to be sexually attracted to a 62-year-old woman. Mirren took the publicity in her stride, saying the photo would haunt her for the rest of her life, because she could never hope to live up to it. Instead, in 2011, she auctioned off the bikini to raise funds for the British charity Age UK and their Spread the Warmth Campaign, which provides seniors with blankets, food, and heaters. She said, "I love the idea of this little flimsy summer thing going towards helping old people stay warm and comfortable and toasty in the wintertime." So the bikini that created an international discussion about whether elderly women could be sexy is now being used to help keep elderly people warm!

Experiences of aging

A variety of factors shape a person's experience of aging, including gender, class, race, and ethnicity. For example, because men die sooner than women, in most countries, older women outnumber older men, so elderly women are more likely to live alone as widows. In addition, thanks to the importance of youth to a woman's beauty, a woman is disqualified from being a sexual and thus valuable being decades earlier than a man is. (Consider Hugh Hefner, who at the time of this writing is 86 and living with his 26-year-old girlfriend.) Literary theorist Susan Sontag wrote an essay called "The Double Standard of Aging" (1978) where she discussed the fact that while men in the United States have two standards of attractiveness – the boy and the man – women only have one: the girl. This results in a lifetime of unrelenting pressures on women to maintain a youthful appearance at any cost. The costs are both financial – some beauty creams can cost hundreds of dollars per ounce – but also emotional. Because no cream, injection, or surgical procedure can actually turn back the clock and make a woman more youthful, the older a woman gets, the greater her anxieties, self-consciousness, and sense of failure. Because while boys are allowed to grow into men and then into old men, girls can only grow into trying to stay a girl, and the older she gets, the more desperate that attempt becomes.

Since racial minorities have a lower life expectancy than whites, whites live longer than minorities on average – at least five years longer. In addition, elderly minorities are more likely to be poor. For the poorest Americans, Social Security benefits account for the vast majority of their retirement benefits, and the average earner only receives $13,406.40 per year, just above the poverty line. But that is the average earner, and would not apply to those who earned, say, the minimum wage during their working careers. Those people would receive a smaller Social Security check, leaving them with even less to live on. On the other hand, people of color in the United States are experiencing greater longevity today so the elderly are becoming more diverse, and in the future will become even more so.

There are two competing perspectives regarding the treatment of minority seniors in the United States. One suggests that seniors of color are at a double disadvantage: they continue to suffer discrimination because of their racial position, and they now experience discrimination because of their age. The other perspective suggests, on the other hand, that as we age factors like racism begin to fall away and our experiences begin to even out; aging is, in this perspective, the great equalizer. This may be becoming more common today.

Another factor shaping differences in experiences of aging has to do with how connected or disconnected people are with the social roles that they once occupied in their lives. Sociologists have developed a number of theories to account for some of these differences in experiences. For example, **disengagement theory** suggests that as people age they gradually withdraw from their previous roles and activities and at the same time are relieved of social responsibilities. This withdrawal is viewed as functional for both the individual and society, since it makes way for younger people to take on the roles evacuated by the aging. **Activity theory**, on the other hand, suggests that the more active and involved in society older people are, the more likely they are to feel life satisfaction as they age, and that disengagement from roles is negative for elderly people and contributes to their social isolation and depression. **Continuity theory** suggests that the elderly will be more satisfied if they can continue to engage in many of the same activities that they engaged in earlier in life.

For many seniors, they have no choice but to disengage from many of the roles that they occupied when they were younger. Many are forced to

the scientific and biomedical body

retire from their jobs, and for parents, their children will grow up and move away. But that does not mean that they cannot still stay actively involved with their families – assuming that their children and grandchildren still want them in their lives – nor does it mean that they should not stay active by volunteering at a non-profit organization in their community. For many seniors, they can have a more fulfilling life once they stop working for pay, because they can concentrate on doing things that are socially or personally meaningful. For many minorities in the United States, as they age they find it easier to retain family bonds than aging whites do, because extended family ties among people of color tend to be stronger and elders tend to remain more closely linked to the family.

One problem is that while the process of growing up is filled, in many cultures, with **rites of passage** – rituals that mark the transition from one life stage to another – aging is typically marked by the lack of such rituals. There are few celebrations involved with aging, and there are few opportunities for learning new information and for taking on new roles. Instead, the elderly are often simply forced into a permanent medicalized state, with their role being that of the permanently ill. In addition, because they are closer to death than the rest of society, this contributes even more to their isolation, because of society's general fear of death, and in the West, our fear of aging.

The aging prison population

One population that is also aging in the United States that not too many people think about is the prison population. While the vast majority of crimes are committed by the young, for those men (because most of the prison population is made up of men) who receive a life sentence for their crimes, they will get old and die in prison, making prisons *de facto* nursing homes. In fact, *Mother Jones* magazine reported in 2012 that one in 12 American prisoners, or almost 125,000, is 55 years or older, and these numbers are expected to continue to rise, as many of the prisoners sentenced under the new mandatory minimum guidelines instituted by Ronald Reagan in the 1980s start to get older. By 2030, there should be 400,000 inmates in state and federal prisons over the age of 55. Human Rights Watch noted in 2012 that the number of prisoners over 65 jumped 63 percent during a time, from 2007 to 2010, when the overall prison population in the United States, increased just 1 percent. Just as in the general population, caring for the elderly is more expensive than caring for the young – in Louisiana, for example, it costs $80,000 for each elderly inmate per year – and in prison, all health care costs are born by the taxpayer. In addition, prisons are not set up to handle disabled prisoners, and as more prisoners become disabled, thanks to the process of aging, there will need to be a number of adjustments made to the buildings as well as to the prison processes to accommodate them.

Should very old, and very compromised, prisoners be released for compassionate reasons? Doing so would alleviate the prison system from the burden of having to care for such compromised prisoners and would give them a chance to die in surroundings of their own choice. But what if they committed a heinous crime? In 2009, Scotland released Abdelbaset Al Megrahi from the prison where he was serving a life sentence for the 1988 bombing of Pan Am Flight 103; the plane left London for New York but exploded over Lockerbie, Scotland, killing 270 passengers, crew, and people on the ground. Al Megrahi had prostate cancer and was expected to die within three months, so his defense team asked for his release on compassionate grounds, even though he had only served eight and a half years of his life sentence. The decision to release Al Megrahi caused widespread outrage in the United States (from where most of his victims came), especially since, after his return to Libya, he ended up living another three years in a villa in Tripoli.

Even so, because so many crimes are committed by the young, it's unlikely that aging prisoners will pose a danger to society; elderly prisoners who are released have a very low **recidivism rate**. Death-row prisoners, too, are aging. As with other prisoners, those who commit murders generally committed them when they were young. But because it can take up to 15 years from the time of an inmate's crime to the time of their execution, the prisoner is much older than he was when he was first arrested. In fact, the median age at arrest for a death-row inmate is 27 and the median age at execution is 43. While 43 is by no means senior, and no one is arguing for the compassionate release of 43-year-old death-row prisoners, it does bring up some interesting questions about the point of the death penalty. If it's to bring peace and closure to the victim's family, and revenge for the killing, then the age at which the suspect dies does not matter. But if it's to eliminate dangerous criminals, then simply keeping them behind bars until they age out of the violent stage of their lives might do the same job as killing them once they're older does.

In Chapter 14, we will once again take up the question of prisoners and how they should be treated. But for now, we will move on to Chapter 4, where we will look at another "natural" phenomenon, reproduction, and address the many ways in which culture and society shape it.

the scientific and biomedical body

Key terms

Activity Theory
Age Norms
Ageism
American Culture of Youth
Baby Boomers
Brideprice
Care Vacuums
Compression of Morbidity
Continuity Theory
Cougar

Disengagement Theory
G.I. Bill
Gerontocracies
Hypergamy
Medicare
Old Age Dependency Ratio
Polygyny
Recidivism Rate
Rites of Passage
Symbolic Annihilation

Further reading

Bass, S. A., Kutza, E. A., and Torres-Gil, F. M., (eds). (1990). *Diversity in Aging*. Glencoe, IL: Scott, Foresman.

Lock, Margaret. (1993). *Encounters with Aging: Mythologies of Menopause in Japan and North America*. Berkeley, CA: University of California Press.

Sontag, Susan. (1979). "The Double Standard of Aging." In *Psychology of Women*, ed. J. H. Williams. New York: W.W. Norton & Company, 462–78.

chapter 4

Reproducing Bodies

On July 25, 1978, Louise Brown, the world's first **test tube baby**, was born in a hospital in Oldham, Great Britain, after having been conceived in a petri dish in a hospital laboratory. Her conception was attended by two scientists, Patrick Steptoe and Robert Edwards, her parents Lesley and John, and her doctor, all of whom were also present at her birth. At the time of this writing, Louise Brown is 34 years old, and the number of babies resulting from **in vitro fertilization** has now passed five million worldwide. As more women delay childbearing in order to pursue educations and careers, as gays and lesbians begin to have families, and more couples find themselves beset with infertility, technological and cultural changes have created new opportunities for childbearing.

Of all the topics discussed in this book, reproduction is perhaps the best example of a biological concept that is deeply culturally constructed. Today's new reproductive technologies bring with them a whole host of cultural changes, but also illustrate the ways in which reproduction is not nearly as simple as we may think. In addition, reproduction is, it hardly needs to be noted, deeply gendered. Not only do men and women play different roles – both biological and cultural – in reproduction, but men and women's reproductive lives are very differently shaped by, and controlled by, social, economic, cultural, and political realities. Biological determinism, discussed in Chapter 1, refers to the fact that our bodies often determine the course of our personal and social lives. As we'll see in this chapter, this is especially true for women.

Menstruation, fertility, and menopause

Women are largely defined by their reproductive abilities. Biologist Lynda Birke puts it quite plainly; she says that women are defined primarily as "wombs on legs" (1999: 12). Their fertility or lack thereof is a source of discussion and concern for members of their families, the wider communities, the church, and sometimes the state itself. Judith Butler (1993) points out that one reason why women's bodies are associated with the material has to do with the origin of the word "matter" which derives from *mater* and *matrix*; mother and womb in Latin. In addition, women's bodies are subject to a wide variety of norms, taboos, and laws that do not affect men. For women, about three decades between menstruation and menopause mark the time in which other people and institutions often share some level of control over their reproductive lives.

Prior to menstruation, girls around the world are often given a great deal of freedom. After the onset of menses, a young woman often experiences menstrual rituals which isolate her from the community and treat her, and her bodily functions, as if she's dirty. **Menstrual taboos** demand that a menstruating woman, for example, refrain from cooking, cleaning, having sex, or even being near men. The **menstrual hut**, where women are concealed during menstruation in many societies, is one of the most visible ways in which the woman is marked as "polluting." One of the reasons that menstruation carries such heavy cultural connotations may lie in the evolution of human menstruation. While some other primates do menstruate, none do so to the extent that humans do. In fact, while human females conceal their ovulation – not going into heat as do most other mammals – which means that they can and do have sex whether or not they are fertile, menstruation can be a very public signal which gives out information about a woman's fertility – especially in societies which utilize menstrual huts. This may be one reason why societies feel the need to conceal menstruating women.

Menstruation and menopause represent the beginning and end of a woman's reproductive life, and as such are fraught with a great deal of symbolic baggage. Modern Western cultures may not have the menstrual taboos found in other cultures (although many men still refuse to have sex with a menstruating women, considering it to be a dirty practice), but even so, menstruation and menopause are still seen to be largely negative phenomena.

In addition, even fertility and conception are often understood in ways in which women's contributions are largely minimized. Anthropologist Emily Martin, in her groundbreaking book *The Woman in the Body* (1987), as well as in an essay titled "The Egg and the Sperm: How Science Has Constructed a Romance Based on Stereotypical Male–Female Roles" (1991), analyzes the Western, scientific understanding of women's reproductive processes, finding an inherent bias even in our scientific discourses.

Martin analyzed biology textbooks and focused first on the ways in which the sperm and the egg are discussed in such books. When men produce sperm, a process known as **spermatogenesis**, the process is constructed in a way that is largely seen as active and heroic. Egg production, on the other hand, is seen as passive and rather dull. During sexual intercourse, when fertilization of the egg occurs, the process is told from the perspective of the ambitious, heroic sperm swimming bravely towards the fat, bloated, and lazy egg. Cultural stereotypes about male and female, masculine and feminine, then, filter down towards the cellular level and shape how we think about these important processes.

Other cultures, too, minimize or even deny the role that women play in fertility. Anthropologist Carol Delaney, in her book *The Seed and the Soil: Gender and Cosmology in Turkish Village Society* (1991), notes that in many cultures, it is assumed that men are the major, if not the only, contributors to the creation of children. In the Turkish community in which she worked, men provided the seed, the spark of life, for the child, while women provide the soil, or the nurturing material that keeps it alive. In cultures like these, women do not create life; they simply sustain it. This also relates to their notion of sexuality, which is similarly gendered. She says that "women as fields are the ground on which male sexuality is played out" (41).

Another way in which cultural biases influence our understanding of biology comes from Martin's analysis of menstruation, which is generally seen as wasteful. Not only does a women not produce eggs during her lifetime (they "ripen" each month during ovulation, but were already produced prior to her birth), but each month, if she does not get pregnant, the egg gets washed away as menstrual "waste." The productivity of sperm production is seen as amazing and fabulous, while the shedding of the eggs is seen as wasteful and sad. Martin asks us to, hypothetically, reverse the situation. Why not see the billions of sperm produced by men – of which very very few are ever actually "used" in a man's lifetime – as wasteful rather than amazing?

Feminist Gloria Steinem once wondered what would happen if men could menstruate and women could not. In a now-classic article (1978), she suggests that if only men could menstruate, menstruation would be seen as enviable, amazing, and a sign of power and strength. Men would brag about how long they bled and how much, cultures would mark the onset of menses with rituals and ceremonies, and, in the United States, "Congress would fund a National Institute of Dysmenorrhea to help stamp out monthly discomforts. Sanitary supplies would be federally funded and free." Steinem's point was that whatever men do is to be celebrated, while what women do is to be seen as unworthy of such celebration. While her article was tongue-in-cheek, it did point out the ways in which phenomena associated with women are denigrated while phenomena associated with men are celebrated.

With the end of menstruation comes menopause, a term that was invented in the 1880s by a doctor named C. P. L. de Gardanne. Prior to this time, other indicators were used to mark this new stage in a woman's life, such as becoming a grandmother. With this new definition came a focus on the end of reproduction. It should not surprise us, then, that in the West, menopause is now seen as pathological. It is largely described in biological and medical texts as a breakdown, as a loss, as a deficiency, and as the body becoming unresponsive to the normal hormonal commands. Because menopause is now seen as a disease, it also should not surprise us to learn that many Western doctors prescribe medication to treat the disease: **hormone replacement therapy**.

By the way, many of the emotional and physical changes that accompany the end of menstruation differ from society to society, which suggests that they are, at least partially, culturally constructed as well. For instance, medical anthropologist Margaret Lock (1993) shows that Japanese women experience the end of menstruation very differently from American women. While in the United States, not only is menopause pathologized, consistent with America's valuation of youth above all, but menopause is seen as risky and dangerous for older women, so hormone-replacement therapy is typically prescribed for years after a woman stops menstruating. In Japan, on the other hand, Lock demonstrates that menopause is unmedicalized, and elderly women are valued in terms of the care that they provide to the young members of their extended families. Lock also shows that how menopause is embodied in Japan is shaped by *both* biology and culture, not just one or the other; Japanese women, for example, typically experience hot flashes much less severely than American women, and some do not experience them at all.

In addition, in many cultures, menopause is often associated with a level of freedom not experienced since childhood. Many of the social controls that childbearing women experience – which serve to ensure that they not only take on the role of mother, but that they only give birth to legitimate children – fall away after menopause and women in many cultures often find that they can travel more freely, engage in political practices, behave much more independently in terms of practices like joking, cussing, smoking, or drinking, and in general engage in non-normative gendered behaviors. Post-menopausal women also tend to have more political power or decision-making ability than younger women. These freedoms, how-ever, tend to be absent in the United States, where instead we find that as menstruation disappears, with it comes both new embarrassment associated with menopausal symptoms (in particular, the need to hide one's hot flashes), and a heightened focus on reclaiming one's lost youth.

Contraception, abortion, and reproductive rights

While many people think of reproductive rights as dealing with contraception and abortion, in reality, reproductive rights refer to the right of a woman to bear a child as well as the right to *not* bear a child. As we noted in our introduction, women's reproductive lives are largely controlled by people and institutions other than women themselves. Family, husbands, communities, the church, and the state all play a role in regulating what a woman can or should do with her body. That process often centers around birth control.

Birth control, including contraception – which prevents pregnancy – and abortion – which terminates pregnancy – has been practiced for thousands of years around the world. The earliest birth control methods were probably barrier methods in which women inserted substances (like crocodile dung!) into their vaginas which acted like diaphragms to block sperm from entering the cervix. Other early methods included herbal abortificents to terminate unwanted pregnancies, and, beginning in the fifteenth century, condoms made from leather. Condoms became popular in the eighteenth century, but not as a form of birth control. They were primarily used to protect men against sexually transmitted diseases.

Until the 1960s, though, there were no birth control methods that were both reliable and in a woman's control. In fact, for many men and women in the Western world, the **withdrawal method** remained the most popular form of birth control. While condoms, when used properly, are relatively reliable (with a 98 percent success rate if always used correctly; the more typical success rate, however is 82 percent, according to Planned Parenthood), their use depends on a man wanting to wear them. For many women, making a man wear a condom is easier said than done. With the development of the hormonal birth control pill in the 1960s, which prevents ovulation, women for the first time had a method that was both in their control and reliable.

Unfortunately, the pill was not terribly safe as many women experienced strokes and other major health problems from the early use of the pill. Today's pills are much safer than they once were, although they can still pose a health risk. This is of course the irony: women pay the penalty for an unwanted pregnancy, so ensuring that birth control methods are firmly in women's hands is a major goal of the reproductive rights movement. But if birth control methods are used by women, then any health problems will

the scientific and biomedical body

be suffered by women as well. Scientists have been working on a male birth control pill for years, and it may be ready for release in the next few years. However, given the potential health problems associated with any new medication like this, many men may not want to use it. In addition, given the fact that women pay by far the greatest cost with an unwanted pregnancy, many women may not trust that their partners are using a male pill.

Birth control is about far more than just preventing births. The subject is fraught with tension and controversy in societies around the world, as a variety of people and institutions continue to debate about what rights women should have with respect to their reproductive lives. Many young Americans do not realize, for example, that prior to the 1960s, not only was there no effective means of birth control that could be controlled by women, but in many states it was illegal to use any form of birth control at all. Many states had laws called **Comstock laws** which made it not only illegal to buy, sell, or use contraceptives, but which criminalized even *talking* about birth control. Birth control pioneer Margaret Sanger, who later founded Planned Parenthood, was jailed multiple times during her life for challenging those laws. The result of Comstock laws? Millions of women were forced to bear and raise children, and many men were forced to support those children, while others chose not to pay child support.

While birth control, including abortion, is now legal in the United States, that does not mean it is easily available. Until the passage of the Affordable Health Care Act (which took effect in 2012), birth control drugs were not covered under many women's health insurance plans, and when the new law was being debated, advocates of birth control were harassed and threatened for their attempts to ensure that contraception be covered like any other aspect of health care (like, for example, Viagra). In 2012, conservative radio host Rush Limbaugh called student health care activist Sandra Fluke – who asked that her college cover birth control in her health insurance – a slut and a prostitute, claiming that she wanted to make taxpayers pay for her sexual activities (he went further and demanded that she, and all women, post videos online showing them engaged in sex, so that all taxpayers "who paid for it" can enjoy it). The reality is that taxpayers do not pay for women's birth control when it's covered through health insurance. Women do, through their health insurance premiums. In addition, if a woman uses contraceptives to prevent pregnancy, by definition that means she is having sex with a man. Yet no man is responsible for paying for the birth control pill.

It's debates like this, continuing to rage in twenty-first-century America, that illustrate how little control women continue to have over their own bodies. Not only have health insurance companies been allowed to deny women coverage for birth control, but four states have what are called **conscience laws** which allow pharmacists to deny birth control to patients

FIGURE 4.1 Project Defending Life, an anti-abortion organization, located right next door to Planned Parenthood, an abortion provider, in Albuquerque, New Mexico. Photo courtesy of Tom Young.

to whom it has been prescribed. Today, the American College of Obstetricians and Gynecologists are advocating that birth control pills be sold over the counter, which will improve women's access to birth control and reduce unintended pregnancies which cost, according to the group, an estimated 11 billion taxpayer dollars per year.

Abortion, legalized in 1973 with the Supreme Court case **Roe v. Wade**, has also come under increasing levels of attack in recent years. Most states now have laws restricting abortion in a variety of ways, such as imposing mandatory waiting periods, parental consent for teenagers, counseling requirements, gag rules, insurance prohibitions, and mandatory vaginal ultrasounds (which make the fetus seem less like a fetus dependent on a woman and more like a baby). A handful of states have even attempted to ban abortion altogether, in opposition to federal policy. In 2011, for example, 60 state laws restricting abortion were passed across the country, and by mid-2012 another 40 laws were passed. Emergency contraception, too, which only became publicly available in 2006, has been subject to a great deal of hand-wringing on the part of conservative politicians and the religious right. Emergency contraception, which prevents ovulation when taken immediately after unprotected sex, is seen as a form of abortion by those who are opposed to it, and that opposition – and the concern that it would make women promiscuous – led the FDA to repeatedly block it from being released to the public.

the scientific and biomedical body

Even with all of the public debate, it's clear that the availability of birth control in the United States in the 1960s, and later the world, has radically changed women's lives, providing them with not only sexual freedom, but the freedom to plan their families, go to college, obtain jobs, and become financially independent. When women have no control over their reproductive lives, none of this is available.

Even today, with the availability of so many birth control methods, the poor still have more unplanned pregnancies than anyone else. Women in poverty are four times more likely to become pregnant unintentionally than other women, and have both more unplanned births and more abortions as a result. One reason for this is that when public health programs are cut, women's access to birth control has been cut as well. In addition, the focus on abstinence education in the United States results in a lack of education about birth control. Internationally, we see this too: today, the average European woman has 1.4 kids, but Middle Eastern and Mediterranean women have 4.3 children apiece, thanks in part to poverty, lack of access to birth control, lack of education, and religious beliefs.

Interesting issues: project prevention

Project Prevention is an American organization that pays drug-addicted women to get themselves sterilized or to go on long-term birth control. It is one of a number of organizations that target poor women who cannot provide for their children. The organization pays $300 for each woman who agrees to have a tubal ligation, an IUD, Depo-Provera shots, or Implanon. Occasionally the group will also pay for men to have vasectomies. Project Prevention and organizations like this advertise, usually with billboards, in low-income neighborhoods. The group has received heavy criticism from opponents who suggest that they are simply a modern eugenics organization – targeting poor people of color and others who the group deems unfit to reproduce, and offering them cash in exchange for ending their reproductive lives. Barbara Harris, the group's founder, refers to drug-addicted women as having "litters" of children, comparing them to dogs, and one of the more controversial billboards reads "Don't let pregnancy get in the way of your crack habit."

Population control, race, and the loss of women's choice

Nation-states have larger concerns about population fertility rates and demographics which impact women's bodies as well. For example, we tend to see societies restricting women's rights to birth control, and thus encouraging more births, when there is a great demand for labor. This was the prominent trend throughout the nineteenth and early twentieth

FIGURE 4.2 *Concerning Race Suicide*, by S. D. Erhart. Illustration shows contrasting views of population growth: "The Idle Stork" on the left has little to do as the upper class chooses not to make babies, whereas "The Strenuous Stork" is being worked to death by a population explosion among the lower class. Illus. in: Puck, v. 53, no. 1361 (1903 April 1), centerfold. Photo courtesy of the Library of Congress.

centuries, as the United States was becoming increasingly industrialized. Where a nation's prosperity is linked to a large population of workers, women are expected to be mothers. On the other hand, in the twenty-first century, a large workforce is no longer demanded, as we have de-industrialized our economy and millions are out of work. Fertility rates are down, and middle-class women are delaying childbirth.

Population control refers to practices and policies by the state that are aimed at restricting population numbers within the nation. China's infamous **one child policy**, which penalizes parents for having more than one child, is an example of a population control policy. Most population control policies are aimed at women, either by restricting the number of births a woman can have, as in China, or by sterilizing women.

Who it is that is giving birth is also a subject of concern. In nations with racism or ethnic conflict, one result is often state policies that restrict access to birth control for the dominant ethnic group, and encourage it for the minority group. In other words, **pro-natalism** is encouraged for the dominant group, with those women being encouraged to have many children, while eugenics policies are often implemented for the minority group, with, in the most extreme cases, sterilization being offered to, or mandated for, those

the scientific and biomedical body

women. Why are women the targets of such policies, and not men? It is women, after all, who reproduce not just children, but ethnic groups, so it's the reproductive lives of women which must be controlled.

As we discussed in Chapter 2, in the first half of the twentieth century, compulsory sterilization programs were instituted in many countries around the world, usually as part of eugenics programs, but sometimes as part of larger population control efforts. The United States, which first tested sterilization methods on Puerto Rican women, had compulsory sterilization policies in 33 states, which targeted women who were "mentally retarded," blind, physically disabled, epileptic, and deaf. (Sterilization is still the most prevalent method of birth control in Puerto Rico today.) Poor African-American and Native American women were often sterilized without their consent and knowledge, and women in prison were also subject to this. Even leading feminists and birth control advocates of the time, like Margaret Sanger and Marie Stopes, supported eugenics policies and wanted to control the reproductive abilities of the "unfit." In fact, after the development of the birth control pill in the United States, many African-American activists discouraged the use of the pill, saying that it was a form of genocide against blacks.

As recently as 1985, the forced sterilization of the mentally retarded was allowed in 19 states.

More infamously, the Nazis sterilized thousands of men and women who were retarded, deaf, blind, mentally disabled, or even alcoholic in a program called Action T4. Prior to the **Final Solution** when Jews were sent to their deaths, hundreds of thousands of Jews, Gypsies, gays, and others deemed undesirable were sterilized as part of the Law for the Prevention of Genetically Diseased Offspring, passed in 1933. At the same time, the Nazis were encouraging Aryan women to bear children, and made birth control very difficult to get for them.

Today, Israel is undergoing what some observers are calling a "demographic race" with Palestinians. Here Ashkenazi Jewish women are encouraged to have more babies, in part to make up for the number of Jews killed in the Holocaust, and are given two free treatments of in vitro fertilization to help infertile couples do so. On the other hand, Palestinian women can get free birth control and Ethiopian Jews are encouraged to use Depo Provera, an injectible contraceptive that lasts for three months. France is another example of a European country in which Muslim immigrants are reproducing at much higher rates than ethnic French, causing much consternation among politicians, the press, and the public.

In the United States, some whites are concerned that by the end of the twenty-first century, Latinos will be the dominant ethnic group in the American southwest, leaving whites behind. In addition, long after the end of the eugenics movement, the threat of poor people of color having babies has not disappeared in this country, but has taken on a new guise. In the 1980s, with the threat of the crack cocaine epidemic at an all-time high, politicians and the media began talking about "crack babies:" babies with a host of developmental problems, born to crack-addicted mothers. While sociologists later discovered that many of these crack babies were really just "poverty babies," and that their low birth weight and other problems were primarily indicative of a lack of prenatal care, poor maternal nutrition, and other problems associated with poverty, many states nevertheless passed laws criminalizing drug use by pregnant women.

Ultimately, all of these debates are part of a larger movement called the **Reproductive Justice** or Reproductive Rights movement, a movement which challenges the dichotomy between pro-life and pro-choice and instead focuses on providing true reproductive rights – i.e., the right to bear children *and* the right to not bear children – to all women, regardless of class, nationality, or color.

Interesting issues: China's one child policy

In 1978, because of China's overpopulation problem, the Chinese government instituted what is known as the One Child Policy. Under this policy, each Chinese couple, with some exceptions, is only allowed to have a single child. Unfortunately, China is a patrilineal, patrilocal society, which means that the line of descent and inheritance is passed through men, and men stay with their families to not only inherit any family property but to take care of their elderly parents. That means that if a family only has a single child, and that child is a girl, then there is no one available to take on the family name, to inherit the family property, or to take care of the elderly parents, since the daughter will be expected to marry out and live with another man's family. Because of these economic and social realities, the one child policy has been extremely detrimental to rural families in particular, and has resulted in countless families abandoning or killing their first-born daughters, in the hope that they can have a son on their second attempt. Some parents will have an ultrasound to detect the sex of the fetus, and, if female, will abort. For families who have a first-born girl and choose to keep her and then try for a boy, they must pay a heavy fine which poor families cannot afford. The result of the policy is now a gender imbalance in China as high 117 boys to 100 girls; by the year 2020, there may be 30 million more men in China than women, leaving millions of men without spouses and families. In addition, thousands of girls are now living in orphanages throughout China awaiting international adoption. Today, thanks to these negative results, the policy has been relaxed for rural families, who can now petition the government to have a second child if their first child is a girl, to prevent girls from being abandoned or killed; if the first child is disabled, the parents are also allowed a second child. Another exception was made in 2008 after many families lost their children in the Sichuan earthquake; those families were allowed to have a replacement child. In urban areas, however, where land ownership is not an issue, the one child policy remains in practice. Another result of the practice, besides the gender imbalance and the loss of tens of millions of girls (sometimes through forced abortions), is the phenomenon known as "little emperors," where single male children are raised with everything that they could ever desire, becoming spoiled and, in many cases, fat.

Pregnancy, childbirth, and lactation

In between menstruation and menopause, society expects that women fulfill their "biological destiny" by getting pregnant and giving birth to children. For some cultures, that destiny is not really fulfilled until a woman has given birth to a male child. With the birth of a child, a woman is finally an adult.

The process of pregnancy, childbirth, and lactation are also heavily culturally constructed, and it goes without saying, heavily gendered. No matter how natural the process of pregnancy or childbirth may seem, how it takes place, how it is viewed, and how it is valued is heavily dependent on the cultural and social context.

On the other hand, even pregnancy is associated with taboos. Taboos associated with pregnancy are many, and primarily involve activities the woman should or should not engage in, so as not to endanger the baby. Some cultures isolate a woman from others in the community after birth, because of the dangers associated with her, and the placenta is often seen as especially dangerous. Many cultures have **postpartum sex taboos** which restrict men's sexual contact with women after birth. Because childbirth is a liminal activity, which straddles the boundary between life and death, it makes sense that this activity is fraught with such danger. Even the pain of childbirth can be interpreted a variety of ways. In some cultures, women who experience pain during childbirth are thought to have done something wrong during pregnancy, or may be suspected of having engaged in adultery.

Pregnancy is tightly controlled by the state and by the wider society, so pregnant women often find that their lives are no longer their own once they are carrying a child. In the West we have a great deal of rights to our own bodies, to our own bodily integrity. That's why, for the most part, we cannot force the mentally ill to take medications if they do not want to, even when it may protect people around them. Yet even today, pregnant women have fewer rights than other people. Pro-life legislation, which is passed in states every year, grants greater rights to fetuses and embryos than to adult women. **Fetal protection laws** can put women in jail for delivering babies who are born with drugs in their systems, but there are no laws that provide rehabilitation for those women; just jail time. The whole notion of **fetal rights**

– that the rights of an unborn fetus should be protected by restricting the rights of the pregnant woman – is extremely controversial, pitting society against pregnant women, who are called irresponsible for choosing to drink, take drugs, smoke, or work in dangerous jobs while pregnant. Once the children are born, however, they have no rights to health care, safe housing, good nutrition, or good schools. Only while in the womb does society give them so much care and protection.

While pregnancy is clearly gendered – only women (and transmen) can get pregnant and bear children, after all – there are a handful of cultures in which men symbolically share the burdens of pregnancy with their wives. In these cultures, including communities in Russia, Thailand, and China, men engage in what is known to anthropologists as **couvade**: fathers-to-be participate in the same food taboos as women, sometimes isolate them-selves from the rest of the community during their wives' pregnancies, and sometimes even experience some of the same physical signs of discomfort as their wives. Jeffery and Karen Paige (1981) argue that this ritual functions as a way to allow for men to claim control of paternity over their children, and simultaneously to control their wives' sexuality.

Even in the United States, many men are afraid to have sex with pregnant women, which suggests that even here there is still a notion that pregnancy is polluting. In recent years, many women have begun to challenge the practice of hiding one's pregnant body under mumu-like maternity clothes, instead showing them off in form-fitting fashions, and some women have begun showing off their "baby bumps" in nude or semi-nude photographs.

In recent years, in the West, childbirth has become increasingly medical-ized. While childbirth has never been a truly "natural" phenomenon – after all, how women give birth is determined entirely by the values and prac-tices of their culture – it has moved entirely into the realm of science today. Most Western births take place in hospitals where women's bodies are largely under the control of doctors, nurses, and machines. Sociologist Robbie Davis-Floyd (1992) writes of the "American way of birthing," in which women's pregnant bodies are seen as defective and unable to handle what billions of women have handled throughout history. Today, man-made machines are thought better able to handle childbirth.

Davis-Floyd writes of childbirth as a rite of passage marking three new social beings: child, mother, and father. But it is especially the mother who is transformed. The symbolic manifestations of her liminal position include the fact that she's wheeled to her room in a wheelchair like a disabled person; she's confined to a bed in a hospital like a sick person, with an IV stuck in her arm, and she's entirely dependent on the machines that monitor her and her unborn baby's functions. She notes that a healthy baby, or successful product, is the goal, and that the mother's experience during childbirth is only secondarily considered. Not only is the birthing process controlled,

the scientific and biomedical body

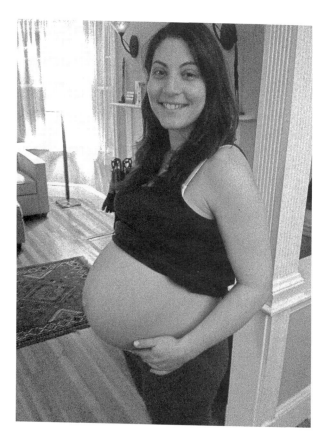

FIGURE 4.3 Lisa Brown, nine months pregnant. She gave birth to her son twelve days after this photograph was taken. Photo courtesy of Lisa Brown.

it is timed, according to the **Friedman Curve**, which is a standardized bell curve which represents the stages that a woman is supposed to go through during labor, and when. When a woman goes through one stage too slowly, then drugs or surgery are used to bring her body into compliance with the norm.

Today, nearly one third of American births are via c-section, either for medical necessity or for other reasons. Some middle- and upper-class women want to schedule their births and other women are either afraid of the pain of childbirth or the potential disfigurement of their bodies from a vaginal birth. In some cases, doctors and hospitals encourage c-sections because they are both easier to control and less expensive for the hospital than a potentially long labor. In Ireland, in the 1950s, women who were having difficult births were not given c-sections, however; instead they had their pelvises broken, a procedure known as a **symphysiotomy**. In Catholic Ireland, the procedure was thought to permanently widen the pelvis, allowing for unlimited future vaginal deliveries, while c-sections were thought to limit women's future fertility. Sociologist Davis-Floyd suggests that because only women have babies, the way a society treats childbirth and pregnancy reveals how it treats women.

Lactation is another "dangerous" activity associated with women. In Victorian England, upper-class women were discouraged from breastfeeding their children right after birth, or sometimes at all, because the colostrum was seen as dangerous. The result was that many mothers used dogs to suckle their breasts to relieve the pressure of milk in their breasts, and many women used **wet nurses** – typically poor and sometimes black women who nursed the babies of wealthier women – to nurse their children. Another concern was that the mother, or the wet nurse, would transmit her anxieties and "passions" to her baby via her breast milk, so the emotions of the nursing woman needed to be tightly controlled.

Today, it is recommended that mothers breastfeed their babies, because it is healthier for the baby and helps to create a bond between the baby and the mother. Yet breastfeeding is shaped by a number of cultural factors, including nation and class.

In non-Western countries, thanks to decades of advertising by American companies like Nestle, many women in the developing world think that powdered milk is the best for their babies, and do not breastfeed. In addition, poor mothers who breastfeed must stay with their babies to do this, keeping them from work that they need to do to earn money to eat and feed their other children. Breastfeeding, for this reason, is often incompatible with working mothers, or with poverty and malnutrition, especially to overworked and underfed women, for whom breastfeeding may even be dangerous.

In the West, breastfeeding is so highly valued and encouraged today that women who choose not to breastfeed are often stigmatized. In addition, because breastfeeding is positively correlated with social class (in other words, the higher the social class, the more likely one is to breastfeed), choosing not to breastfeed has come to be seen as a sign of low education and low class. To further reinforce the class distinction, upper-middle-class women are more likely to have jobs that provide them with not only the breaks needed to pump breast milk, as well as lactation rooms in which they can pump in privacy, but also the income needed to provide for high-quality child care. For other working women, pumping breast milk at work is difficult if not impossible.

When women have their children with them, breastfeeding is not always easy to do either. Because of the taboos associated with both breast milk and the female breast, women often have trouble finding a spot to breastfeed in public, even on their days off work. Some countries, such as Australia, explicitly allow breastfeeding in public, while other countries, like China,

the scientific and biomedical body

consider it to be embarrassing and taboo. In the United States, breastfeeding laws differ by state and region, although the trend is moving towards allowing it in public. Still, for all of these reasons, working women – of all classes – often continue to have a hard time with breastfeeding.

Assisted reproductive technologies

Today, thanks in part to the delay in childbearing for many women in the West, infertility rates have skyrocketed, with approximately one in six American couples experiencing such problems, and with them, the use of assisted reproductive technologies (ARTs). Others use assisted reproductive technologies because they cannot, or choose not to, have a child through conventional methods; gay men and lesbians, for example, often bear children this way. One in seven couples in the United States seek treatment for infertility or use ARTs. Where infertility was once seen as a personal failing, reflecting poorly on either the maternal qualities of the woman or the virility of the man, today much of the moral judgment has disappeared as infertility has become increasingly medicalized in the West.

Today there are a variety of treatments available for infertility or to produce a child without sexual reproduction, including artificial insemination with donor semen if the male partner is infertile or for single women or lesbian couples; in vitro fertilization (IVF), where an egg and sperm are fertilized in a petri dish and the embryo is placed inside the mother's uterus; in vitro fertilization or artificial insemination with a surrogate womb; gamete intrafallopian transfer (GIFT), where the egg and sperm are mixed in a test tube and then placed into the fallopian tubes to fertilize; and intra-cytoplasmic sperm injection (ICSI), where sperm is injected directly into the egg. All of these procedures, and many more, can utilize either the mother's egg, a donor egg, the father's sperm, or a donor's sperm. In the United States, in 2006, 55,000 babies were born thanks to assisted reproductive technologies.

These procedures have been a godsend to many individuals and couples who have been unable to conceive or bear a child naturally. But they have also created a whole new set of social, ethical, and economic concerns. In addition, the whole concept of mother and father has shifted with these new technologies, which often produce distinctions between social and biological mothers and fathers.

One point to make is that these technologies are very expensive. The cost in the United States is about $30,000 for a single IVF cycle, and it often takes two or three to produce a viable pregnancy. Most insurance plans do not cover these procedures, making them primarily available to the well-to-do. In addition, because of the fact that IVF generally results in multiple births (because doctors implant multiple embryos at once), the births are often premature, and the babies generally need expensive care in the hospital before they can go home.

This issue became well known to the public in 2009, when Nadya Suleman, known as Octomom, gave birth to octuplets conceived via IVF. Suleman, a single mom with six other children at the time, was living on public assistance and it is unclear how the IVF treatments were paid for. In addition, because her doctor disregarded embryo transfer guidelines which recommended only implanting two embryos into the patient (instead, he transferred 12 of which eight survived; he later lost his medical license because of this), the babies were born nine weeks early and required millions of dollars of care, paid for by Medicaid, for their survival.

There are other economic and class implications as well. Working-class women can sell their eggs for thousands of dollars to middle- and upper-class women who need them. Lower-class men, on the other hand, cannot sell their sperm to sperm banks because people looking for sperm donors are looking for "high-quality sperm" which they define as coming from men from "good" backgrounds (tall white men with post-graduate degrees are the most highly sought). Sperm, eggs, and even babies are now commercial products which are sought for by consumer-slash-parents.

Surrogacy is also subject to economic concerns. Sometimes surrogates are paid for their services, and sometimes they are not, but when they are, there may be ethical issues involved in paying poorer women to bear children for wealthier women (and men). Today, the class inequality often found in the surrogacy relationship has now been globalized, as Indian surrogates carry babies for wealthy foreign couples; the Indian surrogacy industry now generates more than $2 billion annually. In addition, surrogacy brings up the question of how much a woman should be allowed to do with her body, and how much she should be forced to do. Can a surrogate be forced to abort a baby who is not healthy? And why is surrogacy legal and prostitution, largely, is not? Surrogacy is an interesting type of labor contract in that what is being paid for – the carrying and birth of a baby – is a very different kind of a service than that involved in other kinds of legal contracts. Like prostitutes, women's bodies are being commodified through surrogacy, as are the products of that commodification. One of the legal questions to emerge from surrogacy is whether surrogates, especially those who are not simply gestational surrogates (i.e., those who are carrying an embryo from another couple), but actually are carrying their own biological child, are selling their own children to other people. Selling babies is illegal, and yet through surrogacy it apparently is not.

Another interesting implication of these technologies is the separation of sex from reproduction. Here, babies are conceived thanks to the skills and equipment of medical specialists, and the moment of conception might happen in the uterus (as with artificial insemination or GIFT) or in a petri

the scientific and biomedical body

dish (as with IVF). When, then, does life begin? And what do we do with the millions of leftover embryos produced through IVF, currently sitting in freezers in doctors' offices around the world? These questions are confounding to medical ethicists, theologians, and pro-life and pro-choice advocates alike.

Other questions relate to who gets to have children via these technologies. Should very old women be allowed to get pregnant and give birth? Should doctors be able to deny treatment to gay men or lesbians? Should the number of embryos implanted be restricted, and should doctors force women to abort "surplus" embryos? Today, some countries have begun to regulate some of these issues, while in other countries it is a free for all. It is rumored that a Danish company will soon be offering "fertility cruises" in international waters that will allow patients from countries like England, where these technologies are strictly regulated, to have whatever procedures they like.

And finally, assisted reproductive technologies challenge us to think about what is "natural" when it comes to something like conception or pregnancy. Is it more natural to want a child that you have given birth to yourself, even if the child does not share your genes? Is it more natural to have a child who shares his parents' genes, but was delivered by a surrogate? Or is it more natural to adopt a child? And what of the implications and actions to the woman's body? As Gena Corea (1985) points out, all of the assisted reproductive methods in use today originally were developed from livestock; from developing more efficient ways to make female livestock create more animals to eat come new techniques aimed at making human females produce babies.

Prenatal testing and the threat of the designer baby

Another new development in new reproductive technologies is prenatal testing. While certain practices have been around for many years, like amniocentesis, other practices are much newer. Prenatal diagnosis is used to detect abnormalities and diseases in the fetus, while prenatal screening is used for elective things like sex selection. But in all of these cases, the technology allows for parents and doctors to have more control over the outcome of births than ever before.

In the case of prenatal diagnosis, parents can elect to find out if their fetus has a condition that can either be surgically or medically treated before birth, and they can find out if the fetus has a condition that will be untreatable. In the latter case, parents can choose to either abort the fetus or give birth to a special needs baby, or a baby who will die soon after birth.

Anthropologist Rayna Rapp (1999) has looked at prenatal testing via amniocentesis, and notes a number of interesting ethical issues surrounding the procedure. For those who choose to abort babies with physical defects, or who struggle with that decision, Rapp found a whole array of motivations, based on her interviews with parents. White middle-class women, for example, felt guilty about the fact that they were so "selfish" that they did not want to raise a child with, for example, Down's Syndrome, while immigrants were worried about whether a disabled child could assimilate into the culture, and Latinas were concerned with the child's possible suffering. Middle-class parents were more concerned about their child not being able to achieve and accomplish what they hope for them, while working-class parents were worried about the child's impact on the rest of the family's needs and aspirations.

One of the more modern ways of prenatal diagnosis is through Preimplantation Genetic Diagnosis (PGD), in which, during IVF, the embryo is screened prior to implantation in the uterus. In this case, parents can elect to only have embryos implanted which are healthy. In addition, parents can choose whether to implant male or female embryos. It has also been used to select *for* a disability, such as deafness, so that the child can share that disability with the parent. This kind of genetic testing brings up a whole host of ethical questions: Will parents be able to select for racial characteristics in the future? What about sexuality? How will we begin to define "defect" and which kinds of defects will be aborted in the future? Gay babies? Babies with big noses? Babies with genes that predispose them towards being fat?

In this chapter, we covered the beginning of life – birth – and ended by touching a bit on the ethical issues surrounding which fetuses should be allowed to live or die, based on the genetic conditions that they might have. In Chapter 5, we will look at death, and will begin to answer some of the questions regarding what happens to our bodies when we die.

Key terms

Assisted Reproductive Technologies	Hormone Replacement Therapy
Comstock Laws	In Vitro Fertilization
Conscience Laws	Menstrual Hut
Couvade	Menstrual Taboos
Fetal Protection Laws	One Child Policy
Fetal Rights	Postpartum Taboos
Final Solution	Pro-Natalism
Friedman Curve	*continued ...*

the scientific and biomedical body

<table>
<tr><td>continued</td><td>Surrogacy</td></tr>
<tr><td>Reproductive Justice
  Movement</td><td>Symphysiotomy
Test Tube Baby</td></tr>
<tr><td>Roe v. Wade</td><td>Wet Nurse</td></tr>
<tr><td>Spermatogenesis</td><td>Withdrawal Method</td></tr>
</table>

Further reading

Becker, Gay. (2000). *The Elusive Embryo: How Men and Women Approach New Reproductive Technologies*. Berkeley, CA: University of California Press.

Davis-Floyd, Robbie. (1992). *Birth as an American Rite of Passage*. Berkeley, CA: University of California Press.

Delaney, Janice. (1988). *The Curse: A Cultural History of Menstruation*. Urbana, IL: University of Illinois Press.

Franklin, Sarah. (1997). *Embodied Progress: A Cultural Account of Assisted Conception*. London: Routledge.

Franklin, Sarah and Helene. Ragoné (eds). (1988). *Reproducing Reproduction: Kinship, Power and Technological Innovation*. Philadelphia, PA: University of Pennsylvania Press.

Martin, Emily. (1987). *The Woman in The Body: A Cultural Analysis of Reproduction*. Boston, MA: Beacon Press.

Rapp, Rayna. (1999). *Testing Women, Testing the Fetus: The Social Impact of Amniocentesis in America*. London and New York: Routledge.

Reilly, Phillip R. (1991). *The Surgical Solution: A History of Involuntary Sterilization in the United States*. Baltimore, MD: Johns Hopkins University Press.

chapter 5

Dead Bodies

Dawn of the Dead, a 2004 remake of George Romero's 1978 zombie film by the same name, opens with a nurse named Ana, played by Sarah Polley, who wakes up to find her husband being killed by the next door neighbor's daughter. Less than a minute after her husband's brutal death, he stands up, reanimated, and begins to attack Ana, who eventually escapes through the bathroom window. All of this takes less than three minutes, and sets the stage for what many people consider to be one of the best zombie movies of all time. What makes this scene so compelling, besides the gore – Vivian, the little girl, has had her mouth ripped off and her face is covered in blood and guts, and Luis, Ana's husband, has his throat ripped out and dies, gurgling, in a pool of his own blood – is the fact that Ana is being threatened by two people who she once knew, trusted, and loved, but who no longer behave like themselves. Instead of a loving husband and sweet neighbor, Luis and Vivian are now monsters. Another thing that makes zombie movies like this so frightening is that one of the facts that we think we know for sure is that once someone has died, no matter how loved he was or how horribly he died, he should stay dead.

Zombie movies have turned that simple understanding upside down: in the zombie movie, your loved ones may still look like themselves (if you discount all the blood), but now they are mindless killers, and dying is no longer a permanent condition. What can be more frightening?

Zombies are now big business. Even though the first modern zombie movie, George Romero's *Night of the Living Dead*, came out in 1968, the 2000s was truly the decade of the zombie, with well over 300 zombie movies released from 2000 to 2009. In the years since then, dozens more films have been released, and one of AMC's most popular television shows,

The Walking Dead, is set in a zombie apocalypse. Why have zombies gotten so popular lately?

English professor and zombie expert Kyle William Bishop (2010) notes that one of the reasons that zombies are so frightening is that although they were were once human, they have no real connection to humanity aside from their physical form. In addition, the zombie embodies one of our most central fears: that of our own deaths. By watching our loved ones die, and then re-animate, in front of our eyes, we see before us our own eventual death.

If death is the thing that all humans most fear, it is also the thing that all humans will, at one time, experience. Death is the great universal. And while zombie movies may be fantasy, the idea that death may not be quite as simple as we think is not a fantasy at all. In this chapter, we will look at death: how and where people die, how we treat the dead, and the rituals celebrating the dead. While dying is a clearly a biological phenomenon, common to all humans, the conditions under which we die and the attitudes and rituals associated with death are, like the other subjects in this book, socially constructed.

How and where people die

According to the World Health Organization, about 57 million people died in 2008. But more interesting than the number of deaths is the way in which people die, and how those methods of death differ by country, by income, and by other demographic factors.

Poor countries, for example, not only have higher death rates than wealthy countries (with Botswana as the leader, with 29 deaths per 1,000 people per year), but the causes of death there tend to be rare in wealthy countries. Over one and a half a million people in developing countries die each year from malaria, tuberculosis, and diarrhea, for example. These deaths from infectious diseases are exacerbated by poor sanitation, overcrowding, and lack of access to vaccinations. Other deaths are due to a lack of access to antibiotics – over a million people per year die just from treatable lower respiratory infections – and problems associated with giving birth account for three-quarters of a million women and babies per year. AIDS is also a major killer in poor countries, because it spreads more easily without prevention tools and education, because testing is rare, because of the stigma and shame associated with the disease, and because treatment is inaccessible and expensive.

In Myanamar, also known as Burma, for example, as in so many poor countries, there are not enough AIDS drugs to go to all who need them. While the World Health Organization recommends that people with **CD4** (a type of white blood cell that fights infection) counts below 350 start treatment with anti-retroviral drugs (in the United States, people with AIDS who can afford the drugs take them as soon as they are diagnosed with HIV, regardless of their count), in Myanamar, one can only get access to the drugs when one's CD4 count drops to 150. By the time one's CD4 count drops that low, the patient is deathly ill. The result is that half of all people (estimated at 240,000) in the country do not get the drugs in time, leaving 18,000 of them to die each year.

Children also die much more frequently in low-income countries, thanks to a lack of food, poor sanitation, and lack of access to medical care. In high-income countries, infant mortality stands at about two deaths per 1,000; in Africa, on the other hand, that number is about 30 deaths per 1,000. And where children die with such frequency, mothers may not necessarily respond in ways that we may expect, as anthropologist Nancy Scheper-Hughes shows in her book *Death Without Weeping: The Violence of Everday Life in Brazil* (1993). In the poor shantytowns where she worked, infant mortality was so high that mothers learned to distance themselves emotionally from their babies, and doctors, the church, and the rest of society encouraged this type of detachment. People in the most productive years of their lives, too, die in greater numbers in poor countries. In Africa, four times as many working adults die than those in rich countries, which means that the overall economy of those countries is adversely affected.

In high-income countries, however, most of these conditions are rare or non-existent. In fact, as we noted in Chapter 2, in wealthy nations, death often comes from the prosperous conditions in which we live. Because people in wealthy nations live much longer than those in poor countries – in high-income countries, 71 percent of all people live beyond 70, while in poor countries, only 17 percent live to 70 or above – and eat a more abundant (and fattier) diet, we die of chronic diseases associated with the end of life: cardiovascular disease, cancers of various kinds, pulmonary disease, diabetes, and dementia. In Japan, there is a cause of death known as *karoshi*, which translates to "death from overwork." It's associated with white-collar businessmen in Japan, who often work up to 12 hours a day, and while the true cause of death is often heart attack, it is clearly caused by the Japanese culture which demands huge amounts of overtime with very little time off. These are all examples of how death is socially constructed: we do not die from the same causes, or in the same ways. Nor, as we shall see, do we see death in the same ways.

Understanding how and why people die around the world tells us not only about the efficacy of those nations' health care systems, but also about inequality: those who have the most suffer the least. Unequal access to health care is a major factor in mortality and morbidity rates around the world, but so is unequal access to nutritious food, clean water, safe living conditions, and education. For instance, it should come as no surprise that people who live in shantytowns like those outside of Manila in the Philippines have a life expectancy decades lower than the average American's. Here, the desperately poor live in "homes" constructed of cardboard, cloth, and salvaged wood that are perched on top of tombs in a graveyard – tombs which, once these shantytown dwellers die, they could never afford to reside in after death.

Even in the United States, the poor die earlier and more frequently than the wealthy, and often from very different conditions. Women who live below the poverty line die of heart disease and diabetes at much greater rates than those who live above it. Men without a high school education, for example, are far more likely to die of injury, communicable diseases, and chronic diseases than those with a college degree. African-Americans, who are more likely to be poor than other ethnic groups, die of cancer, liver disease, diabetes, AIDS, violence, and heart disease at greater numbers than whites. In fact, the poorest Americans have life expectancy rates very similar to those found in India or Africa. This is true even though the poorest Americans have far greater incomes than the poorest people in developing countries.

Racism is another contributing factor in African-Americans' higher rates of death from circulatory disease. Racism may also contribute to the fact that Native Americans commit suicide at three times the national rate and die of alcohol-related conditions at 17 times the national rate. These issues will be discussed further in Chapter 6.

Finally, it's not just the relative poverty in the United States that contributes to higher death rates among this country's poor. Studies have shown that the greater the gap between the rich and poor, the lower the overall life expectancy rate, which illustrates why the United States, which is the richest country on the planet but is the fourth most unequal (behind Mexico, Poland, and Turkey), only ranks 38th in terms of overall life expectancy. In fact, a 2009 study in the *British Medical Journal* claims that the United States has 884,000 "excess" deaths per year, all of which are attributable to income inequality. Why would that be? Epidemiologist R. G. Wilkinson suggests that in countries with a large income and wealth gap, like the United States, the wealthy are less likely to pay taxes for public services that benefit the poor, like public schools, public hospitals, and other social services. In addition, societies like ours may also have a lesser degree of social cohesion; we cannot rely on each other, and we rarely participate in community organizations and activities that benefit us all. In addition, homicide is most prevalent when income inequality is greatest. Ultimately, we can say that poverty is the world's number one killer.

It may also be worth pointing out that when the *Titanic* sank in 1912, of the 1,308 passengers and crew on board, 416 survived. Of those survivors, 60 percent came from first class, 40 percent from second class, and 25 percent from third class. The different classes, of course, represent the

dead bodies

FIGURE 5.1 A tomb in a Spanish cemetery. Photo courtesy of Jeff Hayes.

amount of money paid for one's ticket, and covered the room, the food, and the overall experience on the cruise. One of the reasons for the differential death and survival rate had to do with the fact that the third class passengers had rooms far below deck, while those in first class were closer to the top of the boat, and thus had an easier time accessing the lifeboats. Similarly, in 2005, when Hurricane Katrina hit New Orleans, and the levee broke, the greatest number of casualties came from the poor neighborhoods which were situated beneath the water line. So where people live also affects how they die.

For most of human history, people died, except in the cases of accidental death, in their homes, often surrounded by loved ones. Today, at least in the West, this has radically changed. Now, most Westerners, and others who live in societies where access to health care and hospitals is common, die in hospitals or nursing homes. It's been predicted that by 2030, only one in

the scientific and biomedical body

ten British citizens will die at home. Unfortunately, when polled, most people say that they would like to die at home, and those who die at home have a measurably better quality of life in their final days than those who die in an institution. Many elderly people, too, are often moved from nursing home to hospital and sometimes to other types of institution in their final days, making their death even less comfortable. Unfortunately, when dying of a chronic condition, home death is only really possible for those with the resources to provide for an at-home nurse, specialized medical equipment, and of course the social support to make such a death possible. Where one dies, then, is shaped by both economic factors as well as social factors.

On the other hand, sometimes dying at home is not a cause for celebration. Many elderly Americans die alone at home, and sometimes their bodies are not found for days. This points to the increasing isolation of the elderly in the United States, a situation outlined by sociologist Eric Klinenberg in 2001. He found that many seniors, and especially those with little in the way of economic resources, are isolated, afraid, and unlikely to leave their homes to get medical care or to see friends or family. The result is that they die alone and afraid.

Organized death

Death, as we have discussed, does not occur randomly. It is shaped by a variety of social factors, most important among them being access to economic resources. But death can, of course, be far more intentional. When a person is murdered, for example, then the death of that person was predicted and made possible by the person who killed them. On a similar note, there are instances throughout history in which death is not just intentional and predictable, but widespread and organized.

In the twentieth century, most Americans look to the Holocaust as the best example of this type of clinical, intentional, and systematic death. We call these types of killing systems **genocides** – the systematic elimination of one ethnic group by another group. In the Holocaust, the Nazi party in Germany, led by Adolf Hitler, killed at least six million Jews, alongside of countless thousands of Gypsies (also known as Roma), gays and lesbians, Communists, physically and mentally disabled, and political prisoners: the total death toll may be as high as 17 million people. By the end of World War II, when the Allied Armies defeated the Germans, two out of three European Jews had lost their lives. While the killings during the Holocaust began rather informally, by the end of the war, the Germans had created the most organized system of death in the history of humanity.

After years of discriminatory laws aimed at Jews, whom the Nazis blamed for the German losses in World War I, with the rise of Hitler's **Third Reich** in 1933, Jews and other "racial enemies" of the state like Gypsies were targeted for sterilization, prevented from marrying Aryans, and, in some areas like Poland, placed into ghettos, where thousands died from overwork, disease, and starvation. Jews began to be sent to the new concentration camps set up in Germany and Poland in the mid-1930s, where up to 50 percent of all inmates died from overwork, torture, and disease. Systematic killings began in 1939 as specific groups of Jews and others were targeted for murder and killed by German death squads as well as regular citizens, and in 1942, the true extermination camps were founded when the Nazis agreed on what was called the Final Solution.

These death camps were locations set up with the sole purpose of processing and killing Jews, and were supported by the entire infrastructure of German society, including churches, the post office, private companies, schools, the transportation sector, the mass media, and the financial sector. When shooting the victims became too slow and cumbersome, the Germans developed new ways to implement mass slaughter, including the use of vans equipped with poisonous gas, which led ultimately to the use of gas chambers at the death camps, and allowed the killing of millions of men, women, and children in a relatively short time; the gas chambers at Treblinka, for example, could kill 2,000 people at a time. The Nazis disposed of the massive number of bodies through mass graves and through cremation at the death camps. This was the first time in human history that targeted killing has ever taken place on such a grand scale and with such social and institutional support.

Even though the Holocaust was unique in both the numbers of the dead as well as the systematic nature of the killings, history is full of wars and genocides that have killed millions of people. For example, the British have a long history of subjugating, racializing, and killing groups through colonization: first the Irish in the sixteenth century, who were considered to be savage, thus justifying the taking of their land and the killing of their people, then the Native Americans later that same century, who were treated much the same way (by first the British, and later other Europeans and Euro-Americans), and finally the Australians, Tasmanians, and the Maori of New Zealand in the eighteenth and nineteenth centuries. Because the British, Europeans, or Americans were after the land that was occupied by these people, the people that lived there needed to be controlled, removed, and sometimes killed. Even in the United States, when some native groups were successfully "civilized," like the Cherokee, once the British (now Americans) needed their land, their assimilation into American culture, language, and practices was not good enough and they were still forcibly removed on the **Trail of Tears**, resulting in the deaths of 4,000 Cherokee, as well as countless members of other tribes. The **Indian Removal Act**, passed by Congress in

the scientific and biomedical body

FIGURE 5.2 These are slave laborers in the Buchenwald concentration camp; many had died from malnutrition when U.S. troops of the 80th Division entered the camp on April 16, 1945. Photo courtesy of the National Archives and Records Administration. •

1830, allowed for the forcible removal of all Native peoples east of the Mississippi, who were to be relocated to the area known as the Indian Territory (today known as Oklahoma). That law, of course, was only the beginning, because as European-Americans continued to expand westward across the continent, using **Manifest Destiny** as their justification, they continued to move Native Americans further west, killing them as they went, sometimes in organized massacres like Wounded Knee. As anthropologist Mary Douglas said, "dirt is matter out of place." Because Native Americans were seen as dirty and polluting, it was easy for European-Americans to justify their removal by almost any means possible. In addition, since they were already considered to be dirty, their women could be raped without a concern.

The twentieth century has seen yet more instances of genocide, such as that by the Ottoman Turks against the Armenian people, the Bosnian genocide of the 1990s, and the Rwandan genocide of the same period. And while one of the reasons that we still teach children in school about the Holocaust is so that, by remembering history, we will never repeat it, the reality is that mass, targeted killings continue to occur today. The current

dead bodies

killings in Darfur, Sudan by the Sudanese government and the Janjaweed militia is considered to be a genocide by many international observers. It seems that we do in fact continue to repeat history.

Interesting issues: the killing fields of Cambodia

The killing fields refer to a number of mass graves in Cambodia dating to the 1970s when the Khmer Rouge ruled the country. During that time, from 1975 to 1979, at least 1.5 million people either died of starvation, disease, or forced labor, or were killed outright by Khmer forces. Well over a million people were buried in thousands of mass graves scattered throughout the country. The Khmer, led by Pol Pot, took over leadership of the country following the end of the Cambodian Civil War in 1975 and instituted a number of policies intended to create a Communist and nationalist utopia. The result was famine, starvation, deaths from treatable illnesses like malaria, and, as political opposition rose, the torture and execution of dissidents, intellectuals, artists, ethnic minorities, Christians, and Muslims. Because ammunition was scarce, after being tortured, victims were killed by being beaten or hacked to death, and were then buried in one of 20,000 unmarked graves. Today the torture and deaths are memorialized at the Tuol Sleng Genocide Museum, a former school-turned-prison used by the Khmer security forces, in Phnom Penh, and the Choeng Ek Killing Fields, a collection of 129 mass graves outside of Phnom Penh in which about 20,000 bodies are buried.

How do we know when we're dead?

We opened this chapter with a scene from a zombie film which demonstrates that, at least in Hollywood movies, sometimes it's unclear whether someone is alive or dead. The fact that a zombie, or a vampire for that matter, can start out as a living person, die, and then come back as an "undead" person may not be all that fantastic, however. How do we really know if someone has died?

In the past, the defining feature of death was the heart – if it stopped beating, the person was considered dead – or the breath – if the person stopped breathing, then the person was dead. However, thanks to developments in medical knowledge and technology, patients can be revived even after they stopped breathing or their heart stopped beating; sometimes a person can be dead for minutes and can still be revived. On November 6, 2012, at a polling place in the suburbs of Detroit, an elderly man stopped breathing while in the middle of voting during the Presidential election. A nurse who was present found that his heart had also stopped, but after a few moments of CPR he revived the man, who, upon returning to life, asked

the scientific and biomedical body

"did I vote?" (He wanted to make sure that he finished his civic duty before going to the hospital. Had the nurse not been present, there is a good chance that the man may have stayed dead.) In addition, breathing machines, pacemakers, organ transplants, artificial lungs, and other medical technologies can sustain life well beyond the time when a person would have otherwise died.

Even before the development of such technology, however, the cessation of breath or of a heartbeat was not always a foolproof indicator of death. People have revived themselves after being declared dead, and sometimes even after burial or just before embalming. This was such a common occurrence at one time (or people's fear of it was so strong) that in the nineteenth century some coffins and burial vaults were built with escape mechanisms to allow the living to get out; other coffins had bells or other devices to allow the living to notify others of their accidental burial.

Today, in the West, the scientific concept of **brain death** is used to determine life or death. In brain death, brain activity, which can be measured on an electroencephalography (EEG), has stopped. Brain death is complicated, however, because if a person is brain dead, the rest of their body can still be kept alive so that they may be harvested for organs to be donated to others. Some pregnant women, too, who are considered to be brain dead, can be sustained with life support machines until their fetuses can be delivered. This creates an interesting and complicated situation whereby a person can be, by some measures, both dead *and* alive.

One of the most famous cases to challenge the notion of brain death was the case of Terry Schiavo, a 27-year-old woman who collapsed at her Florida home from a cardiac arrest. She was ultimately diagnosed as being in a persistent vegetative state thanks to the loss of blood to her brain while she was unconscious. Schiavo's husband and family hoped that she would recover and spent years and countless dollars trying to revive her. The case reached public awareness in 1998 when her husband tried to have her feeding tube, which was keeping her alive, removed (while she could not feed herself, she was able to breathe on her own); her parents, on the other hand, challenged his petition, claiming that she was conscious, and, thus alive. Even though Schiavo's EEG showed no brain activity, and a CAT scan showed extensive atrophy of her brain cells, doctors hired on behalf of Terry's parents argued that she was minimally conscious. The case was battled in court for seven years, but in March 2005, her husband prevailed and her feeding tube was removed; she died two weeks later. The case was extremely controversial, and Americans on both sides of the case weighed in on whether Schiavo was technically dead or alive, and who – her parents or her husband – should be able to make the ultimate decision about her fate. Even the governor of Florida, Jeb Bush, and the President of the United States, George W. Bush, weighed in on the case.

The Terry Schiavo case helped spur debate regarding the **right to die movement**. The advocates of this movement demand that patients be allowed to choose the time and method of their own deaths, rather than having to linger with painful chronic illnesses, or in vegetative conditions for which there is no hope of recovery. In the Netherlands, for example, since 2001 **voluntary euthanasia,** where a doctor ends a patient's life in the case of unbearable suffering, is legal, and in a few American states (Oregon, Washington, and Montana) **assisted suicide**, where a doctor provides the medication for a patient with a terminal illness to kill themselves, is also legal. For right to die advocates, it's not the quantity of life that's important but the quality of life, and the quality of death. Prior to the Terry Schiavo case was the Karen Quinlan case, which spurred the passage of the first **living will** law in the United States. Like Schiavo, Quinlan was in a persistent vegetative state; but when her parents wanted to remove her from the ventilator that was keeping her alive, the hospital refused, resulting in a court battle that was ultimately resolved in the parents' favor, and in Quinlan's death.

It has long been rumored that no one is allowed to die on Disney property. In other words, when a person collapses at Disneyland in California or Disney World in Florida, the person cannot be declared dead until the ambulance carrying them has left the Disney property. The reason that this alleged Disney policy can be followed is that in the United States, a person is not truly dead until the time of death is called by a medical practitioner and a death certificate is issued. So in the case of Disney deaths, medics will perform CPR on patients on site and en route to the hospital, where they will finally be declared dead, and thus Disney can continue to maintain that no one has ever died at the "happiest place on earth."

In addition, there are a number of places on the planet where it is illegal to die. Generally, these laws have been passed in response to laws banning the development of new cemeteries, but sometimes they are used to protect a sacred site from the polluting qualities of death. In Japan, an island called Itsukushima is sacred to practitioners of the Shinto religion. After the Battle of Miyajima in 1555, fought on the island, not only were the dead bodies removed to the Japanese mainland but the blood-soaked soil was removed as well. Today, the elderly, the terminally ill, and pregnant women are asked to leave the island, to prevent them from dying there.

Treating the dead

What happens after we die is just as culturally and socially constructed as how we die. All human cultures – and some animal species – take care of their dead in some way, by burying, burning, embalming, or otherwise treating the dead. In addition, all human cultures mourn the dead in some way, providing some sort of cultural event or ceremony in order to say goodbye to the dead.

In the Catholic tradition, the dying are given **last rites**, including anointing the dying and providing penance, by a priest just before death, which is thought to prepare the soul for the afterlife and cleanse the person of their sins. For those who die in a hospital, often the people who surround one at death, however, are doctors, who are sometimes the least qualified in terms of handling the wishes and care of the dying.

In Europe until about the nineteenth century, after a person died, a death messenger was a person who traveled around the village letting other villagers know about the death, and inviting them to attend the funeral. Sometimes they rang a bell while announcing the death. Death messengers were generally paid based on the distance that they had to travel. Another paid professional in death rituals is the professional mourner. In some cultures, these people, who are not related to the dead, are paid to wail, moan, and cry, as a way to show the importance of the deceased and to encourage other mourners to cry as well. These are commonly used today in China and in Chinese communities around the world, and help the deceased enter the afterlife quicker.

After death, the body is treated in a variety of ways. Sometimes the body is preserved after death via embalming and mummification. For instance, the ancient Egyptians embalmed the bodies of the dead by removing the organs and bodily fluids and preserving them in pots, where they would be reunited with the dead in the afterlife. After embalming, the corpses would be mummified, preserving them for posterity. Many families mummified their pet cats as well and buried them in the family vault, in the hope that they would be reunited together in the afterlife. Cats and other sacred animals were also mummified because they were thought to be incarnations of gods, so they were buried in an appropriately respectful fashion. Some animals were sacrificed to the gods, and mummified and buried, while still other animals were mummified and buried as food to be eaten by humans in the afterlife.

In the contemporary West, bodies are embalmed too, in preparation for burial, but not for mummification. The exception to this practice is found among Jews and Muslims, who do not embalm their dead; instead, they bury them as soon as possible after death.

In embalming, the fluids of the body are removed and replaced with formaldehyde. In the West, the practice began when people died far away from home; embalming the body preserves it, keeping it from decaying, so that it could be returned home for burial. (Sometimes embalming will not preserve the body for as long as is necessary for burial. In July 2012, actor Sherman Helmsley, who starred in *The Jeffersons*, died, but because of a dispute over his will, his body was embalmed and then frozen in a funeral home in El Paso. After four months of legal dispute, the case was finally resolved and his body has finally been buried.) Today, embalming is also used to allow for open-casket funerals, often held many days after a person's death. By embalming the body, and making it up with paints and other forms of makeup, undertakers can help families to see their loved ones again after death. When the deceased die by violent means, often the face must also be reconstructed to hide the damage caused by the death.

In some cases, bodies are embalmed but not buried. For instance, both Vladimir Lenin and Joseph Stalin were embalmed so that their bodies could be placed on permanent display. Lenin's can still be seen in Moscow today but Stalin was ultimately buried in 1961.

In other cultures, the dead are fitted with a mask after they die. Among Inuits and other native peoples from the Pacific Northwest and the Arctic, burial masks were common, and were especially used for deceased shamans. With bone eyes inserted into the eyeholes, and decorated with feathers, hair, and other items, these masks were placed on the face of the dead to prevent spirits from entering the body and reanimating it. Covering the eyeholes was thought to be especially important, both to keep out the spirits, and also perhaps to let the deceased see their way to the afterlife.

In Western countries, if a person dies under suspicious circumstances, their bodies may also be subject to an autopsy; a medical procedure whereby a pathologist cuts open and examines the body to determine the cause of death.

Burial rites

In cultures around the world, the body's ultimate disposition is very often burial. Burial is a way to move a decaying body out of sight and to treat it with respect, protecting it, for example, from scavengers. According to archaeologists, the first known human burials occurred before we were even modern humans; our ancestors, known as archaic homo sapiens, not only buried their dead in graves as old as 130,000 years, but buried them with burial goods (which presumably would be used in the afterlife). Neanderthals, too, close relatives of human beings, buried their dead at least 50,000 years ago along with items like panther paws and flowers.

Generally, bodies are buried within boxes or caskets; coffins slow the process of decomposition and also provide a formal "shell" for the body to go into the ground. In many cultures, these can be extremely elaborate and expensive. In Ghana, for example, people can be buried in caskets that are carved and painted to look like giant fish, Coca-Cola bottles, cars, or birds. Brightly colored and fabricated by artists, these coffins can cost as much as an average yearly salary, but are a way to send loved ones to the afterlife in style. Today, however, in some Western countries, "natural burials" have become popular whereby people can be buried without a coffin, to help them decompose quicker.

While Jews and Muslims bury their dead immediately after death – generally within 24 hours – other groups wait much longer. The Toraja, an indigenous ethnic group from Sulawesi, Indonesia, wait months to bury a loved one. That's because a funeral is the most expensive event in most people's lives, and the higher status the person, the more expensive the funeral. Because funerals are so expensive, it can take a family months or even years to save up for it. During that time, the deceased is wrapped in cloth and kept in their home, and the soul remains with the body until after the ceremony is complete. During the ceremony, water buffalo (sometimes huge numbers of them) are sacrificed because the dead buffalo will help the deceased to find their way to Puya, the afterlife. After the ceremony, the coffin is placed in a stone grave or cave.

The idea that animals are needed to accompany the dead to the afterlife is common in a number of cultures. In the ancient Zoroastrian religion of Persia, dogs were intermediaries between the profane and the sacred realms, and were especially important in rituals surrounding death. If a person died, for example, dogs were brought in to witness the body, and they played a role in funerals as well: after death, the soul was accompanied to the after-life by two dogs. Many of the cultures of ancient Meso-America like the Olmec, Toltec, Maya, and Aztecs saw the hairless dog as the guardian of the dead. They were used to accompany the souls of the dead to the underworld; for this reason, mummified dogs were buried in the tombs of the deceased throughout Meso-America.

Bodies cannot be buried anywhere at all. They are typically buried at cemeteries – locations that are set aside by the city or state as an exclusive area for bodies to be buried. In some cultures, however, bodies may be buried in the home itself, as in some parts of Africa as well as in ancient Greece. In Christian countries, these resting places are often associated with churches (in which case they are called graveyards), because bodies at one time had to be buried in consecrated ground. Today, they may still be associated with churches, but can also be totally independent and secular as well. In fact, it's more common today to find cemeteries located outside of the bounds of cities, because with the various plagues throughout European history it was safer to keep the dead separated from the living. In some cases, cemeteries are found outside of city limits because the land within the city was too valuable to give to the dead. That was the case in San Francisco in 1900, when they banned the development of any new cemeteries. From that point on, the city's dead were buried just south of the city, in a small town named Colma. Today, Colma has a living population of 1,792, but, thanks to its many cemeteries, a dead population of over 100,000.

FIGURE 5.3 Crypts on "Millionaires' Row" at Mountain View Cemetery, Oakland, CA. Photo courtesy of Ian Elwood.

Another reason why cemeteries are typically located outside of town has to do with taboos and superstitions regarding the dead. It should not surprise us that in many cultures, the lowest caste of people are the people assigned the tasks of dealing with the dead – burying them, handling them, burning them, and even digging their graves. That's also why graveyard dirt is symbolically powerful and is used in a number of forms of sorcery. Even widows and widowers are sometimes socially isolated, because they carry the stigma and impurity of the dead on them. And in some cultures, as with the nomadic Tuaregs of the Sahara desert, the camp moves to another location after a death, and no longer refers to the dead by name, in order to distance themselves from the dead. (On the other hand, poverty can do a lot to reduce the fear of death. In Cairo, hundreds of thousands of Egyptians live and work in tombs in the Cairo Necropolis, a massive cemetery known as the City of the Dead.)

As with how we die, how we are buried reflects our social position in life as well. Those with great resources can be buried in elaborate crypts or mausoleums, while the poor may be lucky to have a burial with a small grave marker. The very poorest members of society may be cremated, may be buried in simple wooden boxes in paupers' graveyards, or may even be buried in mass graves. Criminals were sometimes, as in Renaissance Europe, publicly executed and their heads, or sometimes their whole bodies, displayed as a warning to others.

the scientific and biomedical body

Cemeteries were once divided by religion as well as race, with African-Americans, Chinese-Americans, and other minorities being buried in different cemeteries, or different parts of the cemetery, from whites in the United States. Simple grave markings might be basic wooden crosses, but for those with more money, headstones would sit on graves, carved by stonemasons, with not just the name of the deceased but also the salient details of his or her life. The wealthy dead could also have statues decorating their grave. In the past, in the United States, families marked off their graves within fenced-in lots, a practice that is also seen in Russia, and families continue, in cemeteries around the world, to bring flowers and other items to their loved ones' graves. Some cemeteries, however, have standardized both the type of headstone allowed (some allow only small ground-level plaques), as well as the type of decoration allowed. Artificial flowers, teddy bears, and other items are forbidden in such cemeteries in order to provide a more consistent appearance.

Generally, most cultures which practice the burial of the dead offer funerals before the dead are interred. Sometimes those include an open casket visitation, where the mourners can look at the body, either at or prior to the funeral, and they generally are officiated by a religious leader. Following the funeral, which often occurs in a church, is the burial service, which takes place at the cemetery, and following that, there is often, in many countries, a party or meal at the home of the closest survivors. They are opportunities for the mourners to reflect upon and celebrate the life of the deceased, and to reinforce the cultural view of death and the afterlife. They differ according to both culture and religion, as well as the socio-economic position of the deceased.

In New Orleans, African-Americans have funeral practices that are unique to the region and to the culture. Known as jazz funerals, the family and friends of the deceased march with a jazz band from the funeral home to the cemetery, while the band plays somber music known as a dirge. Once the funeral is complete, the mourners and the band march again to the home where the party will take place, while the band plays upbeat jazz music, and participants, including onlookers, dance along to celebrate the life of the deceased.

In many areas of the world, people are not just memorialized at the cemetery, but at the place where they died. Such **roadside memorials**, known as *descansos* in Spanish-speaking areas, are usually composed of a cross, and are decorated by loved ones with items commemorating the dead. Sometimes they're more informal and just include memorial items in a pile on the ground. They are often found on highways where people were killed in automobile accidents, and thus serve as reminders to viewers about safe driving. In some states in the United States, **ghost bikes** – bicycles that have been painted white – are erected to commemorate a cyclist who was killed by a car.

Because of many people's love of their pets, today pet cemeteries are an increasingly popular way of handling the death of companion animals. Founded in 1896, The Hartsdale Pet Cemetery and Crematory in Hartsdale, New York, was the first pet cemetery in the United States, housing the bodies of over 75,000 animals. What makes this so notable is that prior to that time, animals had no formal place to be laid to rest. No matter how loved individual animals were, our society had not yet come up with a way to honor and memorialize them when they died. Dead animals, whether livestock or working animal or pet, were often treated like garbage and thrown away with the rest of a city's refuse. With the rise of the pet cemetery industry, not only did people have a way to deal with the bodies of their dead companions (a problem for urban residents who could not simply bury a dog in their back yard), but they had a way to permanently memorialize them as well.

At pet cemeteries, the grieving person can invite their family and friends to a funeral and there, surrounded by those who knew the animal, people can reminisce, and, for those with religious sentiments, they can have a member of the clergy present to lead the mourners in prayer. The grave marker is another way to make concrete the memory of a special friend. One grave at Hartsdale, for an animal named Grumpy, had this written on the headstone: "August 4, 1915–September 20, 1926. His sympathetic love and understanding enriched our lives. He waits for us." The love and grief of Grumpy's family is palpable in that message, as is the idea, which many subscribe to today, that humans and animals will share in an afterlife together. Unlike most pet cemeteries, Hartsdale is unusual in that humans can elect to be buried along with their pets, and indeed, the cemetery hosts hundreds of people who want to remain close to their companions after death.

Other methods of disposing of the dead

In the West today, cremation is an increasingly popular option for people who do not want to burden their loved ones with the costs of burial, or who do not like the idea of their remains rotting in the ground. Cremation in the West is performed in crematories, where the body, in a simple wooden or cardboard coffin, is burned in a furnace. The loved ones then receive the "**cremains,**" or pulverized bone fragments, which they can display at home in an urn or box, can store in a columbarium (usually associated with a cemetery), or can, within some legal limits, scatter. In Japan, on the other hand, the bone fragments are not pulverized and are simply stored whole by the family. In 2012, the cremains of James Doohan, the actor who played Scotty in the 1960s television series *Star Trek*, were sent into space on the

SpaceX Falcon 9 rocket. Doohan, along with 300 other space fans, sent their remains (at a cost of $3,000 apiece) aboard the Falcon 9 so that they could orbit the earth before ultimately incinerating when re-entering earth's orbit.

While a number of religions – such as Judaism, Eastern Orthodox Christianity, and Islam – forbid cremation, it is an important practice in a number of other religions. For instance, almost all Hindus cremate their dead, and then dispose of the ashes in the Ganges River. Untouchables are responsible for handling the bodies, but the eldest son of the deceased is responsible for lighting the funeral pyre, which takes place in the open air on the banks of the river. In the past, widows were expected to throw themselves onto the funeral pyre of their husbands, a practice known as *sati*. Other Indian religions like Jainism, Sikhism, and Buddhism also practice cremation, which is seen as the best way to allow the spirit to disengage from the body. Among the Yanomami of South America, the dead were once cremated and the remains mixed with banana paste and then eaten.

In Tibet, dead bodies are left on the top of the mountain; called a "**sky burial**," this allowed carrion birds to eat the body, and is also called *jhator*, or "giving alms to the birds." Leaving bodies out to be scavenged by animals has been practiced in a number of other societies as well, such as among some Native American cultures. Among the Masai of East Africa, only village leaders with great status were buried; everyone else was placed outside of the bounds of the village to be eaten by animals, and their names were never uttered again.

In the West today, some people donate their corpses to science as a way of both disposing of their bodies after death and aiding in the advancement of science. For those opposed to animal experimentation, it's also a way of making sure that medical students have human bodies on which to practice surgical techniques or learn anatomy. We will discuss the issues surrounding the trafficking in bodies and body parts in Chapter 15, and the fact that those body parts often come from poor, non-white, and non-Western bodies. In the next chapter, Chapter 6, we will look at all of the ways that race and ethnicity shape the body – both living and dead.

Interesting issues: Georgia Tri-State Crematory scandal

The Tri-State Crematory was a crematorium located in Noble, Georgia. It was a family-operated business and offered cremation services for funeral homes in the tri-state region of Georgia, Alabama, and Tennessee. In 2002, bodies were discovered on the crematorium property, on which the Marsh family, which operated the business, lived. Ultimately, investigators found 339 decomposing bodies which had never been cremated, and which had been left in various locations around the property to rot. Brent Marsh, who operated the business, told authorities that the oven was broken, although it was found to be operational, so there was never any explanation for why the bodies were never cremated, and why they were simply left around the property. The families of the deceased never realized there was a problem because they were given what they thought were cremains, but was simply concrete dust. Marsh was sentenced to just 12 years in prison, much less than the prosecution wanted, because it was found that corpses do not have monetary value. However, he was also sued by the families of the deceased as well as the funeral homes he served; the lawsuits were ultimately settled by Marsh's insurance company.

Key terms

1830 Indian Removal Act
Assisted Suicide
Brain Death
CD4 Cells
Cremains
Genocide
Ghost Bikes
Last Rites
Living Will

Manifest Destiny
Right to Die Movement
Roadside Memorials
Sky Burial
Third Reich
Trail of Tears
Voluntary Euthanasia
Whitehall Study

Further reading

Bishop, Kyle William. (2010). *American Zombie Gothic: The Rise and Fall (and Rise) of the Walking Dead in Popular Culture*. Jefferson, NC: McFarland & Co.

Kastenbaum, Robert. (2001). *Death, Society, and Human Experience*, 7th edn. Boston, MA: Allyn & Bacon.

Roach, Mary. (2003). *Stiff: The Curious Lives of Human Cadavers*. New York: W.W. Norton & Company.

Scheper-Hughes, Nancy. (1993). *Death without Weeping: The Violence of Everyday Life in Brazil*. Berkeley, CA: University of California Press.

PART III

Mapping Difference onto Bodies

chapter 6

Racialized and Colonized Bodies

In 2008, the United States elected its first African-American president, Barack Obama. (Actually, he's bi-racial, but according to the American racial classification system, which we will discuss in this chapter, he's classified as black or African-American.) Many observers and commentators thought that his election would usher in a post-racial America: a new era in our nation's history marked by a decline in racism and a movement away from the concept of race.

Unfortunately, this did not occur. During the 2008 election, a huge number of racist jokes and images emerged, equating Obama and his wife with apes, or associating him with watermelons, fried chicken, welfare, and other stereotypical African-American images and items. After the election, hate watch groups noted a rise in the number of white supremacist groups operating throughout the country. In the 2012 election, race continued to play a role in the election, with Mitt Romney supporters seen wearing shirts reading "Put the white back into the White House," or "Don't Re-Nig in 2012." Photographs have surfaced of effigies of the president being lynched in people's front yards, and prominent celebrities like Donald Trump continue to assert that Obama is not an American or a Christian, suggesting that he's both Muslim and from Africa (and also demonstrating how very different concepts like race, culture, and religion are often confused and conflated in the minds of many Americans). Such accusations and attacks have never been aimed at other presidents in our history. Even without those elements, racism, and race, certainly did not disappear in the United States.

As Ta-Nehisi Coates writes in the *Atlantic* (2012), President Obama needs to be "twice as good and half as black," meaning that in order to appeal to white Americans, he needs to work harder and be twice as successful as everyone else, but must also appear minimally black so as to be unthreatening to those same whites. As (now Vice President) Joe Biden had said, during the 2008 primary season, "I mean you've got the first sort of mainstream African-American, who's articulate and bright and clean." If Obama was not so "bright and clean," he certainly would not have been elected. And yet, his blackness is still a major threat to a great many Americans.

A recent study demonstrated that successful African-American businessmen tend to have "baby faces," or faces with smaller facial features than other African-Americans, and that those features made their wearers seem warmer and less threatening, which led to their success. This demonstrates that for many whites, African-Americans are still considered to be threatening, and it is only when their features are "less African" that they can be successful. Even though President Obama does, in fact, have relatively small facial features, his relative blackness is still quite threatening to quite a few Americans.

The reality is that in the United States, as is the case elsewhere in the world, race matters; it is among the most salient features that we notice in another person, and more importantly, we attribute meaning to our understanding of race. And while anthropologists, sociologists, and other scholars now know that race is a social construct, rather than a biological fact, it still lives on in the minds of most as a biological feature. For that reason, no understanding of the body in society can be complete without looking at how race is embodied, and how that embodiment plays out on the social level.

What is race?

Most people think that races are biological divisions, or sub-species, of humanity; sort of like breeds of dogs. Most natural and social scientists today, however, see race as a social construct, rather than something that exists in nature. In other words, while we may look different from each other, those differences do not translate into sub-groups of humans the way we think of races. They are simply superficial physical differences.

Races are artificial categories of people that are distinguished from each other on the basis of arbitrary criteria – like skin color or eye shape. Those groups are then ranked in a graded hierarchy; those at the top of the hierarchy – in Western countries, that would be people of northern European descent – are then granted more privileges and opportunities than those at the bottom of the hierarchy. Race is a social, economic, and political system of division and inequality.

We know that racial categories are artificial because each year that the United States has taken a census (every ten years since 1790), there has never been a census that has used the same racial terms from a previous census. Each census a different set of terms are used, showing that the United States government cannot even agree on what the racial terms should be.

But while we are arguing that race is a social construct, race does have roots in the body, and in a misunderstanding of bodily difference. Humans look different from each other because our ancestors evolved in regions of the world with differing environmental conditions. Those conditions led to populations evolving with different physical features, which are better adapted to those environmental conditions. For example, skin color is created through a combination of genes and environment. Variation in skin color is determined primarily by the amount of **melanin** in the skin cells. Melanin protects the skin from too much ultra-violet radiation, so people whose ancestors come from environments with a great deal of sunlight have darker skin than those whose ancestors come from areas with little sunlight. Facial features, too, evolved in specific populations as a result of the environmental conditions in the region in which those people evolved. For example, longer noses develop in areas where temperature is cold and dry; shorter noses where temperature is hot and moist. The **epicanthic fold** of the eye developed in far northern climates like North Asia, North Europe, and the Arctic, because it protects eyes against harsh sunlight and cold.

But just because our ancestors passed on traits to us that make us look different from each other does not mean that we can be broken into subgroups on the basis of those differences. And more importantly, just because we look different from each other does not mean that we *are* different – especially on a group level. "Racial" differences are superficial and are not correlated with how smart a person is, whether a person is musically inclined, or even whether a person is athletic. Furthermore, there is no way to say that a whole population of people who share a number of physical characteristics also share intellectual or emotional characteristics. There is simply no connection between external physical traits and other characteristics. However, thanks to racial stereotyping and discrimination, once people begin to believe that certain people are smarter, thanks to their skin color, those perceptions can become self-reinforcing, as lighter-skinned people will get hired and promoted more often, leading to more light skinned people in positions of power and authority.

If race is not biologically real, how did the concept develop, and why is it so pervasive in social thought today?

Interesting issues: the shooting of Trayvon Martin

Trayvon Martin was a 17-year-old African-American boy who was shot to death by a neighborhood watch coordinator named George Zimmerman in a gated community in Florida in 2012. Martin was walking to his father's fiancée's home, wearing a hoodie, from a convenience store where he had purchased a fruit drink and a bag of Skittles, and Zimmerman spotted him and thought he looked suspicious. Zimmerman called police to report his behavior, telling them that he was going to follow him; the 911 dispatcher told him not to do so. Zimmerman followed Martin and at some point the two got into a physical altercation which ended with Martin hitting Zimmerman and Zimmerman shooting Martin, who was unarmed, in the chest. Zimmerman was not charged with a crime thanks to a Florida law known as "stand your ground," which means that someone can shoot someone, and does not need to back off, if they feel that they or their property is being threatened. The case caused a national uproar over an unarmed black youth being shot by an adult Hispanic man who was not even charged in his murder. Supporters of Zimmerman claimed that he legitimately acted in self-defense while supporters of Martin claim that the law allows any young black person wearing a hoodie to be shot to death without provocation. Martin's supporters held a number of "Million Hoodie Marches" in his honor and even President Obama weighed in, saying that if he had a son, he would look like Trayvon. On the other hand, reporter Geraldo Rivera blamed Martin for his death, saying that because of the "thug wear" that he was wearing, he was killed. Eventually, Zimmerman was charged with second degree murder, after having allegedly racially profiled and shot an unarmed Martin, and in July 2013, after a 19-day trial during which the jury could have found him guilty of either second degree murder or manslaughter, they found him not guilty of all charges.

Colonialism and the emergence of race

Race emerged as a concept during the age of European expansion which brought Europeans into contact with, and dominion over, people from the Americas, Asia, and Africa. As the Spanish, English, French, and other European superpowers began to establish colonies around the world, and especially with the rise of the African slave trade, the idea began to emerge that non-Europeans were not just culturally different from Europeans, but were biologically different as well. One of the many world-altering results of colonialism was the birth of the system of **racialization** whereby groups of humans are categorized and ranked by a new concept known as "race."

During the centuries of European colonial expansion, the peoples of Asia, Africa, and the Americas were not just dominated, with their land, resources, and labor taken from them, but were assigned places within a new hierarchy of races with Europeans placed on top. Different systems of classification emerged which attempted to categorize the variety of people on the planet – but especially those under European control – by skin color and facial features, but also by religion, language, and culture. By overemphasizing the similarities within these groups, and de-emphasizing the differences, Africans, Asians, and Native Americans started to be thought of as cohesive, and inferior, "races." From here, the physical characteristics were correlated with what were thought to be the intellectual and cultural characteristics of each group. This became the basis for the racial system of classification that we have inherited: the idea that we can predict human behavior from something as simple as the color of one's skin or the shape of one's eyes.

The trans-Atlantic slave trade was another major impetus for the development of racial thinking. In the United States, the notion of creating a permanent category of enslaved people was not compatible with its ideology of equality for all that our founding fathers shared. However, the system of racial thinking which said that some groups are biologically inferior to others provided an easy exception to the American ideology of equality. If Africans were truly inferior to whites, then they could not be given the same treatment as others, and thus, by this thinking, slavery – which, like colonialism, developed to further European and American economic gain – was not inconsistent with the ideals of the founding fathers. So a system of racial inequality emerged to justify a system of economic greed, and to reconcile the practice of inequality alongside of a philosophy of equality for all.

The artificiality, and indeed ludicrousness, of the race concept is especially visible in concepts like **hypodescent**. Hypodescent (also known as the "one drop rule"), is the way in which children of mixed-race parentage are classified. In this system, any child born of a white and a black parent is automatically assigned the race of the socially subordinate parent, i.e., the black parent. This system arose to keep the children of slaves and their masters black, and thus enslaved. This rule allowed white men to have sexual access to black women (but not the reverse) and at the same time, did not threaten white domination. Hypodescent explains why Barack Obama, Tiger Woods, and Halle Barry are all considered to be black, even though all have parents from different backgrounds.

Ultimately, the physical differences that we call race mean really very little biologically. However, they mean a great deal culturally and socially.

The display and eroticization of racialized bodies

Colonialism and racialism were also enabled by the **World Fairs** which started in the nineteenth century and were used to display to the world the new technological and cultural developments of the West.

One of the major elements of these fairs was the national pavilion, created by participating countries, in which participants could expose international audiences to the best their countries had to offer in terms of culture, food, music, dance, and art. Related to the national pavilions, but quite different in spirit, were the **human zoos**. At these displays, visitors could gawk at native people from colonized nations in reconstructed villages. Circus showman P. T. Barnum was a major promoter of native people, whom he displayed as anatomical and cultural oddities, as was Robert Ripley, who founded the Ripley's Believe It or Not shows. German animal trader and zoo founder Carl Hagenbeck also played a major role in finding and displaying native people in zoo-like conditions for a paying public to watch. Sometimes the people actually *were* displayed in a zoo. Hagenbeck, for example, displayed his collection of Inuit peoples at the Hamburg Zoo, Geoffrey de Saint-Hilaire exhibited Nubians, Zulus, and Bushmen at the Paris Zoo, and in 1896, one hundred Sioux lived at the Cincinnati Zoo. In 1906 the Bronx Zoo exhibited an African pygmy man named Ota Benga with the chimpanzees until the city's African-American community protested. He was billed as a "missing link" between chimpanzees and humans.

At the 1876 Centennial International Exhibition in Philadelphia, native people were for the first time exhibited in the United States in what was called the "ethnographic display." "Negro villages" were found at the 1878 and 1889 fairs in Paris, the Chicago Expo in 1893 had exhibits showcasing the lives of Algerians, Apaches, Navajos, Samoans, Japanese, and Javanese, the 1900 Exposition Universelle in Paris had a living diorama featuring natives from Madagascar, the 1901 Pan-American Exposition in New York had both The Old Plantation, depicting the lives of happy slaves, and Darkest Africa, an African village, and in 1904, the St Louis World's Fair had displays of such recently conquered people as people from Guam and the Igorots of the Philippines.

The exotic appearance and behaviors of the natives served to draw in paying customers. The Igorots of the Philippines, for example, were both tattooed and were known to eat dogs. Even though they only ate dogs for ceremonial occasions at home, the organizers of the St Louis Expo fed them dogs daily so that Americans could watch the spectacle. Human zoos and other native exhibits like this were contrasted with the highest achievements of Western society to both accentuate the primitiveness of the natives and to emphasize the civilization of the Western world. While these displays were both reflective of, and contributed to, the colonial ideology, they were also influential in constructing a narrative about native people as savages and racial inferiors. The exhibitions not only promoted the colonial agenda, but helped to implement it, as Christian missionaries visited world's fairs in order to learn about the cultures that they planned to "civilize."

Figure 6.1 Padaung girls from the South Shan States, 1887–1890. Photo courtesy of the Library of Congress.

While these displays largely disappeared by the 1960s, a current example exists in Thailand, where Padaung refugees from the civil war in neighboring Burma are living in refugee camps set up like human zoos, where tourists can pay the Thai government to take photos of the Padaung women, who are known for wearing long coiled brass rings around their necks. Another example is found in India's Andaman Islands, where women from India's Jarawa ethnic group dance for visitors who, according to at least one report, throw bananas and biscuits at them.

Outside of the world's fair, native men and women were showcased in sideshows at carnivals, dime museums, and circuses. When women were displayed, their sexuality was often highlighted. One of the saddest and most notorious examples was the case of Saartjie Baartman, a Khoi San woman from South Africa with steatopygia, a condition whereby a large amount of fat accumulates around the buttocks; she also had elongated labia, both found commonly among Khoi San women. She was a slave owned by

Dutch farmers who was exhibited throughout Europe and billed as the "Hottentot Venus." She was displayed in 1810 and 1811 in a cage in London where customers were invited to pinch her butt, and then sold to a French animal trainer who exhibited her in France. After her death in 1815, anatomist Georges Cuvier dissected her body, giving special attention to her labia. He preserved her body parts for future study, comparing them to those of white women. Her skeleton, along with her preserved brains and genitals, were displayed in a French museum until 1974. In 2002, her remains were finally returned to South Africa where they were buried.

The notion that people of color are more sexual than whites has a long history. In the slave colonies of the New World, black men were seen as hypersexual and dangerous, and were kept far from white women, who needed to be protected from them. Asian men, too, were once seen as sexually threatening. The practice of smoking opium in the United States was criminalized in the late nineteenth century in many locations because Chinese men were said to lure white women into opium dens, where they would be defiled. Black women, on the other hand, were considered to be ready sexual objects for white men's use; already degraded, constantly available. In addition, there were few white women in many of the colonies; they were not encouraged to travel from the safety of their homes in Europe, which meant that European men used slaves for sexual services, especially in the Caribbean, where white men took black women as concubines. Anthropologist Verena Martinez-Alier (1974) calls this the **dual marriage system**, whereby in the Caribbean, even after the arrival of European women, white men had a legal white wife, and a black concubine.

The threat posed by black men was controlled by beatings and other measures, while after slavery, it was controlled by lynchings. Between 1882 and 1946, it is thought that almost 5,000 black men were killed by lynching; many of those men had been accused of raping, accosting, or, in some cases (like that of teenager Emmett Till, killed in 1955), whistling at a white woman. Even today, the notion that black men pose a special danger to white women is still an extremely persistent belief. Black women's virtue, on the other hand, was not similarly protected, and during slavery, black women could be legally raped by their masters. In other words, this racialized and sexualized system has two equal and opposite poles: at one pole lies the sexual exploitation of black women by white men, and at the other pole, the extreme concern with purity of white women, and the threat posed to them by black men.

Even today, non-white women are often thought to be more sexual, erotic, and exotic than white women. Black women in particular are represented through advertising, pornography, and art as more primitive, savage, and sexual than other women. Asian and Latina women, too, are often considered to be more sexual than white women; the international sex tourism industry is built on the stereotypes of women from various cultures. Men, generally from Western countries, travel to the Caribbean, Asia, and Latin America in search of the exotic, hypersexual fantasy woman, to contrast to the uptight white woman back home. In places like Bangkok, where poverty and desperation (as well as human trafficking) forces young women and girls into prostitution, tourists tell themselves that these girls are "hot for it," and are naturally more sexual than the women back home are. The mail-order bride business, too, is built upon stereotypes of foreign women; Asian women are sexual, yes, but will make obedient wives to American husbands fed up with the feminism of Western women. Black men, too, are still thought to more "naturally" sexual than whites; in fact, blacks in general continue to be defined more by their bodies – they are natural dancers, natural athletes – while whites continue to be defined by their intellects.

In the twenty-first century, the term "bootilicious" has come to refer to a woman, either black or Latina, with a curvy body and a large butt. This woman, represented by celebrities like Jennifer Lopez, Beyoncé, and Kim Kardashian, has been fetishized in our culture, ogled by men, and seen with jealousy, fear, and perhaps disgust by many women. That women of color are more hypersexual than white women is also thought to be confirmed in the higher rates of teenage pregnancy among young African-American and Latina women, and the way that poor women of color are featured on television shows like *Jerry Springer*, where their sexuality is made into a public spectacle.

Interesting issues: good hair

Race is also an important factor in what different cultures consider to be beautiful. Especially in those regions of the world that once experienced either European colonialism or slavery, people with Caucasian facial features and hair are seen as more attractive than those with features and hair associated with Africans. For African-Americans today, hair continues to be an area where standards of beauty and acceptability are strongly racialized. Long, straight, silky hair has long been considered to be not only the most beautiful but most feminine form of hair in the United States, which leaves African-Americans, who typically have curly or kinky hair, automatically excluded from this standard of beauty. Thus the importance and proliferation of hair-straightening products (a $45 million annual market) aimed at African-Americans; products that demand a great amount of time, money, and sometimes pain, as the chemicals in these products can often burn the skin. But curly vs. straight hair (known as "good hair") is not just a question of beauty for many African-American women. It's also a question of fitting into a society that is still dominated by white people and white values. Comedian Paul Mooney, in the 2009 Chris Rock film Good Hair, *said that "if your hair is relaxed, white people are relaxed; if your hair is nappy, they're not* *happy." Today, many African-American women choose to wear straightened weaves, sometimes made from human hair (which itself comes from poor women in India), camouflaging their own hair. Oprah Winfrey, one of the most powerful women in the world, only just wore her hair "natural" for the very first time on her own magazine cover in 2012. In every other issue in the 150 issues on which she has appeared, she has either had her hair straightened or worn a wig. On the other hand, many African-American embrace hair styles that signify their ethnic heritage, such as braids, cornrows, or the "Afro," although in many places – especially at work – these styles are seen as "too ethnic" and still too threatening to white people.*

Mapping and measuring bodies in the era of biological racism

With the rise of biological science in the seventeenth century, scientific theories were harnessed into the new racial thinking, leading to the emergence of scientific racism and the hardening of racial thinking in the West.

Carolus Linnaeus, for example, who is credited with creating the taxonomic system used to scientifically catalog plants and animals today, came up with the idea that there were five biological races, each with their own physical and intellectual characteristics, while naturalist Georges Cuvier felt that there were three races; of course both Linnaeus and Cuvier placed Europeans on top of their new scientific racial hierarchies. All of the other scientists throughout the nineteenth century agreed with these early thinkers, and all saw Europeans as being biologically superior; the debate primarily centered on how the races developed, and who – Native American or African – was the most inferior. In all of these cases, the idea of racial superiority and inferiority was a given, and was used to justify slavery, since, after all, Africans were thought of as being biologically suited for slavery. After the end of slavery, scientific theories of race continued to be used to deny rights to people of color in the United States and around the colonial and post-colonial world.

A number of pseudosciences developed which were used to prove the superiority or inferiority of the races. For example, eighteenth-century Dutch anatomist Petrus Camper claimed that the races could be distinguished by the angle at which the forehead slopes to the nose and jaw; whites had the most refined angle with Africans having an angle closer to apes, demonstrating their evolutionary inferiority.

Another approach was called **physiognomy**. Physiognomy refers to discerning the character of a person from their facial features or body parts. An Italian doctor named Cesare Lombroso was an advocate of this approach

mapping difference onto bodies

and examined the bodies of hundreds of criminals in the nineteenth century in order to ascertain the physical characteristics shared by criminals and what he called "primitive man." He found that those primitive traits were found most commonly among Africans, a group he knew to be inferior to whites. Another nineteenth-century theorist who subscribed to this theory was Francis Galton, who was also, not coincidentally, a leading eugenicist. Whether the subjects were Italians, Irish, Jewish, or African-Americans, the result was the same – those groups deemed racially different were seen by the scientists at the time as racially inferior in character, intelligence, and morality.

Physiognomy has also been practiced in the twentieth century. For instance, the Nazis used special calipers to measure the facial features of Jews and those who were suspected to be Jews; Nazis thought that Jews had larger, more animal-like facial features, so the size of a person's nose, ears, or brow ridge could mean the difference between life and death. The Nazis were advocates of what they called **criminal biology**, based on Lombroso's theories. They used this approach to detect who was more likely to become a criminal based on their facial features. They taught criminal biology alongside courses in racial hygiene, and used their data to show that Jews were more likely to be criminals and murderers than Aryans. The irony, of course, is that the Nazis were the real murderers.

More recently, evolutionary psychologist Satoshi Kanazawa has revived Lombroso's theories and claims that criminality really can be detected by facial features. As in the nineteenth century, physiognomy continues to be linked to racism, with many proponents, such as Kanazawa, continuing to find in non-white facial features evidence of criminality, aggression, or bad character.

Another scientific approach to racism was **craniometry**. Promoted by anthropologist Samuel Morton, this approach was based on the comparison of human skulls. Morton compared the skulls of Native Americans, African-Americans, and European Americans in order to show that the group with the largest cranial capacity, and thus the largest brains, was the most intelligent. Morton's research showed that, not surprisingly, Europeans were the most intelligent race, followed by Native Americans, and finally African-Americans. His theory was used to prove the theory of **polygenism**: that the races were created separately. In the twentieth century, however, biologist Stephen Jay Gould (1996) showed that Morton used faulty data in order to prove his thesis. One result of Morton's work, and the work of others like him, was that American natural history museums were at one time full of the skulls, bones, and artifacts of Native Americans. In fact, at one time it was perfectly legal to dig up Native American graves and use the bones and other items found therein for scientific purposes or display. It was not until the passage of the **Native American Graves Protection and Repatriation Act**, which passed in 1990, that Native American bones were finally given back to Native Americans, and that grave looting of this type was prohibited.

Race, health, and race purity

In racialized cultures like the United States, on every health and mortality measure, including life expectancy, infant mortality, maternal mortality, prenatal care, infant birth weight, cancer survival rates, and more, whites have better health and survival prospects than other groups.

These differences are due to lifestyle differences between racial groups, the fact that people of color are disproportionately poor, and thus lack access to health insurance and quality health care, the fact that poor people of color will have less healthy living and working conditions, the higher rates of violent crime in non-white communities, and racial discrimination by health care providers.

Because historically African-Americans have had worse health outcomes and higher rates of mortality than whites, thanks to the horrors of slavery and the post-slavery inequalities experienced by blacks, some took that as proof of their natural inferiority. On the other hand, during slavery, it was also thought that blacks suffered less from some diseases, such as yellow fever, than did whites. This was used to justify slavery, since whites would suffer more severely from working in the swampy hot conditions in which diseases like this flourished.

A similar process occurred with Chinese Americans. It was said that the Chinatowns in which Chinese immigrants lived in the United States were cesspools of filth, crime, overcrowding, and disease. Animals were raised alongside humans and were slaughtered openly, in the streets. But it's not thanks to Chinese preferences that Chinatowns exist – they were created by white Americans as a segregated site where Chinese people were forced to live and work, because they were excluded from living and working in white communities. Similarly, when the Chinese were blamed for the spread of Avian Flu in 2003, or Mexican slaughterhouse workers were blamed for the Swine Flu epidemic of 2009, both groups were blamed for conditions of poverty that were not of their choosing.

Sexually transmitted diseases are another a good example of how health and illness can be racialized. In the nineteenth century, when doctors realized that African-Americans in the south had contracted syphilis in high numbers, this was used to further the belief that African-Americans had lower morals, and were more promiscuous, than other groups. AIDS is another example. While in the 1980s, AIDS began in the United States as a disease largely confined to two groups – men who have sex with men and

mapping difference onto bodies

FIGURE 6.2 Oakland Chinatown. Many people don't realize that Chinatowns like this one were initially set up to ensure that Chinese people did not mix with whites. Photo courtesy of Ian Elwood.

injection drug users – it has spread throughout the population into new groups. Today, one of the groups with the highest infection rate is people of color. Here too, it is sometimes thought that blacks (like gays before them) lack the self-control that is necessary to fend off sexually transmitted diseases. The reality is that poverty, lack of education, lack of access to health care, and a lack of information about AIDS (which is, after all, supposed to be a "gay disease") all contribute to the spread of AIDS in the black community.

Another example is addiction. We know that drug consumption patterns exist within racial and ethnic groups, such that, for example, African-American men have more alcohol-related problems than do whites, and Latino men are more likely to have alcohol abuse issues than both blacks and whites. One reason why people of color are more inclined than whites to use harmful substances is because they are targeted by tobacco and alcohol companies. Another reason has to do with the higher rates of poverty and unemployment, combined with the lack of good schools and access to health care. On the other hand, contrary to popular assumptions, blacks do not use crack cocaine in greater numbers than whites. However, in the United States, they are arrested and imprisoned in far greater numbers for crack cocaine use than whites, pointing towards the racist nature of the criminal justice system.

racialized and colonized bodies

One result of these differentials in health outcomes between racialized groups is the race purity movement, or the eugenics movement. This was a European and American movement, which began in the nineteenth century, that was concerned with keeping the "white race" pure, and controlling both the intermixing between the races as well as the reproduction of the non-white races. One of the reasons for its emergence was the idea that non-whites were diseased, compared to whites. For instance, in Germany, Jews were medicalized: they were turned into a health threat that needed to be solved, through segregation, sterilization, and ultimately, extermination.

In the United States, one of the driving forces behind the development of the race purity movement was the waves of immigrants who began arriving in the late nineteenth century. Attracted by the new industrial jobs, these immigrants, who were mostly uneducated and unskilled people from eastern and southern Europe, arrived in American cities and were forced to live in crowded urban ethnic neighborhoods which quickly became filled with crime and disease. The result was a series of laws enacted to both restrict immigration from non-white nations and to control the immigrants once they had arrived. The 1920s and 1930s were possibly the most racist period in the American nation's history. Immigration laws, intelligence tests, **anti-miscegenation laws**, segregationist policies, and even forcible sterilization laws which mandated sterilization for the "unfit," were all examples of the racist nature of the period. As long as non-whites' existence was seen to threaten the health of white people, and more generally, the health of the body politic, then non-white bodies needed this type of intensive control.

The animalization of non-white bodies

Another way in which racial control operates on a bodily level is through **animalization**. People of color have been compared to animals since at least colonialism, and certainly since the African slave trade emerged in the seventeenth century. By the nineteenth century, with the rise of evolutionary thought, some people felt that while humans may be related to apes, some humans were *closer* to apes than others, and Africans in particular were thought to be the "missing link" between apes and humans. By using animals – especially monkeys and apes – to refer to Africans, and by implying or stating that Africans and African-Americans were closer to these animals than whites, whites asserted their superiority over them.

In addition, African-Americans were not just thought of as animals; they were treated like animals. Treating a human like an animal is a way to degrade and dehumanize them. African slaves were shackled and muzzled like animals, beaten like animals, branded like animals, bought and sold like animals, had their children taken from them like animals, and had their

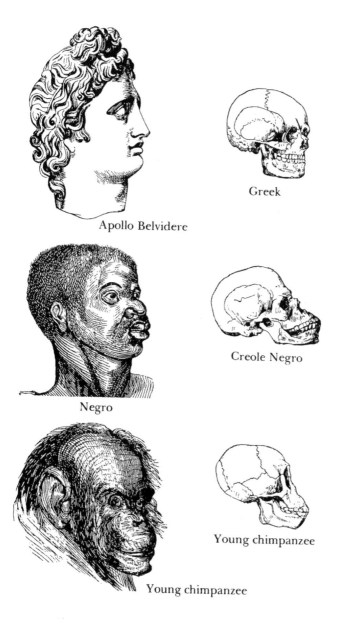

Apollo Belvidere

Greek

Negro

Creole Negro

Young chimpanzee

Young chimpanzee

FIGURE 6.3 This image, a comparison of African-Americans to apes, is from Josiah Clark Nott and George Robert Gliddon's *Indigenous Races of the Earth* (first published 1857), and was reprinted in Stephen Jay Gould's *The Mismeasure of Man* (1981).

racialized and colonized bodies

humanity and individuality ignored, just as humans do with animals. They were property just as animals were, and could be legally killed by their property owner, just as animals could. Huge numbers of Africans died in transit from Africa to America; a loss of life that was absorbed into the prices of the remaining men and women. (Animals who are transported to pet stores in the United States also experience high rates of what the pet industry calls "shrinkage," and those losses are also figured into the prices of the remaining animals.)

Marjorie Spiegel's 1997 book, *The Dreaded Comparison*, makes clear the similarities in the ways that African slaves were treated, and how animals were then, and are still, treated today. Further, she shows that whites justified their use of, and treatment of, slaves with many of the same justifications that humans use today to justify their use of animals as food or medical subjects. Blacks were thought to not feel pain, they were thought to not feel love towards their children, and they were thought to be happier under slavery than living on their own. In addition, slavery was an important part of the economy of the American south – how could plantation owners expect to do without it?

Other groups have been animalized too. Both the Chinese and the Japanese were called vermin and were compared to rats in the nineteenth century by white Americans, and during World War II, the Japanese described the Chinese as pigs during their invasion of Manchuria. Even Disney's animated cartoons play a role in this animalization. If we look at Disney cartoons over the years, you can see how animal characters are racialized. Crows, monkeys, and apes are played by African-Americans, Chihuahuas by Latinos, and cats by Asians, and all are negatively stereotyped.

But perhaps most well known is the treatment of the Jews by the Nazis in the 1930s and 1940s. The German word for "race," *rasse*, is also the word for a purebred animal, demonstrating not only the Nazis' tendency to animalize people but also their concern with maintaining "blood purity" in both animals and people. Jews were called vermin, rats, and cockroaches in Nazi speeches and in the German media. Minister of Propaganda Josef Goebbels said, "It is true that the Jew is a human being, but so is a flea a living being – one that is none too pleasant ... our duty towards both ourselves and our conscience is to render it harmless. It is the same with the Jews," while the Nazi Party Manual had the following line: "All good Aryans should squash Jews and members of other 'inferior races' like 'roaches on a dirty wall.'" The Nazi propaganda film *Der Ewige Jude* (1940) included the following line: "Rats ... have followed men like parasites from the very beginning ... They are cunning, cowardly and fierce, and usually appear in large packs. In the animal world they represent the element of subterranean destruction ... not dissimilar to the place that Jews have among men."

But as with slavery, the animalization of Jews went far beyond name calling. During the eugenics movement in the United States and Germany during the early part of the twentieth century, the practice of animal breeding – breeding those with the desirable characteristics and killing and sterilizing the rest – became the inspiration and example for eugenic efforts to upgrade the human population in both countries. These efforts led to compulsory sterilization of the disabled in the United States and compulsory sterilization, euthanasia killings, and, ultimately, genocide in Nazi Germany.

From 1942 to 1945, European Jews were transported in cattle cars to the camps, some were tattooed with ID numbers like livestock, and millions were slaughtered en masse, with their humanity and individuality completely extinguished. The camps themselves were modeled on American stockyards and slaughterhouses: Nazis borrowed features intended to make the processing of Jews at the camps as speedy and efficient as possible, and to streamline the final part of the operation which took the victims to their deaths. In the gas chambers, Zyklon B, a pesticide normally used on mice, was used for the mass killings. Rudolf Höss, the commandant of Auschwitz, called that camp "the largest human slaughterhouse that history had ever known" (Patterson 2002: 122). Jews, Gypsies, and others were also experimented on in the infamous experiments of Josef Mengele, who called a group of Polish women who were subject to grotesque experiments the "rabbit girls."

In this chapter, we have discussed what to many of us is one of the most common-sense ideas of all: the idea of race. But in reality, race is not common sense at all; it is a term and a system of classification that was created just a few hundred years ago in order to divide humans and to provide privileges and benefits to some, at the expense of a great many. As we have seen, the consequences of that system have been devastating. In Chapter 7, we will look at another system, that of gender, which will probably seem even more natural to you, but which may be just as socially constructed as the racial system discussed in this chapter.

Key terms

Animalization
Anti-Miscegenation Laws
Craniometry
Criminal Biology
Dual Marriage System
Geishas
Human Zoos

Native American Graves
Protection and Repatriation
  Act
Physiognomy
Polygenism
Racialization

---

racialized and colonized bodies

Further reading

Blanchard, Pascal. (2008). *Human Zoos: Science and Spectacle in the Age of Colonial Empires*. Liverpool: Liverpool University Press.

Gould, Stephen Jay. (1996). *The Mismeasure of Man*. New York: W.W. Norton & Company.

Herring, Cedric, Keith, Verna, and Horton, Hayward Derrick. (2004). *Skin Deep: How Race and Complexion Matter in the "Color Blind" Era*. Chicago, IL: University of Illinois Press.

hooks, bell. (1990). *Yearning: Race, Gender and Cultural Politics*. Boston, MA: South End Press.

Spiegel, Marjorie. (1996). *The Dreaded Comparison: Human and Animal Slavery*. New York: Mirror Books.

mapping difference onto bodies

chapter 7

Gendered Bodies

Women's bodies are everywhere in Western culture. They are used in advertising to sell everything from cars to movies to hamburgers, and clothed or naked, they are among the most commonly seen images in magazines, on television, and on the Internet. *Sports Illustrated's* annual "swimsuit issue" is the best-selling issue every year, and the British tabloid The *Sun* features a topless woman on page 3 in every day's paper. Whether clothed, veiled, or naked, women's bodies are on constant display, and every woman knows that she is subject to being looked at, judged, and defined by her appearance and her sexuality. In fact, in 2012, American soccer star Alex Morgan appeared in the *Sports Illustrated* swimsuit issue without a swimsuit; instead of a swimsuit, she was nude and covered in body paint. The idea that a female athlete should appear nude in a magazine devoted to sports is unsurprising; we live in a society in which gazing at women's bodies is simply commonplace. After the 2012 Olympics, which many observers called the "Year of the Woman," because of the prominence of female athletes at the games, NBC produced a video highlighting female athletes which featured scantily clad, beautiful women in slow motion set to music which sounded like a soft porn film.

Perhaps no topic, in the realm of body studies, has been as thoroughly discussed as gender. Women's bodies, in particular, are subject to an unlimited variety of social and cultural control: how big they are, how beautiful they are, how well dressed, made up and coifed they are – women are judged by their appearance in a way that men rarely are judged. They are also more defined by their bodies than men are. Thanks to women's biological capabilities to bear children, they are defined by those same capabilities: for women, biology sometimes feels like destiny, defining what women can, and cannot, do. The body is not the only place where women are controlled and defined, but is a site on and through which gender is constructed and inscribed.

Recent scholarship, too, has begun to focus on men's bodies and the ways that they, too, are shaped by culture and society. In this chapter, we will look at how gendered norms and expectations shape and constrain both male and female bodies. In addition, transgender bodies – bodies which blur the lines between male and female – are of course shaped by the same factors that shape male and female bodies, but often in new and different ways.

The gendered body

Men's and women's bodies differ in a number of respects. Men and women have a different set of reproductive and sexual organs, although it's worth noting that human embryos, until about the seventh week of gestation, are sexually undifferentiated. In other words, male and female embryos are almost exactly the same, and each carries the material which will develop into the gonads. After about week six, these rudimentary organs turn into either ovaries or testes, and secondary to these internal changes, the external genitalia develop accordingly. Further sexual differentiation does not really begin until puberty, when males and females each develop body hair, males grow taller and more muscular, and females develop breasts and increased body fat. Women also have lighter skin, on average, than men of the same ethnicity.

But while it's true that men's and women's bodies differ, on average, in terms of body size and body hair, as well as reproductive and sexual organs, many of the differences between men's and women's bodies are culturally constituted. We *expect* men's bodies to be larger, hairier, and more muscular than women's, and we expect women's bodies to be softer, smaller, and hairless. To encourage these differences, we create cultural imperatives that mandate that women remove most or all of the hair from their bodies and faces, that they maintain an unnaturally thin shape, and that they do not build their muscles too much. Conversely, we demand that men build up their bodies through weightlifting and sometimes steroids so that they can be as muscular as possible, creating what some scholars call the "**Adonis complex**" for men. Researchers at the University of Minnesota School of Medicine, for example, have found that 40 percent of teenage boys use protein powders to build their muscles and 6 percent use steroids.

Gender difference, then, is largely culturally constructed, yet appears entirely natural. It's that "naturalness" that makes it so hard to detect, and

mapping difference onto bodies

so hard to challenge. Sociologist Cynthia Fuchs Epstein coined the term "**deceptive distinctions**" to refer to what appear to be differences between men and women that are based on sex and gender, but that in fact come from the cultural surroundings and the social positions occupied by men and women.

We learn what a woman is, should look like, and should be, thanks to the visual images that surround us. Popular culture shows us how our bodies should be shaped, what our faces should look like, how much hair we should have, where it should be located, and whether it should be silky straight or fall in waves. We learn what kinds of clothes we should wear to highlight our best features and to camouflage our "problem areas." Since every woman's genitals are by definition problematic, women can douche, to cover up their natural odors, can wax their pubic hair to make themselves seem child-like, or can dye their pubic hair pretty colors. They can even purchase a vaginal colorant called My Pink Button which makes one's genitals appear pinker. And for women who are worried about "camel toe" (where the shape of their vulva shows through their pants), they can purchase a new panty called Camelflage, which comes with a flexible insert to prevent the dreaded camel toe. None of this is natural and yet none of us question it.

One of the problems with these unnatural norms for male and female bodies is that most men and most women cannot possibly conform to the standards laid out for them. Men are different from other men, and women are different from other women, and some of those differences have to do with class, sexuality, religion, nationality, and ethnicity. Yet the standard is universal, at least in Western culture. As Susan Bordo writes, "Our bodies are trained, shaped and impressed with the prevailing historical forms of . . . masculinity and femininity" (Bordo 1993, 91).

Another issue that many scholars have noted is that, in most cultures, male bodies are the norm and female bodies are considered somehow deviant from that norm. The Greek philosopher Aristotle, for example, saw women as imperfect versions of men. In 1972, anthropologist Sherry Ortner wrote an article titled "Is Female to Male as Nature Is to Culture?" This article attempted to understand why women are universally subordinate to men, and Ortner locates her explanation in the biological characteristics of women's bodies, and how those characteristics are interpreted culturally. She argues that women are subordinated to men because women are associated with nature, and men are associated with culture, and nature occupies a subordinate position to culture. Women's bodies, in that they are occupied much of the time with reproductive activities, seem to place them closer to animals. Women are, as she put it, the prey of the species, since many of their bodily features and functions do not help women to survive (and may in fact hinder them, such as large breasts, reproductive cancer, menstrual discomfort, pregnancy, etc.), but only exist to help the

gendered bodies

species. Females are more enslaved than males, and males are free to turn to other things, like creating culture. This explains, according to Ortner, why male activities that destroy life (like hunting or warfare) are given greater prestige than female activities that create life, which are seen as involving no skills whatsoever. Ortner's theory, however, does not account for cultural differences and or even individual distinctions, and clearly does not account for all women in all contexts.

A related idea, which goes back to Aristotle, is the idea that men are associated with the mind, and thus with rationality, while women are simply bodies. Susan Bordo, too, notes that while both men and women have bodies, women are much more associated with bodies than are men; not only that, but women's bodies, like the bodies of animals, can then be considered the property of men, and thus are exchanged by men.

Gender is embodied in other ways as well. In 2012, photographer Hanna Pesut created a projected called "Switcheroo," in which she photographed male/female couples. In the first of the photos, the men and women were wearing their own clothing, but in the second photo, each man was wearing the woman's clothing, while each woman was wearing the man's clothes. In addition, the men and women took on the poses that each other displayed in the first photo. The result was a clear demonstration of not just the gendered nature of men's and women's clothing, but the ways in which men and women so often enact gender through their posture, their stance, and even their facial expressions.

Men are instrumental; women are ornamental

Men, as it has often been noted by feminists, are often defined by what they do and what they have achieved. Women, on the other hand, are often defined by how they look, as well as their reproductive abilities. For instance, while both men and women practice a number of body modifications in cultures around the world, the purpose behind those practices differs, and that difference is strongly gendered. Men's tattoos, circumcisions, scarrings, or piercings, for example, often signify an achievement: success in a hunt or in warfare, for instance. Because so many of these practices are painful, they also serve as an important test of a man's strength and courage, which demonstrates his fitness as a man. Women, on the other hand, often receive their tattoos or scars to enhance their beauty and to make them marriageable. Many times those marks are thought to also enable their fertility, and when, as in the case of scarification among the Yoruba of West Africa, the marks are painful, they are sometimes seen to measure whether the woman will be able to undergo the pain of childbirth. While childbirth is no doubt an achievement, it is rarely celebrated as a cultural achievement the way that men's activities are.

mapping difference onto bodies

FIGURE 7.1 High-heeled shoes. Photo courtesy of Tom Young.

As noted above, women, because of their need to appear beautiful, must adhere to standards of beauty that demand perpetual youth and fertility. Thus in the West, diet and exercise are geared towards producing very thin and childlike bodies. Even fashionable trends such as long fingernails or the wearing of high heels are geared to make women appear sexual and youthful, even while they make the woman less useful. In addition, sociologist Michael Kimmel (2000) has pointed out that small breasts are seen as more attractive on women in societies where women's economic and political status is higher; where their status is lower, large breasts are more highly valued, demonstrating the link between women's status and how important their beauty and sexuality is.

Men, on the other hand, are celebrated by their achievements, so men's physical appearance is not as important – to men or to women. While men largely created the standards of beauty that define women, they themselves are free from those standards. When it is measured, men are expected to be strong and powerful, explaining the importance of sports like body building to men (and the ambivalent position women hold in that sport). Even though men are largely defined by their achievements, masculinity still derives, at least in part, from the body. The popular understanding of evolutionary theory says that men are naturally more competitive, more aggressive, more violent, and better at protecting and providing for their families than women. That's why for at least some men, maintaining an appearance and set of behaviors consistent with this mandate is essential. Biological determinism, then, shapes our understanding of both men and women.

The differences between men's and women's footwear can serve as an enlightening example. While it is typical for men's shoes (especially for working men) to be functional and comfortable, allowing them to move easily from place to place and to do a variety of things, it is often just as typical for women's shoes to be created and worn primarily for aesthetic reasons. Women's shoes are made to adorn the female body, but not to allow her mobility, and in fact, many of the most popular women's shoes impede women's mobility, and thus impede women's opportunities. Where women's footwear impedes women's mobility, however, it also enhances their beauty and femininity, even while causing them pain and health problems.

This is not easy to say, by the way, that only men demand that women conform to standards of beauty that leave many women wanting, and other women suffering physically and financially. Women play a major role in both the continuing definition and re-definition of female standards of beauty and in policing other women to ensure that they are in conformity with them. Many women also take advantage of the benefits of conformity. Sociologists use the term **patriarchal bargain** to refer to women who accept rules that disadvantage all women in exchange for whatever small degree of personal power an individual woman can gain from the system. For example, reality star Kim Kardashian has made millions of dollars by using her sexuality (remember, she originally gained fame through a private sex video that mysteriously went public) to her advantage. So while many women dislike, or even attempt to challenge, unrealistic standards of beauty, many more exploit them to their own advantage.

Interesting issues: the removal of Hillary Clinton from the Situation Room photo

On May 2, 2011, a special team of U.S. Navy SEALs, on a CIA-led operation, killed Osama bin Laden, the mastermind behind the September 11, 2001, terrorist attacks on the United States. White House photographer Pete Souza took a now-iconic photo of President Obama's intelligence team, in the White House Situation Room, monitoring the attack while it was happening. The photo included the President, the Vice President, and 11 other officials including Secretary of State Hillary Clinton and, in the back of the shot, Audrey Tomason, Director for Counterterrorism. The photo was widely distributed and published in newspapers around the world. However, Brooklyn-based Hasidic newspaper Di Tzitung, when it published the photo, removed both Hillary Clinton, who was

mapping difference onto bodies

a central figure in the photograph, as well as Audrey Tomason. The White House has a standing policy against press agencies altering White House photos, but Di Tzeitung, in their explanation, noted their own policy: "In accord with our religious beliefs, we do not publish photos of women, which in no way relegates them to a lower status . . . Because of laws of modesty, we are not allowed to publish pictures of women, and we regret if this gives an impression of disparaging women, which is certainly never our intention. We apologize if this was seen as offensive."

Becoming male or female: circumcision and clitoridectomy

If gender is socially and culturally constructed, and if the body plays a major role in that construction, how one comes to *be* male or female in society is important to discuss. While babies may be born male or female, based on their chromosomes, they learn the norms associated with their gender and their society encourages the development of those norms. One way in which this occurs is through gendered puberty rituals. These rites of passage, found in societies all over the world, mark the transition from adolescence to adulthood, teaching the initiate the skills and information needed as adults, and demonstrating to the larger community that they have earned the right to be seen as adults. While both males and females can participate in such rituals (although male puberty rituals are far more common than female ones), the focus is often very different.

It has often been said that men are made, and women are born. This expression refers to the fact that men are celebrated for their achievements and must, in many cultures, earn the privilege of adult masculinity. Adult womanhood, on the other hand, is often seen as no accomplishment at all. Women, after all, menstruate without any prompting, demonstrating no skill. That's why it is so rare to find coming of age rituals that celebrate femininity. The Apache in New Mexico are one of the rare cultures that still have such a ritual (after it had been banned by the American government, which found it distasteful, it was later resurrected by the Apache). The ritual celebrates female power and fertility and prepares the young female initiate for adulthood and marriage. It's worth noting that the focus is on readying the girl for the responsibilities of motherhood and marriage – roles that are only seen as appropriate for females. But at least the Apache have a celebration. Many cultures restrict women's freedom at the time of puberty, and begin the process of confining them during their menstruation.

Male coming of age rituals, on the other hand, demand that young men demonstrate bravery, strength, heroism, or an accomplishment in hunting or some other highly valued but difficult activity. Many rituals involve pain;

circumcision ceremonies are a good example of this. For instance, among the Okiek of Kenya, boys undergo a circumcision ritual between the ages of 14 and 16, after which they are excluded from the world of adults and the opposite sex for a number of weeks. Following anthropologist Arthur Van Gennep's three-part description of a rite of passage, the Okiek are first separated from the tribe, kept in isolation with members of their sex and age cohort (during which time they wear white body paint and are given secret tribal knowledge), and are, in the third and final part of the ritual, reintroduced to society as adult men. Because circumcision in these rituals is done without anesthesia, it is painful, which is one of the important aspects of a male initiation ceremony – to test or challenge the boys to ensure that they are strong enough to earn adulthood.

Among Australian aboriginals, circumcision is also used to mark male adulthood. For Australians, as with Africans, both pain and physical transformation are critical aspects of the ritual, and as in Africa, boys are expected to demonstrate strength and courage and not flinch under the pain. During the boys' separation from society, they witness secret religious ceremonies and are given information about the origins of the universe; because they are separated from their mothers, their relationship with other boys and men is solidified as well, a relationship that may also involve **ritual homosexuality**, and which also bonds a boy to the men of the family to whom he will ultimately be married. Some Australian groups that use circumcision also use other practices to transform boys into men, including tooth evulsion (in which a boy's front tooth is knocked out with a rock), scarification, and, a year or two after the circumcision, **subincision**, in which the penis itself is split down the shaft.

In both Africa and Australia, circumcision makes a boy into a man, through physically transforming his body and, not coincidentally, shedding blood which is often seen as symbolically female and, thus, polluting. The rest of the ceremony, including the isolation from community (especially women), the bonding with other men, and the transmission of secret knowledge, all play an important role alongside of the circumcision in making a boy into a man.

And while many African societies do also perform a similar operation on women, known in some circles as female circumcision and in others as **female genital mutilation** or **clitoridectomy** – the removal of a young girl's clitoris – these practices are very different in terms of the physical transformation of the body and the meanings associated with it.

While circumcision is painful, the practice does not harm or impede a man's sexual function, and, in fact, some men see it as an improvement to sexual function. It shows as well his strength and courage, both important attributes of masculinity. Male circumcision binds young men with other men, and excludes women from these important and powerful bonds.

It's not surprising that societies that celebrate male circumcision are simultaneously societies that have great degrees of male dominance and female subordination.

On the other hand, in the United States, there is a strong and growing anti-circumcision movement. This movement calls for an end to the involuntary circumcision of infants without their consent; some opponents claim that many men have reduced sensitivity after circumcision, scarring, pain, and/or sexual dysfunction. Anti-circumcision movements are found in other countries as well, such as in South Africa, where traditional circumcision practices have left many young men dead from infection, or Germany, where a German court ruled in 2012 that circumcision inflicts harm on boys "too young to consent."

Female circumcision, on the other hand, is used to control female sexuality: to ensure that women do not engage in pre-marital or extra-marital sex. By keeping her virginal before marriage, she is more marriageable, and can bring in a higher bride price; it also ensures that she does not bring shame onto her family. Unlike circumcision, female genital mutilation does not celebrate a woman's maturity, but ensures that her pleasure and her independence will be limited, in order to ensure fidelity to her husband. In addition, a woman who does not stray in marriage will only bear children who are legitimate heirs to her husband's lineage, which is also critical in the patrilineal societies in which clitoridectomy is practiced. Finally, the clitoris is seen as a masculine organ in some cultures so a girl with a clitoris is seen as masculine, not to mention dirty.

Today, clitoridectomies and **infibulations** (in which the clitoris and labia minora are removed and the labia majora is sewn together; not only does this practice ensure a woman's virginity and fidelity, but also, once married, provides the man with extra sexual pleasure) are performed in West Africa, North Africa, East Africa, and the Arab Peninsula, and it is also found in any country with large immigrant populations from these areas, such as France and the United States. In total, the World Health Organization estimates that 100 million women have undergone genital mutilation procedures while Amnesty International estimates that 130 million women have been operated on, over two million each year, with many women suffering from scarring, infections, or infertility as a result.

While Western and non-Western feminists as well as health and human rights organizations are opposed to female genital mutilation, women continue to perform the procedure on their daughters and granddaughters, and many resent the opposition by Western women who may not understand the practice. For them, there are a great many benefits. When women's only opportunity in life, for example, is tied to getting married, then a procedure that ensures marriage and increases the odds of finding a higher status husband will not easily be discarded. Also in countries where adultery for a woman may be punishable by death, or at the very least where a woman who strays from her marriage is ostracized forever, then ensuring chastity by any means is certainly an important concern. Advocates also note that girls who undergo the procedure will have a stronger bond with their husbands since there will be little risk of her cheating on him, he will treat her better knowing that she will not stray, and she will love him even more because her love will not be based on sexual passion.

Female genital mutilation is not just a non-Western issue. It's important to note that Victorian doctors in the United States and England performed clitoridectomies on women who were thought to be suffering from hysteria, lesbianism, or "nymphomania." It was first documented in Europe in 1822 when a German doctor removed the clitoris of a teenage girl who was known as an "imbecile" who was masturbating. For at least a hundred years, doctors throughout Europe and the United States used it to cure any number of mental and physical maladies, and also thought that masturbation itself, in girls and women, caused epilepsy (which is perhaps what they thought a female orgasm was), hysteria and other problems. Ironically, other doctors, on the other hand, used masturbation as a cure for hysteria and prescribed the use of vibrators for the problem. Today, while Western women rarely (but sometimes) get their clitorises removed in a doctor's office, many women do elect to get labiaplasty, an elective procedure during which the labia is reduced in size to be more "appealing."

Hair matters

According to the biblical story of Samson and Delilah, Samson was a great hero whose strength came from the fact that he, following God's orders, did not cut his hair. Delilah, his lover, was paid by the Philistines to cut off his hair, thus removing his strength and allowing his capture. While today we generally look at hair as a woman's issue, and see it as a source of women's beauty, for both men and women, hair – on the head as well as the face and body – is a way of differentiating the genders and reinforcing the differential status of men and women.

For much of human history, women wore their hair long while men kept theirs short. In the Grimm fairy tale "Rapunzel," Rapunzel's great beauty derives, in part, from her long flowing blonde hair. When men or women wear the hairstyles associated with the opposite gender, there is generally a great degree of social concern, as when, in the 1920s, women in the United States began wearing short hairstyles, or during the 1960s when men began wearing their hair long. Because it is often the case that women's hair is a visible sign of her beauty and sexuality, widows are often required to remove or cut their hair after their husband's death. Hindu widows, for instance,

mapping difference onto bodies

traditionally cut their hair after their husbands' deaths in order to prevent other men from being attracted to them. In other cultures, the type of hairstyle worn by a woman signified her marital status. In medieval Europe, girls wore uncovered flowing hair, while matrons bound theirs under veils. And among the Hopi Indians of the American southwest, girls demonstrated their marriageable status by wearing their hair patterned into two squash blossoms over the ears, a style that they abandoned after marriage.

In addition, if a woman's hair signals her gender and sexuality, covering a woman's hair is often mandatory, especially during worship services. Orthodox Jewish women cover their heads with wigs or scarves, and Muslim women often cover their heads with scarves or veils. Amish women keep their hair covered as well; unmarried Amish girls wear a black covering and married women a white one. The Christian apostle Paul once wrote, "does not nature itself teach you that for a man to wear long hair is degrading to him, but if a woman wears long hair it is her pride?" (1 Corinthians 14–15) The idea that women's hair cannot just be prideful but can be sexually dangerous is also found in legends that tell of women who bewitch and entrap men with their long, dangerous hair.

Body hair is gendered as well. Men and women, after puberty, each develop patches of coarse body hair as well, known as **androgenic hair**. The presence of androgenic hair is generally seen as a sign of masculinity in men, and femininity in women when in the "right" place, and as a sign of effeminacy in men and masculinity in women when in the "wrong" place, as when Western women have facial hair, hairy legs, or underarm hair. Where the right and wrong places for body hair growth are differ from one culture to another, however. While an abundance of chest hair on men is often seen as a sign of masculinity and virility, some cultures prefer men to be bare-chested as a sign of youth, or good hygiene. But generally, body hair is associated with masculinity, and women are expected to be much less hairy.

In the modern West, body hair removal did not become popular until the mid-twentieth century, when women's clothing became more revealing, and as the sexualized female body became a mainstay of advertising, television, and film. Most women in the United States now wax or shave their lower legs, underneath their armpits, and the "bikini area" on their upper thighs. In the 1970s, it was common for women involved in the developing women's liberation movement to stop shaving their legs and armpits, and counter-cultural groups like hippies often resisted shaving as well. Today, however, women who do not remove most or all of their body hair often find themselves as the objects of scorn or ridicule. When actress Julia Roberts appeared at the premiere for the 1999 film *Notting Hill* in a sleeveless dress with unshaven armpits, the photos caused a media uproar.

In the late twentieth century, many women in the United States and other Western countries also began removing or shaping their pubic hair, a trend that began in Brazil among women who wanted to wear thong bikinis but did not want their pubic hair to be seen. In some groups, natural pubic hair is seen as unhygienic or messy.

In the late twentieth century, young fashionable men in the United States and some European countries began removing (usually via waxing) their chest hair, a trend that may have started in beach areas in California. Male body hair removal, trimming or styling is often known as **manscaping** but has not become popular with most men. Many Westerners still see body hair as a sign of masculinity, and some groups, such as the **bear** subculture within the gay community, prefer men with abundant body hair.

Like body hair, facial hair, too, is gendered. Because women naturally do not have a great deal of hair on their faces, it is considered a sign of femininity to have as little facial hair (except for eyebrows and eyelashes) as possible. Because of this, most women in Western cultures shave or wax and sometimes bleach the hair that grows on their upper lip, chin, and sometimes elsewhere, and carefully tweeze the hair on their eyebrows in order to keep the eyebrows controlled and to conform to current style. On the other hand, eyelashes are considered a sign of femininity and are encouraged, via makeup and other products, to grow as long and thick as possible. Because of the social stigma associated with facial hair in women, women who do have what would be considered "excess" facial hair are generally considered to lack femininity or to appear mannish.

In 2012, a Sikh woman named Balpreet Kaur was photographed surreptitiously and her photo posted on Reddit, where she was made fun of because she had facial hair. When she found out about the photo and commentary, she posted a response to Reddit which read, in part, "Sikhs believe in the sacredness of this body – it is a gift that has been given to us by the Divine Being [which is genderless, actually] and, must keep it intact as a submission to the divine will." She went on to say,

> When I die, no one is going to remember what I looked like, heck, my kids will forget my voice, and slowly, all physical memory will fade away. However, my impact and legacy will remain: and, by not focusing on the physical beauty, I have time to cultivate those inner virtues and hopefully, focus my life on creating change and progress for this world in any way I can.
>
> (Reddit)

Thanks to her brave response, not only did the original poster apologize, but thousands of people learned about her religion and also may have learned to think twice about judging a woman by her appearance in the future.

Women's bodies: smaller is better

We have noted already that in Western cultures, women are expected to be smaller than men – less muscular, thinner, and more child-like. Even women's feet are expected to be smaller than men's. Because of this, women's shoes are often made to be smaller than her feet – often uncomfortably so. The fairy tale "Cinderella" is a good illustration of the cultural imperative, found in European, African, and Asian countries, for women to have tiny feet. In "Cinderella," the heroine of the tale attends a ball, thanks to the help of her fairy godmother, where she meets a prince. But in her haste to leave the ball, she accidentally leaves behind one of her tiny glass slippers. The prince then brings the slipper from house to house to find the woman who wore it. Cinderella wins the hand of the prince in marriage after she is the only woman in the village whose foot is small enough to fit into the shoe. Some variants of the tale have the wicked stepmother, who wants her own (large and ugly) daughters to marry the prince, cutting off her own daughters' toes or heels in order to fit into the slipper (in one tale the stepmother says "if the shoe will not fit the foot, make the foot fit the shoe;" in another, she says, "cut the toe off, for when you are queen you will never have to go on foot"); it is the presence of the blood in the glass slipper which lets the prince know that he has chosen the wrong girl.

It is clear that the motif of the small slipper, found in folk tales around the world, only has power in cultures in which large feet are considered unattractive and unfeminine, and where the woman with the tiniest feet must automatically be the most beautiful and well-bred of all (and the stepsisters, with their large feet, are considered grotesque). Certainly that is the case in China, and it may have been the case in the classical world as well. Even today, it is becoming more common for American women to undergo elective foot surgery so that they can fit into increasingly narrow shoes. Known euphemistically as "foot facelifts," these cosmetic procedures range from narrowing the feet (either before or after bunions occur), shortening or removing the toes (usually the pinky toe), slimming the toes, and straightening the toes, all so that a woman may fit into a pair of narrow stiletto heels.

Foot binding is the practice of binding a young girl's feet with cloth in order to restrict their growth and control their appearance. Foot binding was practiced in China by the Han ethnic majority from the tenth century until the early twentieth century. Like many other markers of feminine beauty, bound feet were considered beautiful in China partly because a woman with

FIGURE 7.2 Small-footed Chinese woman. LC-USZ62–80735. Photo courtesy of the Library of Congress.

bound feet could not work (and often could not walk), demonstrating her high status and wealth. In addition, in China, to have bound feet meant that a woman was disciplined and virtuous, and that she was brought up correctly. Women with bound feet would also have to take tiny steps when walking, which demonstrated grace. The fact that a girl with bound feet could not walk also most likely meant that she was a virgin, making her even more attractive.

In the West, feet are not the only part of a woman's body that is seen as more attractive when small. In general, women in Western cultures are expected to be thin, and one area of the body that generates the most attention is the waist. Because of the demand for women to have tiny waists, corsets were once a major element of a Western woman's wardrobe. At one time, corsets were worn primarily by upper-class women who competed with

mapping difference onto bodies

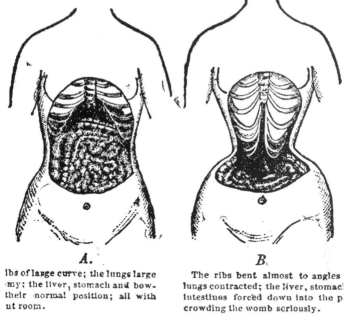

A.

lbs of large curve; the lungs large
my; the liver, stomach and bow-
their normal position; all with
ut room.

B.

The ribs bent almost to angles
lungs contracted; the liver, stomac
intestines forced down into the p
crowding the womb seriously.

Nature versus Corsets, Illustrated.

FIGURE 7.3 Two pictures of a woman's torso; one showing a woman without a corset, the other showing the effects on the internal organs and bones when wearing a corset. Illus. in: *Golden thoughts on chastity and procreation* / John William Gibson. Toronto, Ont., Naperville, Ill.: J. L. Nichols & co., [1903], p. 107. Photo courtesy of the Library of Congress.

one another for the most feminine shape; by the nineteenth century, and especially after the Industrial Revolution which allowed for more inexpensive corsets to be produced, corsets were commonly worn by European and American women of all classes, although the narrow waist and hourglass figure were still seen as emblematic of the upper classes. Attaining the hourglass figure was so important, in fact, that baby girls wore a belt around their waist and young girls wore training corsets. In addition, an upright posture, for both men and women, was associated during the Victorian era with virtue and discipline, while women who kept their bodies unbound were seen as immoral and lazy.

Many women who wore tight corsets had trouble breathing, and prolonged corset wearing permanently changed the shape of women's skeletons. In addition, wearing corsets over a prolonged period of time could result in the back muscles atrophying due to disuse. Of greater concern to the medical establishment, however, was the dangers the corset could bring to a woman's fertility or to the health of her unborn offspring (there were even corsets to be worn during pregnancy). Women wearing corsets could eat very little, denying themselves food in exchange for beauty, a practice which continues to this day.

Another practice in which women's bodies are reshaped is **breast ironing**, found among some tribes in Cameroon, Africa, in which adolescent girls' breasts are artificially flattened. In Cameroon, as in many countries, large breasts are seen as sexually attractive to men and a girl's breasts are a sign of sexual maturity. So in order to protect daughters from rape or early marriages, mothers will pound or massage their growing daughters' breasts in order to make them disappear, allowing the girls to finish school without interruption. According to some studies, a quarter of all Cameroonian girls, primarily in the southern region of the country, have had their breasts flattened with heated tools like wooden pestles, rocks, spatulas, coconut shells, and other hard implements, a process which is quite painful.

Interesting issues: pens for women

In 2012, the pen maker BIC introduced a new ball-point pen called BIC for Her. This pen, which BIC markets as having an "elegant design – just for her!" and a "thin barrel to fit a woman's hand" has received more ridicule than any product in recent memory. The Amazon product reviews have pointed out the inanity of creating a pen just for women (which, by the way, costs 70 percent more than the regular BIC pens, according to Forbes Magazine*). One reviewer writes, "I love BIC Cristal for Her! The delicate shape and pretty pastel colors make it perfect for writing recipe cards, checks to my psychologist (I'm seeing him for a case of the hysterics), and tracking my monthly cycle. Obviously, I don't use it for vulgar endeavors like math or filling out a voter application, but BIC Cristal for Her is a lovely little writing utensil all the same. Ask your husband for some extra pocket money so you can buy one today!" while another writes, "I see this comes in a sleek design. But as a 'full-figured' woman, do these pens come in 'curvy and carefree'?" A male reviewer is disappointed in the product, however, writing, "No good for man hands." While BIC for Her seems to be unbelievably dumb, it seems like every month there's another product that is released that is made "just for women." From deodorant (Secret: "strong enough for a man, but made for a woman") to cigarettes (Virginia Slims: "it's a woman thing"), the assumption is that women need special products just for them. There are even products made just for men, like a blow dryer called the Man Groomer, a loofah called the Axe Detailer Shower Tool, and Hungry Man TV dinners ("you are what you eat; so make it a hungry man . . . you can eat like a man and be full like a man!"). Through product marketing, manufacturers and marketers produce and reinforce gender difference.*

mapping difference onto bodies

The problematic male body

If femininity is constructed in part through the body, via practices like dieting and cosmetic surgery today, or foot binding and **tightlacing** in the past, then masculinity, too, is constructed at least partially through the body. We have said that men are celebrated by their achievements, so physical appearance is not as important as it is for women.

But when physical appearance is measured, men are expected to be strong and powerful. As we have noted, men are expected to be naturally tall, large, and muscular, and when that cannot be attained through "nature," culture steps in. Men can now use cosmetic surgery to modify their own bodies, and have long used body building and other sports to create the normative athletic male body. Steroid use is becoming more common in boys and men as one side effect of the emphasis on muscularity and fitness. They even wear "elevator shoes" to covertly increase their height, because short men make less money in the workplace and are considered less attractive sexual partners than tall men.

The emphasis on physical strength and competition for men has a number of pitfalls. Men have a shorter life expectancy than women, and die more often from violence. Men are expected to compete with other men, via sports, in warfare, and on the streets, which leads to greater rates of homicide, accidents, injury, and heart problems. Because they are expected to be more self-sufficient than women, they also do not go to the doctor as often, and thus die sooner from preventable diseases. Many of the practices associated with traditional masculinity, many scholars have noted, often result in death for men, especially young men. For example, fighting in the military, competitive drinking, aggressive driving, fighting, competitive sports, and a whole host of other activities are linked to greater injuries and shorter life expectancy in men.

In addition, men who cannot or will not conform to the demands of normative masculinity suffer as well. Because expectations of masculinity call for men to be strong, independent, active, and able to do anything, disability certainly does not fit into this definition, and thus men who are disabled are stigmatized in many cultures; they are sometimes seen as not being "real men." After professional cyclist Lance Armstrong survived testicular cancer, the notion that "real men" beat cancer, thanks to their courage, strength, and self-reliance, emerged in the popular media. Unfortunately, the corollary to the idea that one can beat cancer through strength is the idea that men who succumb to cancer are somehow less than real men. In addition, while Armstrong became an international hero thanks to not only overcoming cancer but winning the Tour de France seven consecutive times, in 2012, his medals were taken away after it was discovered that he had been taking illegal performance-enhancing drugs during his cycling career. This demonstrates how high the stakes really are for athletes of Armstrong's caliber, and, by extension, all men.

Even aging can be responsible for stealing masculinity. While it is true that men often gain power as they get older, that power usually derives from wealth. Without wealth, aging for men is just a loss of the attributes of physical masculinity: power, strength, and virility. The ability to be sexual (and heterosexual, in particular) is one of the defining features of masculinity around the world, so the loss of erectile function is often linked to the loss of manhood. Thankfully, for men, erectile dysfunction drugs are one way to reverse one of the most stigmatizing signs of aging in men – the loss of sexual prowess.

Male *and* female: transgendered bodies

We know that gender does not come in only two "flavors." The term **transgendered** is generally applied to individuals whose appearance and behaviors do not conform to the gender roles ascribed by society for people of a particular sex. Transgender people may also identify as both male and female or may adopt behaviors or characteristics of both genders. Transgendered people include transvestites who cross-dress, those who choose to be androgynous in appearance and/or behavior, and biological men or women who identify with the opposite sex, or with neither sex. Some **transsexuals** also could be considered, or may identify as, transgendered. Some transgendered men or male to female transsexuals in the United States as well as other countries inject themselves with silicone in order to feminize their faces or bodies. While in the United States, cross-dressers are the most commonly known form of transgendered person, there are various forms of transgendered people around the world, many of whom have culturally defined roles available to them.

In India, for example, **Hijras** are a cultural category which includes those who were born **intersex** (i.e. with ambiguous genitalia), men who have been defined as "impotent," or men who choose not to live as men (Nanda 1998). Because Hinduism embraces alternative genders and gender transformation, Hijras have a sacred role in Indian society, and form a quasi-religious community. Hijras are created through ritual surgery, performed by a Hijra called a midwife, in which their penises and testicles are removed. Hijras are defined by their sexual impotence and liminal gender status, and adopt exaggerated female mannerisms and appearance. Because Hijras cannot reproduce themselves, they can confer fertility on others, via blessings at childbirths and weddings. While they renounce sexual desire, many do work as prostitutes or even serve as wives to men.

In Brazil, there is a category of transgendered people known as **travesties**. Travesties dress and behave like women, and inject silicone and consume

mapping difference onto bodies

FIGURE 7.4 We-Wa, a Zuni berdache, weaving. Photographed by John K. Hillers, Smithsonian Institution. Bureau of American Ethnology. Photo courtesy of the National Archives and Records Administration.

hormone pills to mold their bodies to look more feminine. They are not transsexuals and do not feel that they are or should be women, nor do they seek to remove their penises (Kulick 1997). As with the Hijras in India, travesties have sex with straight men, who are not considered to be gay as long as they are in the "top" role sexually.

Dozens of Native American societies also at one time had culturally defined roles for transgendered people known as **two spirits**. Two spirits were biological men or women who adopted the roles, appearances, and behaviors of the opposite sex, forming a third or fourth gender. Men-women or women-men would have been recognized as "different" as children and allowed to grow up as the opposite gender, marrying into the opposite gender as adults. Like Hijras, two spirits, sometimes known as berdaches, often had a special ritual function as well as their assigned gender role. Two spirits did not, however, receive any sort of surgery which modified their bodies, although they dressed, spoke and behaved like the opposite gender.

In the United States today, most people only recognize two genders and two sexes. There is no room for third genders; instead, there are transgendered people who fit somewhere in between but do not have a specific cultural role. They cannot even easily navigate which public

gendered bodies

bathroom to use! Transsexuals are allowed to move from one sex and gender to another, however. But recognizing transgender people would, according to some transgender feminists, allow the breaking down of some of the socially constructed hierarchies in American culture which are, after all, based at least in part upon bodily differences. By allowing for gender non-conformity, it may be possible someday to disrupt the power structures behind various oppressions and privileges.

Where gender is, in many cultures, a binary system that limits opportunity for men, women, and transmen and transwomen, sexuality often works the same way. In Chapter 8, we will look at sexuality, and at the myriad ways in which bodies are shaped by sexuality, and at how societies, in turn, control sexual expression.

Key terms

Adonis Complex
Androgenic Hair
Bears
Breast Ironing
Circumcision
Clitoridectomy
Deceptive Distinctions
Female Genital Mutilation
Foot Binding
Hijra
Infibulations

Intersex
Manscaping
Patriarchal Bargain
Ritual Homosexuality
Subincision
Thinspiration
Tightlacing
Transgender
Transsexual
Travesti
Two Spirits

Further reading

Birke, Lynda. (2000). *Feminism and the Biological Body*. New Brunswick, NJ: Rutgers University Press.
Bordo, Susan. (1993). *Unbearable Weight: Feminism, Western Culture, and the Body*. Berkeley, CA: University of California Press.
Butler, Judith. (1990). *Gender Trouble: Feminism and the Subversion of Identity*. New York: Routledge.
Kimmel, Michael. (2000). *The Gendered Society*. New York: Oxford University Press.

mapping difference onto bodies

chapter 8

Sexualized Bodies

Sex is, for many of us, like art or pornography. We may not be able to define it with any scientific accuracy, but we think we know it when we see it. In fact, we think that sex is so simple that we come up with expressions like "men are from Mars and women are from Venus." But is it really that simple? And what exactly does a phrase like that refer to anyway – sex, gender, or something else?

In 2009, South African runner Caster Semenya won the 800-meter women's race at the World Championships in Berlin. She became a figure of international controversy when it was alleged that she might not be "entirely" female. In fact, she was tested by the International Association of Athletics Federation which found that she was intersex, and had internal testes that were producing testosterone. Given this information, should she be allowed to compete as a woman, or would this make her participation in races unfair to the other competitors? For that matter, does any genetically well-endowed athlete pose an unfair advantage to other athletes who are less well-endowed? In Semenya's case, the IAAF ultimately ruled that she could compete as a woman, and indeed, she competed for South Africa in the 2012 Summer Olympics. But this decision did not put to rest the issues and conflicts surrounding Semenya's sex and gender.

Sex, like so many of the issues discussed in this text, is partly a biological construct but is also heavily a social construct. In other words, everything related to sex – and by that, we refer to your biological sex, the sexual relations that you may have, and your sexual identity and orientation – is shaped by, and understood through, the lens of culture. For philosopher

Michel Foucault, sexuality is historically and socially constructed within relations of power. There is no such thing as an inherent or essential sexuality. We create discourses about sex, and those discourses then shape our understanding of sex.

How sex is produced

Humans are born either male or female – or somewhere in between – thanks first to the sex chromosomes that they inherit from their parents. We each receive an X chromosome from our mothers, and from our fathers, either an X, making us female, or a Y, making us male. For the first six or seven weeks of gestation, every embryo is sexually undifferentiated. That means that they have neither male nor female reproductive organs, but undifferentiated gonads. Instead, embryos have two sets of ducts: Mullerian and Wolffian. At about six weeks, a hormone called SRY, in fetuses with the XY chromosome combination, stimulates the undifferentiated gonad into testes. For those with XX chromosomes, ovaries instead develop.

After that, the body begins to produce either estrogens, in the female, or androgens, in the male. The presence of androgens makes the Wolfian ducts turn into the male reproductive organs, while the presence of estrogens turns the Mullerian ducts into female reproductive organs. The alternative set of ducts will disappear in the male and the female, only leaving the "correct" reproductive organs for each sex. Eventually, the external genitals will emerge from the genital tubercle, urogenital groove, and labioscrotal folds, which both male and female fetuses possess. Males will end up with the penis and scrotal sac, while females will end up with the clitoris, labia, vaginal opening, and hymen. Because these organs develop from the same root organs, male and female sexual organs are **homologous**: testes and ovaries, penis and clitoris, scrotum and labia, vas deferens and fallopian tubes, and prostate gland and g-spot, all serve essentially the same function in the male and the female. Men and women, then, are just variations on the same basic pattern, rather than entirely different creatures. And finally, long after the baby is born, and years later, after puberty, the secondary sex characteristics will appear in both males and females, further differentiating the sexes.

Intersexuality: are there just two sexes?

The result of this process is that perhaps as many as one out of every 2,000 births result in a child who cannot be neatly categorized as either male or female. Intersexuality refers to an individual who is born with what are called **ambiguous genitalia**. This means that the genitals of the child do not clearly point to either male or female, or the child possesses reproductive organs that either do not match the genitals or the chromosomes. An older term for this condition is hermaphroditism, and hermaphrodites were once displayed as human oddities in freak shows. But because the medical establishment and society as a whole cannot really cope with the notion that there are more than two biological sexes, these children are surgically "corrected" shortly after birth or at some point during their childhood, turning them, for the most part, into girls (because it's easier to cut off or shorten a penis into a clitoris than to make a penis from a clitoris). The surgery is done so early because the doctors feel that the condition is a "social emergency" warranting immediate medical attention.

The most common cause of sexual ambiguity is congenital adrenal hyperplasia, an endocrine disorder in which the adrenal glands produce abnormally high levels of masculinizing hormones in a genetic female fetus. This leads to an appearance that may be slightly masculinized (such as having a large clitoris) but the individual may also appear very masculine, especially after puberty. Another common condition is androgen insensitivity syndrome, which occurs in genetic male fetuses. In this case, there is an inability to respond to testosterone which leads to a genetic male with female external and sometimes internal organs. In all of these cases, the conditions are managed medically through surgical intervention, and often, hormone administration.

Intersex advocates are opposed to this type of social and sexual determination, because they argue that no doctor, whether surgeon, endocrinologist, or urologist, can determine with 100 percent accuracy the "true" sex of a child. One reason this is so problematic is because this determination is often made from something as arbitrary as penis length, or whether or not the penis/clitoris will respond to testosterone.

Once intersex babies undergo surgery, they are raised in accordance with the gendered norms associated with their assigned sex. For many such children, they grow up with no gender conflicts, but for other children, their gender identity is at odds with their bodies and with the way they were raised. Because these children do not consent to the surgeries, which are in effect **sex reassignment surgeries**, and many are emotionally and physically scarred, with impaired sexual functioning after the surgeries, there is a movement, led by the **Intersex Society of North America**, to end "normalizing" surgeries on infants and children. According to ISNA, the distress caused by the birth of intersex children should not be treated via surgery on the children, but by therapy for parents and children, and tolerance in society in general.

In addition, in the intersex community, there are increasing calls for recognition of the various degrees of intersexuality as healthy variations on a sexual continuum which should not be subject to correction or stigmatization. Despite the recent attacks on the practice of surgical correction, most of the medical profession still supports it, and American society, like most societies, is still firmly committed to the idea that there are only two sexes, and that anything otherwise represents a deviation.

Interestingly, prior to the modern period, those who assigned gender to intersex persons did so in a more humane fashion than today, often waiting until puberty to observe the direction in which an intersex person was developing, and only then assigning them their sex and gender identity. In other cultures too, as in India, intersexed individuals can openly exist as a third gender, without being forced to live as either men or women. Today, physicians make this decision and typically do it right at birth, making a decision that will affect the child for his or her life based on functionality and expected fertility.

The modern medical practice of determining the sex of an intersex infant via medical intervention is notable in not only what it does to intersex people (making them one or the other sex without their knowledge or consent, and without an understanding of whether or not their own gender and sexual identity will conform to the choice that was made for them), but also in the fact that it effectively erases and suppresses intersexuality, and all forms of sex that do not conform to a male/female binary. Women with clitorises that are "too large" are not seen as feminine, and men with penises that are too small are likewise seen as lacking masculinity. In both cases, surgery is used to fix the problem. This is a good example of **biopower**: when the medical profession can control the very sex and identity of a person.

Biologist Anne Fausto-Sterling has argued that there we should instead recognize five sexes, to take in all of the varieties of sexual variation that can occur during gestational development. For her, and for scholars and advocates like her, sex is a continuum with a variety of physical expressions, and not a strict male/female binary.

Why does society care so much if people do not fall easily into male or female? Intersex people blur the divide between male and female, challenging our own beliefs about sexual difference, sexual orientation, and the proper role of men and women. But if we lived in a world in which intersex people were given a place, it would mean that our most critical oppositions – male/female, hetero/homo – would have to dissolve, and there would be no more power imbalance based on those distinctions.

Changing sex: transsexuality

Transsexualism is a condition in which a person feels that they were born in the wrong body, and not only want to adopt the behaviors, mannerisms, and roles associated with the opposite sex, but see their sexual identity as incorrect as well. Most transsexuals want to not only want to live as a member of the gender with which they identify, but want to surgically and chemically alter their bodies so that their bodies match their internal gender

FIGURE 8.1 Hellen Madok aka Pamela Soares, winner Miss Brazil Transsexual 2007. Photo courtesy of Silvio Tanaka, via Wikimedia Commons: http://commons.wikimedia.org/wiki/File: Transwoman_at_Gay_Pride_in_S%C3%A3o_Paulo,_2008.jpg.

identity. Transsexualism is sometimes considered to be a type of trans-gendered behavior.

Transsexuals are thought by the psychiatric profession to suffer from **gender dysphoria** or **gender identity disorder**, both psychiatric conditions. Those who choose to change their bodies to match their gender identity must, in the United States, receive psychological therapy (known as **sex reassignment therapy**), because the mental health profession does not consider surgery to be the only necessary treatment for the condition. Transsexuals who are planning to undergo surgery are known as pre-operative (or pre-op) transsexuals and generally take hormones and dress and behave as their desired sex and gender during this period of time, which generally lasts at least a year. These requirements are intended to prevent people who are not genuinely transsexual from changing their sex and later regretting having done so.

Once an individual has completed the requisite counseling, he or she moves to the next phase, which is receiving sex reassignment surgery. Once the surgery or surgeries are completed, these individuals are known as post-operative or post-op transsexuals. Male-to-female (MTF) transsexuals are those who have transitioned, or are transitioning, from biological male to biological female, and female-to-male (FTM) transsexuals are those who have transitioned, or are transitioning, from biological female to biological male.

Some transsexuals, either because they cannot afford surgery in the United States or because they find the requirements of sex reassignment therapy too restrictive, instead choose to seek surgery in developing countries or with American doctors who are not properly licensed to perform the surgery. Many, including those who never do undergo surgery, will also order hormones on the black market.

While transsexuals probably exist in all cultures, in many they are considered to be sexual and social deviants. Thailand is an example of a country that assigns a special social category to transgenders and male-to-female transsexuals called **kathoey**, or ladyboys. Kathoey dress and behave as women, occupy female gender roles, and many undergo hormone replacement therapy, sex reassignment surgery, and breast implants to legally become women. Like Brazilian travesties, many kathoey have achieved high status careers as models or celebrities, but also like the travesties, many work as prostitutes. Because of the high incidence of transsexuals in Thailand, sex-reassignment surgery is a commonly performed surgery in the country, both for native Thai people as well as Westerners seeking low-cost surgery.

Male and female sexualities

When we talk about bodies and sex, we may be referring to both sexual identity, as previously discussed, or sexual preferences, practices, and feelings. Sexuality in most cultures is strongly gendered. In other words, males and females are socialized into very different sexualities.

In most of the world, girls are socialized to be sexually passive and to guard their virginity closely. Girls, and by extension women, are taught to curb their sexual desires and to closely monitor and guard against the sexual advances of boys and men. On the other hand, in the United States as in other Western countries, girls are also highly sexualized via the mass media. Western popular culture is filled with images of sexually desirable girls and women, and girls are encouraged to look and act sexual from a very early age. In addition, since the development of the birth control pill and the resulting sexual revolution, women now have more opportunities than ever to experience their sexuality. This mixed message – that girls need to guard their sexuality, yet they are to be sexually attractive to boys and men – is at least partly to blame for the schizophrenic way in which female sexuality is seen and approached in the West.

Boys and men, on the other hand, are encouraged to be sexually aggressive and sexually active. Boys are socialized about sex through their peers and through the mass media (pornographic magazines in an earlier age; pornographic websites today). During childhood and adolescence, boys talk about sex and girls, and encourage the development of a form of competitive heterosexuality amongst themselves. In particular when boys engage in sports, the culture of the field and the locker room is very much centered around this sort of masculine heterosexuality in which hooking up becomes a sport in and of itself. Sociologist Michael Messner (2002) goes further and shows that sports are a primary vehicle in which boys and men learn, reinforce, and perform a form of masculinity that is based on compulsive, competitive, heterosexuality.

While girls are seen as sluts if they engage in sexual activity, boys are heroes for doing the same thing. This **sexual double standard** is found throughout the world, to a greater or lesser extent. Even as young girls are becoming more sexual, and having sex earlier, much of that sexual activity is still aimed at pleasing boys. More young girls are engaging in fellatio and even anal sex than ever before, yet the focus often remains on seeking popularity and approval by providing sexual pleasure to boys and men. Similarly, many young women today are "experimenting" with same-sex sexual expression. While there are a variety of reasons for this, one factor that should not be overlooked is the desire of many young women to gain male attention by publicly making out with other women. The video series *Girls Gone Wild*, for example, has made its creator, Joe Francis, millions of dollars by featuring drunk young women showing off their breasts and making out with other women for a bit of attention and fame.

It is certainly true that girls and women face far greater consequences over sexual activity than men do, so there are good reasons for women to guard their sexuality. As long as women get pregnant and women give birth, there will be very real dangers surrounding female sexuality. Unplanned pregnancies, or being called a slut, are not the only danger. Women also face sexual assault and for women who are, or appear to be, sexually active, the risk of such assault is often greater. In addition, in recent years, conservatives in the United States have gained a great deal of ground in restricting access to abortion and contraceptives, making female sexuality even more dangerous.

At the same time, there is a growing abstinence movement in the United States, aimed at both boys and girls. In 2012, NFL quarterback Tim Tebow shot to popularity, in part thanks to his performance as a member of the Denver Broncos, but also in part thanks to his public displays of his Christian faith during football games. Tebow, 24 at the time of this writing, has also publicly come out as a virgin, attracting derision from some, but admiration from others. Typically, however, girls are expected to maintain their virginity beyond the time when boys lose theirs.

Another way that sexuality is gendered is that in the West, the "vaginal orgasm" has long been thought to be the most legitimate expression of female sexuality. Even after pioneering sex researcher Alfred Kinsey wrote about the importance of the clitoris for women's orgasms in his 1953 book *Sex Behavior in the Human Female*, the conservative climate of the time rejected that notion. Instead, doctors, ministers, and the general public alike counseled women to focus on the vaginal orgasm as the standard of "normal" femininity. Because women were, and still are, to some extent, expected to have an orgasm through sexual intercourse alone, needing to have one's clitoris stimulated to achieve orgasm is often seen as a sign of sexual dysfunction. The reality is that clitoral stimulation is key to the vast majority of women's orgasms, so to suggest that women who do not have orgasms through penetration alone are dysfunctional or "frigid" does women a great disservice.

Interesting issues: Toddlers & Tiaras *and the sexualization of little girls*

Toddlers & Tiaras is an American reality television show that airs on TLC that covers child beauty pageants and the families of the girls who enter them. The show has created a great deal of controversy because of the way that the girls' performances and costumes sexualize the performers, who begin performing as infants. The girls wear makeup, wigs, sexy outfits, padded bras, and dance in suggestive routines. In 2012, the mother of one Toddlers & Tiaras *pageant queen sued a number of media outlets for "sexualizing her daughter" after they posted a video of the 5-year-old singing "I'm Sexy and I Know It" at a New York City nightclub. The video was only posted after the parents had their daughter perform the song at the nightclub, but the parents felt that the sexualization only occurred when the media reported on it.* Toddlers & Tiaras *is only the latest example of the sexualization of extremely young girls. Everyone knows about Bratz dolls, extremely popular dolls which come with very sexy clothes and makeup. But now there are Bratz Babyz which are baby dolls which wear the same sexy clothes that the older Bratz dolls wear. Other items that are now marketed to girls include stripper poles: the kit comes with a garter belt that girls can wear that other kids can stuff play money into. Abercrombie & Fitch now makes push-up bras and thongs for 7-year-olds, and* Playboy *markets merchandise for children. Finally, no Halloween would be complete without the ubiquitous sexy costumes (nurse/witch/police officer/devil, etc.) for women. These costumes are now available for teenagers and pre-teens as well.*

Gay, straight, bi, and ?: a diversity of sexualities

In the West, sexuality is seen, like gender, as a binary. One is either hetero-sexual, which is the norm, or homosexual, which is not. While many people understand that bisexuality exists, it seems even more unusual and non-normative than homosexuality. In other cultures, however, sexuality is not seen on such a binary, and may come in more flavors than simply straight or gay.

Defining sexuality – homo, hetero, or other – is difficult not just because the categories themselves are so limiting, but because the terms we use may refer to very different categories of thought and behavior, including sexual behavior, emotional affiliation, and self-definition, and these categories may not all overlap neatly.

For example, in many parts of Latin America, what makes a man gay is the fact that he is sexually penetrated by another man. The man who does the penetrating (in American lingo, the "top" or "pitcher") is not gay, on the other hand. In the United States, men who work as gay prostitutes, or hustlers, may identify as straight, but engage daily in anal and oral sex with other men, often exclusively acting as the "bottom" or "catcher."

How same-sex relationships occur is often strongly shaped by cultural factors. (The presence of people who engage in same-sex relationships, or who want to, is universal, however.) Anthropologists have noted that, historically, there have been at least four different patterns that homosexual relationships might take: egalitarian, gender structured, age structured, and ritualistic.

Egalitarian relationships are those that we see in the West, and largely parallel heterosexual relationships. In other words, two men or two women, of relatively equal status, form a loving relationship. These are not only becoming more common in Western cultures, but are becoming more socially acceptable as well.

Gender structured relationships have been found in cultures around the world, and are associated with transgendered people. In this case, one partner in the relationship takes on the gendered norms of their own sex, while the other partner adopts the gendered norms of the opposite sex. These relationships, then, are same-sex but different-gender relationships. They have been found among many of the most well-known transgendered communities in the world, including Thailand's kathoey, India's hijras, Brazil's travesties, and the two-spirits of Native America.

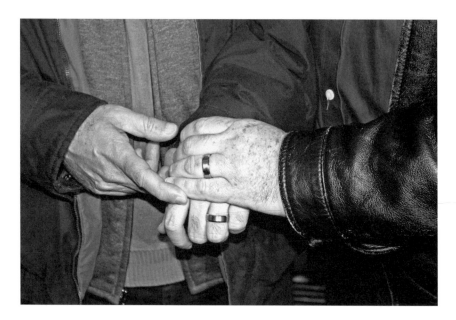

FIGURE 8.2 Gay weddings are becoming increasingly common in the United States; as of 2013, gay marriage is now legal in thirteen states. Bob Mitchell and Randy Huff got married in 2011 in a civil ceremony. Photo courtesy of Janet Kazimir.

Age structured homosexual relationships include one older partner and one younger partner. These types of relationships were well known among the ancient Greeks, for whom it was completely normal. In this case, adult men, married with wives and children, had sexual relationships with much younger men. When the younger men got older, they left those relationships to marry, have wives of their own, and often take younger male lovers.

Finally, **ritual homosexuality** refers to practices most commonly seen in Melanesia where boys participate in homosexual practices with older men, as a part of their initiation into adulthood. Anthropologist Gilbert Herdt (1994) has studied such cultures and has shown that in cultures like these, men may engage in homosexual practices for much of their lives, even though they are not only expected to marry and have children, but are defined as masculine, and, therefore, heterosexual. Sexuality, then, is not only strongly influenced by culture but may be far more flexible than most of us think. Even in the animal world, where hundreds of species of mammals and birds engage in homosexual behavior alongside of heterosexual behavior, sexuality may be more flexible than we sometimes think it is.

In the West, homosexuality and heterosexuality are much more narrowly defined, and they are generally defined as a permanent orientation. About 4 percent of adults in the United States self-identify as homosexual, but because our definition is so narrow, this number does not take into account

mapping difference onto bodies

all of those who may have, or may have had, sexual relations, or even sexual thoughts, about members of the same sex. In fact, researchers are finding that among young men and women, the number of people who have had sexual experiences with members of the same sex is closer to 10 percent, and for young women it may be as high as 18 percent. An important point to note here is that accurately judging the number of people who self-identify as homosexual is difficult in a society that still mandates heterosexuality as the norm. There's no way to know how many men and women who might prefer to engage in same-sex relationships, either some or all of the time, because it is still socially unacceptable in many places to do so. For example, in the eighteenth and nineteenth centuries, many elite European and American women engaged in what were called **Boston marriages**: romantic and sexual relationships with other women. These relationships were rarely public, and when they were, the women were accused of being mentally ill.

This brings up the fact that sexual behavior, and sexual preferences, can change for some people over the course of their lifetime. While most people are firmly committed to heterosexuality, and some are firmly committed to homosexuality, it appears that there are millions of men and women who may have a more fluid sexual orientation.

But does that mean that millions of people are bisexual? According to sexologist Alfred Kinsey, most human beings in fact are bisexual, and it's simply culture that forces most of us to behave strictly as heterosexual. For Kinsey, sexuality can be better seen as a continuum rather than a binary, with most people on the heterosexual side of the continuum, some on the homosexual side, and most of us situated, or moving, along the many points in between.

The idea that sexuality may be fluid or changeable does not challenge the fact that for many people, sexuality appears to be fixed. In fact, the consensus view today among scientists, as well as in the gay community, is that for most people, sexuality – for both straight and gay people – is shaped very early in one's life, if not at birth. Some scientists have theorized that homosexuality may develop in the fetus because of the mother's hormones, which may cause a slightly different brain structure than found in heterosexuals, while others have postulated the presence of a "**gay gene**" or set of genes, which may have evolved to give the recipient, or the recipient's family, some sort of selective advantage. In recent years, there's been a great deal of research looking at sexuality among identical twins, sexual dimorphism of finger length, birth order of siblings, and left- or right-handedness, and that this research provides proof that sexuality is at least partially biological.

One of the problems with these types of explanations is that they assume that not only is heterosexuality the norm, but they imply that homosexuality represents some sort of mutation or abnormality. In fact, prior to 1973, the

American Psychiatric Association considered homosexuality to be a mental disorder, although that's no longer the case today. On the other hand, if sexuality is biologically determined, even if it's seen as a defect, that means that people are born that way, and the various religious and reparative therapies that attempt to "cure" it should be discontinued. (In 2012, California made the news by passing the first law in the country that in fact bans such therapies.) So there are strong political pressures on both the gay rights side and on the fundamentalist Christian side to prove that homosexuality is either biological or a "choice." If homosexuality is biologically determined, there can be no legal justification for discrimination. But if it is a choice, then the religious right can justify discrimination. But in order to account for the wide variety of forms that sexuality take around the world, we need to at least accept the idea that culture may play a role in shaping sexual behavior as well.

Another problem with the terms "heterosexual" and "homosexual" is not only the fact that they are so restricting, and that they imply a norm (heterosexual) and the deviation from the norm (homosexual), but that they define people exclusively in terms of their sexuality. In other words, straight people are not defined as "straight" for the vast majority of their lives. Instead, they are women or men, mothers or fathers, architects or gardeners, volleyball players or runners. But gay people are defined as gay; homosexuality is their master status, and for that reason, society sees them as a "special class" of people who are demanding "special rights." But gay people, like straight people, are volleyball players, architects, and fathers. Sex and sexuality are not their primary forms of behavior, identification, or status. It is only through the construction of the terms, and the binaries on which they are supposed to rest, that this notion that gay people are all about sex has developed. Without the binary definitions, and certainly without the stigma associated with homosexuality, gay people would be seen as the same as everyone else.

Body play, bondage, and fetishes

Sex, of course, refers to more than the biological sex of a person, or their sexual orientation. It also refers to sexual behaviors, as we have already discussed in this chapter. Sexual behavior, as we mentioned, is strongly shaped by cultural norms, but that does not mean that there are no people who engage in sexual behaviors well outside of the cultural norm. **BDSM** (from Bondage and Discipline, Domination and Submission, and Sadism and Masochism), refers to a number of sexual behaviors that include the use of consensual pain, submission, or dominance, and which are seen as deviant by much of mainstream society. Being involved in BDSM or dominant/submissive relationships on a regular basis is often referred to as being "in the lifestyle."

mapping difference onto bodies

A dominant person enjoys controlling his or her sexual partner. A submissive person is one who seeks out a partner to dominate them. Partners can also be tops and bottoms without formally being in a dominance/submission relationship. A top is the person who, when performing sexual acts that include bondage, humiliation, or pain, is the person who controls the activities; bottoms would be the partners to whom the acts are being done, and unless the partners are in a formal dominance relationship, they often will switch roles.

Many if not most of BDSM activities involve pain. Sensation play is one way that one person will inflict pain on the other, without actually injuring them. Participants enjoy the release of endorphins that occurs during these activities. Another motivation is that sensation play is about exploring and pushing one's personal limits, physically and emotionally. While men and women have most likely enjoyed enduring pain with sex for centuries, like pornography, it was probably not seen as a special category of sexual behavior until the eighteenth century when European society began categorizing (and stigmatizing) certain sexual practices.

In the twentieth century, BDSM has most been associated with the gay leather scene that emerged from of a group of gay soldiers after World War II. These early sexual pioneers experimented with a variety of non-mainstream sexual practices such as erotic spanking, flogging, sex toys, paddling, sensory deprivation, and movement restriction, and were the first group of Westerners to really experiment with body piercing, facial piercing, branding, and genital piercing. For instance, branding and ownership tattoos are often used by dominant partners to mark ownership of their submissives, and some submissives will go to the extreme step of having some or all of their genitals removed.

Many people engage in non-normative sexual behaviors on their own, without being members of a community like the BDSM community. For instance, many people have sexual **fetishes** – sexual attractions to an object, body part, or animal. While there are both male and female fetishists, the majority of the documentation on fetishists, including foot and shoe fetishists, is on men, and the most fetishized feet and footwear belong to women.

Foot and footwear fetishes are the most commonly documented form of fetish. A foot fetishist's sexual arousal centers on the foot – stroking, caressing, and kissing the feet, or sometimes using the foot or toes as part of lovemaking. Foot fetishists will typically find certain features of the foot, or of particular feet, to be arousing, such as foot odor, long toes, high arches, or painted toenails. Small female feet have been highly valued in many cultures, and represent femininity and vulnerability, most famously expressed through the Chinese practice of foot binding. On the other hand, some find very large feet in women to be arousing.

Shoe fetishists find shoes to be sexually arousing. The types of shoes valued by shoe fetishists are often very high heels (because of the way they impact a woman's back, hips, buttocks, and breasts), very tight, thigh-high boots, or boots that are laced up like corsets. Fetishists will sometimes caress or lick shoes, or will ejaculate into them; other times the fetish involves being stepped on by the shoes, or watching someone in high heels step on someone or something else, as in a crush fetish. On the other hand, sometimes the smell of the shoe is arousing. (While it has been most common throughout history that women's feet and shoes were sexualized, there have been cases where men's shoes were eroticized as well. The *poulaine*, a men's shoe with a pointed toe as long as 24 inches, was popular in Medieval Europe among wealthy men, while reviled by the Catholic Church, which considered its phallic connotations degenerate. The toes of the poulaine had to be stuffed with wool and horse hair in order to keep the toes erect. It is said that men stood on street corners and waved their toes while women walked by.)

Some theorists postulate that foot fetishism becomes more popular as sexually transmitted diseases rise; using the feet for sexual release becomes a form of safe sex. Another theory suggests that periods of high morality when feet – in particular, female feet – are kept from public sight are also correlated with increases in foot fetishes. So during the Victorian era when women's feet were covered in shoes and concealed under long layers of clothing, they were subsequently more eroticized by fetishists (during the mid-nineteenth century there was a busy underground market in foot fetish pornography and accessories). In fact, foot and shoe fetishism were first defined as a sexual issue in nineteenth-century England, and it may be that these developments were rooted directly in the Victorian morality of the time. Freud, for example, thought that shoes are fetishized because little boys see shoes when trying to look up their mother's long skirt.

Stilettos, too, are both fragile looking and very dangerous, a combination that comes into play in the crush fetish, in which men derive sexual pleasure from watching a woman's stillettoed foot crush objects or small animals, generally in videos called crush videos. The impulse behind a crush fetish is, for many, similar to the impulse behind BDSM: adherents enjoy fantasizing about themselves being crushed, and experience that vicariously through watching a woman in very high heels crush inanimate objects or animals. Even fetishists without a specific crush fetish often fantasize about or enjoy having a woman in high heels walk on them, causing them both pain and humiliation, and making them feel insignificant.

Sex as a weapon: rape and castration

It is clear that sexuality is a core part of who we are as animals, and as humans. We are a sexually reproducing species, so sex is needed to create

mapping difference onto bodies

future generations of humans. But because sex is shaped, viewed, and controlled through culture and society, sex can be used as a tool to oppress or even violate individuals or communities. Rape and castration are both tools used to control the behavior of others, and both women and men can be victims of sexual violence.

Rape is generally defined as forced sexual contact. As simple as this concept seems to be, the definition of rape has been changing over time. While at one time, it only referred to forced intercourse, and supposedly could only happen to women, in Western countries today it is more broadly defined. In addition, in the past, and in many cultures today, women could not be raped by their husbands (so what we today call spousal or partner rape was not a crime), and in a great many places today, men cannot be prosecuted for rape if it is thought that the women invited sexual attention from the man.

Rape is an extremely common crime in the United States, where most victims are young, most know their attackers, and most are female. College students are at the greatest risk of rape of any other population in the United States. But because so many young victims know their attackers, or were attacked at a party or on or after a date, about half of all victims do not report the incidences as rape and many blame themselves for the attack. Many of the attackers may not even realize, or may deny, that they raped someone.

In other cultures, rape is less prevalent among friends or intimates and more common among strangers. But in all cases where rape is common, or in societies that we call **rape-prone cultures**, there tend to be a number of cultural factors that play a role in its prevalence. For instance, factors like masculine violence, sexual violence, victim-blaming, low female status, and poor relations between the sexes are all correlated with cultures with high degrees of rape. Rape is often a product of socialization processes that occur in certain rape-prone societies. These processes glorify masculine violence, teach boys to be aggressive and competitive, and demean the role of women in society. One example of a rape culture is Southern Africa, with its high tolerance for violence and for violence against women, women's low ability to exercise control in sexual relationships, and the general dominance of men and submissiveness of women. The United States is another rape-prone culture, perhaps because of the ways in which the media glorifies and normalizes violence, sexual conquests, and the objectification of women. While women arguably hold higher status in the United States than in many other countries, they still find that their power in sexual relationships remains low and that their role as sexual objects remains quite high. Where women, and women's bodies, are commodified, and where men compete with each other for control over women, rape is often the result.

Feminist pioneer Gloria Steinem calls rape, as well as serial murder, "supremacy crimes." They result, according to Steinem, from men's expectation that they should be dominant over others. Another result of male domination is the fact that women are frequently blamed for being raped. In an environment of male domination, it is believed that women "asked for it," by wearing revealing clothing, by going on a date with men, or by getting drunk. In rape trials, these issues are frequently brought up by the defense, often leading to the acquittal of the rapists, and not surprisingly, leading to a high number of women never reporting their rapes in the first place.

For men who are raped, we find that many of the same factors exist. Where masculinity is highly valued and femininity is devalued, then men who are gay, perceived as gay, or perceived as less feminine tend to be victimized. This holds true both in prison, where male rape is common, and in society as a whole. Here rape is a sign of dominance and power, just as it is when men rape women.

Castration is a form of sexual violence that is aimed exclusively at men, and refers to the surgical removal of the testicles. Human castration has a long history throughout many of the early civilizations and has primarily been used for punitive purposes, religious reasons, and to control certain categories of slaves and servants.

In the civilizations of the Mediterranean and Middle East, for instance, as well as in China and Medieval Europe, castration was often used as a punishment for rape, homosexuality, or adultery. In more modern times, the Nazis sometimes used castration as a punishment and as a way of controlling the reproduction of "unfit" populations.

Castration has also been used throughout history during wartime; invading armies would castrate either their captives or the corpses of the defeated, in order to demonstrate their victory over the conquered people, as a form of ethnic cleansing, and sometimes as a method of torture; castration of men was often used alongside of the rape of women during war. This has been seen in ancient Persia, Egypt, Assyria, Ethiopia, and among the ancient Hebrews, as well as among the Normans, the Chinese, and in modern times, the Vietcong were rumored to have castrated prisoners and dissidents, and the Janjaweed in the ongoing Sudanese conflict castrate men and rape women.

Also found only in stratified societies is the use of castrated men – often prisoners of war – as slaves and servants. In societies in which elite men kept multiple wives, such as throughout the Middle East, castrated men, known as **eunuchs**, were used to guard those women. Eunuchs were preferred as harem guards because one of the side effects of castration, especially when it is performed prior to puberty, is the loss of sexual appetite. (Although some eunuchs could still have and enjoy sex, making them popular, and sterile, sexual partners for the women.) Other societies, such as ancient Rome, Egypt, and the Incan Empire also castrated slaves,

mapping difference onto bodies

FIGURE 8.3 Toronto SlutWalk, May 2012. Photo courtesy of Loretta Lime, via Wikimedia Commons: http://commons.wikimedia.org/wiki/File:Slutwalk_Toronto_May_2012_(1).jpg.

as a way to make those servants more docile, as well as to prevent them from having sexual relations with female members of the household.

Castration has been used in the West as well. During the Victorian era, men were sometimes castrated (as women sometimes had their clitorises removed) as a "cure" for homosexuality. Castration was also used in this way in Nazi Germany.

As we have seen in this chapter, sex is much more complicated than many of us give it credit for. Sex may be natural – that's why we use the phrase "birds and bees" when parents discuss it with their young children – but it is far from simple, and the degree to which society and culture play a role in shaping it is enormous.

Interesting issues: the Toronto SlutWalk

In 2011, at a York University Law School event, a police officer spoke to the students on crime prevention. During his talk, he suggested that for women to avoid being raped, they should "avoid dressing like sluts." His statement provoked outrage among the women on campus, and, as his comments were publicized, around the world, because they were seen as an example of blaming women – their clothing, their bodies, and their behavior – for men raping them. As a response, a number of the students at York decided to hold what became known as a SlutWalk on April 3, 2011. Thousands of women gathered at Queen's Park in Toronto, many dressed in explicitly provocative clothing, and marched to police headquarters. Other slutwalks were held in other areas of the world, and have been held in cities since that time. While feminists around the world have embraced the slutwalk, some have not been in favor of reclaiming the word slut because of its very nature as a male-defined term for female sexuality.

Key terms

Age-Structured Homosexuality

Ambiguous Genitalia

BDSM

Boston Marriages

Castration

Eunuch

Fetishes

Gay Gene

Gender Dysphoria

Gender Identity Disorder

Gender-Structured Homosexuality

Homologous Organs

Intersex Society of North America

Kathoey

Rape-Prone Culture

Ritualistic Homosexuality

Sex Reassignment Surgery

Sex Reassignment Therapy

Sexual Double Standard

Further reading

Butler, Judith. (1993). *Bodies that Matter: On the Discursive Limits of "Sex."* New York: Routledge.

D'Emilio, John and Freedman, Estelle B. (1997). *Intimate Matters: A History of Sexuality in America*, 2nd edn. Chicago, IL: University of Chicago Press.

Dreger, Alice Domurat. (1998). *Hermaphrodites and the Medical Invention of Sex.* Cambridge, MA: Harvard University Press.

Fausto-Sterling, Anne. (2000). *Sexing the Body: Gender Politics and the Construction of Sexuality.* New York: Basic Books.

Foucault, M. (1980b). *The History of Sexuality: Volume I, An Introduction.* New York: Pantheon Books.

Gilman, Sander. (1989). *Sexuality: An Illustrated History: Representing the Sexual Machine and Culture from the Middle Ages to the Age of AIDS.* New York: Wiley.

Herdt, Gilbert. (1994). *Third Sex, Third Gender: Beyond Sexual Dimorphism in Culture and History.* New York: Zone Books.

chapter 9

Classed Bodies

One of the most influential American television shows of all time was *Roseanne*, produced by and starring comedienne Roseanne Barr. It ran from 1988 to 1997 and was one of the few TV series that featured a realistic working-class family, living in a crowded and somewhat unkempt home, with financial and personal struggles. While such TV shows once existed on television (think of the *Honeymooners*, from the 1950s, or *All in the Family*, in the 1970s), they were largely replaced by sitcoms focused on middle-class and upper-class families. Today, it's difficult to imagine watching a television show that does not feature young, gorgeous actors and actresses in the most glamorous fashions and living in beautiful homes or New York City apartments. The Conners were far from anyone you can see today on *Grey's Anatomy*, *Revenge*, *Gossip Girl*, *Modern Family*, or *Pretty Little Liars*. In fact, they were poor, blue collar, lived in a run-down house, did not dress well, and were, quite visibly, fat.

In fact, the weight of Dan (played by John Goodman) and Roseanne Conner was one of the most noteworthy things about the show, and remains notable today. The only other television show in recent years to feature main characters who are overweight is *Mike and Molly*, and the weight of those characters is, as with *Roseanne*, one of the most salient and controversial parts of the show, in part because it remains so rare to see fat people on television. But another reason why Roseanne and Dan's weight was so central to their show was because of the way that it visibly represented their working-class, and blue-collar, positions.

This chapter addresses the ways in which class position is inscribed on bodies. Why would weight, for example, be an indicator of class? And what are some other ways in which class is embodied within us?

How does class shape the body?

In Chapter 1, we discussed the ways that the society and culture shape the body, and in subsequent chapters we covered the ways in which gender, sexuality, health and disease, and other factors are embodied. One of the theoretical concepts that help us to understand this is **habitus**. The term was invented by sociologist Marcel Mauss in an article called "Techniques of the Body" (1979) to refer to how society, through social and cultural practices, is inscribed on the bodies of its members. Later, sociologist Pierre Bourdieu expanded on this idea in his influential book *Distinction: A Social Critique of the Judgement of Taste* (1984). The term, as it's been used by Bourdieu and others, refers to how one's values, habits, taste, and lifestyle are acquired through life experiences, and become firmly entrenched as part of one's culture. These practices and values are then found in and on the body, through bodily habits, skills, and tastes that are shared by a social group. Even things like body posture, body odor, and the manifestation of disease are shared among, and socialized into, social groups. For Bourdieu, habitus refers to the ways that the body "has incorporated the immanent structures of a world" and that in turn structures perception and action (Bourdieu, 1998: 81).

Class is one of the major ways in which we develop habitus. In fact, Karl Marx was the first to suggest that bodies are different, and what makes them different is the type of labor that they do. *Which* body we are discussing matters. Is it the body that works in the factory, that toils in the fields, or that writes out the paychecks? Growing up poor exposes us to vastly different foods, clothing choices, toxins, and illnesses than the rich, for example, might be exposed to. So not only would the rich and the poor embody those class differences in different ways, but those differences would be valued differently as well. Habitus carries symbolic power, just as eating hand-crafted sushi is more symbolically valuable than eating at KFC or McDonald's.

Bourdieu writes of a "universe of class bodies which . . . tend to reproduce in its specific logic the universe of the social structure" (1984: 193). The differences between these "class bodies," according to Bourdieu, is expressed via the differential tastes, appearance, habits, and lifestyles of each. Because members of each class operate from a different habitus, or internalized form of class condition which informs the ways that one inhabits one's body, it is to be expected that their tastes in clothing, food, or sports will differ. Bourdieu's claim that "the body is the most indisputable materialization of class taste" (ibid.: 190) provides a context for our own understanding, in this text, of how the body is shaped by class. In addition, Bourdieu contrasts middle-class and working-class bodies, with the bourgeois body being one without dirt, which provides no challenge to the

mapping difference onto bodies

FIGURE 9.1 Homeless men in Robinson Park, Albuquerque. Photo courtesy of Tom Young.

dominant social order, unlike the working-class body which threatens the social order.

Another major theorist whose work is relevant here is Mikhail Bakhtin. Bakhtin (1984) writes of the relationship between bodies and social classes, and bodily parts and class, with the "classical" body – i.e., the middle-class body – being a refined, laminated, orifice-less body, which lacks the physicality of the working-class body. His work has also informed the work of a number of contemporary studies which deal with the difference between lower-class and upper-class bodies (Stallybrass and White 1986; Fiske 1989; Kipnis 1992). Sociologist Norbert Elias, too, looks at the transformation of social practices through the invention of manners in the upper class, by which standards of privacy, shame, and disgust are transformed.

Media studies scholar Laura Kipnis, for example, in her work on pornography, focuses on how class constructs the pornographic body. She borrows heavily from Mikhail Bakhtin's discussion of the homology between the lower bodily stratum and the lower social classes (as represented in the work of François Rabelais), such that the body becomes a privileged trope of the lower social classes, and through which bodily grossness operates as a critique of dominant ideology. In her reading of *Hustler,* she finds a form of resistance by the working class to middle-class notions about the body. *Hustler*, unlike *Playboy*, is filled with models whose bodies are not airbrushed, and regular men can send in rough-looking photos of their wives or girlfriends for the magazine's "Beaver Hunt" section. In *Hustler*, women are

classed bodies

photographed having interracial sex, sex with dwarves, and engaged in other kinds of boundary-pushing behavior, and the cartoons are not just sexual, but utilize bodily grossness like feces and urine. In addition, their cartoons satirize politicians, conservative public figures, and even the Pope. *Hustler*, then, operates to give working-class readers a way to not only achieve pleasure but, at the same time, to criticize the upper classes.

Another example of how working-class pleasures can challenge the upper classes can be seen in the way that some working-class activities are suppressed, as discussed by media scholar John Fiske. Just as pornography, and in particular the in-your-face kind of pornography embodied by *Hustler*, has long been subject to a variety of social controls (in fact Larry Flynt, the founder of *Hustler*, has been charged numerous times with violating anti-obscenity laws), other activities favored by the poor are often criminalized, while those favored by the wealthy are not. What Fiske calls the working classes' "evasive pleasures," like cockfighting, soccer games, and wrestling, are either spurned by, controlled by, or criminalized by, the middle class.

But if the body has class inscribed on it, just as it does gender, sexuality, or race, it also, according to Foucault, can be a site of resistance, or **counter-inscription**, as people can, and do, mark their own bodies. The working classes, then, can inscribe their own, oppositional values onto their bodies. Sociologist and cultural studies critic Angela McRobbie, in her work on female working-class subcultures (1991), demonstrated that working-class girls in England used what she called the most despised signs of femininity – clothes, makeup, and sexuality – to disrupt the middle-class ordering of the school. Another example is professional wrestling, which is marked by grotesquely huge men and overly dramatic theatrics. But this excessiveness is liberatory for the working-class men (and women) who enjoy the sport. In fact, body-building is an example of how notions of class and gender intersect in interesting ways. Men who are heavily muscled are seen as more masculine than men who are not, as are men who work with their hands. Middle-class men who work in offices, on the other hand, are seen by some in the working class as lacking masculinity. In fact, one of the reasons that professional wrestling is so popular among working-class men today may be that the archetypical working-class male body is undervalued in post-industrial America.

Dirty jobs and clean jobs

In 2005, the Discovery Channel began airing a new television show called *Dirty Jobs*, in which host Mike Rowe takes on dirty, disgusting, or dangerous jobs. The show is entertaining for viewers because most of us cannot imagine doing the kinds of jobs that the show highlights. Some of the jobs featured on the series included pest extermination, pig farming, garbage

mapping difference onto bodies

collecting, septic tank cleaning, bat guano collecting, bridge painting, road kill collecting, hot tar roofing, coal mining, and turkey inseminating. What links all of these jobs, besides the obvious fact that they are dirty, is the fact that the vast majority of them are working-class jobs. In the opening to each episode, Rowe alludes to this by saying,

> My name's Mike Rowe, and this is my job. I explore the country looking for people who are not afraid to get dirty — hard-working men and women who earn an honest living doing the kinds of jobs that make civilized life possible for the rest of us. Now, get ready to get dirty.

In fact, this is one of the primary distinctions between what we call "blue-collar" and "white-collar" jobs. Blue-collar jobs are jobs performed by members of the working class which involve manual labor. The jobs are physical, often demanding, and can be both dirty and dangerous. They involve more workplace accidents, more environmental toxins and fumes, and shortened life expectancy. They are called "blue collar" because of the blue coveralls that are often worn in many of these jobs. White-collar jobs, on the other hand, are those which often require a college education and which demand mental, rather than physical, skills. They are cleaner, safer, and involve no physical activity whatsoever.

The jobs featured in *Dirty Jobs* are dirty, for sure, and most middle-class Americans would never even consider doing them. When we look back in time, however, the working poor in Medieval Europe were forced to take on far worse jobs, like "gong farming," which referred to the activity of cleaning human waste from privies and cesspits, executioners, rat catchers, and those who were tasked with burying those who died of the plague.

Of course in many places today, there are still horrible jobs that must be done, and those jobs are performed by the most marginalized people in those societies. Often called **untouchables**, because they are considered less pure than other members of the society, these are the people who must engage in the jobs that are the most disgusting. **Dalits**, for example, the untouchable caste group in India, are responsible for handling corpses, cleaning human waste, skinning animal carcasses, and executing criminals. Because these activities are so polluting, the bodies of Dalits themselves are considered impure, which is why they are segregated from other members of Indian society and forbidden from sharing food, wells, or even temple space or burial grounds with them.

In most cultures, cleaning houses is a job that is both dirty and performed by the lowest members of society. In the United States, as in so many places, domestic workers are both racialized and gendered; in the United States, African-American and Latina women have long made up the majority of domestic workers, whose work requires them to clean other people's homes, raise other people's babies, and prepare other people's food. In the case of live-in housekeepers and nannies, the work is not just physically demanding, but isolating and demeaning, as the women often have no privacy, no time to themselves, and no respect.

Writer Barbara Ehrenreich, in a year-long experiment, decided to see what it was like to work minimum-wage jobs. She put aside her middle-class lifestyle, her savings account, her health insurance, and her college education, and set out to see what it was like to live among the working poor, an experience she documented in her book *Nickel and Dimed: On Not Getting By in America* (2001). In a series of low-paid women's jobs, one thing that she noted was how physically demanding they were. She wrote, for example, of her job as a maid:

> Ours is a world of pain – managed by Excedrin and Advil, compensated for with cigarettes, and, in one or two cases, and then only on the weekends, with booze. Do the owners have any idea of the misery that goes into rendering their homes motel-perfect?
>
> (2001: 89)

Pink-collar bodies

Pink-collar jobs are service jobs that are performed primarily by women. They tend to involve little physical activity, but, because they feature customer service, they involve what sociologists call **emotional labor**, in which workers are expected to display certain emotions as part of their job: workers must appear cheerful, helpful, and delighted to assist the customer. Dress and appearance codes, especially as they apply to female workers, are another way in which the demands and standards of the workplace are inscribed onto the body. Flight attendants, once called stewardesses (and once exclusively young, unmarried, and female), have long been subject to strict appearance codes, in which their weight, hairstyles, jewelry, and makeup are scrutinized by management. In addition, for years, non-white and working-class women could not get hired as flight attendants because their hair and makeup norms were not acceptable to the airlines. Hooters waitresses, too, are expected not only to be cheerful (even in the face of blatant sexual harassment) to customers, but they must maintain slim figures, and dress in revealing clothing to show off their "hooters" and to appeal to male customers.

Other pink-collar jobs involve what can be called **body labor.** For instance, women's studies scholar Miliann Kang (2010) has written about Korean manicurists, who must display the correct emotions to their clients – generally to make the customers feel better about themselves – and who must also attend to the physical bodies of their customers. Without both high-quality emotional and body labor, which are geared towards pleasing the white middle-class or upper-class client, the working-class Korean worker will not earn repeat business or tips. Kang shows that when the client is African-American, however, the type of emotional and body labor differs; the worker must show the client respect and also must demonstrate a higher level of artistry in terms of their nail work.

In fact, in many jobs, the more physical or manual labor that is involved, the more valuable the finished product is to the consumer. Having a dress, or shoes, made by machine is never as valuable or as valued as a dress or a pair of shoes made by hand. In fashion, *haute couture* refers to clothing that is not only hand-made, but custom-made for a specific client. Seamstresses, employed by the designer, may hand-sew thousands of beads onto a single dress. It's the knowledge of that human toil that both elevates the value of the dress and brings so much satisfaction to the wearer.

Gender and class, as well as race, intersect in other ways as well. During slavery in the United States, African women labored alongside African men in the fields, and lighter skinned African women labored in the home, doing the domestic work that the white women oversaw. These lighter skinned African women also raised white women's babies. With the end of slavery and the Industrial Revolution, white and black women, and women of the upper and lower classes, continued to experience labor very differently. On the one hand, the **cult of domesticity** emerged which asserted that women's true nature forces them to stay home and raise children. This ideology worked well for upper-class, and many middle-class, white women, whose husbands were paid a **family wage** so that their wives could stay home. But working-class and poor women did not have this luxury, and continued to work in the fields, as domestic servants, and in the factories in the emerging industrial period. Not only were black men paid less than white men because of discrimination, but white men were specifically paid a higher wage to allow for white women to stay at home.

Consumption, class, and the body

Another way in which class shapes the body is via consumption practices. What we put into our bodies – whether food, alcohol, tobacco, or other drugs – is first shaped by capitalism, second, it is shaped by class, and third, it reinforces the differences between our bodies in terms of class.

Mike Featherstone, in an essay called "The Body in Consumer Culture" (1991), points out how in post-industrial capitalist culture there are now two bodies: the inner body, which we associate with health, and the outer body, which we associate with appearance and social relationships. "Within consumer culture, the inner and the outer body become conjoined: the prime purpose of the maintenance of the inner body becomes the enhance-ment of the appearance of the outer body" (1991: 171). As the demand for consumer products becomes more important, and satisfying desires, rather than needs, becomes all-important, consumption becomes about managing one's appearance in order to control for imperfections and create "happiness." In addition, health is no longer about warding off the infectious diseases of the past; now it's about warding off aging and presenting a youthful appearance, so for the middle and upper classes, a healthy body is a youthful, slim, and beautiful body.

Chapter 11 will discuss the many issues surrounding body size. One feature of body size today (as opposed to, say, a hundred years ago) is that the poorest people are often the fattest, while the wealthiest people are often the thinnest. While it was once the case that wealthy people were fatter because they had more access to food, and to rich, fatty foods, today, poor people are the fattest, both in the developed world, and in some developing countries as well. Especially in wealthy nations where fast food is easily available and, thanks to government subsidies, very inexpensive, the poor and the working classes eat the least nutritious, and yet most fattening, foods.

At an American McDonald's, you can buy lunch – a double quarter pounder with cheese, a large French fries, and a large Coke – for less than $10, but that lunch will include 1,550 calories – that's about what a 130-pound woman should eat per day, according to most American weight charts. Taco Bell is even cheaper; for less than $5, you can get a beefy 5-layer burrito, a cheesy gordita taco, a chicken quesadilla and a Coke, which will run you 1,870 calories! On the other hand, a healthy salad made up of organic greens and locally grown vegetables – which is not available at any fast food restaurant – will cost much more, and will have far fewer calories.

On top of that, many poor and working-class Americans live in what are called **food deserts**, where grocery stores are rare, and where food is often purchased in small convenience stores, gas stations, or liquor stores. But the poorer the neighborhood, the easier it will be to find fast food restaurants.

One of the results of the poor quality of the food available to the poor and working classes is the high rates of diabetes in those communities. Nursing Professor Claudia Chaufan (2009) has conducted research on medical accounts of type 2 diabetes, and found that there is very little discussion of poverty in those articles. Instead, most medical articles focus on the personal or cultural habits of the patients, while ignoring the role that poverty plays in those habits. One result of this way of framing diabetes, according to Chaufan, is that health policy continues to ignore the role that class and poverty plays in diet and health.

The poor and the working class also tend to consume other unhealthy substances. Smoking (or chewing) tobacco is far more common among the poor today than among the middle classes, who largely gave up smoking

mapping difference onto bodies

FIGURE 9.2 Taco Bell meal. Photo courtesy of Tom Young.

thanks to the anti-smoking health messages of the last few decades. Even though most Westerners now know about the negative health impacts of smoking, it remains a persistent habit among the poor and working classes. One reason why smoking is more common among the poor is because it's a relatively inexpensive way of dealing with stress. Writer Barbara Ehrenreich once suggested that lower classes continue to smoke because it's one of the few ways that they can control their personal space and carve out a little bit of time for themselves. In *Nickel and Dimed*, she writes of blue-collar workers, "because work is what you do for others, smoking is what you do for yourself" (2001: 31). She continues to say that it's as if "in the American workplace, the only thing people have to call their own is the tumors they are nourishing and the spare moments they devote to feeding them" (ibid.).

Interestingly, alcohol is positively correlated with social class. In other words, the higher one is on the socio-economic scale, the more likely they are to drink. On the other hand, binge drinking is more common among working-class and lower-class members, and in fact mortality rates from cirrhosis of the liver are higher among the poor. So while the upper classes may drink more as a form of social lubrication, the working classes and poor probably do so more to deal with the stresses of the day, and thus do so in far greater quantities.

In terms of other drugs, some, such as powdered cocaine, are rare among the poor, because of their expense, while others, like crack cocaine, are much more common among the poor. In the United States, drug policies

classed bodies

have been crafted with these differences in mind; until 2010, being caught with five grams of crack meant that one would get a mandatory five-year minimum sentence – the same sentence given to someone caught with 500 grams of powdered cocaine. Because the person caught with 500 grams of powder, which is far too much for personal consumption, was obviously selling that cocaine, that means that a crack user got the same prison sentence as a cocaine dealer. On top of the obviously biased sentencing law, middle- and upper-class drug users (or dealers) often do no prison time at all, and are instead allowed to enter a drug rehabilitation facility.

Ironically, there was once a time that working people were actually *given* drugs. When the Spanish colonized Peru in the mid-sixteenth century, they found that the Incas chewed the coca leaf, a mildly intoxicating plant (which is the basis for cocaine) used to alleviate hunger, stem the symptoms of altitude sickness, and increase focus and energy. The Spanish first banned the practice of coca chewing, but once they realized that the native people, whom they had enslaved, could work in the mines and the fields more efficiently when chewing coca, they quickly reversed the ban and encouraged its consumption. In the United States, in the late nineteenth century, cocaine was once given to African-American dock workers and fieldworkers by their employers because it made them work harder.

Adorning the classed body: sumptuary laws

Sumptuary laws are laws that restrict certain items of clothing, food, or makeup to certain groups of people. They are typically used to maintain class distinctions in stratified societies by restricting luxury items to elite classes, or forcing the poor or marginalized citizens to wear identifying colors or clothing. They were common in Europe from the thirteenth century into the eighteenth century, and were found in Imperial China and Japan, pre-colonial Africa, and colonial America.

One of the earliest documented sumptuary laws dates from the third century BCE in Rome, and restricted the amount of gold that women could wear and the color of their tunics. In ancient Egypt, for example, only elites could wear dyed, adorned, or otherwise decorated sandals, and only the Pharoah and members of his court could wear gold or jeweled sandals. Greek citizens were allowed to wear sandals decorated with specific adornments, which were prohibited for non-citizens. Roman law dictated the type and color of shoe that could be worn by the classes; free men wore pale colors, senators wore black while Emperors wore red shoes and boots encrusted with precious stones. In addition, only high-status Roman women could adorn their shoes with gold or jewels.

One reason for laws which aim to restrict the wearing of certain clothing and shoes is that governments (and the Church in Medieval Europe) often

mapping difference onto bodies

FIGURE 9.3 Yellow badge Star of David called "Judenstern." Part of the exhibition in the Jewish Museum Westphalia, Dorsten, Germany. The wording is the German word for Jew (*Jude*), written in mock-Hebrew script. Photo courtesy of Daniel Ullrich, via Wikimedia Commons: http://commons.wikimedia.org/wiki/File:Judenstern_JMW.jpg.

saw excessive spending on lavish fabrics to be both a sign of moral decay and vanity, but also a waste of money. The English in particular worried that the excessive spending on foreign materials like silk was problematic for society, and for the local economy. Another reason for these laws is that prices could be regulated by establishing restrictions on the amount of fabric that could be used in a product. Finally, the laws ensured that the lower classes did not appear to be striving to be "above their station." Of special concern, evidently, was that prosperous merchants or craftsmen might be able to dress in clothing finer than members of the nobility.

Sumptuary laws were also used to set apart stigmatized classes of citizens. Jews in Medieval Europe, for example, once had to wear a cone-shaped hat called a *Judenhat,* and under Nazi rule were required to wear the yellow Star of David on their clothing. On the other hand, some ethnic groups were prohibited from wearing items of clothing or hairstyles that were

classed bodies

distinctive to their ethnicity; the Chinese in San Francisco, for example, were once prohibited from wearing their hair in top knots. Prostitutes in most cultures were also required to wear specific colors or fabrics of clothing as well as specific types of footwear. English prostitutes had to wear a striped hood, for example. In some countries, prostitutes began wearing shoes that were prohibited to members of other classes: precariously high wooden sandals, called *chopines* in Italy or *geta* in Japan, were worn by high-class courtesans and advertised those women's sexual services.

Laws prohibiting the consumption of alcohol or other drugs were sumptuary laws as well, and were often aimed at particular social groups. For instance, before the passage of the Volstead Act in 1920, prohibiting the sale and production of alcohol in the United States, a number of municipalities had already banned the sale of alcohol to Native Americans, Hispanics, and African-Americans. On the federal level, Senator Henry Cabot Lodge proposed a law banning the sale of liquor and opiates – then legal – to the "uncivilized races." While it did not pass, the eventual criminalization of marijuana, cocaine, and opiates in the United States was driven in part by racist impulses, as the use of those drugs – opium smoking among Chinese-Americans, marijuana smoking by Mexican-Americans, and cocaine use by African-Americans – spurred a media hysteria that led to their criminalization.

Interesting issues: shoes and class

Footwear, or the lack thereof, indicates the class of the wearer. For example, large feet are not only seen as unfeminine but they signify peasants and other people who have to work for a living, since upper class women could wear shoes that are smaller than their feet, since they do not need to work (or even walk) in such painful shoes. And going barefoot signifies poverty and a lack of opportunity. Removing one's shoes in the presence of a social superior is a practice found in a variety of cultures, such as ancient Egypt and some African kingdoms.

In Europe, from the early Middle Ages through today, elites have always worn very different shoes from commoners, and shoes, like clothing, have been a simple way to note one's class status. As shoe styles multiplied in the late Middle Ages and the Renaissance, elites had more styles to choose from while commoners continued to wear simple shoes. Poulaines, which were shoes with extremely long toes, became fashionable among European noblemen in the fourteenth century, and were confined to elites by legislation which restricted very long toes only to the upper classes, although, given their unusual shape, they could not have been worn by working people regardless of the laws. Other extraordinary shoes arose during the Renaissance, such as extravagantly decorated square-toed shoes with toes as wide as eight or nine inches, and chopines, high platform mules with soles as high as 20 and 30 inches. Both were only worn by elites, and chopines

mapping difference onto bodies

in particular became a symbol of status, as those women who wore them were obviously not working women, and often had to have servants help them to walk or stand. Physical dependency thus becomes associated with wealth and status, and become very desirable attributes for upper-class women. High heels, which developed in Europe the seventeenth century, were yet another footwear innovation that separated the nobility from working men and women. As industrialism influenced the manufacture of shoes, shoes became cheaper to produce and more widely available to members of all classes in Europe and America, reducing the class distinctions of footwear, although elites continue to purchase custom-made shoes rather than buy ready-to-wear shoes. Because of intense competition among shoemakers and the influence of the fashion industry, today styles in footwear change throughout the year, forcing those who want to appear fashionable to buy new shoes often. Today, high-fashion shoes and some athletic brands are so expensive that it would appear that only the elite could afford them. Yet even so many poor people today buy expensive brand-name athletic shoes in order to achieve the status associated with the brand, and, thanks to the proliferation of black-market counterfeit shoes and other accessories, many people buy imitation brand-name shoes.

The invisibility of poor bodies

In countries dominated by the middle class, and controlled by the upper class, like the United States, the poor are relatively invisible. They live in inner-city ghettos or rural slums that the middle and upper classes never visit. Especially with the rise of suburbanization after World War II, but especially since the 1960s, the middle class have largely abandoned America's biggest cities, leaving crumbling infrastructures, few jobs, financial disinvestment, high crime rates, health problems (especially poverty-related diseases like asthma, tuberculosis, AIDS, infant mortality, and diabetes), and a concentration of the poor people and people of color in the cities.

When the middle class do return to the cities, gentrifying neighborhoods, it has not reduced segregation. Instead, the poor are pushed out of those neighborhoods where the white middle class settle, and into worse neighborhoods where they continue to lack access to basic resources like health, good food, and safety that the middle class access. Even transportation is less available to the poor, as bus stops are often placed in inconvenient locations so that the middle class who use the shopping malls do not have to see the poor getting on and off of buses.

The poor are virtually absent from popular culture as well, with the notable exception of television shows like COPS which showcase their criminal activities. With the exception of Roseanne in the 1980s, we cannot watch a sitcom or a television drama focused around a poor or working-class family. (Great Britain has long been an exception to this rule.) One of the reasons why we only see middle- and upper-class people on television today has to do with media ownership in Hollywood. Today, more and more of American (and international) mass media is owned by fewer and fewer, very large corporations. The overwhelming majority of the world's television stations, movie studios, radio stations, cable and satellite systems, magazine and book publishers, music producers, and TV producers are controlled by about 50 companies. Of those, nine companies control the vast lion's share, especially in the United States. The result of this monopolization is that the content that we see is limited and is aimed at the widest possible audience. In addition, because all content has to be paid for by advertising, content needs to appeal to audiences with funds to spend on purchasing consumer items. If television shows, for example, featured the poor or working classes, then presumably the audience for those shows would be made up at least in part by those classes, and they would not have the funds to buy many consumer products. Instead, if shows are aimed at middle-class or upper-class viewers, then advertisers could advertise products like cars, jewelry, or other expensive consumer items. In addition, *Roseanne* was controversial because the show criticized the capitalist system which underlies the entire mass media. That type of criticism simply would not be possible today.

Even on the news, the coverage of the poor in the United States is very limited. The result of that is that most people are under the impression that poverty does not really exist in the United States. When the poor are seen, it's often in the context of criminal activity, as on *COPS*, which gives the impression that the poor are criminals or drug addicts, they are undeserving, or at the very least they live in filthy neighborhoods which are an eyesore. Instead, the wealthy are venerated and their values and activities emulated, even when in reality they are not really like most people at all.

In Chapter 10, we will look at another type of body that is represented more frequently in popular culture than other bodies: beautiful bodies. We will also see that whether one is beautiful or ugly is linked fairly closely to one's class position, because beauty is a commodity that is both valuable to purchase and carries economic value within it.

Interesting issues: white trash

*According to scholars Matt Wray and Analee Newitz (1997), the term **white trash** comes from the U.S. Eugenics Records Office which produced a number of Eugenic Family Studies which tried to demonstrate that rural poor whites were genetically defective, destined to continue to reproduce "imbeciles" and criminals in perpetuity. These studies led to the inclusion of such poor whites in the forced sterilization policies that had previously targeted people of color and the physically and mentally disabled, and also led to the call to end social welfare programs*

mapping difference onto bodies

for them, since they were clearly beyond any help. Today, the term white trash continues to be utilized, not necessarily within the realms of social policy, but as a social marker to denote categories of people who embody a set of easily recognizable stereotypes: rural, ignorant, poor, ill-mannered, and often fat. We continue to use this term because it makes the rest of us feel superior; even if we ourselves our poor, or uneducated, or lacking in some way, at least we're not white trash. The stigma associated with the concept helps explain the popularity of the show Here Comes Honey Boo Boo, *the reality show devoted to the family of Honey Boo Boo, a poor beauty pageant contestant whose family engages in practices like dumpster diving, roadkill eating, tobacco chewing, mud wrestling, and ATV riding. We watch the show because the family entertains us, but also horrifies us, and Americans of all races and classes – except those who are white trash – can come together with a sense of unity: "we are not them."*

Key terms

Body Labor	Food Deserts
Cult of Domesticity	Habitus
Counter-Inscription	Sumptuary Laws
Dalits	Untouchables
Emotional Labor	White Trash
Family Wage	

Further reading

Bourdieu, Pierre. (1984). *Distinction: A Social Critique of the Judgement of Taste*. Cambridge, MA: Harvard University Press.

Ehrenreich, Barbara. (2001). *Nickel and Dimed: On (Not) Getting By in America*. New York: Metropolitan Books.

Wray, Matt and Newitz, Analee, (eds). (1997). *White Trash: Race and Class in America*. New York: Routledge.

PART IV

Bodies and Privilege

chapter 10

Beautiful Bodies

In the 1980s and early 1990s, Michael Jackson was known as the King of Pop. According to the *Guinness Book of World Records*, he was the most successful entertainer ever, with the best-selling album of all time (1982's *Thriller*), hundreds of awards (including 13 Grammies), 13 number one singles, and 750 million records sold worldwide.

Yet by the time he died in 2009, he was known by many as a freak, thanks to his history of cosmetic surgeries, which left him looking sickly and bizarre. Jackson was obsessed with his appearance, and reportedly had multiple surgeries on his nose, cheek bones, chin, jaw, lips, eyebrows, and skin. It was said that some of this obsession developed when he was a young boy, when his father repeatedly insulted his appearance, telling him, for example, that he had a big nose. Sadly, his enormous talent was largely overshadowed in his later years by his bizarre appearance (as well as the allegations of child abuse leveled against him).

Why would such a brilliant, talented – and, most would say, handsome – man expend so much money, pain, and effort into changing his appearance? In this chapter, we will look at the importance of beauty, and how beauty is achieved. We will also attempt to answer questions regarding beauty: Is beauty in the eyes of the beholder? Or do standards of beauty stem from culture, and thus are both historically and culturally contingent? Or is beauty universal, stemming from the evolutionary imperative to reproduce? The reality is that while Michael Jackson embodies one of the more extreme examples of the desire to improve one's appearance, for the most part it is women who work, and are expected to work, to alter their appearance. Feminist scholar Andrea Dworkin once wrote, "In our culture not one part of a woman's body is left untouched, unaltered . . . From head to toe, every feature of a woman's face, every section of her body, is subject to modification" (1974: 113–14).

The science of beauty

If beauty is universal – in other words, according to evolutionary psychologists, all cultures have, more or less, the same concept of what is beautiful – then beauty should have developed as an evolutionary adaption. It should help the species to survive. From an evolutionary perspective, there are a number of physical features that both men and women should be programmed to find beautiful. This includes clean, unblemished skin, thick shiny hair, and symmetrical faces. This is because these features should indicate health and good genes. In addition, faces that are average, rather than extreme, tend to be ranked most attractive in cross-cultural studies; average features are considered beautiful because they too signify good health and good genes. On the other hand, facial features that are unusual are often judged more beautiful than those that are not; rarity then can often indicate beauty. Unusual facial features are certainly noticed more often than those that are average.

In addition to health and good genes, female beauty is a combination of features that indicate youth and fertility. In that sense, beauty is temporary – even the most beautiful woman will become old, losing what once made her beautiful. In addition, according to evolutionary theory, men are programmed to find women attractive with high cheekbones, full lips and narrow jaws because those features signify low testosterone and high estrogen, which are indicators of fertility. Large eyes, too, signal youth, and thus fertility. During the sixteenth and seventeenth centuries, for example, European women put eye drops from the belladonna plant (*bella donna* means "beautiful lady" in Italian) into their eyes to make their retinas appear larger; today, it is popular in South Korea to wear "big eye contacts" to make the eyes appear larger. And it was popular in Greece, Persia, and Rome to use the powdered form of the metal antimony in the eyes to make the whites sparkle.

Since women are considered beautiful when they display a set of features that indicate youth and fertility, beautiful women display a combination of adult beauty and baby beauty. Cuteness, on the other hand, refers primarily to "baby beauty," and features a small face, big eyes, a small mouth, and a large head. Parental love is triggered by the presence of these features, which is why they are present in all mammal babies. They are also highlighted in some areas of popular culture, and especially pop culture from Japan, like **anime, manga**, and Hello Kitty, and **Ulzzang** from South Korea.

In terms of male beauty, women are thought to look for indicators of high testosterone in men's faces, such as strong jaws, heavy brows, thin lips, and broad cheekbones, which indicate both good genes as well as the propensity to attain high status. However, studies show that women who are not ovulating respond less well to a hyper-masculine face. In addition, according to such studies, women are attracted to different types of faces when they are looking for short-term, rather than long-term, relationships. Facial scars, for example, may be considered more attractive by women seeking short-term sexual relationships, although they are more commonly considered to be a sign of an untrustworthy or dangerous person. On the other hand, women may forfeit some or all of these indicators of genetic health and reproductive fitness in exchange for men with financial resources, which are necessary to help a woman to raise her offspring.

The irony is that while men and women today use birth control to ensure that women do not get pregnant, according to evolutionary scientists, those same men and women are still attracted to the visible signs of fertility and good genes in their potential mates. In addition, women in particular spend countless hours and huge amounts of money trying to make themselves appear fertile even if they have no desire to bear children at all.

Can we measure beauty from a scientific perspective? Some scientists claim that they have been able to quantify what makes a face attractive. According to this approach, there is an ideal measurement for the space between the eyes, the length of the chin, the height of the eyes, the length and width of the nose, and the width and shape of the mouth. Those men and women who possess such ideal measurements should be the individuals considered, in any society, to be the most attractive.

The Greeks especially valued faces that were symmetrical, in harmony, and in proportion. The ideal Greek face, for example, was two-thirds as wide as it was high, and it could be divided into thirds, from chin to upper lip, from upper lip to eyes, and from eyes to hairline. Greek philosopher Pythagorus, for example, felt that a mathematical concept called the **Golden Ratio** could provide the mathematical model for the most beautiful face.

Other scientists point to other fields of study to prove that the notion of beauty is not just universal, but is innate. The idea that beauty is universal is demonstrated in studies which show that men and women of many different cultures tend to assess the attractiveness of people in photos very similarly. In addition, other studies have demonstrated that infants, when presented with photos of either "unattractive" or "attractive" adults, will spend more time looking at the photos of the attractive people; in particular, they appear to like big eyes, big lips, and clear skin.

On the other hand, there is a tremendous variety in the types of features that societies around the world find beautiful, indicating that beauty may also be culturally constructed. For instance, in India, the traditional ideals

beautiful bodies

of beauty include cleanliness, the graceful use of clothing, how a woman carries herself, whether her skin and hair is well cared for, and the wearing of the **bindi** on the forehead. In many African cultures, on the other hand, unadorned skin is seen as unattractive, and only a woman whose body or face is marked through scarification would be considered beautiful – the scars are both beautiful to touch and to look at. Also popular in some African tribes were large plates inserted into the lower lip (and sometimes the upper as well), which made a woman more beautiful and marriageable. And the Himba of Namibia rub their bodies in red ochre to celebrate the fertility of earth and the life-giving qualities of blood, and which also make them quite lovely.

While the European long nose came to signify beauty around the world after colonization, people in Malaysia, the Philippines, and Indonesia, prior to colonization, considered flat noses to be the most attractive. And for hundreds of years in Japan, the ideal of female beauty was symbolized by the geisha, who wore thick white face paint, shaved her eyebrows, and painted on both thick black eyebrows and rosebud lips. Women in a variety of cultures, from Renaissance Europe to Native Americans to the Japanese, also blackened their teeth.

Whether beauty is indeed universal and innate, or whether it is entirely or partially constructed from cultural standards, beauty is important. It matters. We notice people's faces immediately upon meeting them, and what we see affects what we think about them. But no type of beauty is more important than female beauty.

Interesting issues: the Golden Ratio

The Golden Ratio (or Golden Section or Golden Mean) is a mathematical number, known as phi (which equals 1.618 . . .), derived from taking the ratio of distances in geometric figures. Specifically, it can be found by dividing a line into two parts and calculating the number that can be found when the long part is divided by the smaller part, which is equal to the length of the line divided by the long part. A Golden Rectangle, for example, is a rectangle whose side lengths each conform to the Golden Ratio, and, when a square is removed from it, the remaining rectangle continues to be a Golden Rectangle. The number is said to be found in both the pyramids at Giza and in the Parthenon in Athens. Besides architecture, proponents suggest that the Golden Ratio is found in the ideal human face. Perfect faces are faces which can be divided into a number of Golden Rectangles, all of which conform to the Golden Ratio. Everything from the distance between the eyes, the shape of the nose and teeth, and the relationship between all of the features, is taken into account. Today, the idea that the Golden Ratio can be used to scientifically map beauty is still a relevant one. Los Angeles cosmetic surgeon Stephen Marquardt revived the theory and began mapping beautiful faces, finding the Golden Ratio throughout the proportions of the ideal face; for example, he found that the ideal mouth is 1.618 times wider than the nose. He created what he called the "golden mask," a visual representation of the proportions that should be found on a beautiful face, and according to Marquardt and his supporters, that mask can be fit perfectly over any beautiful face, male or female.

The importance of female beauty

Beauty is gendered, in that not only are there different standards of beauty for men and women, but women, especially in modern society, are held to a much higher and difficult (some would say impossible) to attain standard than men, which explains the multi-billion dollar cosmetics industry, and the thousands of products available to make a woman's face appear more youthful and more beautiful.

Standards of beauty, at least in contemporary society that is dominated by advertising, were largely created by men, but men are not defined by them, because men are valued for things like wealth and status. But in cultures around the world, men view women primarily through the lens of their appearance. It is men who consume most pornography and it is men who, more importantly, produce the vast majority of all images featuring women in the media today. (One exception to this rule is found among the Wodaabe, a nomadic tribe living in Niger. The Wodaabe practice a ritual whereby men dress up in fancy clothing, apply makeup to their faces, and allow the Wodaabe women, who do not wear makeup, to judge them and decide who they will sleep with that night.)

The reality is that the standards of beauty that surround us today are unattainable by the vast majority of women. No human woman, for example, could live with the proportions of a Barbie doll – her back would be too weak to support her large breasts and her tiny waist could not hold most of her internal organs. Standards of beauty today are so unrealistic that even supermodels cannot achieve them. It's well known in the advertising industry that even the most beautiful and highly paid models' photos are heavily photoshopped before the public sees them; their waists are whittled down; their thighs are reduced; their lines are smoothed out, and, if they are too thin, their ribcages are filled out. Sometimes the photoshopping is so overdone that the results no longer even look realistically human.

Because the standard of beauty today is so unrealistic, most women can never even hope to attain it. That means that most women, no matter their educational, occupational, or familial accomplishments, are failures in the one thing – beauty – on which women are judged most harshly. The psychological effects of this failure include low self-esteem, negative body image, eating disorders, stress, and anxiety. It should not come as a surprise that one of the most popular types of television shows today are makeover shows: shows that begin with plain, overweight, or dowdy women, and transform them, through cosmetic surgery, makeup, dieting, or exercise, into beautiful "swans."

But why do we have a system that mandates conformity to an ideal that is almost impossible to attain, and that demands that women, throughout their lives, must use diet, exercise, makeup, and cosmetic surgery to appear to be as youthful and fertile as possible, regardless of one's biological age? Many feminist scholars feel that the system as it exists in modern society is enabled by economics: the diet, cosmetics, exercise, and cosmetic surgery industries are multi-billion dollar industries, and can only exist when women feel bad about themselves. Thousands of advertisements per day assault women with the message that they are not young enough, not thin enough, and not beautiful enough, and women's magazines in particular devote the vast majority of their advertising and editorial content to making women feel inadequate, so that they might buy some of the products that are advertised. And while many women are thin enough, young enough, or beautiful enough, no women will have those qualities forever. Every woman will get older, which means at some point every woman will fail. Thanks to the beauty industry, however, she can buy products to help camouflage that failure.

As women in the past few decades have experienced unprecedented levels of financial, political, and social independence and clout, they have also been assaulted by increasing numbers of images and messages about their appearance. As the messages increase and the standards of beauty became harder to attain, the numbers of eating disorders skyrocket, the diet industry balloons, cosmetic surgery rates take off, and girls' and women's self-esteem plummets. Naomi Wolf (1991) calls this the "**beauty myth:**" the unreachable cultural ideal of feminine beauty that "uses images of female beauty as a political weapon against women's advancement." Women are trapped in an endless cycle of dieting, cosmetics, and surgery to make women's bodies into what Wolf calls prisons, and which keep them from devoting their time and energy to political and social causes that would further all women – not just the beautiful ones who benefit from the current system.

Beauty derives some of its value from its rarity – if most women cannot and do not look like Angelina Jolie, then that makes her beauty all the more valuable. A corollary of this is that for women who are not naturally beautiful, the value of beauty depends in part on the high costs to achieve it. It can cost a great deal of money to pay for the beauty, diet, and hair treatments used by many women today. The result is that beauty is largely confined to the elite classes, who can afford such treatments. In addition, low-income women with natural beauty can parlay their appearance into social mobility

bodies and privilege

AVEDA
THE ART AND SCIENCE OF PURE FLOWER AND PLANT ESSENCES

thicker,
fuller hair
is yours

AVEDA

97% naturally derived* invati™ solutions for thinning hair
REDUCES HAIR LOSS BY 33%*

FIGURE 10.1 Poster advertising hair products. Photo courtesy of Tom Young.

via marriage into a higher class, or modeling or acting (which often lead to the same thing). Yet at the same time, because of the prevalence of cosmetic surgery today, more women are able to at least come close to achieving beauty, making it somewhat less rare.

The prevalence of beauty today is said to decrease men's commitment to their regular partner because there are so many beautiful women to choose from, especially in places like Los Angeles. What is known as the **"contrast effect"** makes men who are surrounded by beautiful women view their own mates as less attractive. Since, thanks to the prevalence of mass media, we are all surrounded by beautiful women, this is bad news for most women (and for the men who are unable to find the partners that they want). In addition, women who constantly see images of beautiful women also rate themselves as less attractive, leading to a drop in self-esteem. Ultimately,

FIGURE 10.2 Thin, beautiful, and photoshopped women appear on the cover of dozens of women's and men's magazines every month. Photo courtesy of the author.

according to psychologists, the overwhelming presence of beauty in our lives makes it harder for men and women to achieve satisfaction in their relationships. But for men who can afford to attract very beautiful women, the presence of those women will increase a man's status, no matter his appearance, making him even more attractive to the wider society.

Beauty also has physical costs. Many women suffer (and some die) from their attempts to achieve beauty. The skin-whitening treatments common in earlier periods (and still common in some countries today) were often carcinogenic, and cosmetic surgery, tanning, and diet pills have major health risks. Singer Kanye West's mother, Donda, for example, died in 2007 from complications from tummy tuck and breast reduction surgery. Even the wearing of high heels or corsets are associated with pain and health problems. Yet no matter how much money, time, or effort that a woman spends on her appearance, that effort must be concealed in order to maintain the fantasy that her appearance is "natural."

A few years ago, Dove, maker of soap and beauty products, produced a video called *Evolution* as part of their "Campaign for Real Beauty." In the video, a "normally" attractive woman had makeup applied to her face, had her hair styled, and then was subject to a variety of digital modifications which resulted in a face that was both more beautiful, but also more artificial, than the woman's real face. The video was made in an effort to "unveil" the efforts that go into making an average woman into a gorgeous supermodel, but yet, for the most part, most of us continue to believe that supermodels look just like they do in the magazine spreads. (On the

bodies and privilege

other hand, the campaign has also been criticized because Dove's parent company, Unilever, sells skin-whitening creams in developing countries, contributing to the continued dominance of whiteness as a measure of beauty in those regions. Some feminists also criticize the campaign because it continues to encourage the purchasing of products to improve one's appearance.)

Beauty pays

Whether beauty is biologically programmed or culturally constructed, beauty is important in human societies, and not only plays a role in whether a man or a woman achieves a mate, but in contemporary Western society beauty plays a role in how much money a person earns in their lifetime, how early they will marry, how soon they will be promoted, and whether they will experience other benefits. Attractive women will get a leg up in all of these areas, while women who fail to meet certain beauty standards find that they earn less (about 13 percent less), will get promoted less, and will get hired less often than thinner or more attractive women. They will also have less luck finding marital partners, while attractive women, on the other hand, will not only be more likely to find a partner, but will be more likely to marry into a wealthy family. Studies show that people view unattractive people unfavorably, while attractive people are thought to be smarter, happier, and better people. Strangers are also more likely to assist attractive people than non-attractive people, and attractive people are less likely to be arrested or

FIGURE 10.3 An aisle of makeup products in the grocery store. Photo courtesy of the author.

beautiful bodies

prosecuted for crimes. What scientists call the "**halo effect**" shows that, in general, beautiful people are judged by others to be smarter, more popular, and better adjusted; those with beauty have a "halo" around them. This is also a function of what others call "**lookism**:" where we judge other people by their looks, and those who do not rate high on the looks scale are treated with prejudice.

Ultimately, this becomes a self-fulfilling prophecy as beautiful people are not only thought to be successful and happy – they become happier and more successful because of how they are treated. For many people around the world today, beauty means happiness.

But what if we did not just think that beautiful people were smarter or better at their jobs? What if beauty was also correlated with internal characteristics like intelligence or good manners? This line of thinking is much more controversial, but there are some evolutionary psychologists who claim that because beauty is, at least partially, an indicator of genetic health, that beautiful people might really be healthier and perhaps even more intelligent than other people. At least one study appears to show a positive association between IQ (which itself is, according to many, a problematic way to measure intelligence) and physical attractiveness. Some evolutionary psychologists say that because intelligence and physical appearance are both measures of genetic fitness, both would increase for healthier individuals.

An alternative explanation, on the other hand, may simply be that if men select female partners on the basis of attractiveness, and women select male partners, at least in part, based on high status which *may* be linked to intelligence, that these mating patterns might lead to intelligence and beauty being linked. But of course both explanations assume, first, that intelligence and beauty are linked, and second, that intelligence is heritable. While intelligence derives at least in part on the structure of the brain, it is not yet known how much of intelligence is inherited and how much depends on development and environment.

Beautiful men

According to evolutionary theory, women judge men to be most attractive when they have symmetrical faces, average facial features, and signs of testosterone and thus fertility: strong jaws, big muscles, and tall stature. Especially when women are looking for a one-night-stand – men who have the outward signs of physical masculinity are chosen before other men. But women also select men with high status, because for women, men who can provide for their offspring are as important as men who can provide good genes to those offspring. That's why, according to evolutionary psychologists, many beautiful women end up not with handsome men, but with unattractive men who are wealthy and powerful.

bodies and privilege

FIGURE 10.4 Male mannequins in Paris. Photo courtesy of David Brooks.

But that's not the only explanation. Many women date and marry men who are not only relatively plain looking, but who lack high status as well. Women, in many cultures, simply do not judge men's appearance as harshly as men judge women's appearance. Men can be valued for a great many characteristics and achievements, while women, no matter their achievements, continue to be valued primarily for their appearance.

When it comes to men choosing men, however, it turns out that men still want beauty. Gay men tend to choose mates the way that straight men do – by focusing on appearance. In particular, strong jaws and facial hair, because they signify adult masculinity, are often heavily preferred by gay men. Just as straight men choose the most beautiful women, gay men choose the most handsome, i.e., masculine, men. Gay men also choose younger mates, just as straight men do.

Beauty pays for men too. While unattractive or overweight men are not penalized to the extent that women are in the job market, they do earn less than their more attractive counterparts – about 5 percent less.

Racialized and classed standards of beauty

Race and class are both important factors in what different cultures consider to be beautiful. In many societies, a body that signifies elite status is

beautiful bodies

considered the most beautiful. So very light skin would be considered beautiful when darker skin is a sign of working outdoors; conversely, darker skin became beautiful as wealthy people could afford to travel to warmer climates during the winter. So both Roman and Elizabethan women used makeup made from white lead on their faces to appear even lighter than they already were. Elizabethan women sometimes would allow themselves to be bled to further whiten their complexions, and in the eighteenth century, French noblewomen drew blue veins on their necks and shoulders to emphasize the whiteness of their skin.

Especially in those regions of the world that once experienced either European colonialism or slavery, people with light skin are almost always seen as more attractive than those with dark skin – even in countries where everyone has darker skin. In India, for example, higher castes are lighter skinned than the lower castes. Even today, actors and actresses in Bollywood films tend to be lighter skinned than most of the Indian population. In Eastern Asian countries as well, pale skin has typically represented nobility and status. It's not surprising, then, that skin whiteners are very popular in these countries. In the United States, women of color have also invested in skin-whitening products, not so that they could pass for white (although those with more Caucasian features sometimes could), but because going back to slavery, lighter skinned African-Americans received better privileges than darker skinned blacks. Skin whiteners were also used by darker skinned Eastern and Southern European immigrants to help them blend into mainstream American society. And in Japan, **Geishas** still use thick white face powder to give the illusion of white skin, which represents beauty and sophistication.

Even in the twentieth century, skin whiteners have been marketed which contain dangerous ingredients, like mercury and hydroquinone. While the Civil Rights and Black Pride movements made a dent in the skin-whitening industry by convincing many black women that dark skin was beautiful, skin whiteners are more popular than ever today, with hundreds of pills, soaps, creams, and lotions on the market in the United States, Asia, Latin America, Africa, and India. In Japan alone, the skin-whitening industry was worth $5.6 billion in 2001.

Another way in which non-white bodies are held to white beauty standards has to do with the eyes. Most Asian cultures now value Caucasian-looking eyes, making **blepharoplasty**, a cosmetic surgery procedure to insert a crease into the epicanthic fold, a very popular procedure in some East Asian countries today. In South Korea, where the standard of beauty means round eyes, pale skin, a sharp nose, and long legs (none of which are naturally found in Koreans), this surgery is so popular that one in ten adults have received it.

FIGURE 10.5 Women utilize a variety of devices to make themselves beautiful. Wigs on wig forms at Beauty Supply Warehouse on Telegraph Avenue, Oakland, CA. Photo courtesy of Ian Elwood.

As anthropologist Eugenia Kaw (1997) notes, women (and some men like action star Jackie Chan) who receive the surgery say that they want to have eyes that look larger, less "sleepy," and that are easier to apply makeup on. Opponents of the procedure, however, charge that its popularity is a direct result of the globalization of Western standards of beauty, which demand light skin and Caucasian facial features, and that women who undergo blepharoplasty are, at least subconsciously, trying to look white. At the very least, say critics, Asians are emulating a standard of beauty found in Asian celebrities or Japanese anime, but in both cases, the beauty being emulated is not found among the majority of the population and seems to echo the big eyes (often green or blue) seen on Caucasians.

Today, as the surgery becomes more commonplace, pressures to get the surgery are often intense, especially within Asian families. Many parents pressure their children to undergo the procedure, and as siblings and peers recover from surgery with their new round eyes, it becomes harder to resist. Those who are born with a natural "double eyelid" are seen as special, and are thanked for saving their parents money. One result is that in some countries like Korea, it is difficult to find young women who have not had the surgery. In addition, many Asians are now having surgery to make their noses longer and more pronounced, to reduce the size of the cheekbones, and even to lengthen their legs.

beautiful bodies

Interesting issues: ulzzang

Ulzzang or uljjang *means "best face" in Korean, and is a phenomenon in South Korea and in other parts of Asia (or Asian communities outside of Asia) that celebrates cuteness, fashion, and style. In particular,* ulzzang *emphasizes a specific kind of female beauty in which very large eyes are featured. An* ulzzang *is someone who has achieved popularity for her appearance, and a number of websites exist which allow users to post their photos and viewers to rank them. The* ulzzang *look takes quite a bit of work to achieve. It involves the wearing of cosmetic circle lenses, which are contact lenses which make the iris seem much larger; false eyelashes and eye makeup which further emphasizes the size of the eye, as well as pale foundation to lighten the skin. Many girls have had upper eyelid surgery to achieve the Western rounded eye, but those who have not can still achieve the look with eyelid glue or tape, which creates the appearance of a double eyelid. Because of the emphasis of this kind of beauty in South Korea, South Korean pop stars and television stars all share these physical features and are considered to be* ulzzang. Ulzzang's *characteristics are borrowed from Japanese anime, a form of animation popular since the 1960s which itself borrows from American animated characters like Betty Boop, Speed Racer, and Bambi. The large eyes and small facial features from these characters are now ubiquitous not only in anime, but in Japanese and South Korean youth culture in general.*

Manufacturing beauty: cosmetic surgery

Cosmetic surgery developed during World War I, when doctors needed to develop new techniques to repair the bodies and faces of soldiers who were wounded in the war. Today, cosmetic surgery generally refers to procedures that have been developed to repair congenital birth defects such as cleft palates, or disfigurements caused by accidents or injury, such as burns, scars, and severe body and facial trauma, as well as to those voluntary procedures which are aimed at making a person look younger or more beautiful.

Of the voluntary procedures, the most common today include tummy tucks, breast implants, breast lifts, eyelid surgery, butt implants, chemical peels, nose jobs, facelifts, chin augmentations, collagen injections, liposuction, and Botox injections. In almost all of these procedures, the aim is to make the patient – usually female – appear younger and slimmer, and therefore more beautiful. For teenagers, the most common procedures are nose jobs, liposuction, ear surgery, breast implants, and for men, breast reductions, while for seniors, the most common procedures are eyelid surgery, facelift, dermabrasion, **rhinoplasty** (nose reshaping), and forehead lifts. Cosmetic surgeries are on the rise in the United States, up 69 percent from 2000; in 2009, there were 12,494,001 cosmetic procedures performed.

Because the standard of beauty in Western society demands youth and slenderness as the ideal, it is not surprising that these procedures would be so popular with women, with 90 percent of all cosmetic surgeries being done on women. On the other hand, in recent years, the number of men seeking cosmetic surgery – including "masculine" procedures like pectoral and calve implants, and for boys, breast reduction surgery – has been increasing as well. While the United States leads the world in terms of numbers of cosmetic surgery procedures, South Korea is the leader in terms of procedures per capita, with Greece and Italy coming in at second and third. The surgeries of choice for Koreans? Blepharoplasty and rhinoplasty.

Cosmetic surgery is not typically covered by health insurance, so beauty is becoming increasingly a sign of upper-class status, as only the wealthy can afford to undergo these procedures. Furthermore, as beauty is becoming a commodity that can be purchased by the wealthy, men and women whose faces and bodies are not naturally beautiful, but who cannot afford to change their appearance, find themselves at a disadvantage, given the preferential treatment that the genetically and surgically endowed receive in most every aspect of social and economic life. Those who can, on the other hand, afford cosmetic surgery rarely try to hide it anymore. It's becoming a further sign of status for wealthy women to publicly flaunt their brand new eyes, noses, lips, or faces.

And while it was at one time the case that only older women underwent facelifts and other procedures to make them appear younger, young women are now getting Botox injections as well as lip plumping procedures at very early ages, in order to "prevent" aging. Indeed, the prevalence of cosmetic surgery in the United States today indicates an increasing need to deny the inevitable; as the physical signs of aging are being pushed further and further into the future, the wealthy can pretend that the biological rules do not apply to them.

A new problem that has developed in those who can afford it is a condition where men and women become addicted to cosmetic surgery, having procedure upon procedure performed on their body. Multiple surgeries to the same part of the body often weaken and damage tissue, as in the case of Michael Jackson's nose, which often leads to further surgeries to correct the damage. Typically referred to as **body dysmorphic disorder**, a psychological disorder in which an individual is desperately unhappy with his or her own body, patients cannot stop getting surgeries because, regardless of the results, they are never happy with their appearance. (Cosmetic surgery, in fact, relies on the patient's unhappiness with their appearance. The patients, after all, are not sick, and if they were not unhappy with their looks, would not need surgery at all.) On the other hand, the overwhelming demand for youth and beauty, which is fueled by our obsession with celebrities, no doubt plays a major role in this condition as well.

A newer area of cosmetic surgery is the **labiaplasty**. With this procedure, women who are unsatisfied with the appearance of their labias can have them reshaped. Some observers blame the rise in labia surgery on the rise in pornography consumption in the West; in particular, some pornography digitally removes labia from photos to make the genitals appear "tidy." Many women, then, see their own labia as sloppy and choose to have the size reduced or reshaped. For many critics of the plastic surgery boom, this surgery not only preys upon women's anxieties about their bodies and appearances, but pathologizes normal female genitals, continuing a long tradition in which women's genitals are seen as problematic in cultures around the world.

Women's bodies, in general, are problematic. They are not beautiful enough, hairless enough, and they are certainly, in Western countries, not small enough. In Chapter 11, we will look at the issues surrounding weight, focusing primarily on the female body.

Key terms

Anime	Halo effect
Beauty Myth	Labialasty
Bindi	Lookism
Blepharoplasty	Manga
Body Dysmorphic Disorder	Rhinoplasty
Contrast Effect	Skin Whiteners
Golden Ratio	*Ulzzang*

Further reading

Chapkis, Wendy. (1986). *Beauty Secrets: Women and the Politics of Appearance*. Boston, MA: South End Press.

Davis, Kathy. (1995). *Reshaping the Female Body: The Dilemma of Cosmetic Surgery*. London: Routledge.

Etcoff, Nancy. (1999). *Survival of the Prettiest: The Science of Beauty*. New York: Anchor Books.

Jeffreys, Sheila. (2005). *Beauty and Misogyny: Harmful Cultural Practices in the West*. New York: Routledge.

Scruton, Roger. (2009). *Beauty*. Oxford: Oxford University Press.

Wolf, Naomi. (2002). *The Beauty Myth: How Images of Beauty Are Used against Women*. New York: HarperPerennial.

chapter 11

Fat and Thin Bodies

In September 2012, a Google search of the term "Lady Gaga" generated over 600 million results, covering the pop star's music (15 million albums sold so far), her awards (five Grammies), her tours, her success (she is on the Forbes Most Powerful Women list), and her outrageous style. But the second entry on Google that month was titled "Lady Gaga gains 25 pounds and is on a diet; does she need to lose weight?" Countless other stories that month discussed the details of Gaga's apparent weight gain, complete with unflattering photos of the star.

Flash back to October 2010 when a columnist for the fashion magazine *Marie Claire* wrote a blog on the magazine's website in which she said that she was "grossed out" watching "two [TV] characters with rolls and rolls of fat kissing each other." She was referring to the actors Billy Gardell and Melissa McCarthy who play Mike and Molly in the television show by the same name. She went further to say that she finds it "aesthetically displeasing to watch a very, very fat person simply walk across a room." The blogger's comments set off a firestorm of protest and resulted in a long discussion on their own website as well in other places regarding "**fat shaming**" in the media.

Whose job is it to police the weight of other people? And who gets to decide how fat is too fat, or, for that matter, how thin is too thin? The same week that photos of "Fat Gaga" began circulating, *Us Magazine* featured two different photos of actress Sarah Jessica Parker, both taken the same week. In one of the photos, which was used in a fashion spread, the actress was complimented on her appearance. In a different photo, on the other hand, which was used in an article about celebrities who are too thin, the author questioned whether or not she was anorexic.

In this chapter, we will look at the issues surrounding fatness and thinness, and how those categories are constructed, defined, and enforced in society. As we shall see, like so much of what is discussed in this text, there is no clear boundary between these two poles, and the distinctions between them are not as clear as they may seem.

The obesity epidemic

In the West, doctors, public health officials, and politicians have been talking with greater frequency about the "**obesity epidemic**" in which more and more children and adults are not just overweight, but obese, defined as having a **body mass index** (BMI) of over 30. Today, 33 percent of Americans meet that definition, with another 32 percent being defined as overweight. The concerns stem from not just the increase in the numbers of people defined as obese, but from the rise in health problems associated with obesity, such as diabetes, heart disease, and cancer, and the resulting rise in mortality (with 300,000 Americans alone dying from obesity-related causes annually). Around the world, too, obesity is at an all-time high, with the World Health Organization estimating that approximately one billion people are overweight, with 300 million obese, which WHO is now calling "globesity." In turn, as more people develop these conditions, health care costs, especially in the United States where they are already astronomical, will continue to skyrocket. (It's worth pointing out, however, that much of the health care costs associated with obesity come from are prescription weight-loss drugs which treat the "disease" of obesity rather than any health conditions associated with it.)

It seems clear that major lifestyle and cultural changes have contributed to the collective rise in America's weight. In particular, Western jobs have moved from blue collar to white and pink collar, which means that more of us spend our work days sitting down in front of a computer. And our leisure time is increasingly spent consuming media: television, video games, and computers and mobile devices like iPhones, iPods and iPads fill a great amount of our leisure time, which means that most of us spend much less time out of doors.

Our bodies have evolved to deal with periodic hunger; that's why they so efficiently store fat. (And that's why evolutionarily speaking, extremely thin people did not have a genetic survival advantage in the past.) Today, however, most Westerners never experience that kind of hunger, but we continue to store fat in our bodies. In addition, fast food and junk food have become a more central part of the diets of people around the world, and restaurant meal portions are bigger than ever. Fast food and junk food companies spend billions of dollars on advertising their products, which are made to be tasty and inexpensive. Unfortunately, they are also high in calories, fat, sugar, and salt. Thanks to the overwhelming amounts of fatty, sugary, and salty foods around us, people have to work very hard to turn down these kinds of foods and restrict ourselves from eating the food that surrounds us.

These problems are magnified in the United States, which has the highest rates of obesity in the developed world and where, not coincidentally, the fast food industry has the greatest foothold and strongest lobbying power. As a result, government officials in a variety of locations are creating new policies to encourage exercise and reduce the dependence on fast food. In New York City, for example, Mayor Michael Bloomberg passed an ordinance in 2012 banning the sale of sugary sodas over 16 ounces; this follows two other major public health initiatives passed in the city which forced restaurants to post calorie counts on menus, and which banned the use of transfats in restaurants; other cities have since adopted those measures. The soda ban, as it's been called, is simply a modern variant on the junk food tax (also known as the **Twinkie Tax**) – taxes that are placed on unhealthy foods, with the idea that the more expensive the food, the less likely folks will eat it. On the federal level, first lady Michelle Obama's major campaign Let's Move is focused on getting children to exercise and eat healthy, in an effort to reduce childhood obesity. More extreme solutions to the problem have also been proposed, such as the suggestion that child abuse laws be expanded so that fat children can be removed from their families' homes and put into foster care.

On the other hand, there are other voices that argue that the obesity epidemic is simply a **moral panic**; that officials are using obesity as a way to frighten citizens, and to encourage yet more money to be spent on the multi-billion dollar diet and bariatric surgery industries. Many, if not most, overweight people do not suffer from poor health or cause society to pay for their health care costs; only at the far extremes of obesity are found the serious health problems. What's happening, according to Paul Campos, author of The Obesity Myth (2004), is that the overweight and obese have become a sort of **folk devil**, ridiculed and scorned for their weight and blamed for a whole host of social problems. Articles appear weekly in American and European newspapers and online media sites informing us of the problem. These are generally accompanied by photos of poorly dressed, slovenly looking obese people – what Charlotte Cooper (2007) calls "**headless fatties**." These fat people, with their heads removed from the photos, can then be presented as objects open to ridicule and scorn. She writes, "As Headless Fatties, the body becomes symbolic: we are there but we have no voice, not even a mouth in a head, no brain, no thoughts or opinions. Instead we are reduced and dehumanised as symbols of cultural fear."

Americans in particular associate obesity with laziness, sloth, gluttony, and stupidity, and the obese – especially women – suffer discrimination in employment and other areas. In fact, fat shaming and **sizeism** seem to be the last remaining acceptable forms of discrimination in the West. But we justify this discrimination by suggesting that not only are fat people lazy and gluttonous – they brought this on themselves, after all – but that they drain the health care system thanks to their sloth. As a remedy to this kind of fat shaming, obesity acceptance and advocacy groups have become prominent advocates for the acceptance of fat people, and have created public awareness campaigns to defend the rights of the obese and to make them socially acceptable.

One thing that fat acceptance groups have pointed out is that dieting is not only profitable to the diet industry, but dieting, for most people who do it, does not appear to work. Eighty-five percent of all Americans who diet, if they lose weight at all, gain it back, often with "interest." Dieting appears to make us fatter, in other words. In addition, there's no evidence

FIGURE 11.1 This young girl's photo was taken at a McDonald's in 2006 as an illustration of childhood obesity. It's also an illustration of a "headless fatty." Photo courtesy of Robert Lawton, via Wikimedia Commons: http://commons.wikimedia.org/wiki/File:Childhood_Obesity.JPG.

bodies and privilege

that having a BMI of 29 means that one is automatically healthier than having a BMI of 31. The lines between normal, overweight, and obese are arbitrary and not based on anything scientific. And finally, it is probably the case that fat shaming contributes to disordered eating like bingeing which itself causes fatness. Children, in particular, are vulnerable to being shamed and stigmatized, so the current moral panic over obesity, and especially childhood obesity, may even be contributing to the problem. In fact, studies now show that there is a link between early dieting among children and both eating disorders and obesity.

Interesting issues: the fat acceptance movement and fatshion blogs

The fat acceptance movement is a social movement concerned with eliminating the shame, stigma, and discrimination aimed at fat people. It does not promote fatness but encourages people who are heavy to not obsess over their weight or engage in self-hatred. It also argues that excessive dieting, which often results in the regaining of that same weight, can be more dangerous than being overweight in the first place. Dieting and obsession about weight can also result in a variety of eating disorders. In addition, the psychological trauma experienced by the overweight can be damaging, as can the financial costs of being overweight. Fat acceptance advocates promote a philosophy known as health at every size (HAES) which promotes healthy eating and exercise for all people, rather than focusing on numbers such as weight or BMI, and argues that fat people can be just as healthy as skinny people. The movement is represented by organizations like the National Association to Advance Fat Acceptance. Loosely associated with the fat acceptance movement in recent years is the development of a number of fashion blogs known as fatshion blogs. These are blogs or tumblrs created by women of size who post photos of themselves in outfits that they have worn that day. Along with the photos, they post information about their clothes and links to the companies from which they purchased them. They are sources of fashion inspiration for other overweight women who want to look better and feel better about themselves and who see these women as demonstrating that fat women can be sexy, confident, and beautiful. Other bloggers also write articles about social justice issues relevant to the fat community, and many of the blogs encourage a lively conversation in the comments section. Typically the only rule in such blogs is that commenters cannot post about dieting.

The drive to lose weight

As we have discussed in Chapters 7 and 10, women are judged by how they look. In the West, because we are surrounded by affluence, women in particular are expected to be slim, as well of course as beautiful and young.

We know this because of the messages that are disseminated by the health industry about the "obesity epidemic" and also because of the images of women that surround us in popular culture.

Television, advertising, music, and movies are full of women who are thin. Women who are not thin are relegated to "funny best friend" roles on television and in film, but are never romantic leads. Women who are not thin were once quite prominent in popular music, but as MTV and music videos took over the music industry in the 1980s, fat singers began to disappear from the scene. In recent years, a handful of overweight singers have re-appeared, such as the Grammy-award winner Adele, but even then, she has experienced quite a bit of public criticism over her weight. Other overweight female singers, like *American Idol* singers Jennifer Hudson and Jordin Sparks, lost weight after experiencing a great deal of criticism for their appearance.

One way in which dieting and weight loss is promoted to the public is through women's magazines. In magazines like *Seventeen*, *Cosmopolitan*, *Marie Claire*, and *Vogue*, the models and actresses featured are uniformly young, thin – about 23 percent thinner than the average woman – beautiful, and mostly white. Women's magazines are filled with ads as well as articles promoting weight loss, and three-quarters of the covers of all women's magazines include messages about how to change one's appearance, generally through dieting, but also through exercise or cosmetic surgery.

Women who read these magazines are constantly told, through advertising and editorial content alike, that their bodies are defective. They are too hairy, too wrinkly, too lumpy, and definitely too fat. Thankfully, the products that will help them to overcome those problems are advertised in those very same pages – often directly opposite an article about diet, weight, or beauty – so that consumers can pick up their diet pills, creams, and powders, or schedule their surgeries, at the next available opportunity. Thanks to the collusion between entertainment aimed at women and the diet industry, the industry rakes in over $60 billion per year in the United States alone.

The reality is, as we've already discussed in Chapter 10, that trying to look like the models in the magazines is impossible for the vast majority of women. The result is that women must constantly work to achieve something which is largely unattainable, and thus will be judged as failures. For girls in particular, the focus on thinness and beauty is so overwhelming that depression, loss of self-esteem, and disordered eating habits often result. Self-hatred becomes a defining part of most women's identities thanks to what feminist writer Kim Chernin calls the "tyranny of slenderness" (1981).

Feminist Jean Kilbourne calls it "cutting girls down to size" (1999). By forcing girls and women to judge themselves by their thinness, they cannot instead focus on their intelligence, their career goals, or larger political ideas about changing society. Instead, generation upon generation of girls who may have grown up to be CEOs and world leaders are spending countless hours obsessing about their weight. Even though women naturally have more body fat than men, and body fat on men is linked to more health problems (because it tends to accumulate around the abdomen), fat female bodies are far more disgusting and shameful than fat male bodies. In addition, while girls are fretting about how much space they take up, literally and figuratively, men are encouraged to take up as much space as they like. Size, visibility, and power are all denied to women, and fat-hatred is simply a symptom of that fact. Dieting, in addition, is about disciplining both the external body but also the internal desires. Women are told to not want too much; they should not desire too much. Women should simply be complacent, submissive, and happy with what they have. A woman's body, and her passions, are her enemy.

One out of every four college-aged women tries to lose weight with unhealthy methods of weight control like fasting, vomiting, laxatives, or meal-skipping. Forty-two percent of all girls ages 1–3 want to be thinner and 46 percent of 9–11-year-olds are on diets. By the time girls make it to college, that number rises to 90 percent, and 35 percent of those who diet engage in some sort of disordered eating habit. One result of this constant attention and focus on female bodies is that as girls grow older, their self-esteem and confidence in themselves drops. But the $109 million spent per day in the United States on diet products is at least good for the economy!

Dieting has been promoted by doctors since the mid-nineteenth century, even though scientists by then knew about the connections between weight and metabolism, and in 2004, Tommy Thompson, the Secretary of Health and Human Services, proclaimed that obesity was a disease, opening the door for Medicare to cover obesity-related treatments. But disease or no, diet continues to be the major focus of the obesity fighters. The rise in the diet and health industries coincided with the new morality by which fat people began to be associated with a host of personal and public evils; unhealthy and unattractive bodies meant an unhealthy nation, so a variety of cures were promoted to force the body back to health. A thin and healthy body also indicated that one was in control of oneself and one's destiny so by restricting one's diet one could take command over one's body and thus one's life.

But the reality is that dieting rarely works. Certainly, it does for some people. But most people who diet, as we've already noted, will simply gain back the weight that they have lost. But from the perspective of the diet industry, diets are not supposed to work. If they did, and all fat people got thin, then there would be no need for a diet industry anymore, and billions of dollars in profit would disappear alongside our corpulence.

fat and thin bodies

FIGURE 11.2 Photograph of a variety of weight loss products at the grocery store. Photo courtesy of the author.

Today, **bariatric surgery** is the last resort for people who can afford it (the cost runs from $10,000 to $40,000), or whose insurance policies will cover the procedures. For some, it's now the first choice for dramatic weight loss, especially for overweight celebrities, over the conventional weight loss methods of dieting and exercise. In fact, it has become so common that any time an overweight celebrity loses a large amount of weight in a relatively short time, the public often assumes that that person lost the weight via surgery.

The most common types of surgeries are stomach stapling, the lap band, and gastric bypass surgery, all of which are gastric restrictive procedures, meaning that the patient's volume of food intake after surgery is restricted. Bariatric surgery does not involve liposuction or tummy tucks or other cosmetic surgery procedures. Instead, through stapling, banding or other methods, the patient's stomach is made much smaller than it was previously, leaving the patient unable to consume large quantities of food in a single sitting. In gastric bypass surgery, the stomach size is decreased and the first part of the small intenstine is bypassed so that fewer calories are absorbed into the body.

Through obesity surgery, large numbers of elite overweight individuals like Star Jones, Al Roker, and Carnie Wilson have been able to lose a great deal of weight in a very short period of time in order to conform to Western society's standards of beauty. On the other hand, as extreme as bariatric

bodies and privilege

FIGURE 11.3 Bariatric surgery billboard. Photo courtesy of Tom Young.

surgery is, it often results, as do other forms of weight loss, in weight gain after the fact. Singer Carnie Wilson has undergone bariatric surgery twice, and still is considered to be obese.

Another radical solution to obesity is the weight-loss reality show. Shows like *Biggest Loser*, *Extreme Makeover: Weight Loss Edition*, *Thintervention*, *Celebrity Fit Camp*, and *Heavy* feature overweight and obese contestants who compete to see who can lose the most weight. Contestants are put on very strict diets and engage in exercise for up to six hours each day. Some lose massive amounts of weight very quickly – one contestant on *Biggest Loser* lost 41 pounds in a week! On the other hand, thanks to the extreme methods of weight loss, most contestants have a hard time sustaining their loss. It's been estimated that just 50 percent of all *Biggest Loser* contestants have been able to maintain something close to their end-of-show weights.

Eating disorders

What is appropriate behavior in terms of dieting and what is disordered behavior? Here again, the line between the two is often very fuzzy indeed, since anorexia is really just the extreme version of what all women are expected to achieve.

Anorexia nervosa is an eating disorder in which the sufferer has a distorted image of their body leading them to undereat and sometimes

fat and thin bodies

over-exercise, sometimes to the point of starvation and death. Anorexics often also struggle with perfectionism, obsessive compulsive disorder – they often feel that they have no control over their hunger, or indeed their lives – and have obsessive thoughts about food and weight. Anorexics also may utilize diet pills or diuretic drugs in order to lose or control weight. Purging through vomiting, exercise, laxatives, or spitting is generally classified as **bulimia**, and many people suffer from both conditions. Anorexia and bulimia primarily affect adolescent girls in the Western world, with perhaps as much as 10 percent of all victims dying from the disease.

While the disease was described at the end of the seventeenth century, it only became a common condition in the twentieth century, thanks to modern standards of beauty in the West that emphasize an extremely thin ideal, combined with a growing and powerful diet and exercise industry and the mass media's heavy focus on the female body. Many feminists feel that the thin ideal is a thinly disguised way to keep women decorative, feminine, and useless, and to ensure that they do not take up too much space – literally or figuratively.

Anorexia can be seen as more than a psychiatric and physical disorder, however, and can be viewed as an intentional form of body modification. While some sufferers do want help for their condition and recognize that they are threatening their health and lives by refusing to eat, others reject the label and the stigma that comes with having a psychiatric disorder. Many anorexics and bulimics have formed "**pro-ana**" online communities in which they support each other's choices, swap weight-loss tips, share photos of extremely thin people called **thinspiration**, as well as advice on how to hide one's condition from family, friends, and medical professionals. For these people, anorexia is a lifestyle choice and they are intentionally molding their bodies in a way that shows that they are able to control them. For others in the pro-ana community, these websites are simply a safe place to escape the scrutiny and stigma of their families, friends, and doctors, and to resist the medicalization of their lives.

While the pro-ana movement is not as popular now as it once was, it still remains true that anorexia is seen by many young women as an alternative lifestyle and that by modifying their bodies in the extreme way they do, they have taken control over their bodies. For these people, anorexia, or extreme dieting, is not about having a psychiatric disorder or a problem with one's body image; instead, at least for some, it is about exercising control and pushing one's body's limits.

Another way to look at anorexia is to see it as a response to a culture that promotes food to women as a source of pleasure, a sinful treat, and a way to satisfy our emotional problems, and that at the same time mandates that women maintain an extreme if not impossible form of slenderness.

bodies and privilege

How can we reconcile these two contradictory positions if not through developing eating disorders?

Another disorder is **binge eating disorder**, a condition in which individuals binge eat, often compulsively, in order to relieve stress or other unpleasant feelings. Like cutting, in which a person cuts into their arms or legs with a knife to release stress and emotional suffering, binge eating is also a way that some people control emotional pain, and thus exercise control over their own lives.

While we typically associate eating disorders like anorexia and bulimia with young, white, middle-class girls and women, many other demographic groups suffer from these conditions as well. For instance, sociologist Becky Thompson (1996) has written extensively about the experiences of Latina and African-American women with eating disorders. For many women, she notes that eating disorders are associated with trauma, rather than the culture of thinness so dominant in Western culture. Some women begin using food to either punish themselves or to disguise pain after sexual abuse or other traumas, as well as as a way to deal with the culture of racism, sexism, classism, and for lesbians, homophobia.

You need some meat on your bones: a preference for fat

Obesity has not always been seen negatively, however. In a number of cultures around the world, obesity has been associated with physical attractiveness, strength, and fertility. For instance, obesity was often seen as a symbol of wealth and social status in cultures in which many people starve or suffer from undernourishment. The more precarious the economy and the scarcer the food, the more likely larger bodies will be valued, and the higher status those people will be. Even today, there are a great many cultures which are traditionally more accepting of obesity, including some African, Arabic, Indian, and Pacific Island cultures.

Some tribal people still gauge female beauty by size and brides are often "fattened" before marriage. For example, girls in the Hima tribe of Uganda undergo a four-month fattening ritual prior to marriage, in which they eat and drink until they are suitably fat. The Efik of Nigeria have a similar ritual for girls between the ages of 15 and 18, in which girls first shave their heads and then spend time in a fattening room until they are ready for marriage. The Okrika of Nigeria also fatten girls from 14 to 16 to make their bodies "come out;" a practice that makes them not only beautiful but makes them attain puberty, and thus marriageability, earlier. In fact, a number of nomadic Nigerian tribes value fatness in women, and there, unlike in the United States where women remove clothes and shoes before getting on the scale, in Nigeria, they put on extra clothes before doing so. While these practices are most commonly associated with Africa, Native American tribes like the Havasupai also fattened girls to make them more beautiful.

One of the most unusual cases is found among the Dinka of southern Sudan. Here, men, not women, fatten themselves. Dinka men compete in a contest to see who among the men can be the fattest. The men who participate isolate themselves from the rest of the society for three months, drinking as much milk as they possibly can, and moving as little as possible. To be able to do this demonstrates one's wealth, because to do so means that one has many cows from which to drink. The winner is judged at a ceremony attended by the whole tribe at the end of the season, and the winner gets a great deal of respect and honor. Some men even die during the trial – their stomachs literally burst – but that represents a most honorable death.

In the West, there are individuals in modern society who actively encourage obesity, and there are also those who are erotically attracted to overweight people. "Chubbies," for example, are gay men who are overweight or obese and the chubby community is made up of chubbies and **"chubby chasers"** – men who are attracted to them. In the straight community, "fat admirers" are men who are sexually attracted to overweight or obese women, known in this community as big beautiful women (BBW). These relationships may or may not be classified as fat fetishes, as admirers may simply appreciate larger men or women, while the fetish admirers are sexually attracted to excess fat itself. One specific fetishistic category includes "feeders" and "feedees;" feeders are people who over-feed their partner in order to see them gain weight, and feedees, or gainers, are the eaters. These relationships are sometimes associated with BDSM, as the feeder is generally the dominant partner and the feedee or gainer the submissive. ("Stuffing" is the temporary practice of overfeeding someone until their bellies are so full that they cannot move.) Related to this fetish is fat porn – pornography that features very fat women engaging in sex or simply posing in the nude. In all of these cases, the arousal comes from the shock and the violation of social boundaries: showing very fat women naked, eating, or having sex (sometimes all at the same time) is transgressive. Rather than featuring thin women's bodies, as the rest of Western popular culture does, fat porn celebrates the most reviled type of woman, and the woman who, in the rest of popular culture, is rendered harmless, non-sexual, and invisible. Chubby gay porn is even more radical than straight fat porn. Gay culture in the West fetishizes the youthful, in-shape, and thin male body, so the display of corpulent (and often hairy) male bodies in chubby porn is revolutionary indeed.

Weight prejudice

There is a long history of fatness being used as a metaphor for moral, psychological, and physical failings. Since the eighteenth century, caricatures were used in Europe to highlight, via artistic exaggeration, a person's most notable features, such as a large nose, bushy eyebrows, or large body size. One of the intentions of the caricature artist was to illuminate the internal characteristics of the subject. Most commonly, caricatures were negative, and were often grotesque; by exaggerating or emphasizing a person's large size, the image highlighted the moral failings of the powerful and their characteristics of greed, lust, sloth, or avarice. The use of fat characters in literature, plays, and film, too, illustrates the negative moral attributes of the overweight and obese. Fat male characters are stupid, greedy, and evil, while fat female characters are lazy, overbearing, or desperate and needy. In addition, fat women are thought to be especially selfish. Women are expected to feed and nurture others. To feed oneself is to reject that exclusively feminine form of nurturing and, indeed, to reject femininity altogether.

It's not just about caricatures and fiction, though. Being overweight is expensive and damaging to the overweight person. Obese people in particular are made fun and bullied of as children, gawked at in public, and stigmatized. They are thought to be out of control, lazy, gluttonous, and lacking all discipline and control. Thin people, on the other hand, demonstrate discipline, control, the ability to shape one's own life, and that they care about themselves. Fat people embody none of those sentiments. As a result, they are avoided in public, and treated as if their condition were contagious. (And the widely used term "epidemic," which refers to infectious diseases, contributes to this sense of contagion.) They face isolation, humiliation, and cruelty.

Children learn from an early age that calling fat people names is acceptable. The overweight are discriminated against in the romantic arena, are humiliated when flying airplanes, find that their children are ashamed of them, often do not eat in public because of the stares, have to shop at special stores for their clothing, and sometimes find that doctors will not treat them. Ironically, while we target fat people for their obvious overconsumption of food, we do not likewise stigmatize those who overconsume with large houses, fuel-guzzling cars, extravagant clothing, or jewelry, because the latter are trappings of wealth, and not poverty.

Another reason we stigmatize the overweight in the West is because of the association between obesity and poverty. Today, the poorest people are often the fattest, because where inexpensive fast food and junk food are available, they will be increasingly consumed by the poor. And because those foods are very high in sugar, fat, salt, and calories, those with the least amount of money will often weigh the most. But unlike in the past, where a person with access to fatty foods might be considered healthier and certainly more affluent than the rest of the population, today, the fat of the poor is simply the modern sign of malnutrition. The south is the region in the United States with the highest obesity rates; Mississippi is the fattest state in the nation, with 30 percent of that state's population considered obese, and, not coincidentally, the greatest number of the poor.

Because the overweight are less likely to be hired, or promoted, than those with normal weight, they make less money than other people and, like the poor in general, must continue to rely on less expensive, and less healthy, foods. And the heavier the job candidate, the more likely it is that they will not get a job. It's been estimated that each pound of fat costs $1,000 per year in lost income. The diet products and programs purchased by the overweight and obese are also expensive, and since most overweight people will gain back the weight they lost on their diet, forcing them to diet again, the costs are spread over a person's entire lifetime. Not only, then, is poverty positively correlated with obesity – in part because of the costs associated with healthy foods, and the lack of education among the poor – but downward mobility is too. The Duchess of Windsor once said, "You can never be too rich or too thin." However, you can certainly be both too poor and too fat.

Because of the way that class, race, and fat intersect, and because of the disgust that so many of us feel about fat people, fat-shaming often takes on a classist and racist tone. The 2012 television series *Here Comes Honey Boo Boo*, about a 6-year-old child pageant queen and her poor, white, overweight family, is a good example of this. Called white trash and redneck by observers as well as themselves, this reality series showcases the behaviors both most maligned in this country and also most associated with the poor: gluttonous eating, farting, belching, cheap and revealing clothing, and extremely poor taste. The children are shown eating cheese puffs off the floor, or bobbing for pigs' feet, while one of the children's daddies spits tobacco chew into a cup and the matriarch of the family, June, makes spaghetti sauce out of margarine mixed with ketchup. The show is criticized as a sign of the end of times, with its glamorization of white trash culture, but many of the angriest remarks from critics have to do with the size of the family, and the fact that they do not seem terribly bothered by the fact that they are fat. Perhaps that's the worst crime of all: to be fat and, notwithstanding all of the public ridicule and name-calling, to be happy and proud.

Interesting issues: Lane Bryant ad: too fat for TV

In 2010, Lane Bryant, the plus-size clothing retailer, produced a television commercial starring size-16 model Ashley Graham for their Cacique line of

bodies and privilege

lingerie. Both Fox and ABC refused to air the ad during primetime, claiming that the cleavage in the commercial was too prominent. A number of commentators pointed out that not only does Victoria's Secret air television commercials with scantily clad models, but they even run a television show of their runway lingerie show. In addition, just a quick perusal of the primetime shows on the American network ABC like Desperate Housewives and Grey's Anatomy, both of which showcase scantily clad women, many having sex, shows the hypocrisy of the networks' decision. Many people called out the networks and suggested that they were opposing the ads not because they were too sexy, but because the model was too fat for TV. The reality is, seeing an overweight woman in sexy clothing – even a beautiful one, as the model in the Lane Bryant commercial clearly was – is almost unheard of in society today. When we do see overweight women, they are fully dressed, and appear in a housewife or best friend role.

Sugar, fast food, and the sweetening of the world's food

While obviously food and exercise – or the lack of – play a major role in weight and obesity, other factors play a role as well, such as genes and the combination of genes and environment. Recent studies have demonstrated that foods high in fat, salt, and sugar – in other words most junk food and fast food – can alter the brain chemistry of those who eat it, in the same way that cocaine and heroin, both highly addictive drugs, do. Other studies show that some people have a slightly different brain composition, and for them, eating these kinds of foods is much more satisfying than for "normal" people. And still another study indicates that some people may have a dulled dopamine – or reward – response to certain kinds of foods, and therefore need to eat more of them in order to feel rewarded and satisfied. These studies together indicate not only that certain kinds of foods are actually addictive, but that some people may be genetically predisposed to want or need to eat more of them. Even with this new research, we still blame fat people for being fat.

That sugar in particular is addictive can be seen by looking at the rise in sugar consumption in the Western world since the sixteenth century. Sugar cane originated in New Guinea and in India, but was brought to the New World by Christopher Columbus, who recognized that the Caribbean was an ideal environment to grow the crop. At that time, sugar was expensive and rare, and its use in Europe was limited to the elites who could afford it. But with the new sugar plantations in the Caribbean, which used African slave labor to plant, process, and harvest the crop, sugar became more widely available and much less expensive. Because sugar was such a labor-intensive crop, the slave trade had to expand to accommodate Europeans' increasing appetites for the sweet product known as white gold. Over the course of the 380 years of the Atlantic slave trade, millions of Africans were enslaved (and died) and millions of Europeans became hooked on sugar.

While sugar was once a luxury of the rich, sugar became so common, thanks to the labor of the slaves, that all peoples of all backgrounds could consume sugar. Sugar became the most important European trade commodity, and European and American diets changed to accommodate it. Sugar also helped usher in the Industrial Revolution as industrial magnates found that workers could work longer and harder after having consumed sugar, which gave them a burst of energy and dulled their hunger pangs. People began eating jams, cocoa, candy, sweetened tea, and processed foods that had never existed before. One of the results, of course, is the modern Western diet – high in sugar – with its resulting obesity, diabetes, and tooth decay. And of course sugar is now most heavily consumed among the poor, who cannot afford a healthier diet. It provides quick energy, but very little nutritional benefit.

Today, the makers of highly processed, highly sweetened products spend anywhere from $1 to $10 billion each year in the United States to advertise their products directly to children. Sugary sodas, breakfast cereals, happy meals, and other sugary products are advertised with cartoon characters, and are linked with popular television shows and often sold with toys to encourage children to consume them. Children see about 100 ads for vegetables and fruit per year, compared to 5,500 for fast food and junk food products. In addition, the more processed a food item is, the more profitable – and less healthy – it is. Selling grains, milk, or vegetables to consumers brings in much less money than turning those products into highly refined – and highly addictive – food products, which explains why refined and processed foods are so much more popular and abundant today. Ironically, the highly processed foods also tend to be less filling than whole foods, causing us to eat even more of them. In addition, like all well-funded industries, the fast food and junk food industry funds lobbying groups which help to ensure that their products are easily available and subject to little or no regulation. Coca-Cola and Wendy's, for example, support the Center for Consumer Freedom, which, through its lobbying dollars, blocks any public health measures that it can.

As discussed in this chapter, whether one is fat or thin – or somewhere in between – is more than just a matter of how much food one eats. What we eat, how much we eat, and what we think about what we eat, what we look like, and what food means to us, is shaped by a variety of social, cultural, historical, and economic factors that are often invisible to us as consumers. But by making those factors visible, we can begin to understand how those factors operate and the impact they have on our lives, and on our bodies.

Key terms

Anorexia

Bariatric Surgery

Binge Eating Disorder

Body Mass Index

Bulimia

Chubby Chasers

Courtesy Stigma

Fat Shaming

Fatshion

Folk Devil

Headless Fatties

Moral Panic

Obesity Epidemic

Pro-Ana

Sizeism

Twinkie Tax

Further reading

Bordo, Susan. (1993). *Unbearable Weight: Feminism, Western Culture, and the Body*. Berkeley, CA: University of California Press.

Braziel, Jana Evans and LeBesco, Kathleen. (2001). *Bodies out of Bounds: Fatness and Transgression*. Berkeley, CA: University of California Press.

Campos, Paul. (2004). *The Obesity Myth: Why America's Obsession with Weight Is Hazardous to Your Health*. New York: Gotham Books.

Gilman, Sander. (2008). *Fat: A Cultural History of Obesity*. Cambridge: Polity.

Kulick, Don and Meneley, Anne, (eds). (2005). *Fat: The Anthropology of an Obsession*. New York: Jeremy P. Tarcher/Penguin.

PART V

Extraordinary Bodies

chapter 12

Modified Bodies

In 2011, a man named Rick Genest, known as Zombie Boy, shot to mainstream popularity. That year, he modeled for fashion designer Thierry Mugler's Fall campaign, was photographed by celebrity photographer Terry Richardson, was featured in an advertising campaign for a theatrical cover up makeup called Dermablend, played a cameo in the Keanu Reaves film *47 Ronin*, and was featured in the video for Lady Gaga's song "Born This Way." What makes Genest's new fame so noteworthy is the fact that Genest is one of the world's most tattooed – and most unusually tattooed – men. His tattoos, which cover 80 percent of his body, were created to represent a decaying body. According to the *Guinness Book of World Records*, Genest has more insects (178) and bones (138) tattooed on his body than anyone else. The result is a tattooed manifestation of "Zombie Boy."

It was not that long ago that tattoos were, in Western countries like the United States, a sign of deviance. The fact that Genest has managed to achieve a measure of mainstream fame tells us how far tattoos have changed, and how far society has come in accepting, at least partially, non-mainstream body modifications.

Body modification refers to the physical alteration of the body through the use of surgery, tattooing, piercing, scarification, branding, genital mutilation, implants, and other practices. Body modifications can be permanent or temporary, although most are permanent and alter the body forever. Humans have been modifying the human body for thousands of years, and most likely, since humans became human. All cultures everywhere have attempted to change their body in an attempt to meet their cultural standards of beauty, as well as their religious and or social obligations. In addition, people modify their bodies as part of the complex process of creating and re-creating their personal and social identities.

From raw to cooked

Today, **tattooing**, **scarification**, **piercing**, **body painting**, and other forms of permanent and temporary body modification are found in every culture around the world, and are seen by anthropologists as visible markers of age, social status, family position, tribal affiliation, and other social features. Scholars who have studied the ways in which humans mark their bodies note that bodily displays create, communicate, and maintain status and identity. This has been found not only in traditional societies, but in state-level societies as well. Succinctly put, the modification of the body is the simplest means by which human beings are turned into social beings – they move from "raw" to "cooked" as the body goes from naked to marked.

Many cultures that practice piercing, scarification, tattooing, and other permanent body modifications believe that one is not fully human if the body is not properly adorned or modified. In fact, even the wearing of makeup and the styling of hair can be seen as ways in which the human body is distinguished from the animal body. Permanent and temporary, all of the ways in which the human body has been altered historically can be seen as markers of civilization, of culture, and of humanity. The more altered the body, often the more human, the more socialized, and the more civilized. Body adornments and modifications are symbolic as well, symbolizing a great many subtle and not-so-subtle social features about the wearer.

Body modification in traditional cultures

Because the body has always been used as a means of expression and self-construction, it is not surprising that we find in both the archaeological record and among the practices of people around the world an enormous variety of techniques and procedures by which the human body is transformed.

In every society, each individual marks off his or her social position by clothing, adornments, and modifications to the body. Most are temporary, but some are permanent, and many involve quite a bit of pain. Temporary markings, such as body painting, are often used in a ritual context to make the individual different, extraordinary, and are often used to celebrate or mark a specific cultural or ritual event. Permanent markings, on the other hand, such as tattooing, scarification, and genital mutilation, are generally used to mark a permanent status onto the body, such as adulthood, marriage-ability, or class or caste status.

FIGURE 12.1 Kenowun, Nunivak woman wearing nose ornament and beaded labrets below her lower lip. Photo courtesy of the Library of Congress.

Tattooing refers to the insertion of pigment into the skin with needles, bone, knives, or other implements, in order to create a decorative design. Tattooing has been found on every continent of the world as well as among most island populations. The earliest evidence for tattooing dates back to the Neolithic period, with mummies and other tattooed artifacts dating from 6,000 BCE in Europe and 4,000 BCE in Egypt. Tattooing probably spread from the Middle East to the Pacific Islands, and later the Americas, by way of India, China, and Japan. By 1,000 BCE it was found virtually everywhere. In the cultures in which it was found, tattoos were deeply embedded in social institutions; they were decorative and also functioned to communicate social status, rank, religious devotion or affiliation, marital status, and other social markers to the world at large. Often received during rites of passage, tattoos were and are critical features of the societies that practiced them. For example, in Samoa, it was once customary for men to wear the torso tattoo known as the *pe'a*, which extended from the belly, down the buttocks, covering the genitals, and both thighs. Receiving a pe'a was once a critical event in a Samoan's man's life, and marked an important transition from boyhood to adulthood. It signified as well his intent to serve his family and

modified bodies

community. It was once the case that without the pe'a, a man could never truly be a man, and having a half-finished pe'a was considered shameful.

Like tattooing, scarification, which refers to the practice of slicing or puncturing the skin in order to create scars which are joined together into decorative patterns, has long been a way in which cultures – predominantly in Africa – mark social status on bodies. Generally, scarification is performed as a part of a rite of passage, generally enabling the wearer to move from youth into adulthood.

Because both practices are painful, wearing a tattoo or scar is a sign of one's strength and bravery, usually for a man, but sometimes also for women. Finally, both scarification and tattooing are often seen as a form of beautification, without which the individual would be less attractive. Tattooing, however, tends to be practiced by people with relatively light skin, through which the tattoos can show, while scarification, tends to be practiced by people with darker skin.

In many African cultures, women are more commonly scarred and wear more elaborate designs than men. Often, women's scars are seen as an indication that she can withstand the pain of childbearing, making her well suited to be a wife. Men in Africa often wear scars received during initiation, or sometimes after having killed an enemy, as a sign of bravery. Among the Barabaig of Tanzania, boys' heads are cut so deeply that the scars sometimes show up on the skulls. Because scars are considered attractive, they are often cut in such a way as to emphasize the contour of the face or body. The Tiv of Nigeria, for instance, mark along the cheekbones with long, linear scars so as to emphasize the cheekbones.

Another very common practice found around the world is piercing, in which the nose, lips, ears, or other part of the body is pierced, so that jewelry may be inserted. While piercing is commonly found in Western cultures as a method of body adornment, in traditional societies piercing was also done for social, magical, and even medical reasons. For example, a number of indigenous North and South American and Inuit peoples once pierced their lower lips and inserted items known as **labrets**, made of stone, wood, or ivory into them. High-status Tlingit girls and women, for example, wore labrets as decoration, to mark rank, and to protect against evil spirits. Labrets would be inserted into the skin after an excision was made, usually as part of a rite of passage for girls who have just experienced their first menstruation. Among the Kayapo of South America, elder men wore enormous lip plugs in their lips which signified the social dominance of these men and their skills as orators. Labrets were also commonly worn in pre-Columbian Mesoamerica. Among the ancient Aztecs and Mayans, labret piercings were only worn by elite men, who wore elaborately sculpted and jeweled labrets fashioned from pure gold in the shape of serpents, jaguars, and other animals.

One of the more uncommon practices of body modification is **head binding**. Head binding refers to the deliberate reshaping of the human skull in order to make it flatter or sometimes cone-shaped. Usually performed on infants, because the skull bones are not yet fused, it has been practiced by a number of cultural groups who associate a flattened or otherwise shaped head with beauty or status. For the Inca of Peru and the Maya of Central America, for example, an artificially shaped head signified nobility. The Maya, for example, used cloth to bind infants, via their heads, to a cradleboard, a process that could last for years until the head reached the right shape.

Body modification in states

In traditional societies such as foraging bands and pastoral or horticultural tribes, the marking of the body was a sign of inclusion in the community, but with the development of agriculture and the nation-state with its centralized government and systems of inequality, markings like tattooing, scarring and branding became signs of exclusion and stigmatization. In early state-level societies, we see for the first time the state and elites marking power onto individual bodies. For example, the origin of human **branding** in the West is to mark the ownership of slaves, as we will discuss in Chapter 14. Tattooing, too, in state-level societies was used to mark both slaves and criminals in societies as diverse as the Persians, the Romans, and among a variety of European societies. Through the use of tattoos and brands to punish criminals, denote slave status, or mark ownership of animals, these are examples of state power being inscribed directly onto the body, as a way to control unruly or criminal bodies. At the same time, elites used very different adornments and modifications – such as elaborate hairstyles, jewelry made of precious stones, beautiful clothing and, much later, cosmetic surgery – to demonstrate their elevated status. The differential marking of criminals and the lower classes continued into the twentieth century in many societies, and of course the use of specialized adornments among the elites to distinguish themselves from the other classes continues as well.

Body modification today

In modern Western society, we have seen new uses of ancient methods of body modification. Today, Westerns use tattooing, piercing, stretching, branding, scarification, and genital modifications to allow individuals to step outside of the bounds of the normal social order, and mark membership in alternative subcultures, such as bikers, punks, convicts, gang members, or among those who practice alternative sexualities.

For example, branding is often used as a form of initiation for groups like fraternities, street gangs, and prisoners. It serves as a test of endurance as well as a demonstration of loyalty and group solidarity, and provides a rite of passage for new group members. It's a lifetime reminder of what their brotherhood means to them. In the fraternity context, the brand is usually the Greek letter of the organization. It is rumored that George W. Bush, while president of the Delta Kappa Epsilon chapter at Yale, may have helped introduce an initiation ritual for pledges that involved branding a D onto the buttocks of new pledges with a heated wire coat hanger. Today, branding is widely used in African-American fraternities, although it is not officially sanctioned by any. Branding is also commonly used in the BDSM community. For instance, in extreme BDSM dominance and submission relationships, a consensual slave may desire or accept a brand as a permanent mark of belonging and commitment to one's master.

Body piercing is also growing more popular in the West today. While once only found on the ears of women, today, men and women both pierce the ears (the lower ear as well as the cartilage of the upper ear), the nose, the lip, the nipples, the genitals, and other areas of the face and body. Here, piercing can either be decorative, as the jewelry worn in pierced ears, noses and lips is often highly elaborate, or it can be used for sexual purposes – especially genital piercings, nipple piercings, and tongue piercings, which are often worn by members of the BDSM community.

Tattooing remains the most popular form of contemporary body modification, associated in the West originally with sailors, and then carnies,

FIGURE 12.2 Day of the Dead chest piece by Jeff Hayes of Rival Tattoo Studios. Photo courtesy of Nick Sanchez.

extraordinary bodies

soldiers, bikers, gang members, and prisoners. Since the 1970s, however, it has moved from the working classes into the middle classes, and is now practiced by both working-class street tattooists as well as highly trained middle-class tattoo artists who do custom-only work and who charge hundreds of dollars per hour. These artists offer their clientele styles drawn from a variety of cultures like Japan, Indonesia, Polynesia, and Native America, as well as American-born styles like Old School, New School, and Biomechanical (which combines organic and mechanical elements together in the tattoo). Tattoos are becoming much more culturally acceptable today in part because the styles and artistry have improved so visibly, but also because the meanings associated with tattoos have transformed. From working-class symbols – "I got it because I was drunk;" "I got it because my buddies got them" – to deeply meaningful symbols with carefully thought out narratives behind them, tattoos are now thought by their middle-class wearers to be the visible markers of a person's internal identity.

Tattooing, gender, and sexuality

We have already noted that when men and women receive body modifications, the reason for those modifications is often very different. When men get scarified or tattooed, for example, it is often to demonstrate their accomplishments while for women, it is generally to make them more beautiful and marriageable. Gender also plays an important role in tattooing because, in many cultures, men and women differ in terms of the designs, meaning, and location of their tattoos. Sexuality, too, is linked to tattooing. In particular, as Westerners began discovering the practice of tattooing during the Age of Exploration, they began to be linked with sexuality, and with European notions of race, sexuality, and exoticism.

Men and women are often differentiated by their tattoos, with some cultures only tattooing men, some cultures only tattooing women, and many cultures reserving certain types of tattoos, or certain tattoo placements, for either men or women. Among the Maori of New Zealand, for example, men once wore the *moko*, a facial tattoo which covered the full face, and which was different for every wearer. Maori women, on the other hand, did not wear a full moko; instead, they wore a tattoo which only covered the region from their lower lip down their chin.

Sometimes cultures go further and use tattoos to highlight the wearer's sexuality. For example, in the Caroline Islands, tattoos beautified women and made the body more sexually attractive. Some women in the far western islands of Yap and Mogmog, for example, wore tattoos on their vulvas, particularly, but not exclusively, women who served as prostitutes to the men in the men's house. Other women wore pubic tattoos for their husbands, or to mark childbirth. A woman on the eastern island of Pohnpei could not hope to get married, or attract the attention of a man, unless her abdominal and pubic tattoo was complete. In Fiji, too, women wore vulva tattoos, which were paid for by the woman's fiancé, who would alone enjoy the designs under her skirt.

Among the hill tribesmen of Laos, the most common tattoo was once known the trousers tattoo. Shan men were tattooed at puberty and the design began at the waist and extended down the front and back of the lower torso, over the genitals, down the legs, and ended at the knees. These tattoos, made up of a series of geometric designs like rectangles, circles, triangles, and squares bordered by plants and animals, marked the fact that a Shan man had reached adulthood, and thus could be married. In fact, the trousers tattoo also symbolized virility; without such a tattoo, it was said that no woman would want to marry a man.

While the above examples show that tattoos were sometimes used to mark or highlight sexuality, for the most part the link between sexuality and tattooing did not really emerge until the Age of Exploration, when Western explorers first encountered non-Western peoples with tattoos.

While tattooing had been practiced, off and on, in Europe for centuries, it was not until the journeys of Captain James Cook and other eighteenth-century explorers that tattooing firmly entered European, and later, American culture. Cook's first journey to Polynesia in 1769 resulted in his crew documenting the practice of tattooing in Tahiti (the term *tatau* comes from the Tahitian and entered the English language after this trip), and his second voyage, in 1772, resulted in a tattooed Tahitian named Omai being brought back to England. This marked the beginning of the exhibition of tattooed native people throughout Europe and America, and the rise of the dime museum, which itself gave way to the freak show. Freak shows created a connection in the minds of Westerners between tattooing and exoticism, and, ultimately, sexuality.

In particular, after Westerners began getting tattooed and working as sideshow attractions, the showman, who marketed the exhibit to the public, told elaborate stories of their capture and forcible tattooing by hostile natives. In the 1880s, tattooed women arrived on the scene, and with that, sexuality became front and center. Tattooed ladies had to show their bodies – initially their calves and then their thighs – to display their tattoos, and, during the Victorian period, to see a woman's thighs was considered quite racy. Another part of their appeal was the contrast between the notion that women were docile and chaste, with the story of their abduction. Here again, even the intimation of female sexuality helped make tattooed ladies successful.

Irene "La Belle" Woodward, who began her career in 1882, said that she got her tattoos to protect her from the sexual attentions of hostile Red Indians in Texas. One tattooed attraction, Olive Oatman, actually *was*

extraordinary bodies

tattooed by Native Americans. Captured by Yavapi Indians as a child and sold to the Mojave Indians, Oatman was found in 1856 with Mohave chin tattoos, and a history steeped in sexual overtones, since it was rumored that she was raped by her captors.

Because tattooing, in the West, has long been associated with deviants and criminals, it has long been a visible mark of the underclass for the men who have worn them. Once women began wearing tattoos, the stigma did not disappear but simply became sexualized. Tattooist and tattoo historian Samuel Steward noted that in the 1950s, when he was tattooing, the only women he saw in his shop were lesbians and "large lank-haired skags, with ruined landscapes of faces and sagging hose and run-over heels" (1990: 128). In order to protect the propriety of the women who came to see him, Steward implemented a policy of refusing to tattoo a (heterosexual) woman unless she was accompanied by her husband. Steward's rule (found among other tattooists of the time as well) served to keep middle-class women from transgressing the class and sexual borders of the time: of turning into tramps. Lesbians, because they already had transgressed those boundaries, were thus fair game, and in fact were among the earliest women to receive tattoos in the United States.

The idea that women who wear tattoos are promiscuous took root during the period from the 1940s through the 1960s, and dovetailed with the larger notion, popular in scientific studies of the time, that the presence of tattooing indicated psychological and social deviance.

Another popular idea in mid-century was the notion that tattooing was not only associated with sexuality, but with homosexuality. A number of psychologists interpreted the variety of sexual images popular in tattoos – primarily nude women – to be an indication of the wearer's homosexual impulses. These same researchers saw the tattoo process itself – where needles prick the skin – as being overtly sexual, if not sado-masochistic, with most tattooists being latent homosexuals. For example, Albert Parry, who wrote *Tattoo Secrets of a Strange Art as Practiced by the Natives of the United States* in 1933, interviewed tattooist Bert Grimm, who said of the interview, "all his questions seemed to deal with sex . . . he said to me that I would have to admit that all tattooers were queer" (Morse 1977: 34).

In modern Western societies, tattoos are used as a sign of group affiliation by groups like soldiers and sailors, gang members, and fraternity members, but they are also an important way in which modern people communicate their personal preferences, desires, and identities to the world. Since the 1960s, when tattooing began to move slowly from the margins of American society into the middle class, women have been using tattoos as a way to reclaim their bodies, and both men and women have been using tattooing as a way to highlight their sexuality.

The gay community, in particular, has long used tattooing, along with piercing and other body modification practices, as both a visible marker of their sexual orientation but also as a form of liberation. Rainbow flags, pink triangles, and the equal sign (representing marriage equality) are all popular tattoos found in the gay community.

Tattooing is also visible part of the BDSM community. In recent years, BDSM has most been associated with the gay leather scene that emerged after World War II. These early sexual pioneers were the first group of Westerners to really experiment with body piercing, branding, and genital piercing, and many were wearing tattoos long before the rest of society even considered the practice. Tattooing, along with other practices like scarification and piercing, have been used for years within the BDSM community as rites of passage and as a means of gaining self-awareness and self-acceptance.

Ownership tattoos and brands are often used by dominant partners to mark ownership of their submissives; sometimes the tattoos are intended to humiliate the submissive, and thus may be tattooed on a hidden part of the body. Participants may also wear a BDSM symbol as a tattoo, such as the BDSM duck – a yellow rubber ducky wearing a hood, a ball gag, and a harness. Another popular tattoo design is the slave heart, which is a heart with a keyhole in it, representing the person (the dominant) who owns the key to one's heart. The practices of the BDSM community have also played a major role in influencing the rise of the modern primitives movement in the West, described below. Modern primitivism borrows the use of pain from the BDSM movement, and many modern primitives have both genital piercings and genital tattoos, also borrowed from the BDSM movement and kinky gays.

Interesting issues: Jean Carroll

Jean Carroll, born Jean Furella around 1910, worked the carnival and circus circuit, first as a bearded lady, and then as a tattooed lady. She was born with a condition known as hirsutism, which creates excessive hair growth. While a 14-year-old girl working in the Hagenbeck-Wallace Circus, she fell in love with a contortionist and sideshow barker named John Carson. Unfortunately, her beard got in the way of a relationship with Carson; he said that he loved her, but could not kiss her as long as she had her beard. Eighteen years later, sword swallower and fellow sideshow performer Alec Linton encouraged Carroll to shave off her beard so that she and Carson could finally become a couple. She decided to follow his advice, and shaved off her beard. But in order to retain her career in show business, she had herself tattooed by tattooist Charlie Wagner, transforming herself from a "born freak" into a "made freak." She continued her career as the "Tattooed Queen" and finally married her beloved, Carson.

extraordinary bodies

Modern primitives and non-mainstream body modifications

As we have noted, according to theorist Michel Foucault, in state-level societies, power is inscribed on bodies through modes of social supervision and discipline as well as self-regulation. But at the same time, bodies also can be sites of resistance as they always entail the possibility of counter-inscription, of being self-marked. Thus the use of body modifications in ways that are not only not socially sanctioned but are explicitly anti-social can be seen as a way in which disaffected or marginalized bodies can mark themselves in accordance with their owners' self-image.

In the late twentieth century we saw the development of a movement that not only uses non-normative and often extreme body modifications but relies on them for aesthetic, spiritual, sexual, and personal growth. This movement, known as the **modern primitives** movement, borrows body modification techniques and religious and cultural beliefs from non-Western societies to resist and challenge modern social practices. Modern primitives assume that the practices found in traditional or "primitive" cultures are somehow more essential and authentic than modern cultural practices, so by wearing tribal tattoos or a penis piercing, participants can tap into their true natures and achieve a higher consciousness.

Contemporary members of the body modification movement who use extreme modifications in non-normative ways see themselves as taking control of their own bodies and expressing their individual identities through these practices. Proponents see their modifications as ways in which they actively transform the self. However, mainstream society typically views them in a very different light, and sees them as a disfigurement or mutilation. Extreme modifications such as heavy tattooing and highly visible tattoos (on the face, hands or head), multiple piercings as well as genital and facial piercings, brands, intentional scars, and especially the use of implants, genital modifications, or voluntary amputations, are seen by some as a symptom of body dsymorphic disorder, and are generally frowned upon and are often criminalized or heavily regulated.

Modern primitivism originated in the practices and ideologies of the radical leather and BDSM scenes, and later moved into the straight, mainstream body modification community with the publication of the Re/Search volume, *Modern Primitives* in 1989. Fakir Musafar, a former advertising executive from South Dakota (he found the name "Fakir Musafar" in an early *Ripley's Believe It Or Not*), is said to have originated the term "modern primitives" in 1967. He describes its meaning as follows: "a non tribal person who responds to primal urges and does something with the body."

Modern primitives, both in its original usage in BDSM, and in its more widespread usage today, implies a critique of contemporary Western society, which is seen as an alienating, repressive, and technocratic place lacking in ritual, myth, or symbol. By rejecting modern society through participating in the primitive rituals of tattooing, piercing, or scarification, participants feel that they are aligning themselves with societies and world-views that are more pure, more authentic, more spiritually advanced than our own. Piercing and other forms of body modification are seen as emblematic of primitive life, used for rites of passage, status marking, and because many body modifications are permanent, they are seen as possessing more meaning than the accumulation of material possessions in "civilized life."

Tattooing, piercing, and branding have become for many a vision quest, an identity quest, an initiation ritual, a self-naming ritual, an act of magic, a spiritual healing, a connection to the God or Goddess, the Great Mother or the Wild Man. For modern primitives who see their body marks as connecting them to ancient or primitive cultures, the *reality* of those cultures is not important. Rather, it is the idealized version of primitive cultures – closer to nature, in harmony with the spiritual realm, egalitarian, non-repressive – that provides the appropriate image.

But while tattooing and body piercing in modern societies borrow the language and practices of primitiveness, they take place within a modern social context, where status and social position are gained through economic and educational achievement. Body marks in primitive society were markers of social membership in socially cohesive groups, wherein life-cycle changes were necessarily marked by tattooing and scarification. Tattoos and piercings today are commercial objects purchased in a capitalist marketplace and are personal and optional accessories for the self.

While the practices used in the modern primitives movement generally serve to include traditional peoples *within* the social order, these practices, when used in the contemporary West, serve instead to *separate* the wearers from society. They're also only possible, as pointed out by sociologist Mike Featherstone (1991), within the contemporary capitalist system which modern primitives protest. Without consumer capitalism, modern primitives could not hope to use tattoos, piercings, implants, and other technologies to transform and create their identities anew. Even more ironically, perhaps, is the fact that many of these traditional forms of body modification have now disappeared from the societies in which they were practiced, often stamped out through Western imperialism, and only exist now in cannibalized form among modern primitives.

Interesting issues: Spanner case

The Spanner case refers to a British court case in which 16 gay men were prosecuted for engaging in consensual BDSM behavior. The case began in 1987 when the Manchester, England, police obtained what they thought was a snuff

extraordinary bodies

film in which a number of men were being tortured and, they thought, killed. The video was taken by some of the participants at a body play party in which the men were engaging in heavy BDSM activities including the beating of buttocks and genitals, the dripping of hot wax onto the genitals, genital bondage and manipulations, scrotal stretching, nipple and genital branding, play piercings, and other activities. Because the men were easily identifiable in the video, the police investigation led to the arrests and prosecutions of all of the men for assault, even though BDSM practices are and were not themselves illegal in Great Britain, and all of the practices were between consenting adults. In December 1990, the men pleaded guilty to a number of offences including assault with bodily harm, sending obscene materials through the mail, and using anesthetic without a license; some were fined, and others were sent to jail, with sentences up to four and a half years (many of which were later reduced). A number of the defendants appealed their convictions to the British Appeal Court, but their convictions were upheld. The case then went to the House of Lords, which in 1993 also upheld the original convictions. Finally, the case was appealed to the European Court of Human Rights in Strasbourg, France, which, like the courts before it, upheld the original judgment in 1997. After the Spanner case was resolved, the British Law Commission published a Consultation Paper called Consent in the Criminal Law which questioned the notion of whether physical assault can take place between consenting parties. BDSM advocates as well as supporters of sexual freedom and the freedom to perform radical body modifications hope that the Consultation Paper can be used in future criminal cases on behalf of defendants like the men who became known as the Spannermen. Another result of the case was the formation of a British organization called the Spanner Trust which works to defend the rights of gay and straight participants in BDSM.

Subversive bodies

Whether members of the modern primitives movement, the kinky gay, or BDSM movement, or whether people are simply fans of extreme modifications, one might call the bodies that result from these practices subversive bodies. Subversive bodies are bodies that have embraced practices that are seen as extreme by mainstream society – heavy tattooing, facial tattooing, multiple facial or genital piercings, and the heavy use of implants, stretching, branding, or cutting.

Punks, for example, have long embraced such practices and their bodies are a good example of the ways in which people can now inscribe themselves with marks representing their dissatisfaction with mainstream society and culture. Since punk is an oppositional subculture, punks have historically used forms of fashion and body adornment from the margins of mainstream culture, and that represent the ideology of freedom, non-conformity, anti-authoritarianism, and rebellion, thus the heavy use of ripped and defaced

FIGURE 12.3 Artist Larkin Cypher. His frontal mound and skull shape are naturally occurring deformities, while his horns are removable appliances that he made himself from polymer clay. His head is tattooed and he has an eyelid tattoo, and he wears blue horns in his stretched ear holes. Photo courtesy of Larkin Cypher.

clothing, messy or crazy hair, ugly and loud makeup, heavy tattoos and piercings, and elaborately decorated jackets and jeans. These stylistic elements, when viewed as a whole, created a coherent style that was intended to shock society. Piercing, for example, was associated with punks since long before the mainstreaming of piercing in the West. And like the other elements of punk style, piercings were and often still are self-made, with punks sticking themselves with needles, pins, staples, and other sharp implements, as well as cutting themselves with razor blades and knives. Punk piercings also tend to be "louder" than piercings in other scenes, with jewelry utilizing knives, long chains, and bones, as well as stretched piercings, and multiple piercings on the face. Punk women in particular use their bodies as a form of rebellion, challenging conventional standards of female beauty with their use of makeup, hair, clothing, and body modifications.

Because many of the practices found in the body modification community today are so extreme, at least by mainstream standards, there has long been a refrain among authorities and mental health professionals that suggest that people who engage in extreme body modifications are mutilating their bodies. Extreme piercings, heavy tattooing, cutting, branding, and other practices are sometimes seen as signs of mental illness, because these practices result in bodies which are so out of line with conventional norms and standards of beauty as to seem ugly. But this perspective assumes that there is a standard by which all bodies should be judged, and that any deviation from that standard is by definition a sign of mental or social distress.

These bodily practices are interpreted in a radically different way in the West than in traditional cultures – even when the practices are identical. One way in which the difference in interpretations can be understood is by contrasting the collectivist nature of traditional societies with the individualist nature of Western culture. Where traditional cultures mark social status onto the body, modern Westerners, and especially those who embrace extreme body practices, mark their own individual identity onto themselves. While Westerners in general favor practices that privilege the individual over the collective, when the individual self is seen as so contrary to social norms, the result is disdain and stigma. These bodies threaten the social order which demands conformity. For example, when gays tattoo and pierce their bodies, they bring their sexuality out into the open, challenging the heteronormativity of dominant society.

But as sociologist and women's studies scholar Victoria Pitts points out (2003), some body modification practices, such as facial piercings, are now becoming normalized, which is both good and bad for the body modification community. It's good because the wearers become less stigmatized, but it's bad because that means that for those who pioneered them, they must continuously push the boundaries of what is acceptable and non-acceptable. Subversive bodies do not necessarily want to become domesticated, after all. In addition, by continuously pushing the boundaries, and developing more extreme forms of body modification, some of the practices may become more dangerous as well.

Clearly, what is normative to one person – perhaps a simple dolphin tattoo on the ankle – is non-normative, or even subversive to another. The changes in, and varieties of, body modification that we have outlined in this chapter demonstrate how important social and cultural context is to an understanding of these quickly changing practices.

Key terms

Body Painting	Modern Primitives
Branding	Piercing
Head Binding	Scarification
Labrets	Tattooing

Further reading

Atkinson, Michael. (2003). *Tattooed: The Sociogenesis of a Body Art*. Toronto: University of Toronto Press.

Camphausen, Rufus C. (1997). *Return of the Tribal: A Celebration of Body Adornment: Piercing, Tattooing, Scarification, Body Painting*. Rochester, VT: Park Street Press.

DeMello, Margo. (2000). *Bodies of Inscription: A Cultural History of the Modern Tattoo Community*. Durham, NC: Duke University Press.

Pitts, Victoria. (2003). *In the Flesh: The Cultural Politics of Body Modification*. New York: Palgrave Macmillan.

Rubin, Arnold, (ed.). (1988). *Marks of Civilization*. Los Angeles, CA: Museum of Cultural History, UCLA.

Sanders, Clinton. (1989). *Customizing the Body: The Art and Culture of Tattooing*. Philadelphia, PA: Temple University Press.

chapter 13

Religious Bodies

In 2011, (now former) Denver Broncos quarterback Tim Tebow became a media sensation, gaining a measure of fame inside and outside of the professional sporting world not generally seen by other professional athletes. He is young, handsome, and talented, but that's not what has garnered him so much fame and attention. It was his practice of kneeling on the field in prayer during and after games that has made him such a magnetic – and controversial – public figure. Now called "**tebowing**," Tebow's public prayers have become both celebrated and mocked, and are the most visible, public show of the player's evangelical faith. The religious faithful love Tebow for the way in which he so publicly embodies his religious fervor and atheists hate him for what they perceive as his smugness (as well as his public opposition to abortion). If bodies become religious, at least in part, through performance of rituals, then Tebow's body, seen by millions of Americans each week during the football season, not only embodies religion but personifies it for those millions of viewers.

The body of Tim Tebow – handsome, white, fit, athletic – is not just a body that exemplifies Christianity during Tebowing. It also illustrates the ways in which athletes, and to a lesser extent, musicians and actors, look to their religion to explain the source of their talents. A win for Tebow was seen by many as a win for God. Conversely, a loss for Tebow was a win for the secular. Tebow, like so many athletes, saw himself as blessed by God, which was why he thanked God for his performances each week. (It's also something that we see in countless high school football games each week in this country when the team gathers in the pre-game huddle and prays together for God to give them a win.)

Tebow did not just credit his performance to God. We can also say that Tebow was created, as per his religion, in the image of God. God is, after all, a man (and a white man at that) in the Judeo-Christian tradition. Whenever a person publicly suggests that God might be a woman, or that Jesus might be a black man (while Jesus has long been depicted in art as northern European in terms of skin color and facial features, he probably was olive-skinned thanks to his Middle Eastern heritage), it often evokes outrage. What God looks like is more than an academic question. It is central to how we see and perceive ourselves as members of particular faiths. According to the Judeo-Christian tradition, for example, since man was made in God's image, to defile that image (as an example, in the case of Judaism, to tattoo the body) is to defile God's image.

This chapter looks at the ways that religions regulate and define the body and bodily practices. Here we'll look at how the body has been shaped by religion, whether through practices such as veiling or circumcision, or more extreme bodily practices such as self-mortification, fasting, and torture.

The veil

Religion has much to say about how we live our lives, and what we do with our bodies. Much of that information is gendered. The Western traditions of the book – Judaism, Christianity, and Islam – all have a great deal to say about how men and women should interact, and about men and women's bodies and appearances. Sikhs, both men and women, cannot cut their hair, because keeping the hair uncut shows respect for God's perfect creation. Some Muslim men are required to wear beards. Male Jews are circumcised eight days after birth as a visible sign of their incorporation into the community of Jews, and as the mark of the covenant between God and the followers of Abraham. These religiously inscribed bodily practices visibly mark on the body the faith of their practitioners.

Perhaps the most common, and sometimes controversial, way in which religion defines bodily practices is covering the head. A whole range of religions require, or encourage, women to wear head coverings, including some Christian groups like Mennonites and Amish, some Christian and Eastern Orthodox sects, nuns in most traditions, including Buddhism and Taoism, orthodox Jewish women, Muslims, and Sikhs.

In the Middle East, where Judaism, Christianity, and Islam developed, privacy is a highly valued concept for women, and seeing a woman's face is often seen as a sign of intimacy, to be reserved only for family. In the Jewish tradition, men are expected to cover their hair during prayer as a sign

FIGURE 13.1 Civil rights activist Samina Sundas, founding executive of *The American Muslim Voice*. Photo by Emily Fitzgerald, www.efitzgerald.com.

of respect for God, but in the Orthodox Jewish tradition, married women are expected to cover their hair at all times. Christianity also distinguishes between men and women. For instance, in I Corinthians 11:4–7, men are to *uncover* their heads in prayer, since they were made in the image of God, while women must *cover* their heads, since they reflect only the glory of man. In both Judaism and Christianity, hiding one's face both protects one's privacy, but can also indicate humility. For example, in the Bible, when men "hide their face" before God (Exodus 3:6; Isaiah 6:2; or Kings 19:13 when Elijah "wrapped his face in his mantle"), it means that they are showing humility and reverence before him, as in the traditions of many cultures which demand that social inferiors not make eye contact with those who are superior to them.

religious bodies

While the veil is most strongly associated with Islam, veiling predates Islam by thousands of years. Veiling for women was a sign of prestige in the Assyrian, Greek, Persian, Indian, and Byzantine cultures. In these cultures, elite women covered their hair or face, but in ancient Rome, servants covered their hair as a sign of respect. Because veiling was a sign of status, many cultures prohibited the wearing of veils by prostitutes, although lower-class women often did wear veils in order to appear as if they were of a higher class. Eventually, Islam embraced the veil, and as Islam spread from Saudi Arabia to other cultures, the wearing of veils spread along with it, becoming common by the eighth century – first by elites, and later by lower-class women. By the tenth century, many countries began instituting laws restricting the behavior of women, and mandating veiling or seclusion.

In Muslim countries, veiling differs by country: women may cover their faces, a portion of their face, their hair, as in the *hijab*, the most popular form of head covering, or, in some cases, their entire bodies, as in the *burqa* worn in Afghanistan. The *chador* is a full-length body shawl that is held together in the front with a pin or by hand and is common in Iran.

Veiling in Islam is a response to the Qu'ranic demand that women dress modestly in public (although veiling itself is not explicitly discussed in the Qu'ran). To be veiled is to be protected and secluded (and as such, is an example of **purdah,** the seclusion of women), and to have one's anonymity maintained. In cultures that have a strong honor–shame complex, as in the Middle East, a woman can bring shame onto her entire family by her personal conduct. If she were to be violated, her whole family, but especially the men, would be shamed. But veiling oneself when appearing in public protects a woman from the gaze of men, protecting her honor, and that honor is then extended to the members of her family. Because men respect the veil, they will be less likely to prey upon a woman who is veiled. The veil then represents respect, modesty, humility, and obedience – to religion, to culture, and to the family. It also shows that she protects her chastity or her fidelity to her husband, thus guaranteeing virginity upon marriage and paternity to her husband.

In addition, as in the past, the veil represents wealth and status. In stratified societies, elite women often experience the greatest amount of control over their sexuality. The veil is one way to protect the wealth, status, and honor of well-to-do families by ensuring that the women in those families do not have sexual relations with lower-class men. In addition, in the past, only wealthy families could afford to seclude their women, so veiling in a variety of cultures has long been a sign of status and prestige as well.

Each culture has different rules about the wearing of the veil. Some cultures have the law of ***hijab***, a mandatory code for women to veil in public. This was the case in Afghanistan under the **Taliban**, in Saudi Arabia, and in Kuwait and Iran today. Failure to comply can result in imprisonment, harassment, or physical punishment. The veil then represents, ironically, freedom because women can use their veils to go out in public; here it acts as a form of portable seclusion. Some countries, like Tunisia and Turkey, prohibit the wearing of veils in public buildings or schools. Most Muslim countries do not have mandatory veiling laws, so women can voluntarily choose to wear the veil.

Today, because of the conflicts between Western Christian societies and Islamic cultures, veiling has become increasingly controversial. In early 2011, France banned the wearing of face coverings in public spaces, after a contentious public debate. Those in support of the law see it as a way to protect Muslim women from control by their husbands, and to force the assimilation of Middle Eastern populations into French society. Those opposed to the law see it as a sign of the increasing stigmatization of Muslims in France. In fact, a great many Muslim feminists voluntarily wear the veil, whether in the Middle East or in Western nations, as a sign of respect for their religion and for their culture, and as a way to resist Western cultural hegemony.

Pollution and the female body

Another way in which religious bodily practices differ by gender has to do with the notion or purity or impurity. Many religions see women's biological attributes as signs of **ritual pollution**. Menstruation and childbirth are both seen as unclean in a variety of religious traditions. In Judaism, for example, women are unclean while menstruating which means that, among Orthodox Jews, anything that she touches during that time becomes unclean as well, so she must be segregated from the rest of the community. Only after taking a ritual bath is she allowed to re-enter social life.

This is a common feature of a number of religions: the idea that there are behaviors, people, or things that are polluting, and that there are behaviors, people, and things that are pure; the former needs to be avoided and the latter to be strived for. The Indian **caste** system is one example of this concern with purity. In the caste system, Hindus are segregated into a rigid hierarchical order on the basis of people's purity or lack thereof. Untouchables, the most unclean of all of the groups, are not only subject to a degree of oppression that most people around the world would find shocking, but they are so physically impure that they cannot be touched. Women, too, in the Hindu system, are often impure, as when, for example, they are menstruating. A dilemma for Hindu men is even though they are dependent on women to cook for them and to bear their children, contact with women's bodies is potentially contaminating to a man, so women must undergo strict menstrual seclusion. In addition, because chastity is extremely important for an unmarried woman, and fidelity for a married woman, a woman's sexuality is controlled throughout the course of her life; she

FIGURE 13.2 A statue of a holy woman at the Cementiri de Montjuïc in Barcelona, Spain. Photo courtesy of Jeff Hayes.

can be severely punished for engaging in behaviors that even suggest something illicit.

Islam is similar in that women are seen as sexually threatening to men, thus in some Muslim cultures, women need to be strictly separated from men in as many aspects of life as possible. Ideally, when in a strict Muslim culture, a woman should be secluded in her home and if she appears in public she must be veiled. Virgin women are seen as pure (although still dangerous since they pose a sexual temptation), but once they have had sexual intercourse, they are seen to have lost their ability to control their sexual impulses, and order must be imposed.

Christian doctrine, too, is filled with ideas about women's pollution. Visions of women as inherently evil, lustful, and destructive are encoded in numerous teachings, such as Eve's central sin. Eve's sin is especially

extraordinary bodies

troubling because it means that all women are themselves sinners and must be punished for their sins (through the pain of childbirth, for example). In the New Testament, the theme continues as Paul writes in Ephesians 5:23 that women are to be subject to their husbands as to the Lord, for the man is the head of the woman just as Christ is the head of the church. Also, for all three religions, the book of Genesis shows that man did not originally spring from woman, but woman was made out of man, and man was not created for woman's sake but woman for the sake of man.

Interesting issues: the witch

In cultures around the world, there are beliefs in either sorcery, witchcraft, or both. Anthropologists distinguish between sorcery and witchcraft. Sorcery is the use of magic in order to benefit the sorcerer or her or his clients. Witchcraft is the belief that certain members of society are inherently able to harm others. Witches sometimes do not even know that they are witches; they are born evil and can cause accidents, illnesses, bad luck, and even death to others. The witch's body is even different. In mythologies around the world, the understanding of the witch and the witch's abilities are remarkably similar. Witches may be able to transform themselves into animals, they may have organs which are reversed in their bodies, they can shape shift, and they have the evil eye: they can curse a person just by looking at them. Witches can fly at night, sometimes by using an ointment made by mixing belladonna, henbane, or another one of the "hexing herbs" with baby's fat, and inserting it into their vaginas with a broomstick. Witches can be easily identified because they have what's known as a witch's teat: a mole, freckle, scar, or bump somewhere on their body that, when pricked with a needle without eliciting pain, indicates their true nature. Finally, in Europe, witches could be identified by what was known as an "ordeal by water." Because witches were thought to be made of wood (that's why they were killed by burning), an accused witch was thrown into a body of water; if she floated to the surface, she was a witch, and she would be fished out and executed. But if she sank, she was not a witch. Others thought that witches floated because water was pure and would repel the witch. In Europe, as in many other societies, witchcraft accusations were often a social tool used by societies to target social deviants. Those accused of witchcraft are often the most marginalized and powerless members of society – the homeless, religious minorities, gypsies, old women, or prostitutes.

Denying the body: fasting, abstinence, and self-mortification

Self-mortification refers to the practice of punishing oneself to atone for wrongdoing. Self-mortification can involve denying oneself bodily pleasures such as sex or meat, or it can involve adopting a simple or impoverished lifestyle. A number of different religious traditions encourage the practice of self-mortification either for their members or their priests, including Islam, Judaism, Hinduism, and Christianity. Various indigenous peoples also incorporate voluntary pain, suffering, and self-denial as part of their spiritual traditions as vehicles to the divine or as part of rites of passage.

In Christianity, **original sin** necessitates that all Christians do penance for that sin as well as future sins to come, and in the Bible, God demanded that his faithful abstain from meat on Fridays, and later, the 40-day period of **Lent** (based on Jesus's fast for 40 days) was instituted during which Christians are also asked to give up meat. The Bible also notes the practice of wearing rags, tearing clothes and hair, and fasting in order to humble oneself before God, or to imitate Christ's suffering. During the early days of the church when the church was still preaching an imminent end of the world, St Paul counseled believers to renounce their earthly and bodily pleasures, since the present world was shortly to end. Even today, some Christians take vows of poverty, others fast or deny themselves sexual pleasure, and still others wear hair shirts or flagellate themselves with whips, switches, or other tools. Still others carry chains with them wherever they go. The goal of such practices could be to achieve union with God, to alleviate one's sins or the sins of others, or to secure a higher place in heaven. For others, suffering is critical to achieving salvation.

Ancient Meso-Americans also practiced ritual mortification. Mayan women pulled studded ropes through holes in their tongues, and Mayan kings used thorns and spines to draw blood from their penises, tongues, and earlobes. Some Native American tribes also practiced self-mortification. For example, the Sun Dance was a Plains Indian ritual that included dancing, singing, drumming, and fasting and culminated in a ritual in which participants attached themselves to a pole via ropes attached to bone or wood skewers, which are inserted into pre-pierced holes in the chest. Dancing around in a circle to the beat of drums and prayers, the participants pulled against the pole to tear the skewers out.

Indian holy men called Sadhus also engaged in fasting and self-mortification, including self-flagellation, laying on a bed of nails, and other practices. Some may stand in one place for years upon end, stand only on one leg, or refrain from speaking. The Kavadi is a Hindu ritual normally performed during the Thaipusam Festival in India. Bearing Kavadi means to bear a large steel basket or other container filled with items to be offered to the god Muruga, as a form of penance. Some participants wear a skewer inserted through their tongue and others through their cheeks, and still others wear skewers through other parts of the body, and some also walk through burning coals during the ceremony. Sometimes the basket itself is suspended from the body with hooks and spears.

extraordinary bodies

Asceticism refers to a life that is characterized by abstaining from worldly and bodily pleasures, through self-denial and often self-mortification. In Christianity, man is a fallen creature and the body, as flesh, represents the opposite of the soul or the spirit; it requires mastery, discipline, and denial: the denial of the body is central to asceticism. The goal of the ascetic is to strengthen one's spiritual life through distancing oneself from the profane world. Other forms of self-denial include refraining from sexual contact (either temporarily or permanently), dressing in old clothing or rags, and giving up all personal possessions, all of which are used to release one's connection to the profane world and also to purify the soul. Asceticism is a part of a number of religious traditions including Christianity, Judaism, and Islam as well as Buddhism and Hinduism. Because not all members of a religious tradition can live an ascetic life, asceticism is usually practiced by monks, nuns, yogis, and other especially devoted adherents. In Medieval Europe, because lay people could not practice such a life, they could pay monks to practice asceticism on their behalf.

With the rise of the Protestant Reformation, this distinction between the holy monks and the unholy lay people broke down, and regular lay people began to try to emulate practices of self-control and discipline in their everyday lives. Later, with the rise of the Puritans in the seventeenth century, new movements arose that attempted to control bodily excesses through diet. For instance John Harvey Kellogg, the inventor of corn flakes, discouraged stimulating foods, advocated a vegetarian diet, and encouraged sexual abstinence. Another reformer of the time, Sylvester Graham (the inventor of the graham cracker) also promoted both vegetarianism and sexual abstinence. Both men encouraged their followers to recognize the links between a moral life and abstinence in both food and sex. Even dancing was prohibited by a great many Protestant reformers of the time; it was seen, for example, by John Calvin as a precursor to sexual activity.

Fasting is a form of self-denial, and is the most common practice associated with ascetism, and involves the temporary abstaining from food in order to punish oneself, atone for one's sins, or to produce visions. Fasting and other forms of spiritual purification is often a step in the process of communicating with God or the gods.

In Portugal, there have been a number of young women who have become famous through fasting. Called non-eaters by anthropologist Joao de Pina-Cabral, these women – all virgins, and all adolescents when they stopped eating – have long been revered by the faithful, and are thought to survive – allegedly for as long as 30 years – either with no food at all or with only a daily Eucharist cracker to sustain them. Their ability to survive without sustenance is attributed to their extreme holiness. According to Lena Gemzoe (2005), that the sanctity of these women comes from their ability to control food should not be surprising to us, since for women, food is often the one thing that they can control. This practice, by the way, has been happening for hundreds of years. While holy men and holy women around the world are often defined by their ability to abstain – from food, from wealth, and from sex – women like Alexandrina of Balasar and Catherine of Siena typically achieve sainthood *only* by abstaining from food, by becoming "holy anorexics." Typically, women are problematic in religions around the world precisely *because of* their physicality. Yet at the same time, female mystics are more likely to bear their mystical experiences in their bodies: through **stigmata**, through self-starvation, and through ecstatic experiences.

Medieval scholar Caroline Walker Bynum (1995) points out that it's also an interesting twist on the notion of the **Eucharist**. The Eucharist, or the Body of Christ, is the symbolic transformation of the cracker or bread into the body of Christ during the Catholic Mass; participants, by consuming the Eucharistic host, symbolically achieve communion, or oneness, with Christ. But the importance of the host for not just contemporary non-eaters but thirteenth-century female mystics went way beyond the Mass. It became a miraculous object in and of itself, and some women would race from church to church to receive the Eucharist as many times as possible. Walker Bynum notes that thirteenth-century Belgian saint Ida of Louvain went so crazy for her love of the Eucharist that she had to be put into chains. It should not surprise us then that the holy eaters could sustain life from its blessed power.

Interesting issues: Christian weight loss programs

According to the Journal for the Scientific Study of Religion, *American Christians are the most overweight of all Americans; of Christians, the Baptists are the most obese. Like the nineteenth-century religious and dietary reformers John Harvey Kellogg and Sylvester Graham, today there are a number of Christians who believe that there are links between a holy lifestyle and a healthy lifestyle. They have formed what are called Christian weight loss programs. These programs encourage an adherence to a Christian lifestyle, a focus on Christian devotionals, and a focus on good dietary practices, all of which should lead to weight loss. Many involve buying books or products, some involve joining support groups, and some involve attending workshops or summits, but all mandate active Biblical study. These programs also focus, as did the programs led by Kellogg and Graham, on the whole person, and saw weight loss as involving not just physical health but emotional and spiritual health as well. Some of the programs also borrow from 12-step programs like AA in that one must surrender one's problems to God and request from God one's solutions. In addition, the motivation to lose weight in these programs should not be personal: God wants you to take care of your body, which you have defiled by filling it with too much fat. In Christian weight loss programs, losing weight is a way to honor God.*

extraordinary bodies

Religion and sex

All cultures, of course, have rules regarding sexuality. Sexuality is not just a universal human behavior, but it's one of the most socially and culturally charged. Who should have sex with whom, and under what circumstances and for what purpose, has always been subject to a wide variety of cultural rules, which are often enshrined in religion.

In the West, the Judeo-Christian religious system shapes how most of us grew up thinking about sex. Many of these beliefs come from St Augustine, who, before converting to Christianity, was a believer of **Manichaeanism**, which taught that sex was evil. After becoming a Christian, Augustine wrote heavily about sexuality, and his ideas – that the ideal Christian life demanded absolute abstinence, but if that could not be fulfilled, God created marriage, but only for the purposes of procreation – have come to shape the Western understanding of sex today.

But even before Augustine, the conservative view of sexuality was shaped by the circumstances in which the early Christians lived. Expecting an imminent end of the world, Jesus and his followers did not encourage sex, marriage, or procreation, since the focus for these Christians was preparing for the afterlife. In Matthew 19:12, Jesus said, "For some are eunuchs because they were born that way; others were made that way by men; and others have renounced marriage because of the kingdom of heaven. The one who can accept this should accept it." This may be interpreted as suggesting that one should embrace abstinence in order to prepare for the imminent Kingdom of God.

It should come as no surprise, then, that Christianity has one of the world's most restrictive views on sex and sexuality. Like Judaism before it, Christianity mandates that children be conceived and raised within a marriage; that is one of the foundations of most legal systems which determine how property is transmitted across generations. But beyond that, Christianity, Islam, and Judaism preach chastity to young people, encourage heterosexuality, and discourage premarital sex as well as adultery. Orthodox Judaism, Islam, and many types of Christianity go further, however, and claim that sex is only to be used for procreation; that is why birth control is prohibited for Catholics, and masturbation (known as "secreting semen in vain" among Jews), oral sex, anal sex, and homosexuality are seen as sinful. In addition, modest dress is encouraged or mandated for women, but not men, in a variety of orthodox and conservative traditions within both Christianity and Judaism, as well as in Islam. Even doctors, while trained in medicine, shared many of the beliefs promoted by the Christian church, and until very recently, tended to see "excessive" sexuality as abnormal and unhealthy. Sexual activity could cause "nervous exhaustion," and masturbation and female desire were especially dangerous to health (and morality).

Today, progressive Christians and Jews often see sexuality very differently. Premarital sex, homosexuality, and masturbation are not decried in progressive traditions. On the other hand, Islam continues to condemn homosexuality.

Eastern religions like Buddhism and Hinduism, on the other hand, have very different views of sex and sexuality. Sexual expression has often been encouraged in Hinduism, and while Hindu ascetics abstain from sex, the fact that the Kama Sutra, a second-century sex manual, is considered a Hindu text indicates that sexuality is not just frowned upon but is embraced within at least certain parts of Hinduism.

The body/soul division

One of the themes running through this chapter so far is that in many religious traditions, the body is dangerous, messy, or unpredictable, and thus it needs to be controlled. Religious practices like fasting, body mortification, and sexual abstinence are all examples of the way that the body is troubling, and needs to be disciplined. We've already pointed out that in a number of religions, women are particularly polluting, and that in a number of cultures, women are associated with the physical body while men are associated with the mind. This is certainly the case in Christianity. In Christianity, in particular, with its focus on Eve's sin and the fallen state of humanity, there is quite a bit of anxiety about the body, and the female body in particular. Christianity inherited from the ancient Greeks and Romans the duality of the mind and the body (Epictetus once said that humans are born with "the body which we share with the animals, and the reason and mind which we share with the gods"), and from there the idea that the former (the mind, spirit or soul) is to be celebrated and aspired to, while the latter (the body) is to be deplored and denied, emerged. The more physical, material, or bodily the person, the more condemned.

This is one of the reasons why idolatry – the worship of an idol or object – is so condemned within much of Christianity, and why abstinence is so revered. Idolatry is an example of the material, corporeal, world, while religion is to be focused on the sacred, the immaterial. After death, after all, the body comes to an end, while the soul continues on. (An exception is found in the Catholic tradition of venerating **relics**: bones or other body parts of saints or other venerated or holy people, a tradition also found in other religions as well.)

Another way of putting it is the distinction between the carnal, which must be negated, and the spiritual, which must be elevated. Protestant reformer Martin Luther wrote of three levels of humanity: the spiritual, the mental, and, last in importance, the bodily. Many fundamentalist Protestants today (as well as fundamentalists of other religions) prohibit or deny many bodily activities that cannot be readily justified, including dancing, wearing makeup, or drinking alcohol or caffeine. For French Reformation theologian John Calvin, the body's only role is to direct the soul.

Buddhism is also based on the idea of the duality of the mind or soul and the body. In order to achieve enlightenment, and liberation from the suffering involved in life and death, one must not cling to the body, or indeed to life itself. The body, for Buddhists, is the enemy. On the other hand, the body in Buddhism is also a vehicle: it can help the adherent to fulfill their spiritual path and can help one to be of service to others.

Bodily practices

The treatment of the body, as we have seen, is central in many religious practices. Because the flesh is subject to impurity and pollution, practices which focus on cleansing the body are found in a variety of religions. One example of this is **foot washing**: of all of the parts of the body, the feet are the most unclean, thanks to their contact with the earth.

Muslims traditionally wash their feet (a practice called *wudhu*) before praying (as well as hands, hair, and face). Feet must be washed three times. The reason for wudhu in Islam is that without purifying one's body, one's mind cannot be purified. Because Muslims pray five times a day, and thus must pray when at work, at school, and in public spaces, foot baths are common sites in predominantly Muslim countries, and a few American communities with large numbers of Muslims have installed foot baths in public places, so that Muslims do not have to wash their feet in public sinks.

In India, traditionally the parents of a bride wash the feet of their daughter's groom as a way of showing respect to the man who will take care of their daughter. In Buddhism, water for foot washing is one of the eight offerings traditionally made to Buddha, which allows the believer to purify one's negative karma and achieve the body of a Buddha.

In Christianity, on the other hand, foot washing has a slightly different meaning. The New Testament tells us that Jesus washed his disciples' feet as a way to serve them during the Last Supper. At the time that Jesus lived, servants would have washed their masters' feet, so Jesus' decision to wash the apostles' feet was a way of teaching humility and submission.

According to the Gospels, during the evening of the Last Supper, the Apostles were fighting over who would have the highest position in the Kingdom of God, demonstrating their pride. The washing of the feet – a humble and menial task normally left to servants – taught the disciples humility. In addition, feet in the Christian tradition often symbolize walking the spiritual path, so foot washing (using water, which often symbolizes the word of God, as well as cleansing away false beliefs) can also be construed as Jesus' message to his disciples to continue on the path of righteousness

FIGURE 13.3 Mary holding Jesus after the Crucifixion. The body of Jesus is central to much of Christianity. Photo courtesy of Robin Montgomery.

after his death. The Gospels tell us that Peter refused to let Jesus wash his feet, but Jesus told him that without having his feet bathed by him, he would "have no inheritance with me."

Today, some Christian groups continue to practice foot washing, following in the teachings of Jesus. In the Catholic Church, the priest or prelate will wash the feet of twelve poor men, who represent the Apostles, during Holy Week. For Christians who practice foot washing today, it is intended to bring them closer to Jesus and to fill them with a sense of humility and service, concepts that should hopefully be reinforced through other aspects of service to community.

Another form of bodily purification involving water is **baptism**. Baptism is a Christian ritual in which an infant, or, in some traditions, an adult who is converting to the faith, is annointed with, or dunked into, water, in order to be admitted into the Church. It is one of the seven sacraments of the Catholic Church.

Baptism derives from the New Testament story of John the Baptist, who may have been Jesus' cousin, who baptized Jesus by pouring water over him while he stood in the River Jordan. At that time, John baptized Jews as a way for them to repent of their sins. From the time of Jesus onward, baptism became the primary ritual by which someone would convert to Christianity.

extraordinary bodies

The practice most likely derived from the ancient practice of washing one's hands before a meal, as well as from purification practices found throughout the ancient world, including in Judaism. Baptism is mentioned in the Gospels, as well as Acts, which recount that after his resurrection, Jesus instructed his disciples to baptize the nations in his name.

Today, the practice of Baptism varies among Christian denominations. While originally, adults were baptized, over time the practice shifted to baptizing children and, ultimately, infants in the Middle Ages. Most Catholic and Protestant groups practice affusion, which means pouring holy water over the head of the disciple, but sometimes aspersion, or sprinkling water onto the head, is practiced. Immersing the disciple in a body of water is practiced by Mormons, and submersion, in which the entire body is covered in water, is practiced in the Eastern Orthodox Church, by Seventh Day Adventists, and by many evangelical and born again groups. Today, most Christian denominations baptize infants, but Baptists, Pentecostals, Mormons, and a variety of born-again traditions only baptize adults or older children, because only adults are able to profess their faith in Jesus. In addition, these groups do not believe that baptism can wipe away sin; it is purely a visible sign of faith.

Other ways in which bodies are purified or consecrated during religious rituals include the rubbing of butter, fat, milk, or other substances on the face and body of ritual participants. For example, Eastern Orthodox men and women are anointed with oil during Baptism, confirmation, when sick, and on other occasions. In Hinduism, one of the most precious substances of all is clarified butter, known as *ghee*, which is used in a variety of Hindu rituals. For instance prior to a cremation, a body is anointed with clarified butter. It is also used to purify someone who has become temporarily impure. Clarified butter can even make impure foods, or foods prepared by impure people pure enough for high caste people to consume. In Christianity, on Ash Wednesday, the first day of Lent (the 40-day period leading up to Easter when believers fast or deny themselves something as a way of paying penance for their sins and preparing for the celebration of Jesus' resurrection), the faithful are anointed on their foreheads with the sign of the cross made of ashes mixed with blessed oil to show the repentance of their sins. This act recalls the ancient Near Eastern practice of sitting in ashes or sprinkling ashes onto oneself as a sign of mourning or repentance.

Dietary habits, too, or proscriptions against certain forms of labor, are ways in which faith is embodied. Whether fasting during Lent, refraining from working on the Sabbath, or abstaining from eating pork, bodies are structured and disciplined according to the principles of the faith.

On a much simpler level, the ways in which we hold and move our bodies during religious worship is also an example of how faith and religious codes for behavior shape our bodies. Muslims, as we have noted, pray five times a day. After ensuring that their environment and clothing are clean, they must further cleanse themselves with water, they must engage in a number of stances, all in the direction of Mecca, from standing to bowing to **prostrating** themselves on the ground. Other forms of prayer found in other religions include clasping the hands, raising the hands, bowing the head, or holding hands with others. In Catholicism, **genuflecting**, or kneeling on the right knee, is required in certain ritual situations, such as in front of the Holy Eucharist. Other Catholics make what is called the sign of the cross when entering a church; by using their right hand to touch their forehead, the chest, the left and then the right shoulder, people profess their faith, show themselves as disciples of Christ, defend themselves against evil, and accept suffering. Members of the Eastern Orthodox faith prostrate themselves, face the east, mark themselves with the sign of the cross, and engage in deep bows – all ways to express their devotion. In some faiths, "**laying-on of hands**," when participants lay their hands on a person, is used to invoke the Holy Spirit, to cure someone of illness, to bless someone, or to confirm them as a member of the church. It is practiced by Jews, Eastern Orthodox church members, Catholics, Mormons, and other groups.

Some religions have much more extreme corporeal practices. In Thailand, a Taoist festival known as the Phuket Vegetarian Festival, which lasts for nine days and attracts Thailand's Chinese community, participants, who must be virgin men or women, abstain from eating meat and pierce their cheeks and tongues with skewers while in a trance state. Participants are said to feel no pain during these practices, because they are possessed by, or being ridden by, spirits, a practice known as *mah song,* which translates to riding a horse.

Spirit possession, stigmata, and resurrection: miracles of the faithful

Spirit possession refers to the practice whereby a person, often a shaman or someone who is trained in the practice, is possessed or taken by a spirit. Spirits can be good, neutral, or evil, and the practice can be culturally institutionalized or considered deviant. In shamanism, Haitian voodoo, or other traditions where spirit possession is a normal part of the culture, a believer goes into a trance, often brought on by chanting, fasting, drugs, or lack of sleep, and during the trance, is possessed by the spirit. When possessed, or as the Haitians say, when "mounted," the possessed will behave in ways very differently from normal, and in accordance with the norms of the particular spirit. In shamanism, the spirits can be asked to aid the living with a variety of problems – health, luck, protection, and divination. The spirits themselves are generally classified by anthropologists as tutelary spirits, a spirit who is assigned to the shaman as guide and protector, and helping spirits, who assist humans in particular tasks. Spirits can be anthropomorphic, taking the form of living or dead humans, or theriomorphic, taking the form of animals. While spirit possession is typically seen as negative in Christianity, in the United States, it does occur in some Pentecostal traditions. In that case, a person is possessed by the Holy Ghost, and it manifests itself when the person exhibits **glossalia**, or speaking in tongues. Many Catholics also believe in demonic possession where a devil possesses a person; in that case, an exorcist must be brought in to remove the demon from the person's body.

In many cultures, shamans, who utilize spirit possession regularly, come into their calling through illness, affliction, or disability. They generally do not choose to be shamans. Many shamans come from marginalized positions in society, and their afflictions, which are interpreted as spirit possession, are in part a response to that social condition. Through shamanism, their marginal status is temporarily reversed, and if the afflicted becomes particularly good at controlling the spirits that afflict them, they can themselves become a shaman, a person of power. Shamans say that those whose lives flow smoothly are rarely summoned by the spirits. In some cultures, marginalized or dispossessed people, often women, participate in what anthropologists call **cults of affliction,** where multiple people become possessed, often at once. Through participation, their marginal status is temporarily reversed, the victims can make demands which would otherwise go unanswered, and sometimes, if the afflicted become particularly good at managing their spirits, they can themselves become a shaman, a person of power. In the words of anthropologist I. M. Lewis, they go "from illness to ecstasy" (1971). Anthropologist Aihwa Ong (1987) studied an interesting case of mass spirit possession, whereby an entire group of young female factory workers in Malaysia regularly became possessed together by spirits known as weretigers. She interpreted their possession experiences – which occurred from time to time – as a form of spiritual and physical protest against the demeaning conditions under which the women worked. Unfortunately, while the possession did provide the women some relief – sometimes the factory would be closed temporarily, while the women were sent home on Valium; sometimes a shaman is brought in to spiritually cleanse the factory before reopening – it never dealt with the source of their stress and mistreatment, which continues today.

Spirit possession is an example of religious **ecstasy,** an altered state of consciousness in which awareness of the physical world is reduced or altered, because the person is in a trance state. Sometimes the person experiences a state of euphoria. It is associated with mystical traditions in religious around the world and can be brought on by meditation, chanting, dance, drugs, or other mind and body altering conditions.

Stigmata are another way in which the spiritual world manifests itself in the physical body. Stigmata refer to the marks or bruises on the body of Jesus Christ from his crucifixion, as well as mystical marks or bruises on devout Christians, which are thought to correspond to the wounds of Jesus. While reported cases of stigmata seen on the faithful are often on the hands or wrists and feet or ankles (which correspond to the areas on which Jesus was thought to be nailed to the cross), stigmata could also be seen on the forehead (where Jesus wore a crown of thorns), on the back (from his scourging), or on other areas of the body. Sometimes stigmata are said to be painful but invisible and sometimes they are said to emit an odor known as the odour of sanctity, a sweet smell that emanates from saints. The stigmatic is often in a state of trance or ecstasy while the wound is appearing. But the original Greco-Roman usage of the term actually means mark or tattoo.

While cases of Christians reporting to bear the wounds of Christ did not develop until the thirteenth century, there are references to stigmata much earlier in Christian literature. For instance, Paul's letter in Galatians 6:17 reads, "I carry the marks/scars/brands of Jesus on my body." The term stigmata was used in this case, and in much early Christian writing, both to refer to the visible wounds of Christ, as well to the Roman practice of tattooing. While Paul's usage here was metaphorical (there is no reason to suggest that Paul was tattooed or that he was encouraging tattoos for the faithful), the usage illustrates that the old term for tattooing common in the Roman world was giving way to a newer, Christ-centered term. It is also clear that there was a connection between the wounds of Christ and the practice of tattooing, commonly used in the ancient world as a form of punishment. In fact, the Romans, like the Greeks before them, tattooed criminals on the forehead, and until the conversion to Christianity of Constantine and whole of the Roman Empire, Christians were commonly tattooed in this fashion. Thus the tattoo on the head of a faithful Roman Christian could be seen as a sign of faith and could be connected with the wounds of Christ.

The first person to have purportedly demonstrated the wounds of Christ, i.e., the modern use of the term stigmata, was St Francis of Assisi. Padre Pio of Pietrelcina was canonized in 2002 for his wounds. Caroline Walker Bynum (1991) points out that most stigmatics have been women, however, just as most holy non-eaters are women; in addition, only women's wounds have allegedly bled. For example, Mary Rose Ferron was the first documented American stigmatist; she was photographed with images of a crown of thorns bleeding on her forehead. Today, there is no consensus about the cause or veracity of stigmata. Some scientists feel they result from self-mutilation or have something to do with the spiritual fasting that is often associated with it. In fact, a variety of women throughout the history of Christendom have in fact engaged in self-mutilation as a sign of their devotion to Christ and as a way to get close to him during the time of his suffering; as with the mystical experiences found in cults of affliction in other cultures, these women too fuse their suffering with ecstasy.

Stigmata derive from what, in Christianity, is the greatest miracle of all: the resurrection of Christ. In Christian belief, the body of Jesus Christ was resurrected three days after his death. Interestingly, even though most Christians believe in the mind/body dualism discussed earlier, the resurrection, and before that the crucifixion, is an example of the physicality of Christ being central to the belief system. Christ's body, while being tortured on the cross, is the vehicle both of suffering, which is shared by the faithful, and of sacrifice: Jesus was sacrificed for all of our sins. But that same body is also the symbol of redemption and atonement for those same sins. After Jesus rose, it was not just his spirit which was resurrected, but his physical body, complete with the nail holes in his hands and his sides, according to the Gospel of John (John 20:24–9). In addition, the resurrection of Jesus is central to the idea that Christians will themselves be resurrected, after the end of the world has come to pass. In 1 Corinthians 15:20–2, Paul writes, "Because of Adam, all people die. So because of Christ, all will be made alive."

Christ's suffering on the cross has been a central, and visible, sign of faith for the most ardent of Christ's followers for centuries. In Chapter 14, we will look at how torture has long been used to punish and discipline bodies. But where Christ's suffering was used as the basis for a global religion, the suffering and torture of convicts in other contexts often goes unremarked.

Key terms

Asceticism	Original Sin
Baptism	Prostration
Caste	Relics
Cults of Affliction	Ritual Pollution
Ecstasy	Self-Mortification
Eucharist	Sikhs
Foot Washing	Sorcery
Genuflecting	Spirit Possession
Glossalia	Stigmata
Hijab	Taliban
Laying on of Hands	Tebowing
Lent	Witchcraft
Manichaeanism	

Further reading

Bell, Rudolph M. (1985). *Holy Anorexia*. Chicago, IL: University of Chicago Press.

Bottomley, F. (1979). *Attitudes to the Body in Western Christendom*. London: Lepus Books.

Brown, Peter. (1988). *The Body and Society: Men, Women and Sexual Renunciation in Early Christianity*. Lectures on the History of Religions, n.s., 13. New York: Columbia University Press.

Bynum, Caroline Walker. (1995). *The Resurrection of the Body in Western Christianity, 200–1336*. New York: Columbia University Press.

Coakley, Sarah. (1997). *Religion and the Body*. Cambridge: Cambridge University Press.

PART VI

State and Corporate Regulation of the Body

chapter 14

Tortured, Punished, and Convict Bodies

Most Americans think that the United States opposes, and does not practice, torture. After all, torture is prohibited under both U.S. and international law – the United States is a signatory both to the Third and Fourth **Geneva Convention** as well as to the United Nations Convention against Torture. Yet since September 11, 2001, and the wars in Iraq and Afghanistan, the line between unacceptable torture and acceptable conduct has blurred, with intelligence officers and military personnel both engaging in what was once considered to be torture. Many people now argue that the need to extract information from suspects in the new "war on terror" outweighs the concerns about torture. Practices like waterboarding and sleep deprivation, typically considered to meet the definition of torture, have been redefined in recent years in the United States as "**enhanced interrogation techniques**," terms like "**extraordinary rendition**" have entered our vocabulary, and the television show 24 created a hero out of fictional character Jack Bauer, who saved the country over and over, often through the use of torture.

How the state controls convicts, criminal suspects, prisoners of war, and slaves – in other words, dangerous bodies – is a topic that is both rich in terms of historical material and also very relevant to the world we live in today. In this chapter, we will address methods of confinement for dangerous and deviant bodies, as well as methods of identifying, marking, and punishing such bodies, via practices like castration, torture, tattooing, branding, and capital punishment.

Marking deviance: branding, castration, and tattooing

In societies around the world, but especially in state-level societies, criminals have commonly been marked in some way by the state either as punishment for their crime, to identify them as a criminal, or to stigmatize them throughout their lives. In addition, **corporal punishment**, in which the body is the site of the punishment via whipping, the removal of a limb, or even death, is another way that punishment is literally "marked" on the body.

Some trace the evolution of these practices to the biblical story in which God places a mark on Cain, the first murderer, to brand him as a criminal and social outcast, but corporal punishment had been practiced throughout the Greco-Roman and Egyptian world. In addition, those cultures all used tattooing and branding as a form of punishment and identification for criminals, practices which were continued throughout Western civilization in Europe and the Americas.

For example, the origin of human branding in the West is to mark the ownership of slaves. It was seen in the Greco-Roman world, and also was used by European slave traders. The Greeks branded slaves with a delta for *doulos* or slave. Runaway slaves were marked by the Romans with the letter F (for *fugitivus*). Robbers, like runaway slaves, were marked by the Romans with the letter F (*fur*); and men sentenced to work in the mines, and convicts condemned to fight in gladiatorial shows, were branded (or perhaps tattooed) on the forehead for identification.

The first known societies to use tattoos in a punitive fashion were the Thracians, Persians, Greeks, and Romans, all of whom tattooed runaway slaves and criminals. The Persians tattooed slaves and prisoners with the name of their captor, master, and sometimes the Emperor, and Roman slaves were marked on the face with either the crime or the punishment (which was commonly being sent to the mines), until the Emperor Constantine outlawed facial tattooing in the fourth century.

Punitive tattooing and branding traveled through the Roman world to Europe where both practices were used in Germany, England, and France to mark slaves, prisoners, adulterers, army deserters, and the like. British Army deserters were branded with a D, and, beginning in the eighteenth century, the British started using cold iron brands for high-status criminals. Theft and many other offenses were punished with a brand, often with the letter T. In France galley slaves and convicts could be branded TF for forced labor (*travaux forcés*) until 1832. The American colonies inherited the practices as well. Slave masters in American and West Indian colonies also used tattooing and branding for the identification of slaves and to punish runaway or insubordinate slaves. Tattoos and brands were a preferred form of punishment in all of these cases because it was a dual-purpose

FIGURE 14.1 Auschwitz survivor Sam Rosenzweig displays his identification tattoo. Air Force photo by Rudy Purificato. Image via U.S. Air Force.

punishment: one purpose was to inflict pain, but another was to permanently, and often very publicly, proclaim the crime, either through the words or letters used, or simply the fact that forehead tattoos were associated with criminality.

In India, another European colony, after 1797, criminals had their criminal status tattooed on them. The word for tattooing in Hindi later came to mean the marking of criminals in the nineteenth century. Indian criminals were sometimes also branded with the English word for thug. Many Indian criminals attempted to cover, remove, or change their markings via wearing their hair longer or turbans over their faces.

tortured, punished, and convict bodies

FIGURE 14.2 One of the modes of punishment in China – a Boxer prisoner, Peking, China. Photography by B. L. Singley. Photo courtesy of the Library of Congress.

In ancient China, the Han used tattooing, along with banishment, as a mode of punishment for criminals. The Han may have used tattoos in this manner because non-Han tribes in China wore tattoos, and those tribes were considered barbaric and uncivilized to the Han. China's use of punitive tattooing influenced Japan (which also had an ethnic minority, the Ainu, who tattooed themselves), to begin marking their own criminals that way. Later, tattoos in Japan moved from punitive to decorative as convicts developed elaborate designs to mask their criminal tattoos. In fact, the modern practice of prisoners tattooing themselves in prison probably derived from punitive tattooing, when convicts turned their mark of criminality into a badge of honor.

Castration is another method that has been used to both mark and punish criminals. Castration in humans most certainly developed after the rise of agriculture and animal domestication, which both provided the impetus for the development of state-level civilization as well as the technology for castration itself. Human castration has a long history throughout many of the early states and has primarily been used for punitive purposes, religious reasons, and to control certain categories of slaves and servants. While castration technically refers to the removal of the testicles, in some ancient states like China it was not just the testicles that were removed but the penis, testicles, and scrotum. (Chinese eunuchs kept their organs in a jar to be buried with the man when he died, so that he would be reborn as a whole man.) In the civilizations of the Mediterranean and Middle East, for instance, as well as in China and Medieval Europe, castration was often used as a punishment for rape, homosexuality, or adultery. In more modern times,

state and corporate regulation of the body

the Nazis sometimes used castration as a punishment and as a way of controlling the reproduction of "unfit" populations. Castration has also been used throughout history during wartime; invading armies would castrate either their captives or the corpses of the defeated, in order to demonstrate their victory over the conquered people, as a form of ethnic cleansing, and sometimes as a method of torture; castration of men was often used alongside of the rape of women during war. This has been seen in ancient Persia, Egypt, Assyria, Ethiopia, and among the ancient Hebrews, as well as among the Normans, the Chinese, and in modern times, the Vietcong were rumored to have castrated prisoners and dissidents, and the Janjaweed in the ongoing Sudanese conflict castrate men and rape women.

While involuntary castration is very rare in the modern world, some American and European states do allow for the voluntary chemical castration of sex offenders. **Testosterone depletion treatment**, often in the form of Depo-Provera injections (a hormonal birth control method used by women), is a way of temporarily reducing the sex drive of sex offenders, although the success rates of these procedures are questionable, and injections must be ongoing. While surgical castration is more effective in eliminating sexual drive than chemical castration, in both cases there are still problems, as post-pubescent men often retain sexual drive even after castration, and the drive to rape is not an exclusively (or even primarily) sexual drive.

Interesting issues: Geneva Convention

As defined by the Geneva Convention, torture is: "an extreme form of cruel and inhuman treatment and does not extend to lesser forms of cruel, inhuman, or degrading treatment or punishment." To be defined as torture, an act must satisfy all of the following elements:

(1) *the act must cause severe physical or mental pain or suffering;*
(2) *the act must be intentionally inflicted;*
(3) *the act must be inflicted for a proscribed purpose;*
(4) *the act must be inflicted by (or at the instigation of or with the consent or acquiescence of) a public official who has custody of the victim; and*
(5) *the act cannot arise from lawful sanctions.*

Torture, rape, and other forms of corporal punishment

Torture refers to using pain or the threat of pain to cause someone to give in to their captor or tormentor. But according to literary theorist Elaine Scarry, in her book *The Body in Pain* (1985), it's about more than causing suffering to the body; it is also about erasing human dignity, and its purpose is to allow political regimes to maintain power and control.

Torture has historically been used by state and religious authorities to extract confessions or incriminating information from alleged criminals or prisoners of war who otherwise would not speak. It has also been used to convert unwilling participants to a new religion and to indoctrinate and "re-educate" political prisoners or political activists. Torture is also used to dehumanize those being tortured, and as a form of punishment for those accused of extremely serious crimes, such as heresy. During the European witch hunts of the fifteenth to eighteenth centuries, torture was also used to get the accused witches to confess, because authorities felt that a voluntary confession was invalid. Roman slaves, too, could not be trusted to confess voluntarily and were tortured for this purpose.

Methods of torture have included forced exercise, the breaking of bones, removal of the nails or teeth, binding the body, roasting the soles of the feet over hot coals, branding, flogging, burning, castration, cutting, water torture, foot whipping, knee capping, the removal of limbs, rape, starvation, tongue removal, as well as various forms of psychological torture. In Medieval Europe, a number of specialized tools were created to torture victims, including the rack, boot, breaking wheel, lash, padlocks, stock, thumbscrew, and Iron Maiden.

Torture has also been used as a method of punishment, once the suspect has been convicted of a crime. Crucifixion, for example, was used to punish criminals in the classical world; crucifixion was both a form of capital punishment as well as a form of torture, because of the suffering it inflicted on the condemned. In fact, for thousands of years, states have used capital punishment methods in which the victim suffered unspeakably before death; usually these methods were reserved for the very worst of the crimes. Less severe crimes would often be treated with less severe, but still violent, punishments, such as public beatings. According to philosopher Michel Foucault (1979), public executions and public torture were once commonly used for two main reasons: in order to reflect the violence of the original crime onto the convict's body for the public to witness, and to physically inscribe the state's revenge upon the convict's body. In addition, cultures which practice slavery have always used practices associated with torture – whipping, raping, and maiming – in order to control and discipline slaves. Ultimately, however, most nations have moved away from such visible, public, and corporal methods of punishment, although over 30 countries still practice some methods of corporal punishment for criminals, such as caning in Singapore, whipping in Sudan, and amputation in Saudi Arabia.

Amputation has also been used at times as a form of punishment. For instance, Don Juan de Oñate, the colonizer of New Mexico for Spain in the late sixteenth century, punished the Acoma Indian tribe, which led the Pueblo resistance against the Spanish, by killing some eight hundred Acoma people, enslaving hundreds of women and children, and amputating the left foot of

state and corporate regulation of the body

every remaining adult man. In 1998, on the four hundredth anniversary of his arrival in New Mexico, the bronze statue of Oñate outside of Española, New Mexico was vandalized: someone had sawed off Oñate's right foot. A note was left by the perpetrator that said "fair is fair."

Rape has long been a tool that has been used to control people, usually in the context of war. In addition to being used as a means to humiliate and control women, **wartime rape**, conducted by overwhelmingly male armies, is also intended to destroy the bonds of family and society. In World War II, Japanese soldiers were responsible for raping tens of thousands of Chinese women in Nanjing, and the Japanese kidnapped and turned into prostitutes another 80,000–200,000 Korean women who they called "comfort women." In addition, millions of women, mostly German, were raped by Russian soldiers during the last months of World War II, and at the same time, Nazi soldiers raped Jewish women in the concentration camps. More recently, 20,000 Muslim girls and women were raped by Serbs during the Bosnian war in the earlier 1990s, and during the civil war in Rwanda as many as 500,000 Tutsi women and girls were raped and often killed by Hutus.

In 2004, Americans were shocked when photos from Abu Ghraib Prison in Iraq emerged; the photos showed American military personally torturing, raping, and humiliating Iraqi prisoners. While the soldiers involved in that case were court-martialed and some sent to prison, many critics felt that the behavior of the soldiers was not deviant, but that they were behaving in accordance with military policy, or, at the very least, in accordance with a military environment that stresses dominance and aggression. The situation was especially unusual because much of the abuse involved sexually humiliating and feminizing the prisoners, yet three of the soldiers performing the abuse were women. Most people see women as "naturally" compassionate, thus their behavior was especially shocking.

In fact, it's always shocking when the public hears about "normal" people who engage in torture. This is one of the issues explored in psychologist Stanley Milgram's famous obedience studies of the 1960s. During these studies, research subjects were told that they would be administering painful electrical shocks to other subjects (who were, in fact, actors) when they answered test questions wrong. Each time the test taker answered a question wrong, the voltage went up and the person (allegedly) experienced much more pain. In the experiment, 65 percent of the subjects continued to give shocks all the way up to the end of the experiment, even though they may have killed their test taker; 35 percent could not complete the experiment and left partway through. What could make a person continue to harm someone else, even though they clearly did not want to? A major part of Milgram's results points to the intimidation felt by ordinary people in the face of authority. People do what they are told to do, even if they know it is wrong, when someone in authority tells them that they must do it. For Nazi soldiers, one consequence for not participating in the horrific behavior in which they engaged was surely death at the hands of one's commanders.

Since the end of World War II, after the atrocities of the Holocaust came to light, many nations have taken a hard line against torture as a form of punishment, and as a method of extracting information from suspects. However, as was mentioned in the beginning of this chapter, it still takes place in countries around the world. Amnesty International, for example, has found that (as of this writing) 81 nations – including the United States – currently practice torture. Elaine Scarry (1985) writes that torture continues to be used today by the most volatile political regimes in order to assert their control over a populace which is no longer willing to accept that control.

Capital punishment

Capital punishment, while controversial today, is one of the world's oldest methods of punishment. Usually reserved for the worst crimes in society (but as late as the nineteenth century, death penalty crimes included crimes as petty as theft), cultures large and small have executed murderers, witches, and escaped soldiers, and some cultures still do so today. In tribal societies, capital punishment was often used as a form of blood compensation – when a member of one clan or group killed a member of another group, the victim's group was allowed to legally kill the perpetrator as a form of blood payment.

In state societies, however, capital punishment, along with other forms of punishment, is carried out by the state, rather than the victim or victim's family. In ancient Rome, on the other hand, gladiators killed each other in public, not as punishment, but in order to elevate the status of those politicians who sponsored them.

Methods of execution vary, often based on the severity of the crime. In Renaissance Europe, for example, decapitation by the guillotine was thought to be a quick and painless method of execution, and thus was seen as a merciful choice for criminals whose crimes were not that severe. In China on the other hand, decapitation was reserved for more serious crimes, while strangulation – while certainly slower and more painful – was chosen for less serious crimes, because of the Chinese belief that the body needed to be whole after death. On the other hand, criminals whose crimes were considered especially heinous could be executed by partial hanging followed by burning, to be followed by being drawn and quartered. Other cultures, too, chose methods that were known to cause an extreme amount of suffering before death, such as crucifixion, crushing, stoning, slow slicing, and disembowelment, for the most serious of crimes.

In many cultures that practiced capital punishment, executions were public, because the public needed to be able to see the victim die in order

state and corporate regulation of the body

for it to act as a deterrent. In addition, in many cultures, such as China and England, the head of the executed criminal was then publicly displayed, often on a stake in the middle of town, to further educate the citizens. **Gibbeting** refers to the hanging or other display of a dead (or sometimes live) criminal, also as a warning to others. Ironically, however, such public displays often incited violence among the witnesses. In the United States, 1936 was the last year such a public execution was held.

Over time, countries that still practice capital punishment have moved from violent and painful methods to methods that are considered to be more humane. In the United States, for example, methods once included burning, breaking on the wheel, crushing, the firing squad, and hanging. In the nineteenth century, the electric chair became a popular method, alongside hanging and shooting, and in the early twentieth century the gas chamber became popular. While hanging, firing squads, gas, and the electric chair are technically still legal methods, death by lethal injection, first introduced in 1982, is the most common method of execution in the United States today.

Today, capital punishment is relatively rare in the world, with more countries having abolished it than those that practice it. The United States is, today, the only modern Western nation that still allows the execution of its citizens (in 33 states; the other 17 have outlawed it); the other major countries that still practice it today are India and China. Proponents of capital

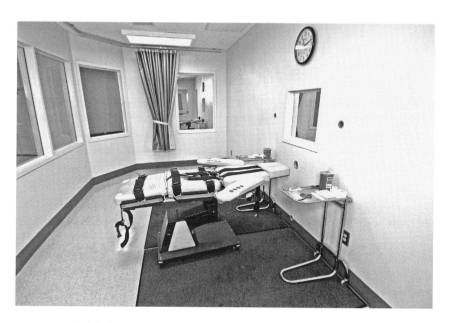

FIGURE 14.3 The lethal injection room at San Quentin State Prison, completed in 2010. Photo courtesy of the California Department of Corrections and Rehabilitation.

tortured, punished, and convict bodies

punishment argue that it is a major deterrent to violent crime, and that it keeps dangerous criminals off the street. Opponents of capital punishment, on the other hand, argue that it is cruel and inhumane, and that since the justice system is not foolproof, innocent people can be (and have been) sentenced to death. In particular, studies have shown that in the United States, men of color are sentenced to death far more than are white defendants, and if the victim is white, the defendant is more likely to be sentenced to death than if the victim is black or Hispanic.

The rise of the prison and the confinement of criminals

According to Michel Foucault, Western nations began moving from public and visceral forms of punishment in the eighteenth century, not because of humanitarian concerns about violent public executions, but because public executions often generated public sympathy for the condemned. In addition, Foucault argues, the state gradually became more concerned with order, and the use of prisons to punish people was a more predictable and orderly way of dealing with crime and its consequences. But while capital punishment and torture are obvious and visible ways of punishing the body, the state devised new ways of using the body which were equally effective. For example, the use of chain gangs and public work crews (which are still used around the world, including the United States, often to pick up trash on the side of the highway) developed as a way to display to the public criminal bodies, both punishing the criminal and demonstrating to the public both the nature of the crime and the punishment – similar to the Roman method of forcing criminals like Christians to work in the mines.

With the rise of the prison as the predominant form of punishment (rather than as a simple form of confinement until the prisoner was tortured, whipped or executed) in the nineteenth century came the focus on carefully controlling, observing, and recording prisoners' bodies. Prisons are designed in order to maximize the state's control over the prisoner's body, as well as to allow prison personnel to closely monitor them, sometimes through closed-circuit television cameras.

Today, the United States has the world's largest prison population, with over two million Americans in prison, thanks to greater federal influence in sentencing (including mandatory minimum sentences), harsher sentences for drug crimes, and more money used for policing and for the building of prisons. One of the results of the increase in the prison population, combined with the racist nature of the criminal justice system, is the wide discrepancy between racial groups in prison. While men and women of color have always made up a greater number, statistically speaking, of the prison population in the United States, since the mid-1980s, when the Reagan administration passed some of the harshest anti-drug laws this country has ever seen, the rate of African-American imprisonment skyrocketed to over ten times the rate for whites. Today, 25 percent of young black men are either in prison or on parole.

Marks of deviance: identifying criminals

As we have seen, the state has been marking criminals for thousands of years, often with tattoos or brands. These practices punish the criminal, but also permanently mark them as criminals, making them easy to identify later in life.

Identifying criminals has long been of concern to governments and law enforcement officials, and a variety of methods have been developed to do this. The most common method in use today, for example, is the fingerprint. Fingerprints may have been used to identify criminals in ancient Babylon, China, and Persia, but it did not become standard practice for identifying European criminals until the late nineteenth century. The practice had already been in use by then for 20 years in India; one reason for its popularity there was that English colonial authorities could not tell Indian faces apart. Today, the FBI has over 55 million fingerprints in their master database.

Another method of identifying criminals was through measurements. French anthropologist Alphonse Bertillion created a system called **"anthropometric signalment"** which involved measuring a suspect's head and body and filing that information on index cards, ordered by each measurement. Through the use of the index cards, law enforcement officials could look individuals up by their height, or, for example, the length of their fingers, in order to see if they had been previously arrested.

Criminals were once identified in other ways as well. It was once thought that criminal tendencies or deviant personalities could be determined by a person's physical appearance. The shape of one's skull, one's facial characteristics, and even one's tattoos could all be used to determine if one had criminal tendencies. As discussed in Chapter 6, physiognomy refers specifically to discerning the character of a person from their facial features or body parts. Criminologist Cesare Lombroso was an advocate of this approach and examined the bodies of hundreds of criminals in the nineteenth century in order to ascertain the physical characteristics, including tattoos, shared by criminals.

The association between tattooing and criminal behavior extended well beyond the work of Lombroso. In colonial India, for instance, British authorities noted the use of tattoos among many of the tribal groups. They also shared Lombroso's theories that criminality was inherent and they thought that they could chart the use of tattoos by different groups in India to show their propensity towards criminality. In addition, hundreds of tribes, with or without tattoos, were considered by the colonial authorities to be criminal tribes under the Criminal Tribes Act of 1871, which allowed the authorities to surveil, register, and control such groups.

In Australia in the nineteenth century, convicts sent from England to the penal colonies there had their tattoos catalogued prior to leaving England, and again upon reaching Australia, as a way of identifying convicts in the days before fingerprinting, and as a way of apprehending escaped convicts. Because the convicts often tattooed themselves on the ship en route to Australia, perhaps out of boredom or collective suffering (and probably due to the proximity of tattooed sailors around them), their new tattoos were a way of subverting English authority in that their body markings would now differ from when they left England. This demonstrates a practice that was also seen in Roman times: of criminals self-marking themselves in order to erase or cover the criminal marks given to them, or even to highlight them, seeing them as a badge of honor.

Today, law-enforcement agencies continue to track the tattoos on former criminals, gang members, and those who have been arrested for a crime. Police maintain tattoo databases which include digital photos and descriptions of tattoos taken from thousands of gang members as well as anyone who has been arrested of a crime. These databases help law-enforcement officials to identify suspects as possible gang members. Other personal characteristics of suspects kept in such databases include scars, and even facial shapes, eye scans, and other forms of **biometric data**. These new electronic databases, which recall the "anthropometric signalment" of Alphonse Bertillion, alarm some civil liberties experts, who worry that these technologies signal a rise in a total surveillance society in which all citizens can expect to have both their personal and physical data, as well as their movements, tracked.

Today, the newest method for suspect identification, and the method with the potential for the greatest accuracy, is DNA identification. When a crime has been committed, crime scene investigators now collect blood, semen, hair samples, and other biological materials, all of which can be tested for DNA, which can, it is hoped, lead to the arrest and conviction of the perpetrator. DNA profiling only results in an arrest, however, when the police already have on file the DNA of the suspect; without the first sample, there is nothing to which to compare samples taken from crime scenes. Proponents of expanded DNA profiling would like to see DNA testing of criminal suspects be mandatory, in order to expand the database needed to solve future crimes. The United States already maintains the largest such database in the world, with over five million records as of 2007, but many people are concerned about the government possessing such intimate information about so many people. In addition, because the government in

state and corporate regulation of the body

the United States can collect such information surreptitiously, many people have no idea that their DNA has been collected by the government. (In the United Kingdom, on the other hand, collecting DNA without consent is illegal thanks to a 2004 law.)

In the United States, which keeps more of its citizens in prison than any other nation on earth, what to do with those people, and how to treat them, is a constant topic for debate. In addition, with the "war on terror" now well into its second decade, the debate over what to do with the prisoners at Guantanamo Bay, and whether or not torture or enhanced interrogation techniques are legal, appropriate, or effective, remain topical and important. As we will see in Chapter 15, some countries like China have chosen new methods to deal with some of these issues.

Interesting issues: mug shots

A mug shot is a photo taken, shortly after arrest, of a person who has been arrested for a crime. The first mug shot was taken by nineteenth-century detective Allan Pinkerton, who used photos of criminals on wanted posters which were distributed throughout the western United States. The term itself derives from the slang term for face, "mug." Today, police and other law-enforcement agencies use these photos, known more formally as booking photos, to track the appearance of arrestees and convicts. In addition, in recent years, celebrity and high-profile arrestee mug shots are released to the media after celebrities have been arrested. For instance, the mug shots of Hugh Grant (arrested in 1995 for engaging in lewd behavior with a prostitute), James Brown (arrested in 2004 for domestic violence), and O. J. Simpson (arrested in 1994 for two counts of murder) are among the most well-known celebrity mug shots. Because mug shots are so firmly associated with the idea of criminality, and because the arrested person often does not look their best in these photos, the mug shot itself can lead the public, the press, and, crucially, potential members of criminal juries to assume that the presence of the mug shot means that the person is guilty. For that reason, many states have laws which are intended to discourage prosecutors from allowing juries to see the mug shot of the accused. After O. J. Simpson was arrested for killing two people in 1994, Time magazine put a digitally altered version of his mug shot on the cover which made his face much darker and sinister than it was in reality. Critics charged that Time was emphasizing the fact that Simpson is African-American and preying on the racial fears of Americans. In a more recent case, Jared Loughner was charged with shooting 20 people, including a Congresswoman, outside of an Arizona supermarket and killing six in January 2011. His mug shot shows a bald man with wild eyes and a crazy smile on his face, and was released by the press under headlines like "face of evil" or "mad eyes of a killer." Most people who see the photo see a person who seems both insane and defiant, and, most importantly, evil. While Loughner ultimately pled guilty to 19 counts of murder and attempted murder, thereby avoiding the death penalty and a lengthy trial, had he undergone a trial, his lawyers would no doubt had argued that his mug shot would have been prejudicial to the jury.

Key terms

Anthropometric Signalment
Biometric Data
Corporal Punishment
Enhanced Interrogation
   Techniques

Extraordinary Rendition
Geneva Convention
Testosterone Depletion
   Treatment
Wartime Rape

Further reading

Foucault, Michel. (1979). *Discipline and Punish*. Harmondsworth: Penguin.
Lombroso, Cesare. (2006). *Criminal Man*. Raleigh, NC: Duke University Press.

chapter 15

Commodified Bodies

In 2005, an email began circulating with a subject line reading "Human parts processing factory in Russia." The email included a number of very graphic photos that appeared to depict dozens of naked corpses piled on the floor and on tables in a filthy room; other photos showed men wearing bloody aprons hacking the bodies apart. The email warned that this body processing factory in Russia was harvesting organs from unclaimed bodies, and selling them to universities and pharmacies. While the email and the images within it are a hoax – in order to be medically viable, the harvesting of organs must be done in a sterile environment and must be taken from the very recently dead or the brain dead – its believability points to the widespread social concerns surrounding organ donation.

In Brazil, these concerns manifested themselves in widely held beliefs, beginning in the 1980s, that children were being kidnapped so that they could be killed and their organs sent to wealthy nations like the United States and Japan. Anthropologist Nancy Scheper-Hughes (1993) heard these stories while working in Brazil; the stories led to many poor Brazilians staying away from hospitals (where they might be killed), opposing international adoption (since adopted children were believed to be used for the same purpose), and even attacking American tourists. While no proof of these mysterious organ abductions ever materialized, the reality is that there *does* exist an illegal trade in **black market organs**, and those organs *do* come largely from poor people like those in Brazil's shantytowns. The reason for this black market has to do both with the rising need for organ donations around the world, but also with economic realities. Those who can profit from the bodies of others will often do so, and often the desperately poor will sell their own bodies, or body parts, in order to alleviate some of their desperation. Bodies, then, carry economic value – whether living or dead.

Slavery and the ownership of people

Slavery refers to the practice of owning people as property, and forcing them to work without compensation. While most Americans think of African slavery in the Americas when they think of slavery, in reality slavery has been practiced since antiquity in a great many societies around the world, and continues to be practiced today. In Western civilization, slavery may go back as far as the town of Jericho, an early farming community in the Middle East from around 10,000 BCE. Slavery was practiced in ancient Mesopotamia, Egypt, Greece, Israel, Persia, Rome, and Byzantium, as well as among the Chinese, Mayans, Aztecs, Indians, and among a number of African, Polynesian, and Melanesian peoples.

Historically, one could become a slave in a number of ways. Slaves are often born into slavery, but other slaves are acquired through warfare: as prisoners of war or war orphans. Colonization is another way that people could acquire the labor of other peoples for free, and **debt bondage** is a longstanding way in which people become slaves. In debt bondage, a parent or relative typically loans a person, usually a child, to someone in exchange for a cash payment. The child then must work off the debt before they can return home, a prospect which is often impossible, because of the price of the debt, and the fact that the new owners take out a set of monthly costs (food, rent, utilities, "protection") that are so high that the debt can never be repaid. In some cultures, people convicted of crimes, or their family members, might be sold into slavery in order to compensate the victims.

Slaves do not own rights to their own bodies, and do not control their own labor, or even their own reproductive labor. In the antebellum United States, for example, African slaves were not just forced to work, but when a slave woman bore children (either as a result of a consensual sexual relationship with a partner – slaves were often not legally allowed to marry – or as a result of rape by a master), her children could be taken from her and sold for profit. In the early years of American slavery, slaves were not encouraged to reproduce and only lived an average of six years after reaching America. After they died, they were simply replenished with new slaves arriving on ships from Africa. After the **trans-Atlantic slave trade** was abolished in 1808, however, slave owners had no choice but to encourage their slaves to reproduce, or even intentionally bred them like animals, selling off some of the children, the "surplus labor," to other plantations, bringing in additional profit. It is clear that slave owners played a major role in the reproduction of slave children based on the extremely high fertility rate of the slaves, especially given the high infant mortality rate. Sociologist Barbara Omolade writes of female slaves:

> Her vagina, used for his sexual pleasure, was the gateway to the womb, which was his place of capital investment – the capital investment being the sex act and the resulting child accumulated surplus, worth money on the slave market.
>
> (1983: 354)

Free women, on the other hand, worked neither in the fields nor in the home, and slave women even raised free women's children. But while slave women were vulnerable to rape by slave owners, free women had their

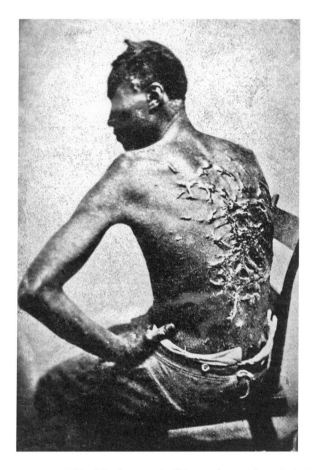

FIGURE 15.1 This 1863 photograph of Peter, a former slave, depicting scars from his overseer's whippings, was widely reproduced as evidence of slavery's cruelty. Photo courtesy of the National Archives and Records Administration.

commodified bodies   263 sexuality tightly controlled; they could only have sex with their husbands and *certainly* could not have sex with slaves.

Because slaves were property, slave owners marked slaves' bodies with a brand or tattoo to demonstrate their claim of ownership; in other times, slaves' heads were shaved to visually distinguish them from non-slaves. Slaves in most societies could also be physically punished by their masters, via branding, whipping, castration, or even murder. In the Americas, slave bodies could also be used for dissection and other forms of medical experimentation. As racialized science developed in the nineteenth century, the skulls and facial features of African slaves were measured by scientists who used the information that they gathered to prove their inferiority. Sometimes slaves were even eaten by their owners, after their utility had ceased, as among the Tupinamba of Brazil.

While slavery in many regions is not racially based, in the Americas it was, and "black" and "slave" became synonymous. The conflation of these concepts played a major role in the solidification of racial practices and racism in the Americas, the legacy of which is still with us today. One of the many justifications of African slavery, in fact, was the idea that not only were Africans and Europeans created differently – a concept known as polygenism – but that Africans were physically weaker than Europeans. They were thought to be less sensitive to pain than whites (thus justifying the beatings), but at the same time more susceptible to diseases like tetanus, colds, or respiratory problems. This was suggested by the fact that slaves' life expectancy was so short, which was believed to be due to their lack of biological fitness rather than the horrific conditions under which they lived and worked. In any case, this apparent physical and intellectual inferiority meant that Africans were well suited to slavery. In a much earlier era, Aristotle also claimed that slaves were born to be slaves, and thus were not suited for anything else.

Today, slavery is still practiced in countries around the world, although it is illegal in every nation. Most slavery today is debt bondage, where children, as well as women, are used as collateral for debts, or are simply sold to pay off debts, and must work as sex slaves or other laborers. Such slaves come from very poor families in very poor countries, and may be kept as slaves in their home countries or may be trafficked to other nations. There may be as many as 20 million slaves in the world today, in places like the Sudan where tribal peoples are enslaved by Arabs, in India where untouchables still often work for no money, in the Ivory Coast where children are forced to work on cocoa farms, in Thailand where young girls work as sex slaves, and in California where Indian girls work without pay in hotels and restaurants.

Prostitution, sex trafficking, and sex tourism

In prostitution, often known as "the world's oldest profession," women or men sell sexual access to their bodies for a price. Among the ancient Greeks and Sumerians, prostitution was once practiced for pay and, separately, **sacred prostitution** took place in a temple but no money was exchanged. While sacred prostitution did not survive the rise of Christianity, prostitution was often tolerated by the Church; in Medieval Europe prostitutes were given a location to ply their trade outside of city walls, because buying and selling sex was seen as less sinful than masturbation or sodomy.

Sander Gilman (2008) points out that during the nineteenth century, the era during which racialized groups were being measured and classified, prostitutes were subject to the same types of analysis. Freud, for instance, said that certain women have an "aptitude for prostitution" based on the anthropological studies of the time which focused on the weight of the women, their skull size, facial abnormalities, and family background.

In some countries (and in the United States, in some counties in Nevada) today, certain kinds of prostitution is legal. Generally, where prostitution is legal, as in much of Europe, Australia, and New Zealand, it is regulated and occurs in brothels where prostitutes are regularly checked for sexually transmitted diseases, where clients must wear condoms, and where conditions are safe and prostitutes are paid a living wage. Street prostitution, however, is typically illegal (women are often the ones who are arrested, while their clients go free), as is **pimping**, because it involves coercion and the control of one person over another person's body. (In Japan, oddly, vaginal prostitution is illegal but fellatio is legal.)

Where street prostitution occurs, women and men (called hustlers or **rent boys**) tend to be young, they are often runaways, they are often addicted to drugs, and have often been coerced into becoming prostitutes. They live dangerous lives – street prostitution is the most dangerous job in terms of occupational mortality than any other female-dominated profession – and are at risk of being abused or killed by pimps, clients (most of whom are married men), and others who prey on the vulnerable. They're at very high risk of sexually transmitted diseases as well.

But even where prostitution is voluntary and relatively safe, many people argue that it should still not be allowed, because by its very nature, it exploits women, by turning them into objects who exist to provide sexual pleasure to men. In addition, many feminists argue that the whole notion of "voluntary prostitution" is illusory because no woman (or man) would become a prostitute if they were not desperate to start with.

In addition, while regulated brothel prostitution often results in women who make good money and are able to exercise a great deal of control over

FIGURE 15.2 A Tijuana prostitute. Photo courtesy of Tomas Castelazo, via Wikimedia Commons: http://commons.wikimedia.org/wiki/File:Prostitute_tj_modificada.jpg.

their bodies and their working conditions, as in the Netherlands, this is not always the case.

In Thailand, for example, where prostitution is technically illegal, but where it is extremely common, young girls and women work in brothels where they service multiple men per day for very little money, most of which goes to pay off the debt that their family owes, as well as their food and other living expenses. These girls were trafficked from countries like Burma and are at the mercy of the people who own them, the clients who have sex with them, and the police who also victimize them. Virgins are sold for as much as $1,000 (money which the girls never see), but after that, their rate drops as they become used up.

Trafficking is an ancient practice which involves forcing women and children into forced labor and often sexual servitude. It's often associated

state and corporate regulation of the body

with war; while conquering armies may kill men in conquered nations, they often bring women and children back as spoils of war and force them to become slaves. During World War II, hundreds of thousands of Korean and Japanese women and girls were kidnapped and enslaved by the Imperial Japanese military and forced to serve soldiers as unpaid prostitutes known as **comfort women**. This practice is an example of wartime rape, a common practice in which conquering armies use rape as both a reward for soldiers as well as a tactic to terrorize the population and humiliate the enemy, destroying family bonds in the process. It's also a method of **ethnic cleansing**, as in the Bosnian war, when over 20,000 Muslim women and girls were raped, and many impregnated, by Serbian soldiers as a program of ethnic and cultural genocide. But it's also an example of the ways in which prostitution and war have also long been linked.

Brothels are often set up nearby military bases during wartime, often with the explicit support of the military, in order to service the needs of soldiers. This was the case in the Korean War when Korean women served as prostitutes, also known as comfort women, to American G.I.s; the brothels were set up as part of the mutual defense treaty signed by South Korea and the United States. During the Vietnam War, American officials set up sites in nearby Thailand for soldiers to get away from the war for R&R (rest and recreation), which was expected to include sex with local women. The United States provided financial investments in cities like Bangkok in exchange for Thailand creating the "recreational" opportunities for American soldiers. This was the origin of the modern sex trade in Thailand today. As with the comfort women in the Korean War, the women who served as prostitutes in the Vietnamese War were desperately poor, and for many, were hoping for an opportunity to marry a soldier and go to America. Called "minor wives," some of these women did get to come to the United States after the war, but many more were left behind, sometimes with children. Because the children were mixed race, they were often ostracized and sent to orphanages where they were raised by nuns or adopted internationally. After the end of the Vietnam War, the prostitution infrastructure set up to serve the soldiers was converted to serve the international sex trade.

Today, human trafficking is the fastest growing form of slavery and, according to the United States State Department, is the second largest and fastest growing criminal industry in the world, particularly in Southeast Asia and Eastern Europe. Traffickers prey on the poor and desperate who are looking for a way out of poverty and believe that they will get a better life by going with the men who offer their families money. These women are transported to other countries, are sorted by beauty and age, and sent to their destinations where they will be purchased and used. Some of the women think they will become domestic servants or even models, but instead they become prostitutes, and once they realize their new situation, they are threatened with violence, or their family is threatened, if they attempt to escape.

Child prostitutes, who are very popular with Western tourists who come to places like Thailand on **sex tourism** vacations, have an especially difficult life, having sex with a dozen or more men per day, often without condoms, and experience pregnancy and disease with alarming frequency. Approximately 1.2 million children are trafficked each year, most for prostitution, according to UNICEF. The National Center for Mission and Exploited Children estimates that 2.8 million children run away from home each year, and that of those one-third end up becoming child prostitutes.

For men who participate in sex tourism, according to sociologist Jacqueline Sanchez Taylor (2006, 2009), the appeal lies in the fact that the women and girls are foreign and exotic, and, preferably, Asian. Many customers apparently do not even consider the practice that they engage in to be prostitution; instead, they think that the women or girls simply want to have sex with them. The sexual exchanges are driven by sexual and racial stereotypes which suggest that while white women are stuck up, too independent, or sexually conservative, Asian women are submissive, ready to please, and sexually voracious. These men are blind to the fact that poverty and desperation underlies one side of the international sex trade.

Today, most women's groups take the position, thanks to activism by prostitutes' rights groups, that all prostitution is not necessarily exploitative, and that prostitution that is truly voluntary should be decriminalized and regulated, so that women who engage in sex work can be protected, and that all forms of forced prostitution should be eliminated.

Interesting issues: virginity for sale

In 2012, a 20-year-old Brazilian woman named Catarina Migliorini auctioned off her virginity. A Japanese man offered the winning bid of $780,000, which Migliorini says she'll use to buy housing for the poor in her hometown. The winner has to pass an STD screening and wear a condom when he has sex with her. The month-long auction was held as part of a documentary called Virgins Wanted, *which will film Migliorini as she's flown to Australia (to avoid prostitution laws, the encounter will be held on the airplane) where she'll be filmed before and after her "date." She says she is not a prostitute because selling sex once does not make one a prostitute. Migliorini is certainly not the first woman to offer her virginity for sale. In 2010, a 22-year-old woman calling herself Natalie Dylan was trying to get one million dollars to sell her virginity at the Moonlite Bunny Ranch in Nevada; she said she was raising the money to pay for graduate school after receiving her undergraduate degree in women's studies. And in 2011, an Australian escort service called MyOutCall was selling the virginity of*

state and corporate regulation of the body

a 19-year-old Chinese girl for $15,000; the price would give the client four days with the girl. Prostitution is legal in Australia and Australian escort services typically take 50 percent of the fee, which means they would take in $7,500 from the girl's work.

Selling love: mail order brides

Related to the international sex trade is the mail order bride trade. **Mail order brides**, also known as migrant brides, are women who advertise themselves on websites – at one time it was done in magazines and newspapers – as looking for a husband. The women are from poor countries in Latin America, Eastern Europe, and, predominantly, Asia, and the men come from Europe and the United States. The marriages are brokered by international agencies that specialize in locating the women and matching them up with Western men; each successful match can result in a price of about $5,000 for the broker. One newspaper advertisement featured a photo of four lovely young Vietnamese women, with the caption: "Buy a wife from Vietnam for only 6,000 USD. 1. Guaranteed virgin. 2. Guaranteed to be delivered within 90 days. 3. NO extra charges. 4. If ran away within a year, you get another one for FREE."

These marriages can be seen as, at least in part, an economic exchange: beautiful young women from desperately poor circumstances trade their youth and beauty for the chance to live in a Western nation with a middle-class husband. For the men, they are offered the chance to have a lovely young wife, one who is often submissive and exotic, who speaks little of their language and is thus dependent on them for all of their basic needs. Many of the men may not be very marriageable in Europe or the United States because they are relatively low status, have low prestige jobs, or are not very attractive. But to a poor Vietnamese, Malaysian, or Russian woman, these men still look quite good. In addition, some Western men feel that Western women have gotten too uppity, and that feminism makes them too independent. Having a wife who knows how to properly take care of a man is seen as an attractive quality for these men; that's one reason why Asian wives are so desirable.

And while the couple may, hopefully, fall in love, love is certainly not a prerequisite for the relationship, since men are expected to come to the country of their choice, pick out their bride, get married, and return home within a single week. Once their wives receive their visas and join their husbands in their new countries, they are expected to assimilate into the new culture and learn to become a loving and accommodating wife. Government and nonprofit agencies who have worked with migrant brides have found that many of the women, after marriage, are isolated and lonely, and sometimes experience physical and emotional abuse. Some women are tricked into prostitution or worse.

Because the same type of economic conditions – poverty and desperation – that drive women to enter the sex trade drive them to enter the international marriage market, the pool of potential young mail order brides continues to grow. According to the International Organization for Migration, 133,000 women from Vietnam alone married foreign men between 2005 and 2010.

Interesting issues: romance tourism

While sex tourism is a well-known, if not openly discussed, international activity, what Deborah Pruitt and Suzanne LaFont (1995) call romance tourism is much less known. They refer to the practice of European or American women who travel overseas for sexual or romantic vacations. The primary destinations for romance tourism are Southern Europe, the Caribbean, Hawaii, parts of Africa, and beach areas in Thailand. Unlike sex tourism, where men go to bars to pay women to have sex, in romance tourism, women meet men on the beach or in other tourist locations. The women do not pay men for sex but instead buy them gifts, pay for meals, and take them out. Women are attracted to the men because not only are they exotic but they are romantic, pay attention to the women, and talk sweetly to them, in ways that American or Northern European men often do not. For the men, they benefit economically, and for the very lucky men, may end up with a permanent relationship whereby they can return to America as a new husband. Like sex tourism, romance tourism is based on stereotypes and economic exploitation, and often results in disappointment, but for both parties, there is the fantasy and hope of romantic or economic satisfaction.

Pornographic bodies

Another way in which bodies are commodified is pornography. Pornography is the graphic representation of nude bodies or sexual activity for sexual gratification. It can be softcore or hardcore, depending on whether sexual penetration and ejaculation occurs.

Pornography, like so many other concepts in this book, is very much a social construct. While the representation of human bodies, and bodies having sex, has long existed, and has existed most likely in every culture, it was not until the nineteenth century when archaeologists uncovered the ruins at Pompeii in Italy that the term pornography first emerged. Pompeii was a Roman town that was destroyed by a volcano, and when it was uncovered in 1860, scientists found a vast array of paintings and sculptures of a sexual nature. They were so shocking that they had to be hidden away from view, and around that time the world's first obscenity law was passed.

FIGURE 15.3 "Elisabeth." Men have enjoyed looking at nude women's bodies for thousands of years. Photo courtesy of Laurence Nixon.

For the first time, it became illegal to view material of an obscene nature, although in reality upper-class men continued to collect and view illustrations and other materials. Women and the working classes, however, were expected to be shielded from such materials.

As different forms of media developed, different forms of pornography developed as well. From the printing press, which popularized not just the Bible but also Rabelais' *Gargantua and Pantagruel*, to photography, which allowed for not only the first battlefield photographs taken during the American Civil War, but the first photographs of naked bodies, to cheap paper which led to dime novels, pulp fiction, and, of course, pornographic

commodified bodies   271 magazines, media has always spurred the development of new forms of pornography. With motion pictures came the first moving images of people having sex and ushered in the era of porn theaters, and with cable TV came the first cable networks devoted to pornography; later, the VCR emerged which allowed people to watch porn in the comfort of their own homes. Not only that, but with the remote control, viewers could fast forward past the dialogue and get right to the good parts, leading to the development of a whole genre of films which only include sex scenes. The latest technological innovation, of course, is the internet and with it online pornography. The internet, it is often said, exists for two purposes: cat videos and pornography. In terms of porn, there is an infinite variety of content available: from still images of naked women and men, to every variety of fetish (feet, butts, dwarves, amputees, the morbidly obese), to professionally shot porn videos to amateur porn to pro-am porn (professionally shot porn which looks like amateur porn), to home web-cams where you can direct the performer yourself to perform according to your own desires. The internet has truly given us everything that we could want in terms of sexual satisfaction, other than a real live person to have sex with.

Pornography is legal in most countries today, although there are certain limits; child pornography, for example, is typically always illegal. In the United States, pornography is considered to be obscenity, and is thus illegal, if it passes what's known as the **Miller test**:

1. The average person, applying contemporary community standards, finds that the work appeals to prurient interests.
2. The work depicts, in a patently offensive way, sexual conduct or excretory functions.
3. The work lacks serious literary and/or artistic, political, or scientific value.

Pornography is threatening to those who oppose it for a number of reasons. Many feminists find it demeaning because, since it is primarily made by men, and for men, it treats women's bodies as objects which exist for male pleasure. It's not the female orgasm, after all, which is the highlight of the pornographic film; it's the male orgasm. In addition, pornography often demeans and humiliates women, and glamorizes violence towards women. Religious conservatives oppose pornography because it encourages sex outside of marriage (although some married couples do use it as a marital aid), because it can encourage sexual addiction and self-destructive behavior, and because it may encourage real world sexual violence (although this last position has been convincingly challenged by studies that show that it does not).

Some cultural critics suggest that politicians oppose it because pornography is a threat to social control. In this reading, pornography can be

state and corporate regulation of the body

seen as a voice of the people. It has long been used as a tool to criticize those in power, and it has often been banned for the poor, but legal for the rich. According to media critic Laura Kipnis, pornography's main purpose has always been to shock, to challenge boundaries, and to invert social norms. In addition, in the United States, the same laws that banned pornography, the Comstock Laws, were also used to ban birth control (and even information about birth control), demonstrating that politicians have long endeavored to use their own forms of morality to control our bodies.

Whether or not you are a consumer of pornography, you cannot deny that pornography has changed our culture. Writer Ariel Levy (2005) calls this the **pornification** of American culture. Not only has pornography acted as a teaching tool for generations of young men (many of whom never heard of a clitoris before watching their first porn film), but it helped, alongside the release of the birth control pill in the 1960s, jump start the **sexual revolution**. The release of *Deep Throat* in 1972, the first pornographic film that got wide release in mainstream theatres, was watched by millions of Americans, and got people talking about sex in a way that they never had before. With the popularity of the video series *Girls Gone Wild*, in which drunk young women are encouraged to show off their breasts for the camera, many young women have a new sense that it's "empowering" to strip, show off one's breasts, or engage in wet tee shirt contests. Where these activities would have been seen as demeaning or slutty a generation ago, they are normal for many young women today. Also normal today are breast implants and waxed pubic regions, both made popular by pornography. And finally, the rising popularity of anal sex can also be traced to its prevalence in pornography, as is the notion that women's role in sex should be to service and provide pleasure to men.

How much are bodies, and body parts, worth?

The scientific use of bodies is not a new phenomenon. For centuries, doctors have been dissecting human bodies in order to understand anatomy, disease, and to develop surgical techniques. The ancient Greeks practiced dissection and other techniques on both animals as well as on living and dead human beings (mostly prisoners and slaves). Herophilus, for example, dissected both dead bodies but also live criminals. Dissection of live humans was largely discontinued after the rise of Christianity in the Roman world, but the use of humans as test subjects in drug trials continued; in fact, it was common for doctors and inventors to test drugs on themselves and their families.

While experimenting on live humans, even prisoners, was largely replaced by animal experimentation, it reappeared, infamously, during World War II, when Nazi scientist Josef Mengele experimented on human subjects, mostly

Jews, Russians, and Gypsies housed at concentration camps, from 1941 through 1945, and when Japanese scientists experimented on Chinese prisoners of war from the 1930s into the 1940s. Also during the 1940s, the United States Army, in conjunction with the University of Chicago Department of Medicine, infected four hundred prisoners from a Chicago prison with malaria to test new drugs on them, and both the American military and the CIA have conducted numerous experiments on soldiers, prisoners, and other test subjects, many without their consent. Perhaps most infamously, starting in 1932, American doctors at Tuskegee Medical School in Alabama ran a trial on patients without their consent in the Tuskegee Syphilis Study. During this decades-long study, poor African-American men who had syphilis were evaluated by doctors in order to see how syphilis would develop in an untreated patient. The men – many of whom died during the course of the study and whose wives and children were infected – were neither informed that they had syphilis nor offered treatment (penicillin was widely available as a cure for the disease as of 1947), until news of the study was leaked in 1972 and the study terminated.

After the end of World War II, once the Nazi atrocities came to light, the **Nuremberg Code** was developed, which established guidelines for human experiments, including the mandate for voluntary, informed consent for any test subjects, the absence of coercion, a lack of suffering and minimal risk for subjects, and a clear scientific gain for both the subject and society in general. Thanks to the Nuremberg Code, most medical testing on living humans is limited to clinical trials.

Dead humans, on the other hand, are an entirely different matter. Donated human heads are used to teach plastic surgery techniques to surgeons, while whole bodies are used in anatomy classes in medical school. Prior to the modern era of body and organ donations, doctors and anatomists also needed access to bodies, and when those bodies were not easily available – people did not at that time donate bodies to science because they believed that it was sacrilegious to have one's body taken apart – nefarious means were often employed to get them. Until 1836, the only legal means to get dead bodies was to get the bodies of executed murderers (part of capital punishment in Europe was in fact hanging followed by dissection). To get around this limitation, doctors began hiring grave robbers to dig up bodies for them, and sometimes they even did it themselves. These were generally poor bodies; those who could afford it had themselves interred in tombs which could not be easily entered. Two **body snatchers** of the time, William Burke and William Hare, ended up killing poor people in order to sell them to anatomists, once they realized how much money they could make from it. Besides the bodies of executed criminals, in the United States, doctors were sometimes given slaves after they were killed.

FIGURE 15.4 Execution of the notorious William Burke the murderer, who supplied Dr Knox with subjects. The execution by hanging is taking place on a platform in a crowded metropolitan street; people are leaning out of windows, sitting on roof tops, and fill the street around the platform and on into the background, Edinburgh, Scotland, 1829. Photo courtesy of the National Library of Medicine.

And finally, the very poor who died in poor houses or orphanages could be given to medical schools after death. To be so poor as to die, and not have one's body claimed by family members and buried in a cemetery, was a fate almost worse than death itself.

Today, however, thanks to the Uniform Anatomical Gift Act in the United States, people can donate their bodies to science after death, where they can be worth up to $200,000. If their organs are in good enough shape, they can also donate their organs to the living who need them after their death. In 1983, cyclosporine, an immunosuppressant drug, was released, making it far easier for people to accept organs from people who are not related to them (before that time, those organs were generally rejected). Since that time, the need for organ donations has skyrocketed, as more lives could be saved through organs from both living and dead donors. In the United States, where many people do donate their organs, a single dead donor can provide enough organs to save the lives of eight people. The knowledge that one's loved one has saved other people's lives is a major factor in encouraging survivors to let doctors remove their loved ones' organs. On the other side of the equation, many organ recipients often want to find out about their donors, and some even reach out to the families of the donors in order to thank them for the "gift of life" that they have received. Additionally, some recipients even begin to feel that they have

commodified bodies

received, alongside a heart or set of lungs, some of the personality or life force of their donor.

One hundred and fifteen thousand people in the United States alone are awaiting healthy hearts, livers, kidneys, lungs, corneas, and other organs, but there simply are not enough organs for all, or even most, of them. Sometimes it's because people do not believe in organ donation. In Japan, for example, cultural values preclude most Japanese from donating organs after death. On average, the waiting period for a kidney is 10 years, and on average 18 people die each day waiting for organs. In addition, it has become clear that a kidney from a living donor can keep a person alive for twice as long as one from a corpse. That means that living organ donors are now more needed than ever. Consequently, there's a thriving black market in organ sales.

While selling organs is illegal in most countries, because of the obvious risk for exploitation, it does continue to happen, primarily in the poorest countries on the planet like India. In general, organs – usually kidneys – in this black market move from south to north, from poor to rich, and from black or brown to white. Certainly the kinds of people who sell their organs could not afford to get them themselves; they could neither afford the surgeries nor the immunosuppressant drugs to keep them alive afterward. The World Health Organization estimates that perhaps one fifth of all kidneys transplanted every year are illegally procured. It even occurs in the United States, where poor Americans sometimes try to sell their organs to the rich.

In India, which only prohibited the sale of organs in 1994, Indian "donors" sell their kidneys, for which they make about $2,000 (but which are sold for closer to $150,000) to pay off debts or to pay for a dowry for a daughter. Families with an "extra" daughter are often especially forced to sell a kidney in order to raise the funds for the dowry. The problem in India is so bad that in 2008, several people were arrested in India in what has come to be known as the Gurgaon kidney scandal in which kidneys were being taken from as many as 500 poor victims, some of whom were drugged and operated on without their consent, and transplanted into patients in other countries, including the United States.

In Brazil, where anthropologist Nancy Scheper-Hughes has worked, organ transfers are done locally, and the buyer and seller pretend that they are friends or relatives, even though one is obviously wealthy and the other obviously poor. In order to stop the sale of organs, Brazil has recently passed a law mandating that all Brazilians, after death, are automatically organ donors, unless they opt out of the requirement. That way, there will be plenty of organs available and no one will need to sell their organs. Unfortunately, poor Brazilians feel that they will be taken advantage of and killed for their

state and corporate regulation of the body

organs, so more people are opting out of the law than expected, and the poor continue to sell their organs to the rich.

In addition, the rich can locate, via brokers, organs taken from the dead – usually executed prisoners – from countries like China or Singapore, a practice that has been banned by the World Medical Association, but still continues today, especially in China. Chinese doctors, in fact, remove organs from Chinese prisoners even before they're executed to be given to wealthy patients from Hong Kong or other countries, who travel to China for their surgeries, a practice known as **medical tourism**. Amnesty International accuses China of increasing the number of death penalty crimes in the country so that they can create a larger pool of organs for sale; Human Rights Watch estimates that 90 percent of all of the organs in China are from executed prisoners; at least 2,000 per year.

What this means is that poor people and criminals (who are, after all, often the same) are often more valuable dead than alive. They are also more valuable as repositories of organs than they are as living, breathing beings. Writer Rebecca Skloot (2010) wrote about the case of Henrietta Lacks, an African-American woman who had cervical cancer and died in 1951. During the course of her treatment at Johns Hopkins University, a doctor there took a sample from the tumor in her cervix; the cancerous cells grew and became the basis for what became the HeLa cell line, an immortal cell line that has been used in countless research projects, including the testing of the polio vaccine. As Anne Enright wrote, "There is more of her now, in terms of biomass, than there ever was when she was alive" (2000: 8). Lacks' family was never told about the existence of her cell line, its use in medicine, and all of the money made by the doctors who have used it since the 1950s. A similar case involved a patient named John Moore whose doctors patented a cell line called "Mo" from his cancerous spleen. When Moore heard about how the doctor was profiting from his cells, he sued. No matter, though: the California Supreme Court has ruled that we have no property rights to cells removed from our bodies and later patented as cell lines, even when those cell lines produce billions of dollars' worth of products.

Who owns our bodies?

To some extent, we all own our own bodies. But what we can do with our bodies is subject to the laws of the nation-states in which we live. Can we sell our bodies for sex? If it is for prostitution, then we can do so only if we live in a state or country that allows it. On the other hand, if it is on film, then most likely we can, as long as we are over the age of consent. Can we sell our organs? If we are talking about blood, plasma, sperm, or eggs, then yes we can. We cannot sell embryos, by the way, but we can give them away, just like we can babies. If we are talking about kidneys, however, then we cannot legally sell them, unless we live in Iran, where it is legal. We can do it outside the law, however, in which case we are most likely going to be exploited and will be paid a fraction of the cost that the organ will ultimately be sold for. Yet the doctors, hospitals, transplant registries, and procurement agencies all profit from them. The only person who does not is the organ provider him or herself.

Key terms

Black Market Organs	Pimping
Body Snatchers	Pornification
Comfort Women	Rent Boys
Debt Bondage	Romance Tourism
Ethnic Cleansing	Sacred Prostitution
Mail-Order Brides	Sex Tourism
Medical Tourism	Sexual Revolution
Miller Test	Trafficking
Nuremberg Code	Trans-Atlantic Slave Trade

Further reading

Fox, Renee C. and Swazey, Judith P. (1992). *Spare Parts: Organ Replacement in Society.* New York: Oxford University Press.

Griffin, Susan. (1981). *Pornography and Silence: Culture's Revenge Against Nature.* New York: Harper.

Phoenix, J. (2001). *Making Sense of Prostitution.* Basingstoke: Palgrave.

Rouselle, Aline. (1988). *Porneia: On Desire and the Body in Antiquity.* New York: Blackwell.

Williams, Linda. (1989). *Hard Core: Power, Pleasure and the Frenzy of the Visible.* Berkeley, CA: University of California Press.

chapter 16

Animal Bodies

In mid-2011, a British newspaper reported that more than 150 **human–animal hybrid** embryos had been produced by that time in British biomedical laboratories. These hybrid embryos were made by mixing the cells of human and non-human animals, and were never intended to survive. Instead, the experiments were (and are) conducted in order to develop new techniques for creating embryonic human stem cells which can be used to treat human illnesses. But the creation of these embryos – and the public outrage which often follows the publicizing of such work – brings up interesting and often disturbing issues. Besides the hybrid embryos, scientists have already been creating genetically modified animals; genetically modified mice, which carry human DNA, are widely used in scientific research today.

Many people wonder where such experiments will lead, and some see the 2011 film *Rise of the Planet of the Apes*, in which scientists created a new type of chimpanzee using human cells, as a cautionary tale. In the film, the fictional apes, made artificially intelligent through the use of human brain cells, rebelled against their human captors, ultimately taking over the world. Animal protection advocates, on the other hand, point to the ways in which such research will result in even more human exploitation of non-human animals. Clearly, this kind of research will continue and human and animal bodies will begin to overlap in ever more interesting – and problematic – ways.

In this chapter, we will look at the ways in which non-human animal bodies are subject to human, corporate, and state control. We will look at the history of human control over animal bodies, including domestication, selective breeding, marking and altering animal bodies, **genetic modification**, and **cloning**, and the implications for those practices. We will also address some other aspects of the human/animal relationship, such as the human–animal bond and the future of our relationship with other species.

Human–animal kinship: evolutionary links

In the mid-nineteenth century, naturalist Charles Darwin's theory of **evolution by natural selection** was a revolutionary challenge to thousands of years of religious and philosophical thought regarding animals, which claimed that animals and humans are separately created and thus categorically different. Darwin's writings (*On the Origin of Species*, published in 1859, and *The Descent of Man*, published in 1871) challenged the notion that humans are a special creation and placed humans and animals into the same category: animals. While animality had long been defined as that which is beneath humanity, Darwin definitively affirmed that humans *are* animals.

Darwin was not the first to claim that humans are animals; eighteenth-century biologist Carolus Linnaeus classified humans in the primate order in 1758 in his *Systema Naturae*, which earned him a reprimand from his Archbishop. And in the seventeenth century, anatomist Edward Tyson demonstrated through dissection the similarities between humans and apes (Tyson 1972). But it was not until Darwin that there was a scientific theory to account for the relationship between the species: not only are humans and non-human animals similar, but they share these similarities due to common descent from a shared ancestor.

Not only that, but Darwin argued that there are no fundamental differences between humans and the "higher animals" in terms of their mental abilities, again challenging the basic premise on which so much of the distinction between the species rested. Darwin proved that not only are humans and all other animals related, but that we together feel pain, share emotions and possess memory, reason, and imagination. Rather than seeing humans and animals as categorically different, Darwin showed that all animals, including humans, share a continuum of mental and emotional capacities. Of course, while *On the Origin of Species*, Darwin's major work, was published in 1859, it would not be fully accepted for another hundred years. And it would not be until the late twentieth century and the rise of modern **ethology** that the idea that non-human animals experience emotions or possess reason would be taken seriously.

Today, ethologists who study the minds and behaviors of non-human animals show that, as Darwin theorized, there is no radical break between the emotional and mental capacities of humans and other animals; instead, there is a continuity of capacities. Ethologists who work with great apes, dolphins, and parrots, as well as a wide variety of other animals, continue to find more and more examples of this continuity. We now know that many animals can feel and experience much of what we once considered to be "human" emotions, that they have self-recognition and self-awareness, that they can communicate to each other (and to us) through sophisticated communication systems and perhaps even languages, can make and use tools, can empathize with others, can deceive others, can joke, can plan, and can understand the past and the future.

Also since Darwin's time, the science of genetics has demonstrated the extent to which we share genetic material with other animals, and especially with the great apes; we share more than 98 percent of our genes with chimpanzees, for example, and chimpanzees are more closely related to humans than they are to gorillas. And finally, research in **paleoanthropology** has proven conclusively that humans share a common ancestor with chimpanzees who lived as recently as eight million years ago – a very short time in terms of evolutionary history.

In fact, we can say that since the nineteenth century, the border between human and animal bodies is narrowing quite rapidly. Through new discoveries in genetic science, paleoanthropology, neuropsychology, sociobiology, and ethology, we find that we are physically, behaviorally, and emotionally closer to other animals than we have ever been before. Where scientists, theologians, and philosophers of the past spent their time over-emphasizing the differences between us and underestimating, or ignoring, the similarities, today's scientists have been closing the gap between the species.

Interesting issues: human–animal transformation

Humans have been transforming into animals, and vice versa, for thousands of years, at least within the stories and songs of cultures around the world. The tanuki is a Japanese animal which resembles a racoon or a badger, but is a member of the dog family. The tanuki is often featured in Japanese folktales as a **shapeshifter** *– a creature who can turn into humans (or even inanimate objects) to get what he wants. According to the tales, tanuki often transform into Buddhist monks in order to beg for food. Werewolves are an example of the transformation from human to animal and back again. Werewolf stories were common in Slavic and Chinese cultures, and often involve a curse which causes the person to transform into a beast. A related folkloric tradition is the marriage between humans and animals. For instance, in the Korean folktale "Silkworm," a princess whose kingdom is at war promises her father that she will marry the first man who kills the enemy's commander. When it appears that a white stallion has killed the commander, thereby winning the war, the princess declares that she will marry the horse. The King, on the other hand, is horrified at the prospect, and orders that the horse be killed and skinned. The princess, however, is filled with grief, and wraps herself in the dead horse's hide, whereby she transforms herself into a silkworm. The King takes the worm and* passes her eggs out to all the people, who benefit from the beautiful silk thread that they produce. In Scottish lore, selkies are seals which can, upon removal of their skin, take on human form and marry humans. The human generally is unaware of the real identity of their spouse, until they find the seal skin. Discarding the skin means the selkie will never be able to return to the sea. In China and Japan, foxes commonly transform into humans who then seduce men into marriage. These fox-maidens, however, can be detected by other animals, and when they are caught, must transform back into foxes and leave their human husbands. A similar idea is behind the Japanese tale "The Crane Wife." This tale tells of the marriage between a poor fisherman and his wife shortly after the man cares for and eventually releases an injured crane. The wife is able to magically weave sails for the husband to sell, saving them from poverty, but warns her husband to never look behind the curtain while she is weaving. One day he looks behind the curtain and startles a crane, who flies away, leaving the fisherman all alone.

Domestication and selective breeding: the creation of animal bodies

Even though the majority of the animals used or kept by humans today were domesticated many thousands of years ago, the process of selectively breeding animals for human purposes continues up to the present. In fact, when we examine the scientific advances since the 1990s (particularly in the field of agricultural sciences and most notably developments made in animal cloning), we might even say that the process of domestication has accelerated in recent years, changing the shape and very nature of today's domesticated animals, and with it creating a radically new set of relationships between people and animals.

As has been long noted by archaeologists and historians, animal domestication (as opposed to simply taming animals) first occurred at least 15,000 years ago, with the domestication of the dog (as hunting partner), followed at least five thousand years later by the first domesticated food animals, the goat, sheep, pig, and cow). Horses (first used for food, but later the first beast of burden), cats, chickens, llamas, alpacas, and camels followed, and were finally followed, less then 2,000 years ago, by smaller animals such as rabbits and guinea pigs. As has been demonstrated by a number of scholars (Zeuner 1963; Diamond 1999) of the 14 or so larger animals to have been domesticated, most (the cat is a notable exception) can be defined by a number of behavioral traits, including a tendency towards scavenging, a rapid maturity rate, reasonable size, a calm disposition, ability to be bred in captivity, a gregarious nature and willingness to live with others in close quarters, and a hierarchical social life, all of which make animals such as the dog or horse amenable to living with humans, in exchange for feeding and care. Of course the animals themselves must have had something to offer to humans as well, such as food, clothing, the ability to work as hunters or beasts of burden, and later the promise of companionship.

While the species that were ultimately domesticated fit the above criteria, making them natural choices for domestication, the process of domestication itself was a result of both natural and cultural evolution. First, specific behavioral and physical traits of individual animals who scavenged or hung around human encampments were favored by natural selection in the process of domestication (for example, those individuals who demonstrated less fear and more curiosity of humans, traits which tend to be found among the juveniles of the species, would be among the first individuals to approach human societies; after reproducing, those traits would continue in their offspring). Second, humans most likely adapted their own behavior to that of the animals, incorporating them into human social and economic structures and later manipulating the physiology and behavior of the animals themselves. As we will see, domestication in the twenty-first century has moved from natural selection to artificial, and has been shaped almost entirely by human hands.

The domestication of animals (especially combined with the cultivation of plants) was a truly revolutionary stage in the development of modern civilizations, allowing for not only development of the early city-states with their complex division of labor and high degrees of inequality, but eventually the political and economic dominance of a handful of European and Asian societies over much of the rest of the world. But the results of domestication for the human–animal relationship, and for the animals themselves, were no less revolutionary. As anthropologist Tim Ingold points out (1994), the relationship between animals and humans among traditional hunter-gatherers was often one of mutual trust in which the environment and its resources are shared by both animals and people; animals that were hunted by humans were seen as equals. Domestication changed this relationship into one of dominance and control, as humans took on the role of master and animals that of property, becoming items to be owned and exchanged.

Domestication also had long-range consequences for the animals themselves, as the very nature of the animals changed throughout the process, typically not in the animals' favor. Through domestication, once-wild animals become increasingly more dependent on humans, both physically and emotionally. Because a handful of traits (like curiosity, lack of fear, willingness to try new things, food begging, submissiveness, etc.) found among the juveniles of species are selected for in domestication, the physical traits of the young (shorter faces, excess fat, smaller brains, smaller

FIGURE 16.1 Pepe, a seven-pound Chihuahua, illustrates some of the most extreme characteristics of neoteny; he cannot survive without human care. Photo courtesy of the author.

teeth, etc.) will also be selected for, leading to modern domesticates who are physically and behaviorally unable to live independently, and who are, in fact, perpetual juveniles (a condition known as **neoteny**).

Since the first animals were domesticated for food, labor, and skin, domesticated animals have been transformed in a whole host of ways, both behaviorally and physically. Natural selection favored those physical and behavioral traits that made individual species, and individual animals, good prospects for domestication – lack of fear, curiosity, small size, and gregariousness, for example – making the earliest domesticates look and behave very differently from their wild relations.

Once humans began selectively breeding animals (and killing those whose bodies or temperaments were unwelcome) in order to emphasize or discourage certain traits, animals changed even further, resulting in animals who are, for the most part, smaller (yet fleshier), more brightly colored, with shorter faces, rounder skulls, and more variations in fur and hair type as well as ear and tail appearance. They also became tamer, friendlier, and more dependent on the humans who cared for them.

As farmers, and later show breeders, learned more about the inheritance of traits, animal breeders began selectively breeding animals for more specific characteristics, such as overall size, fur and wool color or texture,

state and corporate regulation of the body

ear and tail shape, and more. Termed **artificial selection** by Darwin, selective breeding has led to the creation of hundreds of breeds of dogs, for example, one of the most intensively bred animals in the world. In the case of dogs, breeds were created in order to fulfill human desires; some breeds were created to retrieve ducks during a hunt, others were created to herd sheep, and still others were created to race. In the case of cattle and other livestock, animals were transformed through selective breeding to create animals who were tame, easy to breed, easy to feed, and easy to control, with the ultimate goal being to create animals whose sole purpose is to create a food source for humans.

Altering the animal body

With the advent of industrial methods of food production in the twentieth century, changes in livestock breeds accelerated as livestock have become meat-producing machines, manufactured and maintained for the highest profits. To produce the most meat in the shortest amount of time, animal agribusiness companies breed farm animals such as pigs and chickens to grow at unnaturally rapid rates. These changes have been encouraged by new developments in agricultural science, aimed at improving the productivity of food animals. For example, American beef cattle are routinely administered hormones to stimulate growth, and to increase milk yield producers inject dairy cows with hormones. Animal bodies are stuffed into "**concentrated animal feeding operations**," massive facilities in which animals are confined into small spaces and in which food, water, and temperature is controlled and "unnecessary" and "inefficient" animal movements are restricted or eliminated altogether.

Since the early part of the twentieth century, farmers have been experimenting with creating new livestock breeds, via careful cross-breeding, in order to maximize size, fat composition, productivity, or other traits. Since the development of artificial insemination and the ability to freeze semen, cattle farmers are able to more selectively breed their prized bulls and cows to replicate the traits of the parents.

The pet and show industries, too, rely on artificial selection (and today, following the livestock industry, artificial insemination) to create breeds of animals with favorable (to humans) traits. Recent years have seen an escalation in the varieties of dogs, cats, and other companion animals being developed in order to appeal to discriminating consumers.

While the early breeds of dogs were created to highlight working traits, recent breeds have been geared more towards aesthetics. On the other hand, since cats are not working animals, most cat breeds have been created for aesthetic purposes, with an eye towards color, size, fur type, tail, ear, and body type. The result is hundreds of breeds of dogs, and dozens of breeds of cats, rabbits, and other species, all bred by large and small breeders to sell through the pet industry. Another result is a whole host of health problems associated with these breeds. Dogs in particular are at risk of problems associated with the odd proportions in body, legs, and head that are bred into many of the breeds. German Shepherds and Golden Retrievers are highly disposed towards developing hip dysplasia, and Chihuahuas and other toy dogs commonly develop luxating patellas. Even without specific genetic defects associated with certain dog or cat breeds, many modern breeds of dog or cat are unable to survive without close human attention. While dependency has been bred into domestic animals since the earliest days of domestication, it has accelerated in recent years with the production of animals such as Chihuahuas, who are physically and temperamentally unsuited to survival outside of the most sheltered of environments.

To better control the ultimate products – the animal bodies being produced – breeders of pet animals routinely cull those babies who do not conform to breed standards. For example, the American Boxer Club's code of ethics prohibits the sale by a club member of a boxer with a coat color not conforming to breed standards. Because up to 20 percent of all boxers are born white, this code necessitates the routine killing of a huge number of white babies.

Another form of artificial selection refers to the selection of deleterious traits in the breeding process. Japanese Bobtails (cats with a genetic mutation resulting in a bobbed-tail), hairless cats, and Scottish Folds (who have folded down ears) are examples of this type of breeding. More disturbing are cats that go by the name of Twisty Cats, Squittens, or Kangaroo Cats, all of whom have a genetic abnormality which results in drastically shortened forelegs or sometimes flipper-like paw rather than normal front legs, and who are being selectively bred by a handful of breeders. The twisty cat is reminiscent of the days of the circus and carnival freak show, when genetic abnormalities – both human and animal – were displayed to the public for education, entertainment, and profit.

Genetic manipulation of animals represents a new scientific development that has irreversibly changed animal bodies. Because pigs, beef cows, and chickens are created for one purpose – food consumption – their genes have been altered in a whole host of ways to suit that purpose, resulting in, for example, pigs engineered to have leaner meat, tailor-made to suit a more health-conscious consumer. Pig breeders are now able to purchase gene markers to modify their breeder swine in order to control for traits like the number of piglets born in a litter, how efficiently the pigs will process feed, how quickly they will grow, and how much, and of what quality, fat is present. Fast growth genes now allow pigs to reach market weight three days sooner than those without the gene, which increases profits for pig producers, and pigs with the lean gene have less back fat and eat less feed. Producers can

state and corporate regulation of the body

use genomic selection to reduce the prevalence of porcine stress syndrome, a fatal genetic condition that is triggered in conditions of extreme stress – conditions which are endemic to factory farming. Ultimately, pig producers will be able to feed their animals less, and produce more pigs, in less time, with less fat and more vitamin-rich flesh.

Meanwhile, the Meat Animal Research Center has now patented a gene that produces "double muscling" in cattle, producing more lean meat on the same size body. Belgian Blue cattle are the result of this double muscling, and because of their enormous muscles relative to their bones, these cattle are susceptible to a huge number of medical complications, such as swelling of the tongue which interferes with a calf's ability to nurse; congenital articular rigidity, a chronic ailment that affects a calf's ability to stand on its legs; cardio-respiratory problems which can cause death in calves; and birthing complications necessitate caesarian sections 90 percent of the time.

Genetically engineered animals are also becoming more popular among scientists who experiment or test products on animals. Genetically modified mice and rats are especially popular, allowing researchers to study the ways that genes are expressed and how they mutate. Genetic engineering has even found its way into the pet world, with the production of a new hypoallergenic cat (selling for $12,000–$28,000), created by manipulating the genes that produce allergens, and Glofish – zebra fish modified with sea anemone genes to make them glow.

In terms of reproduction, cloning animals is the wave of the future, allowing humans the greatest level of control over animal bodies. Thus far, the livestock industry has been most active in the use of cloning, cloning prized breeder animals in order to ensure higher yields by copying only very productive animals, but cloning is found in the vivisection and pet industries as well. Laboratory scientists are cloning mice, rabbits, and other laboratory animals in order to ensure that the animals used in research are genetically identical, and to control for any imperfections. In the pet world, cloning has been less successful, but a handful of companies today offer cloning for pets at a cost of up to $150,000 per cloned pet. Dog cloning is the most controversial so far – 12 dogs are needed to produce a single cloned puppy, and in South Korea, where cloned dogs are produced, those donor dogs are often slaughtered for food afterwards. According to published reports of cloning studies, 3,656 cloned embryos, more than 319 egg "donors," and 214 surrogate mothers were used to produce just five cloned dogs and 11 cloned cats who were able to survive 30 days past birth.

Another way that animal bodies have been transformed is through surgical procedures. Because the control of animal reproduction is critical to maintaining populations of domestic animals, castration has been used for thousands of years to ensure that undesirable animals cannot breed, or to increase the size or control the temperament of certain animals.

Castration methods include banding (in which a tight band is placed around the base of the testicles, constricting blood flow and eventually causing the scrotum to die and fall off after about two weeks), crushing (this method uses a clamping tool called a Burdizzo, which crushes the spermatic cords), and surgery (in which the testicles are removed from the scrotum by a knife or scalpel). In the twentieth century, with companion animals rising in popularity, surgical techniques to remove the uterus and ovaries of female animals were developed, and spaying is now an extremely common surgery for companion animals, although it is very rarely performed on livestock.

Other forms of surgical modification have also been common for years, particularly in livestock and purebred companion animals. For example the last century has seen a number of procedures performed on livestock as a result of the close confinement necessitated by factory farm production. The **de-beaking** of hens (amputating, without anesthesia, the front of the chicken's beak) is common in the egg industry, where chickens are so intensively confined in tiny cages that they may attack each other out of stress and overcrowding. Even in situations where livestock are not as closely confined, farmers often remove body parts to make caring for them easier. One increasingly common practice is **tail-docking** (without anesthesia, usually via banding) of dairy cows and sheep, in which producers amputate up to two-thirds of the tail, usually without painkiller. Pigs' tails are also docked, to keep intensively confined pigs from chewing each other's tails. **De-horning** cattle is also becoming increasingly popular, as dehorned cattle require less feeding space at the trough, are easier to handle, and cannot injure other cattle, as injuries result in bruised meat which cannot be profitably sold.

In the pet-breeding world, many companion animals undergo surgical procedures in order to make them conform to the artificial requirements of the breed. Breed standards demand that certain dogs, for example, have their tails docked, their ears cropped, or both. In addition, many companion animals today undergo surgical procedures which are used to control unwanted (by humans) behavior. Some people, for example, have their dogs de-barked (by cutting their vocal cords) in order to reduce barking, and many cat owners elect to have their cats de-clawed (which involves amputating the front portions of a cat's toes) in order to prevent harm to their furniture.

Animal bodies are also marked with more explicit signs of ownership. Branding is the oldest form of marking ownership on animal bodies, and has been used since the ancient Greeks, Egyptians, and Romans marked both cattle and human slaves with iron brands. Still popular amongst cattle ranchers today, brands are used to prevent theft, to identify lost animals, to mark ownership, and to identify individual animals. Today, freeze brands (which freeze, rather than burn the skin), ear tags, tattoos, and micro-

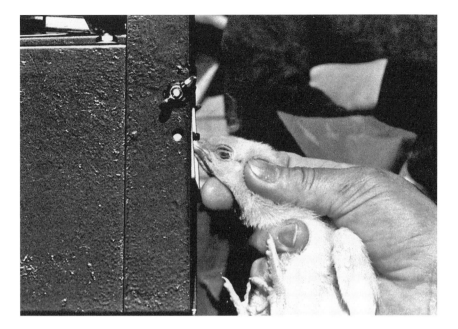

FIGURE 16.2 In a process called de-beaking, baby chicks have part of their beaks sliced off with a heated blade, to prevent them from pecking each other when crowded together into battery cages. Photo courtesy of Mercy for Animals, www.mercyforanimals.org.

chips are another method of marking livestock, laboratory animals, and companion animals.

And finally, in the biomedical world, non-human animals have undergone a tremendous amount of physical alteration. Genetically modified mice and rats are especially popular "research tools," allowing researchers to study the ways that genes are expressed and how they mutate. Laboratory scientists are also cloning mice, rabbits, and other laboratory animals in order to ensure that the animals used in research are genetically identical, and to control for any "imperfections." Ultimately, laboratory animals are stand-ins for humans, so they experience greater levels of genetic manipulation so that they can become more human-like, at least within the context of their status as research tool.

Bodily control

The very act of body modification is a centrally human act. No other animal can change their bodies in the ways that we can, and there is no evidence to suggest that animals want to change the appearance of their bodies. Yet, since the dawn of animal domestication, humans have been changing, sometimes radically, animal bodies through both temporary, but usually permanent, modifications. The modification of animal bodies serves a very

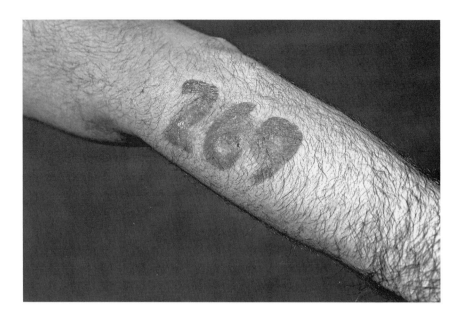

FIGURE 16.3 Project 269 brand tattoo. On October 2, 2012, World Farm Animals Day, three animal rights activists in Israel got branded with the numbers 269, in the same way farm animals are branded. The number 269 was the designated number of a veal calf animal rights activists encountered in one of Israel's intensive factory farms. Photo courtesy of Sasha Boojor and Tamir Bar Yehuda.

different purpose from body modification among humans: it functions to incorporate animals into culture, but *as property*, rather than as persons. Animal bodies are treated by law and common practice as objects which are owned and controlled. They can be bred, bought, and sold, can be used for labor, for food, for entertainment, and as a collection of resources that are both separable and commercially transferable. Their bodies can be patented, manipulated, dismantled, and modified on both the genetic and physical levels.

One of the primary reasons that humans modify their own bodies is to differentiate ourselves from (other) animals – to mark culture onto our bodies. This same reason also underlies all of the ways in which we have changed the shape, appearance, function, and indeed the very nature of animal bodies. Since the **Neolithic Revolution**, humans have been endeavoring to make animal bodies less wild, and less natural. While the goal is not to make them human – although it can be argued that the ways in which many owners dress their pets is an attempt to humanize them – it serves to bring them under human and cultural control. Tattooing, branding, artificially inseminating, de-beaking, de-horning, genetically modifying, and cloning – all of these procedures serve to remove from animals their wild, uncontrolled nature, and much of their own agency, and to replace that with human control, generally in order to profit from them. Through these maneuvers, we turn animals into products of our own making, to fulfill our own desires.

One of the ways in which we justify this control over animal bodies is by our assertion that non-human animals are qualitatively distinct from humans – they exist in nature, not in culture, and their behaviors are said to derive from nature. Humans have not only transcended nature; they have overcome nature, and thus animality. Thus the practice of marking and modifying human bodies serves as a clear visual sign that humans are *not* animals, that they are cultural beings. And humans are not just bodies: they are bodies with a mind, a soul, a self. Animals, on the other hand, as we have seen, lack that key component. Body modifications, then, can be seen as tools to visually mark and enforce the human/animal boundary.

While the human body today may be subject to a handful of commercial practices – prostitution, the marketing of human organs, blood and plasma sales, stem cell research, the patenting of products made from human tissues – there is still a deeply held assumption, grounded in law, that the individual person within that body should ultimately have a say over what happens to that body. While even here we find exceptions – laws which prohibit or restrict abortion, the contemporary practice of slavery, or the trafficking in stolen human organs – there is still broad consensus around the idea that a human being is the only person with rights over their own body and its disposal.

But animal bodies are an entirely different matter. Because non-human animals have not been granted any of the legal rights of personhood, their bodies are not, ultimately, theirs to control. Each and every animal is owned by some (legal) person, or corporate or state entity. Even wild animals are owned by the state. Further, animal bodies are not simply objectified but are commodified, and the body modification practices to which animals are subjected are incorporated into these practices.

While most people do not stop to think about the ways in which humans have changed, to their own detriment, animal bodies, what does evoke public outcry is the use of animal bodies in a way that challenges the human–animal border. **Xenotransplantation**, which is the use of animal organs in human bodies, is troubling to many precisely because of the way that it blurs the border, as are the examples of human–animal hybrids mentioned at the opening of this chapter. While animals are seen as bodies, and bodies alone, which justifies the ways in which they can be bred, sold, confined, manipulated, disassembled, and even consumed, humans are not just bodies. They are more than bodies. Animals can and are used as a set of parts, but when those parts are inserted into human bodies, the hard-fought border begins to dissolve.

Interesting issues: the link between violence to animals and violence to humans

There is now wide consensus around the fact that there is a strong causal connection, known as "the link," between violence toward animals and violence toward people. Cases of serial killers who started out their careers torturing animals are well documented. Some recent studies on children and animal cruelty have shown that half of all school shooters had a history of animal cruelty (Verlinden, Hersen, and Thomas 2000), and a 1985 study (Kellert and Felthous) found that 25 percent of violent criminals had been violent to animals, compared with 6 percent of non-violent criminals. A Canadian study found that 70 percent of people arrested for animal cruelty had past records of violence towards humans, and most animal abusers commit another offense within ten years of their arrest. Another study found that 36 percent of sexual murderers had abused – generally sexually – animals during childhood. Today, "cruelty to animals" is considered by the American Psychiatric Association to be a symptom of conduct disorder, which refers to a pattern of anti-social behavior that can persist into adulthood. Quite often, the children themselves have been the victim of abuse, and often sexual abuse. They may have been victims of bullying, and some were bullies themselves (Henry and Sanders 2007). Up to 88 percent of families with child abuse also had some form of animal abuse (Deviney and Lockwood 1983); one study (Duncan and Miller 2005) finds that children who abused animals are twice as likely to have been abused themselves. Alternatively, they may have witnessed animal abuse, often committed by their father or other adult figure. Witnessing a parent's violence towards another parent is also a causative factor, in which watching a parent get battered leads a child to harm animals. The links go both ways – not only are children in households with violence at more risk of committing violence themselves, but they are at greater risk of being harmed if they live in a household in which an adult harms either another adult or an animal. Unfortunately, while the research is clear that abuse in the home is correlated with abuse towards animals, there are no laws mandating that animal abuse be reported to officials, so early warning signs are often ignored.

A different kind of hybrid

For much of Western history, the idea that animals and humans are categorically different has been a basic component of philosophical, religious, and scientific thought going back to the Greek philosophers and continued through the writings of Christian theologians like St Augustine and St Thomas Aquinas. In Europe in particular, animals were thought to have been created expressly for human exploitation. Nature was considered a force to be subdued, and Christian clergy were especially inclined to emphasize that humans were both radically different from and superior to all other creatures.

With **animality** posited as something inferior to humankind, and as something to be conquered and exploited, early modern Europeans made concerted efforts to maintain distinct boundaries between themselves and animals. Bestiality was thus an extremely serious crime, often considered a capital offence. This concern with the human–animal boundary has also been used to explain medieval Europeans' fear of werewolves, and their preoccupation with monsters and mythical beasts – especially half-human, half-animal creatures.

The rise of the traveling freak show in colonial-era Europe was tied to this preoccupation. One of the most popular of such oddities, or freaks, were humans or animals born with disfiguring diseases or disabilities, and "gaffes," or artificial creatures created out of the parts of multiple beings. Those freaks that crossed the human–animal border were especially horrifying, and thus entertaining. Early documented sideshow attractions included a FeeJee Mermaid (marketed as a mummified body of a mermaid but probably created from the bodies of a fish, monkey, and perhaps an orangutan) first displayed in 1822, and P. T. Barnum's long-running "What is It?" attraction. "What is It?" was played by two men; one who was born with very short legs, and one who was mentally retarded and also possessed a sharply sloping forehead. Both men portrayed "wild men," or missing links between animals and humans.

In all of these cases, the "freak" was freakish precisely because of the freak's blurring of the human–animal border. Animal–human wonders like lobster boys (people with ectrodactyly, which causes the fingers and toes to fuse together), dog-faced girls (with a condition called hirsutism, which causes excessive hair growth on the face), and alligator men (who had a skin condition called ictheosis) were the most astonishing, and led to the new science of teratology – the study of monsters – in the nineteenth century. Ultimately, after Darwin, these creatures were explained as the "missing link" between animals and humans.

The discovery of African apes by Europeans was another example of how unsettling it was for humans to see animals who so clearly challenged the human–animal border. Long before Darwin, chimpanzees and especially gorillas were thought to be savage humans or part-humans, and their existence generated a huge amount of anxiety and excitement when they were first exported from African and displayed in Europe. For example, when Hanno the Navigator, a fifth-century BCE Carthaginian explorer, first encountered gorillas, he thought they were a tribe of hairy, savage women; he called this strange tribe "*gorillai*," after the word given to him by African informants. Even today, 150 years after the publication of Darwin's *On the Origin of*

Species, many are still unsettled by the notion that we are related to apes. The more primatologists discover about their use of tools and language, and their possession of self-awareness, the more fervently anti-evolutionists continue to fight to keep humans and apes separate.

But there are some people who want to blur, or even erase, the human–animal border. Some body modification practices, such as body painting, generally used to mark transitional status within a ritual in traditional cultures, are used to make a person appear animal-like. For instance, during festivals in Papua New Guinea, tribesmen dress up as animals via the use of elaborate headdresses as well as body paint in order to placate spirits and ensure prosperity. Papuan people also pierce their septums and their ears and men wear horns, bones, and tusks through the openings. The Kangi tribe wear bat bones and sweet potatoes in their noses, and other tribes favor pig tusks which make the men look fierce and animal-like for warfare.

Another intriguing exception to the idea that humans modify their own bodies to separate themselves from animals is the practice, still quite rare even in the body modification community, of people permanently modifying their bodies to appear more animal-like. We can date this practice to the 1930s when a circus performer named Horace Ridler transformed himself into a zebra man via full-body tattoos, tooth filing and facial piercings, and who, under the name the Great Omi, was typically displayed in sideshows alongside either wild animals or native peoples.

A subversion of the dominant human impulse to separate ourselves from animals, animality, as cultural studies scholar Annie Potts calls it (Potts 2007), allows humans to tap into a desire to get in touch with their animal selves. Animality in body modification is linked to the rise of primitivism as a philosophy, which posits that humans, and especially Westerners, are out of touch with the environment, physically destructive, violent, and represent all that is wrong with the world. In some circles, however, all humans are seen as bad and the only way to rectify the damage caused by humans is to emulate animals which are seen as good, balanced, sane, in touch with nature, etc. Just as primitive people are seen by modern primitives of representatives of a pure, peaceful, environmentally correct world, animals are now, for some, the highest ideal to aspire to: the ultimate authentic creature.

Examples of the desire to change from human to animal include Lizard Man (Eric Sprague), Katzen, Stalking Cat (Dennis Avner), and Jocelyn Wildenstein, all of whom have, through various surgical, tattooing, and piercing techniques, attempted to become more animal-like.

Another example of a human–animal transformation are people called **furries**. Furries are people who celebrate anthropomorphic animal characters in art and literature. While most furries live normal lives in mainstream society, in their private lives and when they come together as a group, they often take on animal totems themselves, internalizing some of the supposed characteristics of that animal, and, on occasion, dressing up as the animal, for personal satisfaction and social bonding. Both types of human–animals are, not surprisingly, considered freaks by modern society (in the case of Lizard Man, he actually does make his living as a sideshow freak).

Ultimately, animality can be seen as more than just the human emulation of the animal. It can also be seen in the ways that through modern biomedical science, animal bodies and human bodies are overlapping in ways that blur the line, once seen as hard and fast, between human and animal. Developments such as xenotransplanation, genetic engineering, and the creation of human–animal embryos, are all frontiers for the development of scientific animality, concepts which are discussed more in Chapter 17.

Human–animal kinship: coming together

As discussed, humans have, for thousands of years, used animal bodies for their meat, for their skins, for their muscle power, and for companionship. It is this last area – companionship – that offers the most promise for a more positive human–animal relationship. For example, the recent rise of **animal-assisted therapy** could not have occurred if it were not clear that humans benefit from animals in ways that are not strictly utilitarian. Assistance dogs, for example, do not just push wheelchairs or help guide the blind across streets; they make people feel less lonely, and more emotionally and socially connected. Military dogs, too, do not just detect bombs or guard installations; they also give soldiers comfort during extremely stressful times. The wealth of research on the power of the human–animal bond tells us that the benefits that animals can provide to humans go far deeper than we ever thought before.

And not only that: the healing power of animals is not just anecdotal; it has been well documented. For example, we know that animals encourage more exercise in their human companions, which results in better physical health. Seniors who own dogs go to the doctor less than those who do not (Siegel 1990), and cope better with stress life events without entering the healthcare system. Pet owners have lower blood pressure, triglyceride, and cholesterol levels than non-owners (Anderson, Reid, and Jennings 1992), fewer minor health problems (Friedman, Thomas, and Eddy 2000), decreased rates of heart attack mortality (Friedmann, Katcher, Thomas, and Lynch 1980), and higher one-year survival rates following coronary heart disease (Friedmann *et al.* 1980). Children exposed to pets during the first year of life have a lower frequency of allergic rhinitis and asthma.

There are also measurable emotional benefits of living with companion animals. The companionship of animals decreases loneliness (Sable 1995),

FIGURE 16.4 Olivia Montgomery plays catch with Sheba. Photo courtesy of Robin Montgomery.

helps children in families adjust better to the serious illness and death of a parent, and increases psychological well being and self-esteem. Pets provide emotional comfort and support for children whose parents are going through a divorce, and to seniors who have faced the loss of family (Hart 1995), and pet owners feel less afraid of being a victim of crime when walking with a dog or sharing a residence with a dog. The presence of a dog at a child's doctor's appointment or during a jury trial or other court appointment decreases the child's stress and provides comfort (Hansen *et al.* 1999). In children, animals focus attention, enhance cognitive development, and have a calming effect, and may improve attendance in school, compliance with authority, and learning and retention of information. A few studies show that contact with pets develops nurturing behavior in children who may grow to be more nurturing adults. And people with HIV/AIDS who have pets have less depression and reduced stress (Allen, Kellegrew, and Jaffe 2000).

The health and emotional benefits of living with companion animals are so strong that since the 1990s, organizations have emerged to help those with physical disabilities or serious help problems keep companion animals in their lives. Known as human–animal support services, these agencies provide financial or practical support to allow people to keep pets. San Francisco's Pets are Wonderful Support (PAWS) is one such group, giving

state and corporate regulation of the body

aid to people with HIV and AIDS, by providing for veterinary care, pet food, or transport to the veterinary clinic. PAWS volunteers will visit with HIV/AIDS patients in their homes to make sure that their companion animals have what they need, in order to keep the patient happy and healthy.

Finally, living with pets has documented social benefits as well. Animals are known as "social lubricants:" they increase our ability to affiliate with others around us by stimulating conversation and aiding in the reduction of anxious feelings. They stimulate social interaction, conversation, and rapport in a variety of situations (McNicholas and Collis 2000; Wells 2004). For instance, pets in nursing homes increase social and verbal interactions between residents (Bernstein, Friedman, and Malaspina 2000), and children with autism who have pets have more pro-social behaviors and less autistic behaviors such as self-absorption. Children who live with pets are more involved in activities such as sports, hobbies, clubs, or chores, and children who live with pets score significantly higher on empathy and pro-social orientation scales than children who do not. It is clear that animals' presence in human lives may have started out primarily as a primarily utilitarian issue, but has clearly evolved into something that goes to the very heart of how human beings function and feel.

What do animals get out of their relationship with humans? For well-cared for, much loved companion animals, the answer clearly is a lot. Unfortunately, no studies have been conducted on whether animals' heart rates improve when they are being petted, or whether their social behavior improves thanks to their relationships with humans. But they definitely benefit from a loving relationship, just as we do. But for the billions of animals who live and die in the food industry, the biomedical industry, or the fur industry, the human–animal relationship is much less beneficial to the animal.

Key terms

Animal-Assisted Therapy
Animality
Artificial Selection
Cloning
Concentrated Animal
Feeding Operations
De-Beaking
De-Horning
Ethology
Evolution by Natural

Selection
Furries
Genetic Modification
Human–Animal Hybrid
Neolithic Revolution
Neoteny
Paleoanthropology
Shapeshifter
Tail-Docking
Xenotransplantation

Further reading

DeMello, Margo. (2012). *Animals and Society: An Introduction to Human–Animal Studies*. New York: Columbia University Press.

Fudge, Erica, Gilbert, Ruth, and Wiseman, Susan, (eds). (1999). *At the Borders of the Human: Beasts, Bodies and Natural Philosophy in the Early Modern Period*. New York: St Martin's Press.

Henninger-Voss, Mary. (2002). *Animals in Human Histories: The Mirror of Nature and Culture*. Rochester, NY: University of Rochester Press.

Tattersall, Ian. (1998). *Becoming Human: Evolution and Human Uniqueness*. Oxford: Oxford University Press

PART VII

Bodies of the Future

chapter 17

Conclusion

Bodies of the future

In Aldous Huxley's novel *Brave New World* (1932), humans are no longer born, the population is limited to two billion people, and babies are decanted and raised in hatcheries and then conditioning centers. In the novel, life is presented as a utopia that is in actuality a **dystopia**. Countless science-fiction movies have dealt with this theme – that birth and/or death are controlled by the state – and show that state control over human reproduction never ends well. For example, in 1976's *Logan's Run*, society is controlled and resources are maintained by the state killing all citizens once they reach the age of 30. More recently, a similar theme was explored in the 2011 movie *In Time*, where people stop aging at 25. In that film, when they turn 25, poor people just die, but for anyone who can purchase more time, they can live for as long as they can afford to buy more time. (Of course this is somewhat true today: currency does in fact buy us time.) In a slightly different scenario, in the 2012 post-apocalyptic film *The Hunger Games*, the nation of Panem hosts an annual event where a group of teenagers, taken from the poor districts, must fight in a televised – and rigged – contest to the death, for the entertainment of the wealthy.

In all of these cases, the writers have imagined a future where technology has allowed humans to create a world where the very conditions of our lives are now controlled by science, via the state, in a way that should benefit society, but actually only benefits the elites.

While technology has not yet evolved to that stage, we are beginning to reach a point where scientists, religious leaders, and bioethicists are starting to ask questions about what the scientific limits should be when it comes to human bodies. Should there be limits at all, and who should decide what those limits should be? Today, as discussed in Chapter 4, we can already choose a father from a sperm bank with the "right" color of skin, eyes, hair, college education, and musical and athletic skills. We can choose an egg donor with the same qualifications, and if we believe that personality, emotions, and intelligence are heritable, we can raise a child with the "right" kinds of characteristics. We can elect to undergo Preimplantation Genetic Diagnosis in order to screen out any diseases prior to implanting our carefully created embryos, and to pick the sex of the baby. In the future, as the technology develops, we may even be able to select further characteristics. Who knows where it will end?

Cyborg bodies

In the 1970s, one of the most popular American television shows was the *Six Million Dollar Man,* inspired by the 1972 novel *Cyborg,* written by Martin Caidin. It featured an astronaut named Steve Austin who crashed while returning to earth, and had to have his right arm, his legs, and his left eye replaced by **bionic** parts, i.e., mechanical body parts that mimic, and enhance, biological organs. Thanks to these new parts, this "bionic man" had superhuman strength and senses, and was able to work as a secret agent, fighting crimes for the government. The bionic man was not just a fantasy figure. The first true biomechanical limb, using **myoelectricity**, was developed in the 1940s but became available in the 1960s. These prosthetics are attached to the body in a way that allows for electrical signals to travel from the muscles of the body into the prosthetic, causing movement in the prosthetic. The nerves in the arm or leg are surgically modified to control movement in a muscle that has been affixed with biosensors. The biosensors can pick up the movement in the muscle, send it to a controller in the prosthetic, and, when flexed, the muscle then forces the prosthetic to move.

The i-Limb hand is one such device. It is a completely mechanical hand, costing about $40,000, which allows each digit to move independently of the other. It also works with myoelectricity, whereby the muscles in the remaining portion of the arm send signals to the device which allow the fingers to then move. Devices like the i-Limb hand or the Bebionic 3, a similar device undergoing testing, allow users to peel vegetables, pick up coins, and even type. Patients can also choose a cosmesis, which is a custom-made artificial skin, to cover the hand, to make the hand appear more natural, although apparently some soldiers prefer the cyborg appearance of the mechanical hand without the skin.

Another modern device is the fiber prosthetics worn by athletes who have lost their legs. In the 2012 Summer Olympics, for the first time ever, a double-amputee ran in the Olympic Games. His name is Oscar Pistorius, and his performance in the 200- and 400-meter sprints was facilitated by the fact that he wears carbon fiber prostheses shaped like sickles called Cheetahs. Some of his competitors, however, felt that his prostheses gave him an unfair advantage, and might actually make him faster than the "normal" athletes. (He finished last in the 400-meter semi-finals in the 2012 games, silencing at least some of his critics. On the other hand, he is now awaiting trial for the February 2013 shooting death of his girlfriend Reeva Steenkamp; it has been alleged that Pistorius may have killed her because of steroid rage.) Of course, every other Olympic-quality athlete uses the most advanced technology in their shoes, their clothing, and their equipment to give them the greatest edge possible over their competitors, and of course it's an open secret that many use performance-enhancing drugs as well. How do we draw the line between what are acceptable advantages and unacceptable advantages?

The new frontier in prosthetics technology today is developing an artificial limb that can be controlled simply by the brain of the amputee. These brain-controlled prostheses would come closest to being truly bionic in that they would imitate the function of the missing limb perfectly and perhaps even enhance its original capabilities. The military in particular has been working on such technology, thanks to the large number of soldiers returning from the wars in Iraq and Afghanistan with limbs lost to IEDs (improvised explosive devices). In 2006, for example, former Marine Claudia Mitchell, who lost her left arm in a motorcycle accident, was the first woman to receive a truly bionic – in the sense of being mind-controlled – arm. With her new mechanical arm, developed by the Rehabilitation Institute of Chicago, all she needs to do is think about doing something, and her arm will do it. It works by using more than just myoelectricity. Mitchell's chest muscles have not only been rewired to the stumps of nerves that went to her arm, but the skin above her left breast was also "rewired" so that when the area is stimulated by movement from the arm, the skin sends a message to her brain informing it to move her new hand. It's based on the idea that when amputees try to move their missing limbs, their brains still send impulses down the spinal cord and end where their limb ends.

In November 2012, Zac Vawter, who lost his lower right leg in a motorcycle accident, tested the very first truly bionic leg during a stair-climbing charity event in Chicago. This new bionic leg was also made by the engineers at the Rehabilitation Institute, funded by the Department of Defense, and has two motors inside it; it is designed to respond to electrical signals in his thigh, which come directly from his brain. As he thinks about lifting his leg, his leg lifts. The testing of the leg (which will not be on the market for another few years while its performance is perfected) was significant because until now, there are no mind-controlled artificial legs on the market, giving those people who have lost legs fewer options.

Another experimental technology, this time aimed not at amputees but at those who have lost the control of their limbs or even their entire bodies, involves implanting microchips into the brains of the severely disabled, which are then wirelessly connected to robotic devices that they can then control using their brains. For instance, in 2004, quadriplegic Matthew Nagle had a device called BrainGate implanted into his brain which was connected to the outside of his skull and from there to a computer, which read his thought patterns. The computer then allowed him to perform a variety of tasks like control the television, check his email, and control a prosthetic hand. Nagle only wore the device for a year, as part of a test protocol, and died of an infection not too long after having it removed.

According to cultural critic Donna Haraway, we are already cyborgs. We live with pacemakers, artificial limbs – including those, like Pistorius' Cheetahs, which may help him run faster than other athletes – drug implant systems, artificial skin, implanted corneas, and more. When in the hospital, we are sustained with heart monitors, incubators, dialysis machines, respirators, and life-support systems. How do we draw the line between the technological enhancements we already have, and the sci-fi bodies of the future – the Six Million Dollar Man, and his spinoff, the Bionic Woman? According to Haraway, there's no point in drawing that line, as we will all, increasingly, become cyborgs.

As another example, body modification in recent years has become not only more sophisticated but has allowed users to become more techno-logically enhanced as well. People can now wear animated tattoos in which a tattooist tattoos onto a person a QR, or quick response, code. When a smart phone with a QR code reader is laid on the phone, and scans the code (via taking a picture of it), it triggers the online content, showing in the phone's display a moving image of the tattoo on a website previously created for the image. This procedure was first performed by French tattooist Karl Marc in 2011. Anyone with the technical skills can generate their own QR code and direct it to a particular website. That means that while the technology was first used to "animate" a particular tattoo, any tattooist can tattoo any code onto a person and, when scanned, it can trigger any sort of website or image.

In March 2012, the cell-phone company Nokia patented a device that would tattoo or otherwise affix magnetic material onto a person's skin, which would then be paired with a cellular phone. When the phone rings, the tattoo would then vibrate, alerting the wearer to the phone call, text message, or other notification; each type of notification could potentially have a different type of vibration associated with it. The inventors also suggested that the tattoo could serve as a form of identity check, which would only allow the user to open or use the mobile device. In both of these tattoos, technology is harnessed to the tattoo to turn the person into a

FIGURE 17.1 Neil Harbisson, the world's first official cyborg. Photo © Dan Wilton and Red Bulletin, courtesy of the Cyborg Foundation.

moving piece of art, as in the former example, or a mobile identification system, in the latter case.

While science fiction is full of examples of bodies and worlds in which human and machine are merged – think the novels of William Gibson or Philip K. Dick, or the cylons in *Battlestar Galactica* or the Terminators in the *Terminator* films, the reality is that this is becoming more and more possible every day. Not only can **cochlear implants** be implanted into the ear to give the deaf the ability to hear, but implants can now be inserted into the brain to allow some blind people to regain limited sight; a color-blind man named Neil Harbisson wears a device called an **eyeborg** on his head which allows him to hear colors. Harbisson founded the Cyborg Foundation in 2010 to promote the concept of cyborgs and to help other people to become cyborgs.

Virtual bodies

One new technology that allows for a new way in which our bodies can interact with both technology and the world around us is virtual reality technology. **Virtual reality** refers to the creation of computer-enabled environments that allow a person to feel as though they exist in a different world. Explored in movies like *Tron* and *The Matrix*, and prominently featured in video gaming technology and in combat or pilot training in the military, virtual reality technology is becoming increasingly life-like. While most of us may be familiar with virtual reality technology that involves wearing goggles which allows us to see a world that is computer generated (such as the new Google Goggles), another form of virtual reality involves beaming, explored in the early 1960s in the television series *Star Trek*, when the crew of the Starship Enterprise would have themselves virtually beamed from the ship to other planets and back. In that case, beaming involved a person entering a teleporter, having their matter broken down into energy, and then rematerializing when they reached their final location.

In 2008, cable news program CNN tried a more modern version of beaming when they turned reporter Jessica Yellin, reporting from Chicago, into a **hologram**, so that she could interact with Wolf Blitzer in the CNN studio in New York City. They achieved the technology through filming Yellin with 35 different cameras from multiple angles, and merging the information in a number of computers to create the appearance of Yellin standing in front of Blitzer. The effect was less like Spock and Kirk transporting from one place to the other in *Star Trek*, however, than Princess Leia appearing on the Holodeck in *Star Wars*.

In 2012, beaming technology has allowed scientists to beam a person into a rat cage so the rat and the person can interact with each other, on the same scale, for the first time ever.

While the person actually is not in the rat cage – it is a rat-sized robot – the robot is controlled by a human who is operating in a virtual, cage-like environment. The rat, at the same time, is controlling a human-sized robot who is interacting with the human in his own virtual environment. Since both are in their own virtual environments, and both creatures are interacting with a robot who looks like them – a rat-like robot and a human-like robot – this gives both participants a chance to truly interact with the other species in a way that's not normally possible given the intra-species barriers presented by our species differences. Mandayam Srinivasan, one of the scientists involved in the project, suggests that this technology allows scientists to virtually study animals and environments in ways that are both more authentic and less dangerous than those presently used. It is a bit like the human characters in the 2009 science fiction film *Avatar*, who interact with the Na'vi, the creatures who live on the planet Pandora, via their genetically engineered avatar bodies.

It's also clearly a new way of trying to *be* the animal, because as the human moves, his or her robot moves in the same way, and the rat then responds to that movement, causing the rat's human avatar to respond as well. Both human and rat then respond to each other, learning from and through each other, and in some sense each tries to *become* each other.

Hybrid bodies

In some ways, we can now become anything we like. In Chapter 16, we discussed people who choose, through extreme forms of body modification, to become animals. For instance, Dennis Avner, who called himself Stalking Cat, spent much of his life transforming himself into a tiger through a series of radical body modification procedures. Avner, who was part Native American (Huron and Lakota), said that he was told by an Indian chief to "follow the ways of the tiger," and decided to transform himself into his totem animal. He started by behaving like a cat, occasionally hunting his own food and eating raw meat. He began his real transformation in 1981 at the age of 23, and at the time of his death in November 2012 had tiger stripes and fish scales tattooed on his body and face, a surgically modified hairline, surgically shaped ears, a surgically flattened nose, silicone injections in his lips, cheeks and chin, six subdermal silicone implants inserted into his brow, forehead, and along his nose, 18 transdermal implants which acted as whiskers above his lips, a bisected upper lip, and a full set of fangs. He also wore a bionic tail. Most of Avner's work was done by body modification artist Steve Haworth, although he also traveled to Mexico to have some of the work performed by cosmetic surgeons there. He also wore green contact lenses with slits as irises and detachable bionic ears, but wanted to get another set of transdermal implants in his head to act as permanent cat ears and had plans to attach a permanent pelt to his skin. Unfortunately, Avner took his own life in late 2012 before completing his final transformation.

If anything, the human body is now plastic. It is malleable; we can make it into what we like, freeing it ultimately from the constraints of our biology – as long as we have the funds to do so. The body is also interchangeable, as we discussed in Chapter 15; we can sell and exchange body parts, and as we discussed in Chapter 4, embryos and even babies. The body, and its parts, can not only be sold but patented, as was the case with the Mo and HeLa cell lines, and with countless non-human animals which have now been patented beginning with OncoMouse, the first living animal patented by DuPont in 1988. While American bodies (but not their cells) are still prohibited from being patented, thanks to the Thirteenth Amendment to the Constitution which prohibits the ownership of human beings, the European Patent Office has already received patent applications for humans. Outside of the United States, too, tribes in the developing world are finding that their blood has been taken and is being turned into immortal cell lines which are being patented and are now owned by pharmaceutical companies who are now profiting off them. Known as **gene prospecting**, these cell lines are potentially even more lucrative when taken from peoples whose genes may contain unknown antibodies to hard-to-treat diseases, making these people even more vulnerable to capitalist exploitation.

Plastination is another way in which bodies can be turned into something other than simply bodies; they can become both artistic creations and commodities. Plastination is a process by which human or animal bodies are preserved with plastic and can be permanently displayed, either whole, in parts, or with the skin, muscles, or organs removed. It was developed by German anatomist Gunther von Hagens and is used to create models for medical students, but more controversially, plastinated bodies are now displayed as part of the *Body Worlds* exhibitions, which are traveling shows that are attended by the general public for entertainment. While the bodies used in von Hagens' *Body Worlds* shows are all donated for that purpose, the major competitor to Body Worlds are the *Bodies: The Exhibition* shows, run by a company called Premiere Exhibitions, which uses "unclaimed" bodies donated by the Chinese government. (After an investigation by the New York Attorney General in 2006, Premier Exhibitions now posts a disclaimer on their website stating that they cannot "independently verify" that their "bodies do not come from executed criminals.")

Xenotransplantation, which refers to the transplantation of non-human animal organs into humans, is another area in which human bodies are becoming more malleable. Because of the worldwide shortage of human organs available for transplant that we discussed in Chapter 15 – more than 92,000 Americans are currently awaiting an organ transplant and more than half will die while waiting – the result is a growing black market in organ sales as well as illegal harvesting of organs and tissues for transplant. While most organ donation advocacy groups focus on recruiting new donors or improving procurement practices in order to meet the growing demand and some are even proposing incentives for organ donation, there is also support in the biomedical community to focus instead on using non-human animals for human bodies.

Scientists have been working on perfecting xenotransplantation methods for decades. Yet, aside from the ethical concerns about creating "body part farms" where animals are raised in order to provide organs for humans, xenotransplantation has, from a medical perspective, been a total failure. Since 1964, when doctors transplanted a chimpanzee heart into a man, to 1984, when a baboon heart was transplanted into an infant, to 1994, when

FIGURE 17.2 A plastinated human body exhibited at the *Body Worlds* show, Museum of Natural History, San Diego, 2009. Photo courtesy of Patty Mooney, Crystal Pyramid Productions, San Diego, California, via Wikimedia Commons: http://commons.wikimedia.org/wiki/File: Plastinated_Human_Body_Worlds_San_Diego.jpg.

a pig's liver was transplanted into a woman, the result always has been the same: in all cases, the patients died shortly after their surgeries. This failure demonstrates that even the relatively small genetic differences between, say, chimpanzees and humans are actually quite large when it comes down to the ability of one species' organs to survive in another, even closely related species' body.

As biologists Lynda Birke and Mike Michael point out (1998), the ability to raise and kill non-human animals in order to use their body parts in our bodies is only possible because humans argue that we are not just different from other animals but superior to them. We are special. Yet those body parts can only work if we are similar enough to them that the species barrier between us can be breached; that is how biomedicine works, after all. With the breaching of the species barrier, we ultimately create a hybrid species, challenging the notion of what a human ultimately is.

Digital bodies

Increasingly today, our bodies take form and interact online. Through Twitter and Facebook, through online games, and through online pornography, human beings abandon their corporeal beings in favor of their online **avatars** who visit other worlds, take on other personalities, and engage in virtual relationships.

One popular site for increasing numbers of people today is **Reddit**. Reddit is a social news site where registered users upload news, photos, and other items, and other users then vote those items up or down; those items with lots of up votes can end up on the home page. Reddit has hundreds of subreddits which are devoted to every possible type of interest, and which attract every possible type of user. Some of those are extremely controversial, and feature bodies of various kinds. These subreddits have names like jailbait, creepshots, creepsquad, chokeabitch, misogyny, and incest. In most cases, the content is self-explanatory based on the name; other controversial subreddits are dedicated to featuring pictures of dead children or babies, women being beaten, violent car crashes, and mutilated animals.

In fact the Internet is now the one place where bodies that were once taboo in all but the most exclusive of spaces are now open and available to all. Anyone can now Google "Princess Diana car crash," "Michael Jackson autopsy," or "Saddam Hussein execution" and those photos will be instantly available. Any kind of pornography, no matter how repulsive, or illegal, is available. A few years ago, the trailer for a Brazilian fetish porn film called *Hungry Bitches* went viral on the Internet; called *2 Girls 1 Cup*, the trailer showed two nude women eating human feces, vomiting, and eating their vomit as well. Immediately after the video appeared, "reaction videos" began appearing during which someone would be shown the video for the first time, while a camera recorded their horrified (and often hilarious) reactions. But as gross as *2 Girls 1 Cup* is, there is so much graphic and often disturbing material online – naked bodies, dead bodies, celebrity sex videos, open-heart surgery, sex-change operations, babies being born, executions, fetish porn, animal slaughter, and more. There simply is no limit to the amount of pain or destruction or degradation that the human or non-human animal body can endure, nor does there seem to be a limit to the amount of people who seem interested in watching it.

For people interested in body modification and, in particular, interested in extreme forms of body modification, the place to go is **BME.com** (Body Modification Ezine), an online magazine devoted to the documentation of body modification practices. BME's focus is reader stories and photos. The site allows readers a forum for sharing their personal stories about how they got a particular modification, why they got it, the process that they underwent, and the impact on their life since they received it. Because a primary purpose of the site is to encourage the development of community, there are personal ads, event listings, and IAM.bmezine community, which requires members to join. The website is geared to adults as it contains sexually explicit materials, as well as photos of dangerous or life-threatening activities like voluntary amputations, cutting, and torture. The website has a prominent statement on their home page which warns the reader of the possible dangers of some of the activities documented on the site, and which claims no legal responsibility for them.

This book opened with a discussion of the centrality of the body in horror movies, that early twentieth-century technology. It ends with twenty-first-century technologies, and the body still remains central. According to the satirical website *The Scoop News*, the Internet is made of 80 percent pornography, 15 percent cat videos, 4 percent poorly written comments, and 1 percent unknown content. While many would argue that the percentage of cat videos is probably much higher, it is certainly true that pornography has always been a major element of the online world. But other kinds of bodies, and in particular, graphic, subversive, and tabooed bodies, are popular there as well, as we have been discussing, perhaps because of the uncensored, unfiltered nature of the Internet. As long as sites like Reddit and BME exist which promote online freedom and welcome graphic photos that make many people uneasy, then bodies will remain a prominent feature of the online world.

Ultimately, the preponderance of bodies on the Internet speaks to the preponderance of bodies in horror movies, in society, and indeed in the class that you are currently taking. As discussed in Chapter 1 the body is the primary symbol through which we communicate our cultural values and norms, it is the physical form on which society inscribes itself, and it's the vehicle through which we experience the world and our relationships with each other. It serves as the intersection between the physical and the social, cultural, and the historical. And as such, it will continue to be shaped by the technologies of the future, and will continue to be a flexible surface on which we inscribe our wills and desires.

Key terms

Avatars	Gene Prospecting
Bionic	Myoelectricity
BME.com	Plastination
Cochlear Implants	Reddit
Cyborg	Virtual Reality
Dystopia	

Further reading

Featherstone, Mike and Burrows, Roger, (eds). (1995). *Cyberspace/Cyberbodies/Cyberpunk: Cultures of Technological Embodiment*. London: Sage Publications.

Haraway, Donna. (1991). *Simians, Cyborgs and Women: The Reinvention of Nature*. New York: Routledge.

—— (1993). "The Biopolitics of Postmodern Bodies." In *Knowledge, Power and Practice*, ed. Shirley Lindenbaum and Margaret Lock. Berkeley, CA: University of California Press, 364–410.

—— (1997). *Modest Witness @ Second Millennium. FemaleMan Meets Oncomouse: Feminism and Technoscience*. New York and London: Routledge.

Bibliography

Agar, Nicholas. (2005). *Liberal Eugenics: In Defence of Human Enhancement*. Malden, MA: Blackwell.

Ahmed, Sara. (2000). *Strange Encounters: Embodied Others in Postcoloniality*. London and New York: Routledge.

Alcoff, Linda Martin. (2006). *Visible Identities, Race, Gender, and the Self*. New York: Oxford University Press.

Allen, Jessica M., Hammon Kellegrew, Diane, and Jaffe, Deborah. (2000). "The Experience of Pet Ownership as a Meaningful Occupation." *Canadian Journal of Occupational Therapy* 57 (4): 271–8.

Alsop, Rachel, Fitzsimons, Annette, and Lennon, Kathleen. (2002). *Theorising Gender*. Cambridge: Polity Press.

Alter, Joseph. (1992). *The Wrestler's Body: Identity and Ideology in Northern India*. Berkeley, CA: University of California Press.

—— (2000). *Gandhi's Body: Sex, Diet, and the Politics of Nationalism*. Philadelphia, PA: University of Pennsylvania Press.

Althaus, Frances A. (1997). "Female Circumcision: Rite of Passage or Violation of Rights?" *International Family Planning Perspectives* 23 (3): 130–3.

Angel, J. L. and Hogan, D. P. (1991). "The Demography of Minority Populations." In *Minority Elders: Longevity, Economics and Health, Building a Public Policy Base*. Washington, DC: Gerontological Society of America, 1–13.

Armstrong, David. (1985). *The Political Anatomy of the Body*. Cambridge: Cambridge University Press.

Arnold, David. (1993). *Colonizing the Body: State Medicine and Epidemic Disease in Nineteenth-Century India*. Berkeley, CA: University of California Press.

Arnup, Katherine, Andree Leveque, Andree, and Pierson, Ruth Roach, (eds) (1990). *Delivering Motherhood: Maternal Ideologies and Practices in the Nineteenth and Twentieth Centuries*. London: Routledge.

Asad, Talal. (1997). "Remarks on the Anthropology of the Body." In *Religion and the Body: Comparative Perspectives on Devotional Practices*, ed. Sarah Coakley. Cambridge: University of Cambridge Press, 42–52.

Atkinson, Michael. (2003). *Tattooed: The Sociogenesis of a Body Art*. Toronto: University of Toronto Press.

Bakhtin, Mikhail. (1984). *Rabelais and his world*. Bloomington, IN: Indiana University Press.

Balsamo, Anne. (1992). "On the Cutting Edge: Cosmetic Surgery and the Technological Production of the Gendered Body." *Camera Obscura* 28: 206–37.

Banks, Ingrid. (2000). *Hair Matters: Beauty, Power and Black Women's Consciousness*. New York: New York University Press.

Banner, Lois. (1983). *American Beauty*. Chicago, IL: University of Chicago Press.

Barker, Francis. (1984). *The Tremulous Private Body: Essays on Subjection*. New York: Methuen.

Barley, Nigel. (1995). *Grave Matters*. New York: Henry Holt & Company.

Bass, S. A., Kutza, E. A., and Torres-Gil, F. M., (eds) (1990). *Diversity in Aging*. Glencoe, IL: Scott, Foresman.

Baudrillard, Jean. (1995). *Simulacra and Simulation. The Body, in Theory: Histories of Cultural Materialism*, tr. Sheila Faria Glaser. Ann Arbor, MI: University of Michigan Press.

Becker, Gay. (2000). *The Elusive Embryo: How Men and Women Approach New Reproductive Technologies*. Berkeley, CA: University of California Press.

Bell, Rudolph M. (1985). *Holy Anorexia*. Chicago, IL: University of Chicago Press.

Berger, H., Jr. (1987). "Bodies and Texts." *Representations* 17: 144–66.

Berger, John. (1972). *Ways of Seeing*. London: British Broadcasting Corporation.

Bernstein, P. L., Friedman, E., and Malaspina, A. (2000). "Animal-Assisted Therapy Enhances Resident Social Interaction and Initiation in Long-Term Care Facilities." *Anthrozoös* 13 (4): 213–24.

Birke, Lynda. (1999). *Feminism and the Biological Body*. New Brunswick, NJ: Rutgers University Press.

Birke, Lynda and Michael, Mike. (1998). "The Heart of the Matter: Animal Bodies, Ethics, and Species Boundaries." *Society & Animals* 6 (3): 245–61.

Bishop, Kyle William. (2010). *American Zombie Gothic: The Rise and Fall (and Rise) of the Walking Dead in Popular Culture*. Jefferson, NC: McFarland & Co.

Blacking, J., (ed.) (1977). *The Anthropology of the Body*. New York: Academic Press.

Blanchard, Pascal. (2008). *Human Zoos: Science and Spectacle in the Age of Colonial Empires*. Liverpool: Liverpool University Press.

Bleir, Ruth, (1984). *Science and Gender: A Critique of Biology and its Theories on Women*, New York: Pergamon.

Bobel, Chris and Samantha Kwan. (2011). *Embodied Resistance: Challenging the Norms, Breaking the Rules*. Nashville, TN: Vanderbilt University Press.

Bogdan, Robert. (1988). *Freak Show*. Chicago, IL: University of Chicago Press.

Bolin, Anne. (1992). "Vandalized Vanity: Feminine Physiques Betrayed and Portrayed." In *Tattoo, Torture, Mutilation, and Adornment: The Denaturalization of the Body in Culture and Text*, ed. Frances Mascia Lees and Patricia Sharpe. Albany, NY: State University of New York Press, 79–99.

bibliography

Bond, Selena, Thomas F. Cash, (1992). "Black Beauty: Skin Color and Body Images Among African-American College Women." *Journal of Applied Social Psychology* 22 (11): 874–88.

Bordo, Susan. (1989). "The Body and the Reproduction of Femininity: A Feminist Appropriation of Foucault." In *Gender/Body/Knowledge: Feminist Reconstructions of Being and Knowing*, ed. Alison M. Jaggar and Susan R. Bordo. New Brunswick, NJ: Rutgers University Press, 13–33.

—— (1990). "Reading the Slender Body." In *Body Politics: Women and the Discourses of Science*, ed. Mary Jacobus, Evelyn Fox Keller, and Sally Shuttleworth. New York: Routledge, 83–112.

—— (1993). *Unbearable Weight: Feminism, Western Culture, and the Body*. Berkeley, CA: University of California Press.

—— (1999). *The Male Body: A New Look at Men in Public and Private*. New York: Farrar, Straus & Giroux.

Bornstein, Kate. (1994). *Gender Outlaw: On Men, Women, and the Rest of Us*. New York: Routledge.

Bottomley, F. (1979). *Attitudes to the Body in Western Christendom*. London: Lepus Books.

Bourdieu, Pierre. (1984). *Distinction: A Social Critique of the Judgement of Taste*. Cambridge, MA: Harvard University Press.

—— (1994). "Structures, Habitus, Power: Basis for a Theory of Symbolic Power." In *Cultures, Power, History: A Reader in Contemporary Social Theory*, ed. Nicolas Dirks, Geoff Eley, and Sherry Ortner. Princeton, NJ: Princeton University Press, 155–99.

—— (1998). *Practical Reason: on the Theory of Action*. Stanford, CA: Stanford University Press.

Bourgois, Philippe and Schonberg, Jeff. (2007). "Intimate Apartheid: Ethnic Dimensions of Habitus among Homeless Heroin Injectors." *Ethnography* 8 (1): 7–31.

Braidotti, Rosie. (1994). *Nomadic Subjects: Embodiment and Sexual Difference in Contemporary Feminist Theory*, New York: Columbia University Press.

Brain, Robert. (1979). *The Decorated Body*. New York: Harper & Row.

Braziel, Jana Evans and Kathleen LeBesco. (2001). *Bodies Out of Bounds: Fatness and Transgression*. Berkeley, CA: University of California Press.

Breckenridge Carol A. and Candace Vogler. (2001). "The Critical Limits of Embodiment: Disability's Criticism," *Public Culture* 13 (3): 349–57.

Brown, Peter. (1988). *The Body and Society: Men, Women and Sexual Renunciation in Early Christianity*. Lectures on the History of Religions, n.s., 13. New York: Columbia University Press.

Bruch, Hilde. (1973). *Eating Disorders: Obesity, Anorexia Nervosa, and the Person Within*. New York: Basic Books.

Brumberg, Joan Jacobs. (1997). *The Body Project: An Intimate History of American Girls*. New York: Random House.

Burgett, Bruce. (1998). *Sentimental Bodies. Sex, Gender and Citizenship in the Early Republic*. Princeton, NJ: Princeton University Press.

Burton, John W. (2001). *Culture and the Human Body: An Anthropological Perspective*. Prospect Heights, IL: Waveland Press.

Butler, Judith. (1990). *Gender Trouble: Feminism and the Subversion of Identity*. New York: Routledge.

—— (1993). *Bodies that Matter: On the Discursive Limits of "Sex."* New York: Routledge.

—— (2004). *Undoing Gender*. New York: Routledge.

Bynum, Caroline Walker. (1991). *Fragmentation and Redemption: Essays on Gender and the Human Body in Medieval Religion*. New York: Zone Books.

—— (1995a). *The Resurrection of the Body in Western Christianity, 200–1336*. New York: Columbia University Press.

—— (1995b). "Why All the Fuss about the Body: A Medievalist's Perspective," *Critical Inquiry* 22(1): 1–33.

—— (1995c). "Women Mystics and Eucharistic Devotion in the Thirteenth Century." In *Beyond the Body Proper: Reading the Anthropology of Material Life*, ed. Maragert Lock and Judith Farquhar. Durham, NC: Duke University Press, 202–12.

Byrd, Ayana and Lori L. Tharps. (2002). *Hair Story: Untangling the Roots of Black Hair in America*. New York: St Martin's Press.

Campbell, Fiona Kumari. (2009). *Contours of Ableism*. Basingstoke: Palgrave Macmillan.

Camphausen, Rufus C. (1997). *Return of the Tribal: A Celebration of Body Adornment: Piercing, Tattooing, Scarification, Body Painting*. Rochester, VT: Park Street Press.

Campos, Paul. (2004). *The Obesity Myth: Why America's Obsession with Weight Is Hazardous to Your Health*. New York: Gotham Books.

Caplan, Jane, (ed.) (2000). *Written on the Body: The Tattoo in European and American History*. London: Reaktion Books.

Carey, James W. (1993). "Distribution of Culture-Bound Illness in the Southern Peruvian Andes." *Medical Anthropology Quarterly* 7: 281–300.

Chapkis, Wendy. (1986). *Beauty Secrets: Women and the Politics of Appearance*. Boston, MA: South End Press.

Chaufan, Claudia. (2009). "The Elephant in the Room: The Invisibility of Poverty in Research on Type 2 Diabetes." *Humanity & Society* 33 (February–May): 74–98.

Chernin, Kim. (1981). *The Obessession: Reflections on the Tyranny of Slenderness*. New York: Harper & Row.

Clover, Carol J. (1987). "Her Body, Himself: Gender in Slasher Film." *Representations* 20. Special Issue: Misogyny, Misandry, and Misanthropy Fall: 187–228.

Coakley, Sarah. (1997). *Religion and the Body*. Cambridge: Cambridge University Press.

Coates, Ta-Nehisi. (2012). "Fear of a Black President." *The Atlantic*, September, http://www.theatlantic.com/magazine/archive/2012/09/fear-of-a-black-president/309064/, accessed March 31, 2013.

Cohen, Philip. (2011). "Creating Care Vacuums as Nursing Homes Close." *Huffington Post* January 11, 2011.

Comaroff, John and Comaroff, Jean. (1992). "Medicine, Colonialism, and the Black Body." In *Ethnography and the Historical Imagination*, ed. Comaroff and Comaroff. Boulder, CO: Westview Press, 215–34.

Conboy, Katie, Medina, Nadia, and Stanbury, Sarah (1997). *Writing on the Body: Female Embodiment and Feminist Theory*. New York: Columbia University Press.

Cooper, Charlotte. (2007). "Headless Fatties." London, http://www.charlottecooper.net/docs/fat/headless_fatties.htm, accessed March 31, 2013.

Corbin, Alain. (1986). *The Foul and the Fragrant: Odor and the French Social Imagination*. Cambridge, MA: Harvard University Press.

Corea, G. (1985). *The Mother Machine: Reproductive Technologies from Artificial Insemination to Artificial Wombs*. New York: Harper & Row.

Crawford, R. (1984). "A Cultural Account of Health: Control, Release, and Social Body." In *Issues in the Political Economy of Health Care*, ed. J. McKinlay. New York: Tavistock, 60–103.

Cregan. Kate. (2006). *The Sociology of the Body: Mapping The Abstraction of Embodiment*. London: Sage.

Crossley, Nick. (2001). *The Social Body: Habit, Identity, and Desire*. London: Sage.

—— (2004). "Fat is a Sociological Issue: Obesity in Late Modern, Body-conscious Societies," *Health and Social Theory* 2 (3): 222–53.

Csordas, Thomas. (1990). "Embodiment as a Paradigm in Anthropology." *Ethos* 18: 5–47.

—— (1993). "Somatic Modes of Attention." *Cultural Anthropology* 8 (2): 135–56.

—— (ed.) (1994). *Embodiment and Experience. The Existential Ground of Culture and Self*. Cambridge Studies in Medical Anthropology. Cambridge: Cambridge University Press.

Dain, Bruce R. (2002). *A Hideous Monster of the Mind: American Race Theory in the Early Republic*. Cambridge, MA: Harvard University Press.

Darwin, Charles. (1859/1985). *On the Origin of Species*. New York: Penguin.

—— (1871/1981). *The Descent of Man*. Princeton, NJ: Princeton University Press.

Davis, Kathy. (1995). *Reshaping the Female Body: The Dilemma of Cosmetic Surgery*. London: Routledge.

—— (1997). *Embodied Practices: Feminist Perspectives on the Body*. London: Sage.

Davis-Floyd, Robbie. (1992). *Birth as an American Rite of Passage*. Berkeley, CA: University of California Press.

De Beauvoir, Simone. (1970). *The Second Sex*. London: Jonathan Cape.

—— (1972). *The Coming of Age*. New York: Putnam.

Dean-Jones, Lesley. (1994). *Women's Bodies in Classical Greek Science*. Oxford: Oxford University Press.

Delaney, Carol. (1991). *The Seed And The Soil: Gender and Cosmology in Turkish Village Society*. Berkeley, CA: University of California Press.

Delaney, Janice. (1988). *The Curse: A Cultural History of Menstruation*. Urbana, IL: University of Illinois Press.

Demand, Nancy. (1994). *Birth, Death, and Motherhood in Classical Greece*. Baltimore, MD: Johns Hopkins University Press.

DeMello, Margo. (1995). "The Carnivalesque Body: Women and Tattoos." In *Pierced Hearts and True Love: A Century of Drawings for Tattoos* (catalogue), ed. Don Ed Hardy. New York: The Drawing Center, 73–9.

—— (2000) *Bodies of Inscription: A Cultural History of the Modern Tattoo Community*. Durham, NC: Duke University Press.

—— (2007). *Encyclopedia of Body Adornment*. Westport, CT: Greenwood Press.

—— (2012). *Animals and Society: An Introduction to Human-Animal Studies*. New York: Columbia University Press.

D'Emilio, John and Freedman, Estelle B. (1997). *Intimate Matters. A History of Sexuality in America*, 2nd edn. Chicago, IL: University of Chicago Press.

Deviney, E., Dickert, J., and Lockwood, R. (1983). "The Care of Pets within Child Abusing Families." *International Journal for the Study of Animal Problems* 4 (4): 321–9.

Diamond, Jared. (1999). *Guns, Germs and Steel: The Fate of Human Societies*. New York: W.W. Norton & Company.

Diedrich, Lisa. (2001). "Breaking Down: A Phenomenology of Disability." *Literature and Medicine* 20 (2): 209–30.

Diprose, Ros. (1994). *The Bodies of Women: Ethics, Embodiment and Sexual Difference*. London: Routledge.

Dixon, Laurinda S. (1995). *Perilous Chastity: Women and Illness in Pre-Enlightenment Art and Medicine*. Ithaca, NY: Cornell University Press.

Douglas, Mary. (1966). *Purity and Danger: An Analysis of Concepts of Pollution and Taboo*. New York: Praeger.

—— (1973). *Natural Symbols: Explorations in Cosmology*. New York: Vintage.

Dreger, Alice Domurat. (1998). *Hermaphrodites and the Medical Invention of Sex*. Cambridge, MA: Harvard University Press.

Dubois, Page. (1988). *Sowing the Body: Psychoanalysis and Ancient Representation of Women*. Chicago, IL: University of Chicago Press.

Duden, Barbara. (1991). *The Woman Beneath the Skin: A Doctor's Patients in 18th-Century Germany*. Cambridge, MA: Harvard University Press.

—— (1993). *Disembodying Women. Perspectives on Pregnancy and the Unborn*, tr. Lee Hoinacki. Cambridge, MA: Harvard University Press.

Duncan, A., Thomas, J. C., and Miller, C. (2005). "Significance of Family Risk Factors in Development of Childhood Animal Cruelty in Adolescent Boys With Conduct Problems." *Journal of Family Violence* 20: 235–9.

Dutton, Diane B. (1986). "Social Class, Health, and Illness." In *Applications of Social Science to Clinical Medicine and Health Policy*, ed. Linda H. Aiken and David Mechanic. New Brunswick, NJ: Rutgers University Press, 23–46.

Dworkin, Andrea. (1974). *Woman Hating*. New York: Dutton.

Edmonds, A. (2007). "'The Poor Have the Right to be Beautiful': Cosmetic Surgery in Neoliberal Brazil." *Journal of the Royal Anthropological Institute* 13 (2): 363–81.

Edwards, Jeanette *et al.* (1999). *Technologies of Procreation: Kinship in the Age of Assisted Conception*, 2nd edn. London: Routledge.

Ehrenreich, Barbara. (2001). *Nickel and Dimed: On (Not) Getting By in America*. New York: Metropolitan Books.

—— (2007). "Welcome to Cancerland." In *Feminist Frontiers*, ed. Verta Taylor, Nancy Whittier, and Leila Rupp. New York: McGraw Hill, 35–7.

Elias, Norbert. (1978). *The Civilizing Process*. New York: Urizen Books.

Elliott, Dyan. (1999). *Fallen Bodies. Pollution, Sexuality, and Demonology in the Middle Ages*. Philadelphia, PA: University of Pennsylvania Press.

Elshtain, Jean Bethke and Cloyd, J. Timothy, (eds) (1995). *Politics and the Human Body*. Nashville, TN: Vanderbilt University Press.

Emmett, Steven Wiley, (ed.) (1985). *Theory and Treatment of Anorexia Nervosa and Bulimia: Biomedical, Sociocultural and Psychological Perspectives*. New York: Brunner/Mazel Publishers.

Enright, Anne. (2000). "What's Left of Henrietta Lacks?" *London Review of Books*, April 13.

Entwistle, Joanne and Wilson, Elizabeth. (2001). *Body Dressing*. Oxford: Berg.

Epstein, Julia and Straub, Kristina, (eds) (1991). *Body Guards: The Cultural Politics of Gender Ambiguity*. New York: Routledge.

Etcoff, Nancy. (1999). *Survival of the Prettiest: The Science of Beauty*. New York: Anchor Books.

Falk, Pasi. (1996). *The Consuming Body*. London: Sage.

Fallon, P., Katzman, M., and Wooley, S., (eds) (1994). *Feminist Perspectives on Eating Disorders*. New York: Guilford Press.

Fan, Hung. (2013). *AIDS: Science and Society*. Sudbury: Jones & Bartlett Learning.

Fanon, Frantz, (1963). *Black Skins, White Masks*, tr. C. L. Markmann. New York: Grove Press.

Faris, James C. (1972). *Nuba Personal Art*. London: Duckworth.

Farmer, Paul. (1999). *Infections and Inequality: The Modern Plagues*. Berkeley, CA: University of California Press.

Fausto-Sterling, Anne. (1985). "Gender, Race, and Nation: The Comparative Anatomy of 'Hottentot' Women in Europe, 1815–17." In *Deviant Bodies: Critical Perspectives on Difference in Science and Popular Culture*, ed. Jennifer Terry and Jacqueline Urla. Bloomington, IN: Indiana University Press, 19–48.

—— (1992). *Myths of Gender: Biological Theories about Women and Men*. New York: Basic Books.

—— (2000a). "The Five Sexes: Why Male And Female Are Not Enough", *The Sciences* 33 (2): 20–5.

—— (2000b). *Sexing the Body: Gender Politics and the Construction of Sexuality*. New York: Basic Books.

—— (2005). "Bare Bones of Sex: Part I, Sex & Gender." *Signs* 30 (2): 491–528.

Featherstone, Mike. (1991). "The Body in Consumer Culture." In *The Body: Social Process and Cultural Theory*, ed. Mike Featherstone, Mike Hepworth, and Bryan Turner. London: Sage Publications, 170–96.

—— (ed.) (2000). *Body Modification*. London: Sage Publications.

Featherstone, Mike and Burrows, Roger, (eds) (1995). *Cyberspace/Cyberbodies/ Cyberpunk: Cultures of Technological Embodiment*. London: Sage Publications.

Featherstone, Mike, Hepworth, Mike, and Turner, Bryan, (eds) (1991). *The Body: Social Process and Cultural Theory*. London: Sage Publications.

Fee, E., Brown, T. M., Brown, Lazarus, J., and Theerman, P. (2002). "The Effects of the Corset." *American Journal of Public Health* 92: 1085.

Feher, Michel, (ed.) (1989). *Fragments for a History of the Human Body*. 3 vols. New York: Zone Books.

Feinberg, Leslie. (1997). *Transgender Warriors: Making History from Joan of Arc to Dennis Rodman*. Boston, MA: Beacon Press.

Fiske, John. (1989). *Understanding Popular Culture*. New York: Routledge.

Foster, Gwendolyn Audrey. (2000). *Troping the Body: Gender, Etiquette, and Performance*. Carbondale, IL: Southern Illinois University Press.

Foster, Susan, (ed.) (1995). *Corporealities: Body, Knowledge, Culture, Power*. London: Routledge.

Foucault, Michel. (1979). *Discipline and Punish*. Harmondsworth: Penguin.

—— (1980a). *Power/Knowledge: Selected Interviews and Other Writings. 1972–77*. Brighton: Harvester.

—— (1980b). *The History of Sexuality: Volume I, An Introduction*. New York: Pantheon Books.

Fox, Renee C. and Swazey, Judith P. (1992). *Spare Parts: Organ Replacement in Society*. New York: Oxford University Press.

Frank, Arthur W. (1991.) "For a Sociology of the Body: an Analytical Review." In *The Body: Social Process and Cultural Theory*, ed. Mike Featherstone, Mike Hepworth, and Bryan Turner. London: Sage Publications, 36–102.

Frank, G. (1986.) "On Embodiment: A Case Study of Congenital Limb Deficiency in American Culture." *Culture, Medicine, and Psychiatry* 10: 189–219.

Franklin, Sarah. (1997). *Embodied Progress: A Cultural Account of Assisted Conception*. London: Routledge.

Franklin, Sarah and Ragoné, Helene, (eds) (1988). *Reproducing Reproduction: Kinship, Power and Technological Innovation*. Philadelphia, PA: University of Pennsylvania Press.

Freund, Peter. (1982). *The Civilized Body: Social Domination, Control and Health*. Philadelphia, PA: Temple University Press.

—— (1988). "Bringing Society into the Body: Understanding Socialized Human Nature." *Theory and Society* 17: 839–64.

Friedmann, E., Katcher, Aaron H., Thomas, S. A., and Lynch, James J. (1980). "Animal Companions and One-Year Survival of Patients after Discharge from a Coronary Care Unit." *Public Health Rep.* 95 (4): 307–12.

Friedmann, E., Thomas, S. A., and Eddy, T. J. (2000). "Companion Animals and Human Health: Physical and Cardiovascular Influences." In *Companion Animals and Us: Exploring the Relationships between People and Pets*, ed. A. L. Podberscek, E. S. Paul, and J. A. Serpell. Cambridge: Cambridge University Press, 125–42.

Fudge, Erica, Gilbert, Ruth, and Wiseman, Susan, (eds) (1999). *At the Borders of the Human: Beasts, Bodies and Natural Philosophy in the Early Modern Period*. New York: St Martin's Press.

Furth, G. and Smith, R. (2000). *Amputee Identity Disorder: Information, Questions, Answers and Recomendations about Self-Demand Amputation*. London: Author-house.

Gaines, Jane. (1990). "Fabricating the Female Body." In *Fabrications: Costume and the Female Body*, ed. Jane Gaines and Charlotte Herzog. New York: Routledge, 1–27.

Gaines, Jane and Herzog, Charlotte, (ed.) (1990.) *Fabrications: Costume and the Female Body*. New York: Routledge.

Gallagher, Catherine and Laqueur, Thomas W., (eds) (1987). *The Making of the Modern Body: Sexuality and Society in the Nineteenth Century*. Berkeley, CA: University of California Press.

Gallop, Jane. (1988). *Thinking Through the Body*. New York: Columbia University Press.

Gans, Eric. (2000) "The Body Sacrificial." In *The Body Aesthetic: From Fine Art to Body Modification*, ed. Tobin Siebers. Ann Arbor, MI: University of Michigan Press, 159–78.

Garber, Marjorie. (1992). *Vested Interests: Cross Dressing & Cultural Anxiety*. New York: HarperCollins.

Garland Thompson, R. (1997). *Extraordinary Bodies: Figuring Physical Disability in American Culture and Literature*, New York: Columbia University Press.

—— (ed.) (1996). *Freakery: Cultural Spectacles of the Extraordinary Body*. New York: New York University Press.

Gatens, Moira. (1996). *Imaginary Bodies: Ethics, Power and Corporeality*. London and New York: Routledge.

Gay, Kathlyn. (2002). *Body Marks: Tattooing, Piercing, and Scarification*. New York: Millbrook Press.

Gemzoe, Lena. (2005). "Heavenly." In *Fat: The Anthropology of An Obsession*, ed. Don Kulick and Anne Menely. New York: Jeremy P. Tarcher/Penguin, 93–108.

Gil, José. (1998). *Metamorphoses of the Body. Theory out of Bounds*, tr. Stephen Meucke. Minneapolis, MN: University of Minnesota Press.

Gilman, Sander. (1985). *Difference and Pathology: Stereotypes of Sexuality, Race, and Madness*. Ithaca, NY: Cornell University Press.

—— (1988). *Disease and Representation: Images of Illness, Madness to AIDS*. Ithaca, NY: Cornell University Press.

—— (1989). *Sexuality: An Illustrated History: Representing the Sexual Machine and Culture from the Middle Ages to the Age of AIDS*. New York: Wiley

—— (1991). *The Jew's Body*. New York: Routledge.

—— (1995). *Picturing Heath and Illness: Images of Identity and Difference*. Baltimore, MD: Johns Hopkins University Press.

—— (1999). *Making the Body Beautiful. A Cultural History of Aesthetic History*. Princeton, NJ: Princeton University Press.

—— (2000) "Imagined Ugliness: A History of the Psychiatric Response to Aesthetic Surgery." In *The Body Aesthetic: From Fine Art to Body Modification*, ed. Tobin Siebers. Ann Arbor, MI: University of Michigan Press, 199–216.

—— (2003). *Jewish Frontiers: Essays on Bodies, Histories, and Identities*. New York: Palgrave Macmillan.

—— (2008a). *Fat: A Cultural History of Obesity*. Cambridge: Polity Press.

—— (2008b). "The Hottentot and the Prostitute: Toward and Iconography of Female Sexuality." In *Sociology of the Body: A Reader*, ed. Claudia Malacrida and Jacqueline Low. Ontario: Oxford University Press, 45–50.

Ginsburg, Faye D. (1990). *Contested Lives: The Abortion Debate in an American Community*. Berkeley, CA: University of California Press.

Girard, Rene. (2000). "Hunger Artists: Eating Disorders and Mimetic Desire." In *The Body Aesthetic: From Fine Art to Body Modification*, ed. Tobin Siebers. Ann Arbor, MI: University of Michigan Press, 179–98.

Glassner, Barry. (1992). *Bodies: Overcoming the Tyranny of Perfection*. Los Angeles, CA: Lowell House.

Glenn, Evelyn N. (2009). *Shades of Difference: Why Skin Color Matters*. Stanford, CA: Stanford University Press.

Goffman, Erving. (1959). *The Presentation of Self in Everyday Life*. New York: Anchor.

Gould, Stephen Jay. (1996). *The Mismeasure of Man*. New York: W.W. Norton & Company.

Graham, Elaine. (2002). *Representations of the Post/Human: Monsters, Aliens and Others in Popular Culture*. New Brunswick, NJ: Rutgers University Press.

Greenberg, David F. (1988). *The Construction of Homosexuality*. Chicago, IL: University of Chicago Press.

Gremillion, Helen. (2003). *Feeding Anorexia: Gender and Power at a Treatment Center*. North Carolina, NC: Duke University Press.

—— (2005). "The Cultural Politics of Body Size." *Annual Review of Anthropology* 34: 13–32.

Griffin, Susan. (1978). *Woman and Nature: The Roaring Inside Her*. New York: Harper & Row.

—— (1981). *Pornography and Silence: Culture's Revenge against Nature*. New York: Harper & Row.

Griggs, Claudine. (2004). *Journal of a Sex Change: Passage through Trinidad*. Jefferson, NC: McFarland & Company.

Grimm, Veronika E. (1996). *From Feasting to Fasting, the Evolution of a Sin: The Development of Early Christian Ascetism*. New York: Routledge.

Grosz, Elizabeth. (1990). "Inscriptions and Body Maps: Representations and the Corporeal." In *Feminine, Masculine and Representation*, ed. Terry Threadgold and Anne Cranny-Francis. Boston, MA: Allen & Unwin, 62–74.

—— (1994). *Volatile Bodies: Toward a Corporeal Feminism*. Bloomington, IN: Indiana University Press.

—— (1995). *Space, Time and Perversion: Essays on the Politics of Bodies*. New York: Routledge; and Sydney: Allen & Unwin.

—— (2005). *Time Travels: Feminism, Nature, Power (Next Wave)*. Durham, NC: Duke University Press.

Hacking, Ian. (1995). "Making up People." In *Beyond the Body Proper: Reading the anthropology of material life*, ed. Margaret Lopck and Judith Farquhar. Durham, NC: Duke University Press, 150–63.

Haiken, Elizabeth. (1997). "The Michael Jackson Factor: Race, Ethnicity, and Cosmetic Surgery." In *Venus Envy: A History of Cosmetic Surgery*, ed. Elizabeth Haiken. Baltimore, MD: Johns Hopkins University Press, 175–227.

Halberstam, Judith. (1998). *Female Masculinity*. Durham, NC: Duke University Press.

Hall, Ronald E. (2008). *Racism in the 21st Century: An Empirical Analysis of Skin Color*. New York: Springer.

Halliburton, Murphy. (2002). "Rethinking Anthropological Studies of the Body: Manas and Bodham in Kerala." *American Anthropologist* 104 (4): 1123–34.

Hansen, K. M., Messinger, C. J., Baun, M. M., and Megel, M. (1999). "Companion Animals Alleviating Distress in Children." *Anthrozoos* 12 (3): 142–8.

Haraway, Donna. (1990). *Primate Visions*. New York: Routledge, 1990.

—— (1991). *Simians, Cyborgs and Women: the Reinvention of Nature*. New York: Routledge.

—— (1993). "The Biopolitics of Postmodern Bodies." In *Knowledge, Power and Practice*, ed. Shirley Lindenbaum and Margaret Lock. Berkeley, CA: University of California Press, 364–410.

—— (1997). *Modest Witness @ Second Millennium. FemaleMan Meets Oncomouse: Feminism and Technoscience.* New York and London: Routledge.

—— (2003). *The Companion Species Manifesto: Dogs, People and Significant Otherness.* Chicago, IL: Prickly Paradigm Press.

Hart, L. A. (1995). "The Role of Pets in Enhancing Human Wellbeing: Effects for Older People." In *The Waltham Book of Human–Animal Interaction: Benefits of Pet Ownership,* ed. I. Robinson. New York: Pergamon.

Hebidge, Dick. (1979). *Subculture: The Meaning of Style.* London: Routledge.

Henninger-Voss, Mary. (2002). *Animals in Human Histories: The Mirror of Nature and Culture.* Rochester: University of Rochester Press.

Henry, Bill and Sanders, Cheryl E. (2007). "Bullying and Animal Abuse: Is There A Connection?" *Society & Animals* 15 (2).

Herdt, Gilbert. (1994). *Third Sex, Third Gender: Beyond Sexual Dimorphism in Culture and History.* New York: Zone Books.

Herring, Cedric, Keith, Verna, and Horton, Hayward Derrick. (2004). *Skin Deep: How Race and Complexion Matter in the "Color Blind" Era.* Chicago, IL: University of Illinois Press.

Hewitt, K. (1997). *Mutilating the Body: Identity in Blood and Ink.* Bowling Green, OH: Bowling Green State University Popular Press.

Heywood, Leslie. (1998). *Bodymakers: A Cultural Anatomy of Women's Body Building.* New Brunswick, NJ: Rutgers University Press.

Hicks, Esther Kremhilde. (1987). *Infibulation: Status through Mutilation.* Rotterdam: Erasmus University.

Hiltebeitel, Alf and Miller, Barbara D., (eds) (1998). *Hair: Its Power and Meaning in Asian Cultures.* Albany, NY: State University of New York Press.

Hong, Fan. (1997). *Foot Binding, Feminism and Freedom: The Liberation of Women's Bodies in Modern China.* London: Frank Cass & Co.

hooks, bell. (1990). *Yearning: Race, Gender and Cultural Politics.* Boston, MA: South End Press.

Howson Alexandra. (2004). *The Body in Society: An Introduction* Cambridge: Polity Press.

Hummer, Robert A. (1996.) "Black–White Differences in Health and Mortality: A Review and Conceptual Model." *Sociological Quarterly* 37 (1): 105–26.

Hunt, Lynn, (ed.) (1990). *Eroticism and the Body Politic.* Baltimore, MD: Johns Hopkins University Press.

Hyde, Alan. (1996). *Bodies of Law.* Princeton, NJ: Princeton University Press.

Inahara, Minae. (2009). *Abject Love: Undoing the Boundaries of Physical Disability.* Saarbrucken: VDM Verlag.

Ingold, Tim. (1994). "From Trust to Domination: An Alternative History of Human–Animal Relations." *Animals and Human Society,* ed. Aubrey Manning and James Serpell. New York: Routledge.

—— (ed.) (1988). *What Is an Animal?* London: Routledge.

Irigaray, Luce, (1985). *Speculum of the Other Women,* tr. G. C. Gill. Ithaca, NY: Cornell University Press.

—— (1993). *An Ethics of Sexual Difference.* Ithaca, NY: Cornell University Press.

Irvine, Janice M. (1990). *Disorders of Desire: Sex and Gender in Modern American Sexology*. Philadelphia, PA: Temple University Press.

Jackson, Jean. (1994). *"Chronic Pain and the Tension Between the Body as Subject and Object."* In *Embodiment and Experience: The Existential Ground of Culture and Self*, ed. Thomas J. Csordas. Cambridge: Cambridge University Press, 201–28.

Jackson, Michael.(2002). "Familiar and Foreign Bodies: A Phenomenological Exploration of the Human–Technology Interface." *Journal of the Royal Anthropological Institute* (new series) 8 (2): 333–46.

Jaggar, Alison, and Bordo, Susan, (eds) (1989). *Gender/Body/Knowledge*. New Brunswick, NJ: Rutgers University Press.

James, Jacquelyn, McKechnie, Sharon, and Swanberg, Jennifer. (2008). "Predicting Employee Engagement in an Age-Diverse Retail Workforce." *Journal of Organizational Behavior* 32 (2): 173–196.

James, Jacquelyn B., McKechnie, Sharon, P., Ojha, Mamta U., Swanberg, Jennifer E., and Werner, Mac. (2008). "CitiSales Study: Jobs That Work." http://www.issue lab.org/permalink/resource/8677, accessed March 31, 2013.

Jaquart, Danielle and Thomasset, Claude. (1988). *Sexuality and Medicine in the Middle Ages*. Princeton, NJ: Princeton University Press.

Jeffreys, Sheila. (2005).*Beauty and Misogyny: Harmful Cultural Practices in the West*. New York: Routledge.

Johnson, Mark. (1987). *The Body in the Mind: The Bodily Basis of Meaning, Imagination, and Reason*. Chicago, IL: University of Chicago Press.

Johnson, Walter. (1999). "Reading Bodies and Marking Race." In *Soul by Soul: Life Inside the Antebellum Slave Market*, ed. Walter Johnson. Cambridge, MA: Harvard University Press, 135–61.

Joralemon, Donald. (1995). "Organ Wars: The Battle for Body Parts." *Medical Anthropology Quarterly* 9: 335–56.

Kahn Jonathan. (2007). "Race in a Bottle." *Scientific American*. July.

Kang, Miliann. (2010). *The Managed Hand: Race, Gender, and The Body in Beauty Service Work*. Berkeley, CA: University of California Press.

Kasson, John. (2001). *Houdini, Tarzan, and the Perfect Man: The White Male Body and the Challenge of Modernity in America*. New York: Hill & Wang.

Kastenbaum, Robert. (2001). *Death, Society, and Human Experience*, 7th edn. Boston, MA: Allyn & Bacon.

Kaw, Eugenia. (1997). "Opening Faces: The Politics of Cosmetic Surgery and Asian American Women." In *In Our Own Words: Readings on the Psychology of Women and Gender*, ed. M.Crawford and R. Under. New York: McGraw-Hill, 55–73.

Kellert, Stephen R. and Felthous, Alan R. (1985). "Childhood Cruelty toward Animals among Criminals and Noncriminals." *Human Relations* 38 (12): 1113–29.

Kessler, Suzanne J. (1998). *Lessons from the Intersexed*. New Brunswick, NJ: Rutgers University

Kessler, Suzanne J. and McKenna, Wendy. (1978). *Gender: An Ethnomethodological Approach*. Chicago, IL: University of Chicago Press.

Kilbourne, Jean. (1999). *Deadly Persuasion: Why Women And Girls Must Fight the Addictive Power of Advertising*. New York: Free Press.

—— (2000). *Can't Buy My Love: How Advertising Changes the Way We Think and Feel*. New York: Simon & Schuster.

Kimbrell, Andrew. (1993). *The Human Body Shop*. New York: HarperCollins.

Kimmel, Michael. (2000). *The Gendered Society*. New York: Oxford University Press.

—— (ed.) (1990). *Men Confront Pornography*. New York: Meridian–Random House.

King, Helen. (1998). *Hippocrates' Women. Reading the Female Body in Ancient Greece*. New York: Routledge.

Kipnis, Laura. (1992). "(Male) Desire and (Female) Disgust: Reading Hustler." In *Cultural Studies*, ed. Lawrence Grossberg, Cary Nelson, and Paul Treichler. New York: Routledge, 373–91.

Kirk, Malcolm. (1981). *Man as Art: New Guinea Body Decoration*. London: Thames & Hudson.

Klinenberg, Eric. (2001). "Dying Alone: The Social Production of Urban Isolation." *Ethnography* 2 (4): 501–31.

Ko, Dorothy. (2005). *Cinderella's Sisters: A Revisionist History of Foot binding*. Los Angeles, CA: University of California Press.

Kosut, Mary and Moore, Lisa Jean. (2010). *The Body Reader: Essential Readings*. New York: New York University Press.

Kulick, Don. 1997. "Gender of Brazilian Transgendered Prostitutes." *American Anthropologist* 99 (3): 574–85 .

Kulick, Don and Meneley, Anne, (eds) (2005). *Fat: The Anthropology of an Obsession*. New York: Jeremy P. Tarcher/Penguin.

Kunzle, David. (1982). *Fashion and Fetishism: A Social History of the Corset, Tight-Lacing and Other Forms of Body Sculpture in the West*. New York: Rowman & Littlefield.

Lachmund, Jens and Stollberg, Gunnar, (eds) (1992). *The Social Construction of Illness: Illness and Medical Knowledge in Past and Present*. Stuttgart: Steiner.

Lambert, Alix. (2003). *Russian Prison Tattoos: Codes of Authority, Domination, and Struggle*. Atglen, PA: Schiffer Publishing.

Lang, Sabine, Jacobs, Sue-Ellen, and Thomas, Wesley. (1997). *Two Spirit People: Native American Gender Identity, Sexuality, and Spirituality*. Chicago, IL: University of Illinois Press.

Laqueur, Thomas W. (1990). *Making Sex: Body and Gender from the Greeks to Freud*. Cambridge, MA: Harvard University Press.

Latimer, Joanna and Schillmeier, Michael. (2009). *Un/Knowing Bodies*. Malden, MA: Blackwell Publishing.

Leder, Drew. (1990). *The Absent Body*. Chicago, IL: University of Chicago Press.

Lennon, Kathleen, (2004). "Imaginary Bodies and Worlds." *Inquiry* 47: 107–22.

Levenkron, Steven. (2001). *Anatomy of Anorexia*. New York: W.W. Norton & Company.

Levy, Ariel. (2005). *Female Chauvinist Pigs: Women and the Rise of Raunch Culture*. New York: Free Press.

Lewis, I. M. (1971). *Ecstatic Religion*. London: Routledge.

Lock, Margaret. (1993a). *Encounters with Aging: Mythologies of Menopause in Japan and North America*. Berkeley, CA: University of California Press.

—— (1993b). "The Politics of Mid-Life and Menopause: Ideologies for the Second Sex in North America and Japan." In *Knowledge, Power and Practice*, ed. Shirley Lindenbaum and Margaret Lock. Berkeley, CA: University of California Press, 330–63.

—— (1998). "Perfecting Society: Reproductive Technologies, Genetic Testing and the Planned Family in Japan." In *Pragmatic Women and Body Politics*, ed. M. Lock and P. A. Kaufert. Cambridge: Cambridge University Press, 206–39.

—— (2001a). "The Alienation of Body Tissue and the Biopolitics of Immortalized Cell Lines." *Body & Society* 7 (2–3): 63–91.

—— (2001b). *Twice Dead: Organ Transplants and the Reinvention of Death*. Berkeley, CA: University of California Press.

Lock, Margaret and Farquhar, Judith. (1995). *Beyond the Body Proper: Reading the anthropology of material life*. Durham, NC: Duke University Press.

Lombroso, Cesare. (2006). *Criminal Man*. Raleigh, NC: Duke University Press.

Lorber, Judith and Moore, Lisa Jean. (2007). *Gendered Bodies: Feminist Perspectives*. Los Angeles, CA: Roxbury.

Lowe, Maria R. (1998). *Women of Steel: Female Bodybuilders and the Struggle for Self-Definition*. New York: New York University Press.

Lowy, Ilana, (ed.) (1993). *Medicine and Change: Historical and Sociological Studies of Medical Innovation*. Montrogue, France: Libbey. Paris: Institut National de la Sante et de la Recherche Medicale.

Lupton, Deborah. (1994). *Medicine as Culture: Illness, Disease and the Body in Western Societies*. London: Sage.

Lynch, Wilfred. (1982). *Implants: Reconstructing the Human Body*. New York: Van Nostrand Reinhold Company.

McClintock, Anne. (1995). *Imperial Leather: Race, Gender and Sexuality in the Colonial Contest*. New York: Routledge.

McLaren, Angus. (1978). *Birth Control in Nineteenth Century England*. New York: Holmes & Meier.

McMillen, Sally G. (1990). *Motherhood in the Old South: Pregnancy, Childbirth, and Infant Rearing*. Baton Rouge, LA: Louisiana State University Press.

McNicholas, J. and Collis, G. (2000). "Dogs as Catalysts for Social Interactions: Robustness of the Effect." *British Journal of Psychology* 91: 61–70.

McRobbie, Angela. (1991). *Feminism and Youth Culture*. Boston, MA: Unwin Hyman.

Maguire, Henry. (1996). *The Icons of Their Bodies: Saints and Their Images in Byzantium*. Princeton, NJ: Princeton University Press.

Mairs, Nancy. (1990/1997). "Carnal Acts" In *Writing on the Body*, ed. K. Conboy, N. Medina, and S. Stanbury. New York: Columbia University Press, 296–308.

Malacrida, Claudia Jacqueline Low. (2008). *Sociology of the Body: A Reader*. Don Mills: Oxford University Press.

Mansfield, Alan and McGinn, Babara. (1993). "Pumping Irony: The Muscular and the Feminine." In *Body Matters*, ed. S. Scott and D. Morgan. London: Falmer Press.

Martin, Emily. (1987). *The Woman in The Body: A Cultural Analysis of Reproduction*. Boston, MA: Beacon Press.

—— (1991). "The Egg and the Sperm: How Science Has Constructed a Romance Based on Stereotypical Male–Female Roles." *Signs* 16 (3): 485–501.

—— (1992). "The End of the Body?" *American Ethnologist* 19 (1): 121–40.

—— (1995). *Flexible Bodies: Tracking Immunity in American Culture from the Days of Polio to the Age of AIDS.* Boston, MA: Beacon Press.

Martinez, Renato. (1993). "On the Semiotics of Torture: The Case of the Disappeared in Chile." In *Reading the Social Body*, ed. Catherine B. Burroughs and Jeffrey David Ehrenreich. Iowa City: University of Iowa Press, 85–103.

Martinez-Alier, Verena. (1974). *Marriage, Class and Colour in Nineteenth Century Cuba.* Cambridge: Cambridge University Press.

Mascia-Lees, Francis, (ed.) (2011). *A Companion to the Anthropology of the Body and Embodiment.* West Sussex: Wiley-Blackwell.

Mascia-Lees, Francis and Sharpe, Patricia, (eds) (1992). *Tattoo, Torture, Mutilation, and Adornment: The Denaturalization of the Body in Culture and Text.* Albany, NY: State University of New York Press.

Mauss, Marcel. (1979). *Sociology and Psychology: Essays.* London: Routledge and Kegan Paul.

Merleau-Ponty, M. (1962). *Phenomenology of Perception.* New York: Humanities Press.

Messner, Michael. (1992). *Power at Play: Sports and the Problem of Masculinity* Boston, MA: Beacon Press.

—— (2002). *Taking the Field: Women, Men, and Sports.* Minneapolis, MN: University of Minnesota Press.

Messner, Michael and Kimmel, Michael. (2009). *Men's Lives.* New York: Macmillan.

Mitchell, Timothy. (1991). "After We have Captured Their Bodies." In *Colonising Egypt.* Berkeley, CA: University of California Press, 95–127.

Mizumoto Posey, Sandra. (2004). "Burning Messages: Interpreting African American Fraternity Brands and their Bearers." *Voices, the Journal of New York Folklore* 30 (Fall–Winter).

Momoh, Comfort. (2005). *Female Genital Mutilation.* Oxford: Radcliffe University Press.

Moore, Lisa Jean and Kosut, Mary. (2010). *The Body Reader: Essential Social and Cultural Readings.* New York: New York University Press.

More, Kate and Whittle, Stephen, (ed.) (1999). *Reclaiming Genders: Transsexual Grammars at the Fin de Siecle.* London and New York: Cassell.

Morini, Simona. (1972). *Body Sculpture: Plastic Surgery from Head to Toe.* New York: Delacorte Press.

Mulvey, Laura. (1975). "Visual Pleasure and Narrative Cinema." *Screen* 16 (3): 6–18.

Murphy, Robert F. (1987). *The Body Silent.* New York: Henry Holt.

Myers, James. (1992). "Nonmainstream Body Modification: Genital Piercing, Branding, Burning and Cutting." *Journal of Contemporary Ethnography* 21 (3): 267–306.

Nanda, Serena. (1998). *Neither Man Nor Woman: The Hijras of India.* New York: Wadsworth Publishing.

Nettleton, Sarah. (2013). *The Sociology of Health and Illness.* Cambridge: Polity Press.

Noske, Barbara. (1997). *Beyond Boundaries: Humans and Animals*. Montreal: Black Rose.

O'Brien, Mary. (1981). *The Politics of Reproduction*. London: Routledge & Kegan Paul.

Omolade, Barbara. (1983). "Hearts of Darkness." In *Powers of Desire: The Politics of Sexuality*, ed. Ann Snitow, Christine Stansell, and Sharon Thompson. New York: Monthly Review Press, 350–67.

Ong, Aihwa. (1987). *Spirits of Resistance and Capitalist Discipline: Factory Women in Malaysia*. Albany, NY: State University of New York Press.

O'Neill, J. (1985). *Five Bodies: the Shape of Modern Society*. Ithaca, NY: Cornell University Press.

Ortner, Sherry B. (1974). "Is Female to Male as Nature Is to Culture?" In *Woman, Culture, and Society*, ed. M. Z. Rosaldo and L. Lamphere. Stanford, CA: Stanford University Press, 68–87.

Oudshoorn, Nelly, (1994). *Beyond the Natural Body: An Archaeology of Sex Hormones*. London: Routledge.

Outram, Dorinda. (1989). *The Body and the French Revolution: Sex, Class, and Political Culture*. New Haven, CT: Yale University Press.

Paige, Jeffery and Paige, Karen. (1981). *The Politics of Reproductive Ritual*. Berkeley, CA: University of California Press.

Parry, Jonathan. (1989). "The End of the Body." In *Fragments for a History of the Human Body, Part Two*, ed. Michel Feher, Ramona Naddaff, and Nadia Tazi. New York: Zone Books, 490–517.

Patterson, Charles. (2002). *Eternal Treblinka: Our Treatment of Animals and the Holocaust*. New York: Lantern Books.

Pedersen, Susan. (1991). "National Bodies, Unspeakable Acts: The Sexual Politics of Colonial Policy Making." *Journal of Modern History* 63 (4): 647–80.

Pernick, Martin S. (1998). "Back from the Grave: Recurring Controversies over Defining and Diagnosing Death in History." In *Death: Beyond Whole-Brain Criteria*, ed. Raymond M. Zaner. Boston, MA: Kluwer, 17–74.

Perutz, Kathrin. (1970). *Beyond the Looking Glass: America's Beauty Culture*. New York: William Morrow.

Pfeffer, Naomi. (1993). *The Stork and the Syringe: A Political History of Reproductive Medicine*. Cambridge: Polity Press; and Oxford: Blackwell.

Phillips, Katharine A. (2005). *The Broken Mirror: Understanding and Treating Body Dysmorphic Disorder*. Oxford: Oxford University Press.

Phoenix, J. (2001). *Making Sense of Prostitution*. Basingstoke: Palgrave.

Pitts, Victoria. (1988). "'Reclaiming' the Female Body: Embodied Identity Work, Resistance and the Grotesque." *Body & Society* 4 (3): 67–84.

—— (2003). *In the Flesh: The Cultural Politics of Body Modification*. New York: Palgrave Macmillan.

Polhemus, Ted. (1978). *The Body Reader: Social Aspects of the Human Body*. New York: Pantheon Books.

Polhemus, Ted and Housk, Randall. (1996). *The Customized Body*. London: Serpent's Tail.

Porter, Roy. (1990). "Barely Touching: A Social Perspective to Mind and Body." In *Languages of Psyche: Mind and Body in Enlightenment Thought*, ed. G. Rousseau. Berkeley, CA: University of California Press, 45–80.

—— (1991a). "Bodies of Thought: Thoughts about the Body in 18th-Century England." In *Interpretation and Cultural History,* ed. Joan H. Pittock and Andrew Wear. London: Macmillan, 82–108.

—— (1991b). "History of the Body." In *New Perspectives on Historical Writing,* ed. Peter Burke. London: Polity Press, 206–32.

Porter, Roy, (ed.) (1985). *The Anatomy of Madness: Essays in the History of Psychiatry.* London: Tavistock Publications.

Porter, Roy and Teich, Mikulas, (eds) (1994). *Sexual Knowledge: Sexual Science: The History of Attitudes to Sexuality.* Cambridge: Cambridge University Press.

Potts, Annie. (2007). "The Mark of the Beast: Inscribing 'Animality' through Extreme Body Modification." In *Knowing Animals,* ed. P. Armstrong and L. Simmons. Leiden: Brill, 131–54.

Pouchelle, Marie-Christine. (1990). *The Body and Surgery in the Middle Ages.* New Brunswick, NJ: Rutgers University Press.

Price, Janet and Shildrick, Margrit, (eds) (1999). *Feminist Theory and The Body: A Reader.* Edinburgh: Edinburgh University Press.

Proctor, Robert N. (1991). "Eugenics Among the Social Sciences: Hereditarian Though in Germany and the United States." In *The Estate of Social Knowledge,* ed. JoAnne Brown and David K. Van Keuren. Baltimore, MD: Johns Hopkins University Press, 175–208.

Prosser, Jay. (1998). *Second Skins: The Body Narratives of Transsexuality.* New York: Columbia University Press.

Pruitt, Deborah and Lafont, Suzanne. (1995). "For Love and Money: Romance Tourism in Jamaica." *Annals of Tourism Research* 22(2): 422–40.

Qureshi, Sadiah. (2011). *Peoples on Parade: Exhibitions, Empire and Anthropology in Nineteenth-Century Britain.* Chicago, IL: University of Chicago Press.

Rapp, Rayna. (1999). *Testing Women, Testing the Fetus: The Social Impact of Amniocentesis in America.* London and New York: Routledge.

Reddit. (2013). http://www.reddit.com/r/funny/comments/109cnf/im_not_sure_what_to_conclude_from_this/?sort = new#c6bmnym, accessed March 31, 2013.

Reilly, Phillip R. (1991). *The Surgical Solution: A History of Involuntary Sterilization in the United States.* Baltimore, MD: Johns Hopkins University Press.

Reiss, Benjamin. (2001). *The Showman and the Slave: Race, Death, and Memory in Barnum's America.* Cambridge, MA: Harvard University Press.

Rich, Adrienne. (1979). *Of Women Born, Motherhood as Experience and Institution.* London: Virago.

Ripa, Yannick. (1990). *Women and Madness: The Incarceration of Women in 19th-Century France.* Cambridge: Polity Press.

Ritenbaugh, C. (1982). "Obesity as a Culture-Bound Syndrome." *Culture, Medicine, and Psychiatry* 6: 347–61.

Roach, Mary. (2003). *Stiff: The Curious Lives of Human Cadavers.* New York: W.W. Norton & Company.

Robinson, Paul. (1989). *The Modernization of Sex: Havelock Ellis, Alfred Kinsey, William Masters and Virginia Johnson.* Ithaca, NY: Cornell University Press.

Rosenberg, Charles E. (1989). Body and Mind in 19th-century medicine: Some Clinical Origins of the Neurosis Construct. *Bulletin of the History of Medicine* 63: 185–97.

Rosenblatt, Daniel. (1997). "The Antisocial Skin: Structure, Resistance, and 'Modern Primitive' Adornment in the United States." *Cultural Anthropology* 12 (3): 287–334.

Rouselle, Aline. (1988). *Porneia: On Desire and the Body in Antiquity*. New York: Blackwell.

Rubin, Arnold, (ed.) (1998). *Marks of Civilization: Artistic Transformations of the Human Body*, Los Angeles, CA: Museum of Cultural History, University of California.

Russell, Kathy, Wilson, Midge, and Hall, Ronald. (1993). *The Color Complex: The Politics of Skin Color among African Americans*. New York: First Anchor Books.

Russett, Cynthia Eagle. (1989). *Sexual Science: The Victorian Construction of Womanhood*. Cambridge, MA: Harvard University Press.

Russo, Mary. (1985). *Female Grotesques: Carnival and Theory*. Milwaukee, WI: Center for Twentieth Century Studies, University of Wisconsin-Milwaukee.

Ruthrof, Horst. (1997). *Semantics and the Body: Meaning from Frege to the Postmodern*. Carlton, Victoria: Melbourne University Press.

Sable, P. (1995). "Pets, Attachment, and Well-Being across the Life Cycle." *Social Work* 3 (3): 443–342.

Salecl, Renata. (2001). "Cut in the Body: From Clitoridectomy to Body Art." In *Thinking through the Skin*, ed. S. Ahmed and J. Stacey. New York: Routledge, 21–35.

Samuel, Geoffrey. (1990). *Mind, Body and Culture. Anthropology and the Biological Interface*. Cambridge: Cambridge University Press.

Sanchez Taylor, Jacqueline. (2006). "Racism and Child Sex Tourism in the Caribbean and Latin America." *Revista SER Social* 18: 189–208. University of Brasilia, Brazil.

Sanchez Taylor, Jacqueline and O'Connell Davidson, Julia. (2009). "Unknowable Secrets and Golden Silence: Reflexivity and Research on Sex Tourism." In *Secrecy and Silence in the Research Process: Feminist Reflection*, ed. R. Ryan-Flood and R. Gill. London: Routledge, 42–53.

Sanday, Peggy Reeves. (1981). *Female Power and Male Dominance: On the Origins of Sexual Inequality*. Cambridge: Cambridge University Press.

Sanders, Clinton. (1989). *Customizing the Body: The Art and Culture of Tattooing*. Philadelphia, PA: Temple University Press.

Sault, Nicole. (1994). *Many Mirrors: Body Image and Social Relations*. New Brunswick, NJ: Rutgers University Press.

Sawday, Jonathan. (1995). *The Body Emblazoned: Dissection and the Human Body in Renaissance Culture*. London: Routledge.

Scarry, Elaine. (1985). *The Body in Pain: The Making and Unmaking of a World*. New York: Oxford University Press.

Scheper-Hughes, Nancy. (1979). *Saints, Scholars, and Schizophrenics: Mental Illness in Rural Ireland*. Berkeley, CA: University of California Press.

—— (1993). *Death Without Weeping: The Violence of Everyday Life in Brazil*. Berkeley, CA: University of California Press.

Scheper-Hughes, Nancy and Lock, Margaret. (1987). "The Mindful Body: A Prolegomenon to Future Work in Medical Anthropology." *Medical Anthropology Quarterly* 1 (1): 6–41.

Schiebinger, Londa. (1986). "Skeletons in the Closet: The First Illustrations of the Female Skeleton in Eighteenth-Century Anatomy." *Representations* 14 (Spring): 42–82.

—— (1989). *The Mind Has No Sex? Women in the Origins of Modern Science*. Cambridge, MA: Harvard University Press.

—— (ed.) (2000). *Feminism and the Body*. New York: Oxford University Press.

Schilder, Paul (1935/1950). *The Image and Appearance of the Human Body: Studies in the Constructive Energies of the Psyche*. New York: International Universities Press, Inc.

Schillin, Chris, (ed.) (2007). *Embodying Sociology: Retrospect, Progress and Prospects*. Malden, MA: Blackwell Publishing.

Schleidgen, Sebastian, Jungert, Michael, Bauer, Robert, and Sandow, Verena, (eds) (2011). *Human Nature and Self Design*. Paderborn: Mentis.

Scott, Sue and Morgan, David, (eds) (1993) *Body Matters: Essays on the Sociology of the Body*. London: Falmer Press.

Scranton, Philip. (2011). *Beauty and Business: Commerce, Gender, and Culture in Modern America*. New York: Routledge.

Scruton, Roger. (2009). *Beauty*. Oxford: Oxford University Press.

Seidman, Steven. (1990). "The Power of Desire and the Danger of Pleasure: Victorian Sexuality Reconsidered." *Journal of Social History* 24: 47–67.

Sennett, Richard. (1994.) *Flesh and Stone: The Body and the City in Western Civilization*. New York: W.W. Norton & Company.

Shapiro, Ann-Louise. (1989). "Disordered Bodies/Disorderly Acts: Medical Discourse and the Female Criminal in 19th-Century Paris." *Genders* 4: 68–86.

Sharp, L. A. (1995). "Organ Transplantation as a Transformative Experience: Anthropological Insights into the Restructuring of the Self." *Medical Anthropology Quarterly* 9: 357–89.

Shell-Duncan, Bettina and Hernlund, Ylva, (eds) (2000). *Female "Circumcision" in Africa: Culture, Controversy, and Change*. Boulder, CO: Lynne Rienner.

Shildrick, Margrit and Price, Janet. (1998). *Vital Signs: Feminist Reconfigurations of the Bio/logical Body*. Edinburgh: Edinburgh University Press.

Shilling, Chris. (1993). *The Body and Social Theory*. London and Newbury Park, CA: Sage.

Shorter, E. (1983). *A History of Women's Bodies*. Harmondsworth: Penguin.

Siebers, Tobin, (ed.) (2000). *The Body Aesthetic: From Fine Art to Body Modification*. Ann Arbor, MI: University of Michigan Press.

Siegel, Judith M. (1990). "Stressful Life Events and Use of Physician Services among the Elderly: The Moderating Role of Pet Ownership." *Journal of Personality and Social Psychology* 58 (6): 1081–6.

Silliman, Jael and Bhattacharjee, Anannya, (eds) (2002). *Policing the National Body: Race, Gender and Criminalization*. Cambridge, MA: South End Press.

Silverman, Kaja. (1986). "Fragments of a Fashionable Discourse." In *Studies in Entertainment: Critical Approaches to Mass Culture*, ed. Tania Modleski. Bloomington, IN: Indiana University Press, 139–54.

Small, Meredith F. (1998). *Our Babies, Ourselves: How Biology and Culture Shape the Way We Parent*. New York: Anchor.

Smith, R. and Furth, G. (2002). *Amputee Identity Disorder*. Bloomington: Ist Books Library.

Snyder, Sharon L. and Mitchell, David T. (2001). "Re-engaging the Body: Disability Studies and the Resistance to Embodiment." *Public Culture* 13 (3): 367–89.

Sontag, Susan. (1979). "The Double Standard of Aging." In *Psychology of Women* ed. J. H. Willians. New York: W.W. Norton & Comapny, 462–78.

—— (1989). *AIDS and Its Metaphors.* New York: Farrar, Strauss & Giroux.

—— (1991). *Illness as Metaphor.* New York: Farrar, Strauss & Giroux.

Spiegel, Marjorie. (1996). *The Dreaded Comparison: Human and Animal Slavery.* New York: Mirror Books.

St Martin, L. and Gavey, N. (1996). "Women's Bodybuilding: Feminist Resistance and/or Femininity's Recuperation." *Body & Society* 2 (4): 45–57.

Stafford, Barbara M. (1991). *Body Criticism: Imaging the Unseen in Enlightenment Art and Medicine.* Cambridge, MA: MIT Press.

Stallybrass, Peter, and White, A. (1986). *The Politics and Poetics of Transgression.* Ithaca, NY: Cornell University Press.

Stanworth, Michelle, (ed.) (1987). *Reproductive Technologies: Gender, Motherhood and Medicine.* Oxford: Polity Press.

Steele, Valerie. (1995). *Fashion and Eroticism: Ideals of Feminine Beauty from the Victorian Era to the Jazz Age.* New York: Oxford University Press.

—— (2001). *The Corset: A Cultural History.* New Haven, CT: Yale University Press.

Steinem, Gloria. (1978). "What if Men Could Menstruate?" *Ms. Magazine*, October.

Steward, Samuel. (1990). *Bad Boys and Tough Tattoos: A Social History of the Tattoo with Gangs, Sailors and Street-Corner Punks, 1950–1965.* New York: Harrington Park Press.

Suleiman, Susan Rubin, (ed.) (1986). *The Female Body in Western Culture,* Cambridge, MA: Harvard University Press.

Sullivan, Nikki. (2001). *Tattooed Bodies: Subjectivity, Textuality, Ethics, and Pleasure.* Westport, CT: Praeger.

Sweetman, Paul. (1999). "Only Skin Deep? Tattooing, Piercing and the Transgressive Body." In *The Body's Perilous Pleasures: Dangerous Desires and Contemporary Culture*, ed. Michele Aaron. Edinburgh: Edinburgh University Press, 165–87.

—— (2000). "Anchoring the (Postmodern) Self? Body Modification, Fashion and Identity." In *Body Modification*, ed. Mike Featherstone. London: Sage, 171–84.

Tattersall, Ian. (1998). *Becoming Human: Evolution and Human Uniqueness.* Oxford: Oxford University Press.

Taylor, Gary. (2000). *Castration: An Abbreviated History of Western Manhood.* New York: Routledge.

Terry, Jennifer and Urla, Jacqueline, (eds) (1995). *Deviant Bodies.* Bloomington, IN: Indiana University Press.

Tew, Marjorie. (1990). *Safer Childbirth: A Critical History of Maternity Care.* London: Chapman & Hall.

Thevóz, Michel. (1984). *The Painted Body.* New York: Rizzoli International.

Thomas, C. (2002). "The 'Disabled' Body." In *Real Bodies: A Sociological Introduction*, ed. Mary Evans and Ellie Lee. Basingstoke: Palgrave, 64–78.

Thomas, C. (1999). *Female Forms: Experiencing and Understanding Disability.* Buckingham: Open University Press.

Thompson, Becky W. (1996). *A Hunger So Wide and So Deep: A Multiracial View of Women's Eating Problems*. Minneapolis, MN: University of Minnesota Press.

Thompson, Mark. (1992). *Leatherfolk: Radical Sex, People, Politics, and Practice*. Los Angeles, CA: Daedalus Publishing.

Tine Cohen-Kettenis, Peggy. (2003). *Transgenderism and Intersexuality in Childhood and Adolescence: Making Choices*. Thousand Oaks, CA: Sage Publications.

Troyabsky, David G. (1989). *Old Age in the Old Regime: Image and Experience in 18th-century France*. Ithaca, NY: Cornell University Press.

Turner, Bryan, S. (1984). *The Body and Society: Explorations in Social Theory*. New York: Basil Blackwell.

—— (1991). "Recent Developments in the Theory of the Body." In *The Body: Social Process and Cultural Theory*, ed. Mike Featherstone, Mike Hepworth, and Bryan S. Turner. London: Sage Publications, 1–35.

—— (1992). *Regulating Bodies: Essays in Medical Sociology*. New York: Routledge.

—— (1999). "The Possibility of Primitiveness: Towards a Sociology of Body Marks in Cool Societies." *Body & Society* 5 (2–3): 39–50.

Turner, Terence. (1980). "The Social Skin." In *Not Work Alone: A Cross-Cultural View of Activities Superfluous to Survival*, ed. Jeremy Cherfas and Roger Lewin. Beverly Hills, CA: Sage Publications, 112–40.

—— (1994). "Bodies and Anti-Bodies: Flesh and Fetish in Contemporary Social Theory." In *Embodiment and Experience*, ed. T. Csordas. Cambridge: Cambridge University Press, 27–47.

—— (1995). "Social Body and Embodied Subject: Bodiliness, Subjectivity and Sociality among the Kayapo." *Current Anthropology* 10 (2): 143–70.

Tyson, Edward. (1972). *A Philological Essay Concerning the Pygmies of the Ancients*, ed. Bertram C. A. Windle. Freeport, NY: Books for Libraries Press.

Urla, Jacqueline and Swedlund, Alan C. (1995). "The Anthropometry of Barbie: Unsettling Ideals of the Feminine Body in Popular Culture." In *Deviant Bodies: Critical Perspectives on Difference in Science and Popular Culture*, ed. Jennifer Terry and Jacqueline Urla. Bloomington, IN: Indiana University Press, 277–313.

Vale, V. and Juno, Andrea. (1989). *Modern Primitives*. San Francisco, CA: Re/Search Publications.

Verlinden, S., Hersen, M., and Thomas, J. (2000). "Risk Factors in School Shootings." *Clinical Psychology Review* 20: 3–56.

Vertinsky, Patricia. (1990). *The Eternally Wounded Women: Women, Doctors and Exercise in the Late 19th Century*. Manchester: Manchester University Press.

Virel, Andre. (1979). *Decorated Man: The Human Body as Art/Text*. New York: Henry Abrams.

Wacquant, Loic. (1995). "Pugs at Work: Bodily Capital and Bodily Labor Among Professional Boxers." *Body and Society* 1–1 (March): 65–94.

—— (1998). "The Prizefighter's Three Bodies." *Ethnos* 63–3 (November): 325–52.

—— (2004). *Body and Soul: Notebooks of An Apprentice Boxer*. New York: Oxford University Press.

Wallerstein, Edward. (1980). *Circumcision: An American Health Fallacy*. New York: Springer Publishing Company.

Waskul, Dennis D. and Vannini, Phillip. (2006). *Body/Embodiment: Symbolic Interaction and the Sociology of the Body*. Burlington, VT: Ashgate.

Weideger, Paula. (1976). *Menstruation and Menopause: The Physiology and Psychology, the Myth and the Reality*. New York: Knopf.

Weinberg, Thomas S. (1995). *S&M: Studies in Dominance & Submission*. New York: Prometheus Books.

Weiss, Gail. (1999). *Body Images: Embodiment as Intercorporeality*, New York and London: Routledge.

Weitz, Rose. (1998). *The Politics of Women's Bodies*. New York: Oxford University Press.

Wells, D. L. (2004). "The Facilitation of Social Interactions by Domestic Dogs." *Anthrozoös* 17: 340–352.

Wendell, Susan. (1996). *The Rejected Body: Feminist Philosophical Reflections on the Disabled Body*. London: Routledge.

Wijngaard, Marianne Van Den. (1997). *Reinventing the Sexes: Biomedical Construction of Femininity and Masculinity*. Bloomington, IN: Indiana University Press.

Williams, Linda. (1989). *Hard Core: Power, Pleasure and the Frenzy of the Visible*. Berkeley, CA: University of California Press.

Williams, Simon J. (1997). "Modern Medicine and the 'Uncertain Body': From Corporeality to Hyperreality?" *Social Science & Medicine* 45 (7): 1041–9.

Wilson, Elizabeth. (1987). *Adorned in Dreams: Fashion and Modernity*. Berkeley, CA: University of California Press.

Wilson, M. (1980). "Body and Mind from the Cartesian Point of View." In *Body and Mind: Past, Present, Future*, ed. R. Rieber. New York: Academic Press, 35–55.

Wilson, Thomas C. (1996). "Ambiguous Identity in an Unambiguous Sex/Gender Structure: The Case of Bisexual Women." *Sociological Quarterly* 37 (2): 449–64.

Wolf, Naomi. (1991). *The Beauty Myth: How Images of Beauty Are Used Against Women*. New York: W. Morrow.

Wray, Matt and Newitz, Analee, (eds) (1997). *White Trash: Race and Class in America*. New York: Routledge.

Young, Iris Marion. (2005). *On Female Body Experience: "Throwing Like a Girl" and Other Essays*. New York: Oxford University Press.

Zeuner, Frederick E. (1963). *A History of Domesticated Animals*. London: Hutchinson.

Zito, Angela and Barlow, Tani E., (eds) (1994). *Body, Subject, and Power in China*. Chicago, IL: University of Chicago Press.

Index

Paralympics 30, 33
Parker, Sarah Jessica 189
Parry, Albert 217
patents 307–8
patriarchal bargain 122
personalistic disease theory 27
Pesut, Hanna 120
pet cemeteries 94
pets 285–6, 287, 288, 295–7
phenomenology 9
Philippines 81, 104, 176
physical capital 14
physiognomy 108–9, 257
piercing 209, 210, 212, 214; BDSM 149, 218; modern primitives 218, 219–20; religious rituals 232, 240; subversive bodies 221, 222, 223
pigs 286–7, 288
pimping 265
Pina-Cabral, Joao de 233
pink collar jobs 160–1
Pistorius, Oscar 30, 302–3, 304
Pitts, Victoria 223
plastination 308
pollution 35, 39; see also ritual pollution
polygenism 264
polygyny 36, 47
Polynesia 215, 216, 262
Pompeii 270
population control 65–9
pornification 273
pornography 19, 177, 270–3; class and 157–8; fat porn 200; Internet 310, 311; labiaplasty influence by 188; Victorian era 13
Portugal 233–4
postpartum sex taboos 69
Potts, Annie 294
poverty 38, 39, 40, 68; breastfeeding 72; death linked to 80–1; diet and health 162; invisibility of poor bodies 167–8; lack of birth control linked to 65; obesity linked to 201; race and 111
power relations 5, 13, 19, 136, 137–8
prayer 239–40
pregnancy 69–70, 143
prenatal testing 75–6, 302
primitivism 218, 219–20, 294
prison population 55–6, 256–7
prisoners of war 253, 274

"pro-ana" groups 198
Project Prevention 65
pro-natalism 66–7
prosthetics 302–3
prostitution 142, 166, 228, 265–9, 270
prostration 240
Protestantism 233, 236–7, 239; see also Christianity
Pruitt, Deborah 270
puberty rituals 123–4
pubic hair 119, 128
punishment 248–57, 264
punks 221–3
purdah 228
purification 237, 239

Qi 28
queer theory 13
Quinlan, Karen 88

Rabelais, Francois 15, 271
race 6–7, 99–116; aging 45; animalization of non-white bodies 112–15; beauty and 183–5; biological racism 108–10; burials 93; capital punishment 256; colonialism 102–3; health and 34, 110–12; prison population 256–7; racialized bodies 103–7; reproduction issues 67–8; seniors 54, 55; slavery 264; as a social construct 100–1
race purity movement 112; see also eugenics
racialization 102, 110, 183–4
racism 81, 99, 108–10, 111, 199
rape 7, 151–2, 153; HIV/AIDS 37–8; rape-prone cultures 151; of slave women 263; wartime 251, 253, 267
Rapp, Rayna 76
recidivism rate 56
Reddit 310, 311
reductionism 7, 10
relics 236
religion 225–44; bodily practices 237–40; body/soul division 236–7, 243; burial rites 91, 93; cremation 95; divination 27; pollution and the female body 229–31; self-mortification 231–4; sex and 235–6; spirit possession 240–1; stigmata 234, 242–3; wearing of the veil 226–9; see also Buddhism;

267, 268; romance tourism 270;
slavery 264; transsexuals 142, 145
therapeutic abortions 31–2
Thevóz, Michel 7
thinness 8, 130–2, 162, 189, 194–5, 198;
see also dieting
thinspiration 198
Third Reich 83–4
Thompson, Becky 199
Thomson, Rosemarie Garland 32
Tibet 95
tightlacing 133
Titanic 81–2
Toddlers & Tiaras 144–5
Toraja 91
Toronto SlutWalk 153–4
torture 247, 251–2, 253–4, 259, 310–11
trafficking 266–8
Trail of Tears 84
trans-Atlantic slave trade *see* slavery
transgender people 8, 118, 134–6, 145
transsexuals 11, 134, 136, 140–2
travesties 134–5, 142, 145
Turner, Bryan S. 12
Turner, Terence 11
Tuskegee Syphilis Study 274
24 247
Twinkie Tax 191
2 Girls 1 Cup 310
two spirits 135, 145
Tyson, Edward 280

Uganda 199
ulzzang 174, 186
United States: aging 43–4, 45, 46,
49–52, 54, 55; American culture of
youth 44, 46–8; anti-circumcision
movement 125; assisted
reproductive technologies 73; birth
control 63–5; body hair 127–8;
breast cancer 35; breastfeeding 73;
capital punishment 255, 256;
compulsory sterilization 67;
cosmetic surgery 186; death 81, 83;
diet industry 194, 195; disability 29,
31, 33; DNA identification 258–9;
domestic workers 159–60; drugs
163–4, 166; ethnic groups 67–8;
eugenics 115; experiments on
humans 274; food deserts 162; gay
men 145; ghost bikes 93–4; graves

93; health and illness 23, 24–5;
health care 39, 40, 41; HIV/AIDS 36,
38–9, 80, 110–11; Indian Removal
Act 84–5; inequalities 39–40;
invisibility of poor bodies 167–8;
mail order brides 269; menopausal
women 61–2; obesity 190, 191–2,
195, 202; organ donations 275, 276;
pornography 272, 273; pregnancy
70; prison population 55–6, 256–7;
prostitution 265; punishment of
criminals 248; race 6–7, 99–100,
101, 104, 106, 108, 110, 112, 184;
rape 151; sexuality 139–40, 142,
143–4, 146–7; slavery 103, 263–4;
sumptuary laws 164, 166; torture
247, 254; transgender people 134,
135–6; transsexuals 141–2; Vietnam
War 267; *see also* African-Americans;
Native Americans
untouchables 159, 229, 264

values 24, 311
Van Gennep, Arthur 124
Vawter, Zac 303
the veil 226–9
Victorian era 13, 26, 126, 131, 150, 153,
216
Vietnam 251, 267, 269, 270
violence 151, 292; *see also* sexual
violence
virginity, selling of 268–9
virtual reality 306–7
voluntary euthanasia 88
Von Hagens, Gunther 308

Wacquant, Loic 14
Walker Bynum, Caroline 234, 242
Walmart 49
wartime rape 251, 253, 267
weight *see* obesity
weight loss reality shows 197
weight prejudice 201–2
Wendy's 204
wet nurses 72–3
white trash 168–9, 202
Whitehall Study 40
whiteness 184
Wildenstein, Jocelyn 294
Wilkinson, R. G. 81
Wilson, Carnie 196, 197